Railroad Collectibles

An Illustrated Value Guide

4th Edition

Stanley L. Baker

COLLECTOR BOOKS

A Division of Schroeder Publishing Co., Inc.

The current values in this book should be used only as a guide. They are not intended to set prices, which vary from one section of the country to another. Auction prices as well as dealer prices vary greatly and are affected by condition as well as demand. Neither the Author nor the Publisher assumes responsibility for any losses that might be incurred as a result of consulting this guide.

We are always looking for knowledgeable people considered to be experts within their fields. If you feel that there is a real need for a book on your collectible subject and have a large comprehensive collection contact Collector Books.

Additional copies of this book may be ordered from:

COLLECTOR BOOKS
P.O. Box 3009
Paducah, Kentucky 42002-3009

@ $14.95. Add $2.00 for postage and handling.

Copyright: Stanley Baker, 1990
Values updated: 1996

Printed by IMAGE GRAPHICS, INC., Paducah, Kentucky

Table of Contents

Introduction

This fourth revised edition of *Railroad Collectibles - an Illustrated Value Guide,* finds that the collecting of railroadiana is now bigger and better than ever, with prices continuing to rise. This means that you, the dealer (seller) – and you, the collector (buyer) – both need to be aware of the variations in the net worth of items in this field.

All prices shown are based on the current market as of this writing. Be assured that they have not been established by simply pulling them out of the air and attaching them to specific items. All values have been arrived at from careful study of a multiple of sources – Railroadiana Shows and Sales, Railroadiana Mail Order Dealer's lists, railroad advertisements in the Antique Trade Journals, noting railroadiana prices at major antique shows, mall shows, antique shops, flea markets, public auctions, and word of mouth among collectors, thus constantly maintaining a continuous up-to-date price record compilation. Also bear in mind that it is difficult to standardize prices as they fluctuate from coast to coast.

It cannot be emphasized enough that condition, too, plays a very important role in determining value, and you will find this fact repeated over and over again throughout this guide. Also, pieces with railroad markings from long-gone defunct roads carry much higher price tags. Needless to say, supply and demand is the rule governing most pricing, as sometimes a passionate collector is willing to go overboard for a certain item especially needed to round out his/her collection. And, of course, there is always the chance of paying far less should you be lucky enough to come across a "sleeper." Therefore, all prices should be used as a GUIDE and not as a final authority.

The same general format has been followed as in previous editions, with a short narrative at the beginning of each of the categories, summarizing them in as few words as possible in an effort to make the guide easy to use as a handy, take-along reference book. As you will note, a new category has been added, "Pullman Company Collectibles," and others have been enlarged; also, items are described in more detail to ensure your having the right piece. It goes without saying that any attempt at completeness is impossible, as collectors will always come up with things not known to exist before. This is one of the fascinations of looking for railroad memorabilia – new discoveries are being made all the time!

Railroadiana is basically divided into two main categories – paper and non-paper, with a vast quantity of items in each. It is open to question which is the most popular; it is simply a matter of personal preference. Discriminating can make you an expert in your thing, while generalizing provides you with a broader scope of the hobby. Many collectors do both – have a varied collection to which they are continually adding, while at the same time specializing in one particular category.

Buyers and sellers should get to know as much as possible about railroad artifacts in order to be able to recognize a choice piece and make their own evaluation on the spot. Many items are rarities or one of a kind, and their value must be judged subjectively.

Good luck in your search!

All photos by the author.

Key To Railroad Abbreviations

Initial	Railroad Name	Also Known As
AARR	Ann Arbor RR	
A&GW	Atlantic & Great Western RR	
A&S	Alton & Southern RR	
A ST	Atlanta Street RR	
A&StL	Atlantic & St. Lawrence RR	
AC&S	Atlantic City & Shore RR	
AC&Y	Akron Canton & Youngstown RR	
ACL	Atlantic Coast Line RR	Sea Level Route
AT&SF	Atchison Topeka & Santa Fe Ry	Santa Fe
B&A	Boston & Albany RR	
B&F	Boston & Fitchburg RR	
B&MR RR	Burlington & Missouri River RR	
B&Me	Boston & Maine RR	Line of the Minute Man
B&O	Baltimore & Ohio RR	
BAR	Bangor & Aroostock RR	
BCER	British Columbia Electric Railway	
BCR&M	Burlington Cedar Rapids & Minnesota RR	
BCR&N	Burlington Cedar Rapids & Northern Ry	The Iowa Route
BN	Burlington Northern	
BO&SW	Baltimore Ohio & Southwestern Ry	
BR	Burlington Route	
BR&P	Buffalo Rochester & Pittsburgh RR	
C&A	Chicago & Alton RR	Alton The Only Way
C&EI	Chicago & Eastern Illinois RR	The Noiseless Route
C&G	Columbus & Greenville Ry	
C&NW	Chicago & Northwestern Ry	Northwestern Line
C&O	Chesapeake & Ohio Ry	
C&S	Colorado & Southern Ry	
C&WI	Chicago & Western Indiana RR	
C&WM	Chicago & West Michigan RR	
CA&CRR	Cincinnati Atlantic & Columbus RR	
CB&Q	Chicago Burlington & Quincy RR	Burlington Route
CC&L	Chicago Cincinnati & Louisville Ry	
CCC	Cape Cod Central RR	
CCC&StL	Cleveland Cincinnati Chicago & St. Louis Ry	Big Four Route
CGW	Chicago Great Western Ry	The Corn Belt Route The Maple Leaf Route
CH&D	Cincinnati, Hamilton & Dayton Ry	
CI&L	Chicago Indianapolis & Louisville RR	Monon Route
CI&W	Cincinnati Indiana & Western	
CK&N	Chicago Kansas & Nebraska Ry	
CLS&SB	Chicago Lake Shore & South Bend	
CM	Colorado Midland	Midland Route
CI&W	Cincinnati Indiana & Western Ry	
CM&PS	Chicago Milwaukee & Puget Sound RR	
CM&StP	Chicago Milwaukee & St. Paul Ry	Milwaukee Road
CMStP&P	Chicago Milwaukee St. Paul & Pacific RR	Milwaukee Road
CNR	Canadian National Ry	
CNS&M	Chicago North Shore & Milwaukee RR	The North Shore Line
CNJ	Central RR Co of New Jersey	
CO&G	Chocktaw Oklahoma & Gulf RR	
CPR	Canadian Pacific Ry	

Initial	Railroad Name	Also Known As
CRI&P	Chicago Rock Island & Pacific RR	Rock Island Lines
CSS&SB	Chicago South Shore & South Bend RR	
CStP&KC	Chicago St. Paul & Kansas City Ry	
CStPM&O	Chicago St. Paul Mpls. & Omaha Ry	Omaha
CStPM&DM	Chicago St. Paul Mpls. & Des Moines	
C U T	Chicago Union Transfer	
CV	Central Vermont Ry	
CW&B	Cincinnati Washington & Baltimore RR	
D&H	Delaware & Hudson RR	The D & H
D&IR	Duluth & Iron Range RR	Vermillion Route
D&RGW	Denver & Rio Grand Western RR	Rio Grande
D&RG	Denver & Rio Grande	Rio Grande
D&SF	Denver & Santa Fe Ry	
D&SL	Denver & Salt Lake RR	The Moffat Road
DL&W	Delaware Lackawanna & Western RR	Lackawanna
DM&IR	Duluth Missabe & Iron Range Ry	
DM&N	Duluth Missabe & Northern Ry	
DM&V	Delaware Maryland & Virginia RR	
DSS&A	Duluth South Shore & Atlantic Ry	The South Shore
E&TH	Evansville & Terre Haute Ry	
EJ&E	Elgin Joliet & Eastern Ry	Chicago Outer Belt Line
EL	Erie Lackawanna RR	
ERR	Erie RR	Erie
F&NE	Fairchild & Northeastern Ry	
F&PM	Flint & Pere Marquette RR	
FC&G	Fernwood Columbia & Gulf RR	
FDDM&S	Fort Dodge Des Moines & Southern RR	
FE&MV	Fremont Elkhorn & Missouri Valley RR	
FEC	Florida East Coast Ry	Flagler Systerm
FJ&G	Fonda Johnstown & Gloversville RR	
FRR	Fitchburg RR	The Hoosiac Tunnel Route
FW&DC	Fort Worth & Denver City Ry	
GB&W	Green Bay & Western RR	Green Bay Route
GC&SF	Gulf Colorado & Santa Fe Ry	
CF&A	Gulf Florida & Alabama Ry	
GH&S	Gulf Houston & Southern Ry	
GH&SA	Galveston Harrisburg & San Antonio Ry	
GM&N	Gulf Mobile & Northern RR	
GM&O	Gulf Mobile & Ohio RR	The Alton Route
GN	Great Northern Ry	
GRR	Grand Rapids Railway Co.	
GS&F	Georgia Southern & Florida Ry	
GTP	Grand Trunk Pacific Ry	
GTR	Grand Trunk Ry System	
GTW	Grand Trunk Western RR	
H&BT	Huntington & Broad Top RR	
H&NH	Hartford & New Haven RR	
H&STJRR	Hannibal & St. Joseph RR	
HBL	Harbor Belt Line RR	
H&TC	Houston & Texas Central RR	
ICRR	Illinois Central RR	Mississippi Valley Route
ICG	Illinois Central Gulf	
ICStRY	Illinois Central Street Railway Co.	
IHB	Indiana Harbor Belt RR	
IR	Indiana Railroad System	
IRT	Interborough Rapid Transit Co. N.Y.	
IStRy	Indianpolis Street Railway Co.	
MKT aka "Katy"	Missouri, Kansas & Texas Railway	

Initial	Railroad Name	Also Known As
MN&S	Minneapolis Northfield & Southern Ry	
MP	Missouri Pacific RR	Mo-Pac
MRL&M	Minneapolis Red Lake & Manitoba Ry	
MRR	Manistee RR	
MS&NI	Michigan Southern & Northern Indiana Ry	
MSO	Missabe Southern RR	
MStP&A	Minneapolis St. Paul & Ashland Ry	
MSTPR& DETCO	Minneapolis, St. Paul, Rochester & Dubuque Electric Traction Co.	Dan Patch Electric LInes
MStP&SSM	Minneapolis St. Paul & Sault Ste. Marie Ry	Soo Line
MT RY	Minnesota Transfer	
NAT.RYS.MEX	National Railways of Mexico	
N&W	Norfolk & Western Ry	
NC	North Carolina RR	
NC&StL	Nashville Chattanooga & St. Louis Ry	The Dixie Line
NI	Northern Indiana Ry	
NJC	New Jersey Central	Jersey Central LInes
NKP	New York Chicago & St. Louis RR	Nickel Plate Road
NP	Northern Pacific Ry	Yellowstone Park Line
NWP	Northwestern Pacific RR	
NYB&M	New York Boston & Montreal RR	
NYC	New York Central RR	
NYC&HR	New York Central & Hudson River RR	
NY&NH	New York & New Haven RR	
NYNH&H	New York Haven & Hartford RR	New Haven
NYC&StL	New York Chicago & St. Louis RR	Nickel Plate Route
NYLE&W	New York Lake Erie & Western	
NYO&W	New York Ontario & Western Ry	OW, O&W
NY&E	New York & Erie RR	
NYP&B	New York Providence & Boston RR	
O&W	Oregon & Washington RR	
OR&N	Oregon Railroad & Navigation Co.	
OSL	Oregon Short Line RR	
OVE	Ohio Valley Electric RR	
OW	Oregon Western Ry	
P&LE	Pittsburgh & Lake Erie RR	
P&O	Portland & Ogdensburgh RR	
P&PU	Peoria & Pekin Union Ry	
P&R	Philadelphia & Reading Ry	The Reading
PC	Penn Central RR	
PE	Pacific Electric Ry	
PM	Pere Marquette RR	
POD	Post Office Department	
PPC CO	Pullman Palace Car Co.	
PRR	Pennsylvania RR	Pennsy, Penna
PTRA	Port Terminal Railroad Assn	
PORT	Portland RR	
PW&B	Philadelphia Wilmington & Baltimore RR	
QA&P	Quanah Acme & Pacific Ry	Quanah Route
R&I Ry	Rockford and Interurban Ry	
REA	Railway Express Agency	Ry. Ex. Agy. Am. Ry. Ex.
RDG	Reading Ry	
RF&P	Richmond Fredericksburg & Potomac RR	
RI	Rock Island Lines	
RRI&StL	Rockford Rock Island & St. Louis RR	
RUT	Rutland RR	Green Mountain Line
SAL	Seaboard Air Line Ry	Seaboard
SCL	Seaboard Coast Line RR	Seaboard

Initial	Railroad Name	Also Known As
SD&A	San Diego & Arizona Ry	
SM	Southern Minnesota RR	
SP	Southern Pacific Co.	Sunset Route
SP&S	Spokane Portland & Seattle Ry	Columbia River Scenic Route
SR	Southern Ry	
SSCSY	South Sioux City Stock Yards	
StJ	St. Joe Ry	
StL&SF	St. Louis & San Francisco Ry	Frisco Lines
StL&SW	St. Louis & South Western Ry	Cotton Belt Route
StLD&S	St. Louis Iron Mountain & Southern Ry	Iron Mountain Route
StL&OR	St. Louis & Ohio RR	
StP&D	St. Paul & Duluth RR	
StP&P	St. Paul & Pacific RR	
StP&SC	St. Paul & Sioux City RR	
StPCyRy	St. Paul City Railway	
StPM&M	St. Paul Minneapolis & Manitoba Ry	
StPUD	St. Paul Union Depot	
StPUSY	St. Paul Union Stock Yards Co.	
SURYs	State University Railways (NC)	
T RY	Toronto Ry	
T&NO RR	Texas & New Orleans RR	
T&P	Texas & Pacific RR	Sunshine Special Route
T&YR	Toronto & York Radial Ry	
TCR	Texas Central RR	The Lone Star Route
TP&W	Toledo Peoria & Western Ry	
TRRA	Terminal Railroad Assn	
TStL&KC	Toledo St. Louis & Kansas City RR	
UP	Union Pacific RR	The Overland Route
USTVA	United States Tennessee Valley Authority	
UTC OF IND.	United Transit Co. of Indiana	
USY OF O	Union Stock Yards of Omaha	
V RR	Valley Railroad	
VGN	Virginian Ry	
VL	Vandalia Line	
W&LE	Wheeling & Lake Erie Ry	
W&StP	Winona & St. Peter RR	
WAB	Wabash RR	The Banner Route
W RY	Wheeling Ry	
WC	Wisconsin Central RR	
WCF&NRR	Waterloo Cedar Falls & Northern RR	
WCStRR	West Chicago Street Railway Co.	
WM	Western Maryland Ry	
WNRR	Wisconsin Northern Ry	
WP	Western Pacific RR	Feather River Route
WP&YR	White Pass & Yukon Route	
WStL&P	Wabash St. Louis & Pacific Ry	
Y&MV	Yazoo & Mississippi Valley RR	

Advertising Souvenirs

Countless thousands of advertising souvenir items such as paperweights, souvenir spoons, hand fans, letter openers, pocket knives, desk ornaments, pocket mirrors and novelty items of all kinds, were widely distributed by the railroads over the years. Earlier pieces are now bringing high prices while those from the later years are valued according to their scarcity and demand, the rare and unique item realizing record prices at auction.

ADVERTISING CARDS – set of 12 monthly cards for 1885; each shows a respective printed color scene for the month with a poem on the back, WABASH RAILWAY, scarce $60.00

ADVERTISING CARDS – litho of train on Niagara Falls Suspension Bridge; take the GREAT WESTERN & MICHIGAN CENTRAL R.W. LINE, backside has advertising, ca. 1870's $25.00

ADVERTISING CARDS – litho of family at depot waiting for a train; backside has map and advertising, CHICAGO NORTH WESTERN RY, ca. 1890's.........................$12.00

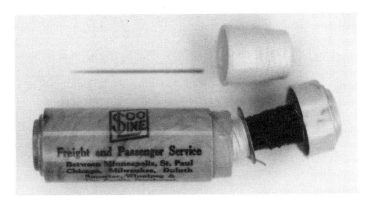

Sewing Kit

ADVERTISING CARDS – litho of man at depot missed train entitled, Time and the Erie wait for no man, N.Y. LAKE ERIE & WESTERN R.R., backside has advertising, ca. 1880's $15.00

BAGGAGE TAG – celluloid, 1½x 2½", on leather strap, SOO LINE, adv. "Tag Your Grip, Take a Trip, The New Train," $18.00

BAKED POTATO COVERED INKWELL – pot metal, NORTHERN PACIFIC RY., potato replica on 3¼ x 5½" base, "Route of the Great Big Baked Potato," scarce $450.00

BOTTLE OPENER – shiny metal head, pearlized handle 2½"L, MISSOURI PACIFIC LINES logo, adv. "Air Conditioned" trains $15.00

CLOCK – cast bronze, locomotive front, 10½" tall, wind-up, CHICAGO MILWAUKEE & ST. PAUL RAILWAY around dial, PIONEER LIMITED on pointed base, ca. 1890, rare $750.00

CORK SCREW – metal, folding type, 3 x 3" opened, "For Hunting, For Fishing, Take The SOO LINE" on handle $35.00

DESK ORNAMENT – grizzly bear, bronze, upright on cube, 4" tall, NORTHERN PACIFIC RY, logo, RWBA initials, "Yellow Stone Park Line, The Orme Co. St. Paul,"

around cube base, scarce $100.00

DESK ORNAMENT – grizzly bear, pot metal, copper finish, 2½ x 4", felt padded base, CHICAGO MILWAUKEE & ST. PAUL RY "Gallatin Gateway to Yellowstone Park," 1920's $125.00

DESK ORNAMENT – locomotive, pot metal, silver finish, model of CHICAGO MILWAUKEE & ST. PAUL RY 10250 electric loco. on padded base, 1¾ x 6", ca. 1920's $155.00

DESK ORNAMENT – locomotive, pot metal, brass finish, model of READING RAILWAY SYSTEM 2100 steam loco. 5"L, mt'd. on wood base, ca. 1930's........................$85.00

DESK ORNAMENT – locomotive, pot metal, silver finish, model of "New York Central 5200" loco. on felt padded base, 2½ x 9¼" base, Van Gytenbeek Co. NY ca. 1928 ....$200.00

DESK ORNAMENT – locomotive, pot metal, silver finish, model of VIRGINIAN RAILWAY "Allegheny-type" loco. on felt padded base, 2¼ x 10½", Lima-Hamilton Corp., 1940's $275.00

DESK ORNAMENT – locomotive, pot metal, silver finish, model of NEW YORK CENTRAL 5445 streamlined Hudson Type locomotive on felt padded base, 2¼ x 10½", ca. 1940's $235.00

DESK ORNAMENT – match holder, cast iron alligator 8½"L, MONON ROUTE on hgd. back, names of cities served on legs, head and tail, early 1900's $450.00

DESK ORNAMENT – match safe, cast iron, black finish, shape of MK&T logo w/hg'd. lid, MISSOURI KANSAS & TEXAS RY, names of RR officials incised on bottom........$150.00

DESK ORNAMENT – vista dome car, pot metal, silver finish,

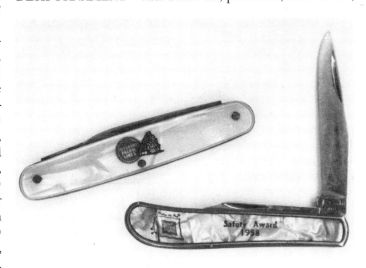

Pocket Knives

model of BURLINGTON ROUTE first Vista Dome car on 2 x 7½" felt padded base, 4 orig. logos, 1945 ..$85.00

GOLF BALLS – set of three in box, mint, Spalding 4, mk'd. w/modern SOO logo, adv. "100 Years" on box $20.00

GOLF TEES – set of four in cardstock case, ea. mk'd UNION PACIFIC RAILROAD, adv. on case $5.00

HAND FAN – cardstock, 7½ x 9¼", on stick handle, CHI-CAGO NORTH WESTERN LINE logo, advertising vacations on reverse $15.00

HAND FAN – cardstock, round 9"D, on stick handle,MIS-SOURI PACIFIC LINES logo, advertising name trains on backside, 1930's...$18.00

HAND FAN – cardstock, 7 x 8½", on stick handle, PENNSYL-VANIA RAILROAD logo, adv. "Keep Cool" ride their air conditioned trains...$10.00

HAND FAN – paper, folding-type, 13 bamboo sticks, opens 21" wide, NORTHERN PACIFIC red/black logo on front, b/w train-boat pic other side, ca. 1900, rare $125.00

HAND FAN – rice paper, folding type, ten bamboo sticks, opens 20" wide, NORTHERN PACIFIC red/black logo front, hand-colored train-boat pic other side, ca. 1890, rare $150.00

HAND FAN – blue floral paper, folding type, 24 sticks, opens 15" wide, "From your Fans at UNION PACIFIC RAIL-ROAD" $7.50

HAND FAN – cardstock, Moolah Shrine Circus hat, 7¼ x 12", on flat wood handle, WABASH RR advertising back-side $5.00

JIGSAW PUZZLE – cardboard, two-sided, Sioux City, Iowa CORN PALACE, map of ILLINOIS CENTRAL RAIL-ROAD routes, orig. box 4 x 4", dated 1889, rare. $95.00

KEY CASE – black leather, 1½ x 2½", gold logo, "Ship and Travel via SOO LINE," $5.00

Picture Puzzle

LETTER OPENER – bronze, 8½"L, NORTHERN PACIFIC "The Great Big Baked Potato" embossed on both sides $95.00

LETTER OPENER – nickel-plated thin brass, 5" L, ornate, CHICAGO MILWAUKEE & ST. PAUL RY, red logo, "Chicago and Omaha Short Line," ca. 1890 ....$35.00

LETTER OPENER – plastic, red, streamliner shape, 8½"L, ROCK ISLAND, Century of Service 1852-1952 ......$8.00

LETTER OPENER – plastic, red, 8½"L, NORTHERN PACIF-IC logo, "Main Street of the Northwest" $6.00

PAPERWEIGHT – metal rim ⅜" thick, round, 2¾"D, CHI-CAGO GREAT WESTERN Maple Leaf Route herald on celluloid covering both sides, ca. 1890's.............$125.00

PAPERWEIGHT – tin, white plastic overlay, round, 3½"D, mirror bottom, NORTHERN PACIFIC YPL logo, "Fargo Diamond Jubilee," made by Fargo Rubber Stamp Wks $45.00

Shaving Kit

PAPERWEIGHT – glass, 1" thick, octagon, 3"D, GREAT ROCK ISLAND ROUTE CRI&PRY on black logo,SOLID VESTI-BULE TRAINS and list of cities, ca. 1880's $100.00

PAPERWEIGHT – lucite, clear, 1" thick, round, 3"D, "ROCK ISLAND   LINES   1852-1952" Centennary logo incased $45.00

PAPERWEIGHT – marble sample 1 x 3 x 4", glued photo of bldgs., "EAST TENNESSEE MARBLE, Compliments of SOUTHERN RY and LOUISVILLE & NASHVILLE RY," 1915 ....$35.00

PAPERWEIGHT — bronze, round, 3"D, St. L. SW.Ry. COT-TON BELT ROUTE logo, lightning bolt, diesel train, flowers raised on surface, 1950's $75.00

PENNANT – green felt, vertical, 30" L, NORTHERN PACIF-IC RAILWAY advertising "Great Big Baked Potato" Dining Car Dept...$175.00

POCKET DIARY – brown celluloid covers, 2½ x 3¾", MIS-SOURI KANSAS & TEXAS RY red logo, figure of Lady Katy and adv. "The Katy Flyer," 1901-1902 calendar $40.00

POCKET DIARY – maroon leather covers, 2¼ x 4", THE

NORTH WESTERN LINE (gold logo) "Compliments of CStPM&ORy.," 1908 calendar $25.00

POCKET DIARY – black grain leather covers, "MPLS. & ST. LOUIS RR CO., THE PEORIA GATEWAY LINE" (gold logo) 1932 calendar $10.00

POCKET KNIFE – single blade, Remington, SOO LINE, red logo on pearlized 2½" case w/ball end $35.00

POCKET KNIFE – two blades, Remington, MISSOURI PACIFIC LINES logo w/train on pearlized 3¼" case $25.00

POCKET KNIFE – two blades, CHICAGO GREAT WESTERN, "Diesel Powered-Route Your Freight," red diesel train on pearlized 2¼" case $35.00

POCKET MIRROR – round 2"D, pictorial train scene, FRISCO SYSTEM "There is Something to See" red logo $95.00

POCKET MIRROR – in green plastic rectangular case, 2½ x 3", BURLINGTON NORTHERN, "We think you're beauti-ful"...$5.00

POCKET MIRROR – round, 2¼"D, celluloid cover, photo of car leaving lower station, MT. TOM RAILROAD, Holyoke, Mass., early 1900's $50.00

POSTAGE STAMP CASE – celluloid, flat 1¾ x 2½", inside book for stamps, MISSOURI PACIFIC, advertising name trains to cities, 1924 ....$37.50

POSTER STAMPS – set of 10, "See America First," Series No. 2, Blackfeet Indians, Glacier National Park, GREAT NORTHERN RAILWAY...$20.00

POSTER STAMPS – set of 10, "See America First," Series No. 7. wild animals, GREAT NORTHERN RAILWAY ..$15.00

POSTER STAMPS – set of 10, "Wonderland," Series No. 2, Yellowstone National Park, NORTHERN PACIFIC RAILWAY $15.00

POSTER STAMPS – set of 10, "The Overland Route Series" scenes out West, UNION PACIFIC SYSTEM.........$15.00

POSTER STAMPS – single, "Go West" Series No. 1, Royal Gorge, Colo. BURLINGTON ROUTE $1.50

RULER – 12" folding, celluloid, WISCONSIN CENTRAL RAILWAY, adv. make "it the Rule" to travel their route, 1905, rare..$75.00

SAFETY RAZOR KIT – Ever-Ready, nickel plated case, razor/blades, Compliments of GREAT NORTHERN RAILWAY, New Oriental Limited, ca. 1920's..........$50.00

SEWING KIT – celluloid, tubular, 2½"L, top unscrews, contains thimble, needle, thread, SOO LINE, Freight and Passenger Service $18.00

SOUVENIR SPOON – silverplate, 6"L NORTHERN PACIFIC, embossed logo, potato, "Route of the Great Big BAKED POTATO"..$75.00

SOUVENIR SPOON – silverplate, 6"L, SOO LINE, embossed logo, view of Locks, Mich. "Through Cars to Atlantic & Pacific Oceans" $75.00

TAPE MEASURE – 36", pictorial celluloid case 1½"D, Summit House, Car Leaving Station, MT. TOM RAILROAD, Holyoke, Mass., early 1900s $45.00

TAPE MEASURE – 36", black/white celluloid case 1¼"D, SOO LINE logo, A new train, "The Winnipeger" early 1900's $27.50

TRAY – tin, rectangular, 10½ x 15¼", brown finish, SOO LINE, "Montana Success," map showing rail lines leading to setting sun's rays, ca. 1907 ....$150.00

WINDSHIELD SCRAPER – ice, white plastic, dust pan shape, 5"L, "Compliments of NEW YORK CENTRAL SYSTEM Road to the Future" $5.00

Advertising Wall Posters

The railroads used many colorful posters down through the years to advertise their trains and special travel features. These were displayed on the walls, bulletin boards and other places in ticket offices, passenger terminals and small town depots. Many of these posters did not survive for long as they were discarded when their usefulness ended. Value depends on condition; those that are fly-specked, soiled and torn are usually discounted in value. An early rare poster in fine shape generally brings an exceptionally high price, as noted here.

B&M – "The Boston and Maine RR Will Sell Round-Trip Excursion Tickets to the GREAT FOREPAUGH AND WILD WEST SHOWS to Wells River & Woodsville Thursday, Aug. 14 afternoon and evening" (2-sided poster picturing various attractions to see at the shows) red/black printing on off-white, 10½ x 28", dated 1890, rare $175.00

BCR&N – this is a scene at IOWA'S Famous SUMMER RESORT SPIRIT LAKE Reached by (logo) The IOWA ROUTE, Burlington Cedar Rapids and Northern Ry (Tourists are shown in swimming attire at the beach of the Magnificent Hotel Orleans) multi-color litho on white, 10½ x 22", ca. 1890, rare $200.00

BCR&N – Harvest Excursions, August 4 and 18, Sept. 1, 15 and 29, Oct. 6 and 20, to points in IOWA, MINNESOTA AND SOUTH DAKOTA. Round Trip Rate ONE FARE plus $2.00. The Cedar Rapids Route (logo), red printing on white, 5½ x 15¼", ca. 1900, scarce...................$75.00

BURLINGTON – COLORFUL COLORADO in multi-color letters on white across wide top, color photo of tourists on horseback on canyon trail at center, across the white bottom stripe is a BR logo and slogan "Best by BURLINGTON," 25 x 40", ca. 1960's $15.00

CM&StP – Through Cars, Quick Time, our DENVER and CHICAGO express via the UNION PACIFIC RAILWAY and the (red logo) CHICAGO MILWAUKEE and ST. PAUL RAILWAY. (tt. schedule listed below) black printing on white, 9 x 22½", ca. 1912 ....$85.00

GN – LOW COACH FARES TO CHICAGO International Livestock Exposition Nov. 29 to Dec. 6, 1941, Round Trip Coach Fares to Chicago (photo of bldg. plus fares from cities listed below, also GN (logo) red/blk printing on white, 8½ x 22" $25.00

GN – SEATTLE Queen City of the Pacific Northwest! in red/blue letters on white across top, color photo of city and space needle at night in center, across the white bottom is a GN goat logo and slogan, "Best way to get there? Go Great Northern," 25 x 40", ca. 1960's $15.00

Framed Early Poster, ca. 1890

LV – LEHIGH VALLEY Coach Excursion to NEW YORK Saturday-Sunday June 8-9, $2.50 round trip, Baseball - New York Giants vs. Boston, Polo Grounds, 3 p.m. DST (tt schedule) dk. blue on pink, 5 x 14½", ca. 1920's $18.00

M&StL – Low Rate EXCURSION to TWIN CITIES and return via Minneapolis & St. Louis RR account North Dakota-Minnesota Football Game at Minneapolis, Oct. 2. (timetable schedule and photo of U of M stadium) below, black printing on white, 8 x 19", ca. 1930's $35.00

NP – NORTHERN PACIFIC RAILROAD, The Dining Car Route to the PACIFIC COAST, passing through Minnesota, North Dakota, Montana, Idaho, Oregon and Washington Territory. (Pullman Palace Cars, The Shortest Line, etc. below). Multi-color printing on yellow, 10½ x 28", ca. 1887, rare $250.00

NP – horizontal color photo reproduction of cowboys and

cattle titled, "Montana Roundup" by Jessamine Spear Johnson, dated 1924, 30 x 40", scarce $150.00

NP – reproduction of a painting showing a passenger train rounding a curve in the mountains by Krollman, titled at bottom "North Coast Limited in the Montana Rockies," a Northern Pacific logo is at the left of the title, 30 x 42", ca. 1920's $55.00

NP – has a border of portraits from life of Indians painted by Marion Glemby with teepee scene in center, bottom titled THE INDIAN COUNTRY (feathered letters) between two Northern Pacific logos, 30 x 40", ca. 1920's $95.00

NP – reproduction of a painting of the Absoroka Mountains, Montana, with passenger train in foreground by Gustav Krollman. Along the bottom is the title MONTANA between two Northern Pacific logos, 30 x 40", ca. 1920's $50.00

NP – multi-color litho depicting Cowboys and Indians on horseback riding down Main Street in town titled RODEO PARADE in the Montana-Wyoming Dude Ranch Country. A Northern Pacific logo is at the bottom corners, 30 x 40", ca. 1930's $75.00

PRR – multi-color litho titled WASHINGTON THE CITY BEAUTIFUL depicting buildings amidst trees and people alongside a locomotive. At bottom is PENNSYLVANIA RAILROAD in red on dark blue, 25 x 40", ca. 1930's $60.00

PRR – Pennsylvania System $3.00 to NEW YORK and return SUNDAYS Sept. 12, 26, Oct. 10, 24, Nov. 7, 21, Dec. 5, 19, 1920 SPECIAL TRAIN (tt schedules and photo Amer. Museum Natural History bldg.) red on cream, 6 x 19" $22.00

PULLMAN – horizontal dark blue cardstock poster, 23 x 29", featuring two 7" x 9" color scenes - one shows a home in the winter, another shows a couple seated in a Pullman car compartment, entitled "Travel in Pullman SAFETY and COMFORT to your Favorite Winter Resort." Along the bottom vacation spots are depicted, ca. 1936..$45.00

READING – Philadelphia and Reading Railway UP-THE-HUDSON to NEWBURGH and return, 300 miles by river and rail, Sunday, Sept. 17, 1922, $4.00 round trip (tt schedule and photo of Steamer Benjamin B. Odell) black on yellow, 5 x 16"..$18.00

SP – KLONDIKERS N.B. If you are going to Alaska by the DYEA or SKAGWAY Route, you can shorten your journey thence from 18 to 48 hours in time by taking the Famous SHASTA ROUTE of the SOUTHERN PACIFIC COMPANY (names of cities, schedule, etc., plus logo and ills. of pass. train) red/green printing on white, 10½ x 28", dated 1898 ....$145.00

UP – ONE DAY SAVED, The OVERLAND FLYER makes faster time to LOS ANGELES, SAN FRANCISCO and PORTLAND via (shield logo) UNION PACIFIC, TheOVERLAND ROUTE than by any other line. Double Daily Trains (names of cities and advertising below.) Black/red/blue printing on white, 9½ x 25", ca. 1890 ....$130.00

UP – GAR Annual Encampment Cleveland, Ohio, September 10-14, 1901. Take The (shield logo) UNION PACIFIC, Greatly Reduced Rates, etc. (Veteran in blue uniform is standing with raised sword at center), red/blue/black printing on white, 10½ x 28" $95.00

UP – like a smooth, cool breeze – that's one way of describing travel on Union Pacific's daily STREAMLINER'S Daily to Los Angeles, San Francisco-Portland-Denver — From Chicago and St. Louis (girl standing wearing white dress, blue hat & purse, yellow streamliner in background) black printing on pale blue, white border, 25 x 38", ca. 1940's $35.00

WABASH – The WABASH Railway, SHORTEST LINE to St. Louis-Kansas City – The West and Southwest, Palace Reclining Chair Cars, etc. (vase of roses depicted at center) multi-color litho, 10½ x 28", ca. 1886, rare $195.00

Art

Most nineteenth century original railroad art is owned by museums or is in private collections. Many artists from the early twentieth century produced railroad art that is now being offered for sale at various prices, depending on the fame of the artist. Original Currier & Ives railroad lithographs command very high prices. Other works such as woodcuts, etchings, engravings, or reproductions of railroad subjects are priced according to their rarity. Old photographs of locomotives and railroad scenes are steadily increasing in value and are now finding their way into collections. Many of these various old pictures hung on the walls of depots and railroad offices. When found intact in their original frames, they usually bring a much higher price.

Paintings and Drawings

Note: Measurements here do not include the frame – only the material that the art work is on, such as canvas, paper, wallboard or panel.

Pen and ink drawing – paper, 19½ x 24½", NP Ry's North Coast Limited (passenger train in country) Helmut Kroening, 1901 ....$250.00

Pen and ink sketch – illustration board, 6 x 8", "Old Time Atchison, Topeka & Santa Fe Train," Herb Mott, 1961 ....$75.00

Pen and ink sketch – illustration board, 7 x 9", engineer at the throttle in cab, Soo Line advertisement, 1924........$95.00

Pen and ink sketch – paper, 4 x 7", two steam locomotives side by side, Helmut Kroening, 1925.....................$50.00

Pen and ink sketch – paper, 7½ x 15" "GN Fast Mail Train No. 27," (out West) Fred R. Wooley, 1937 ....$35.00

Oil, wallboard – 11½ x 14½", "Hezekiah Upjohn," railroad tycoon, (portrait — executive sitting in chair) A. Sheldon Pennoyer, 1942 ....$400.00

Framed Original Water Color Signed and Dated 1961

Original Pen and Ink Sketch Early 1900's

Watercolor – paper, 11 x 20½", NYC & HR RR's "Empire State Express" (speeding passenger train along river), Helmut Kroening, 1908 ....$375.00

Watercolor – paper, 17¾ x 24½", "UP's Fast Mail, Sherman Hill, '55," (2 steam loco's pulling cars) Howard Fogg, 1960 ....$950.00

Watercolor – paper, 12¾ x 17½", "Buffalo Hunt Excursion Train," (tourist shooting buffalo from train) Herb Mott, 1961 ....$275.00

Watercolor – illustration board, 14 x 21", "Hutchinson Local"(GN mixed train) Pat McMahon, 1961 ....$150.00

Watercolor – paper, 14 x 20", The "400" (C&NW steam locomotive) C. Zimmer, 1961 ....$125.00

Watercolor – paper, 10 x 14", "Christmas Greetings" (station agent handing wreath to train) Don Salmela, 1950 ....$45.00

Woodcuts, Etchings and Engravings

Of special interest are the woodcuts, etchings and engravings that appeared in periodicals before the turn of the century, such as *Illustrated London News, Harper's Weekly, Ballou's Pictorial Drawing Room Companion,* and the like, picturing trains and railroad scenes as it was back in those days. These are being collected by railroad enthusiasts and historians as well, and when appropriately framed, bring good prices.

Engraving – 7¼ x 9¼", Interior of a Palace Hotel Car used on the Pacific Railroad, sketched by A.R. Waud, from *Illustrated London News,* 1861, hand tinted $35.00

Engraving – 7¼ x 10¾", THE DEPOT AT HEXAM, Northumberland, published 1836 by Currie and Bowman, New-castle-on-Tyne $75.00

Engraving – 7½ x 11" (mezzotint) LAST RUN steam locomotive put to rest on scrapline track, by Reynold H. Weidenar, 1955 ....$35.00

Etching – 9¼ x 15½", NYNH & HR RR Station, Springfield, Conn., Geo. S. Payne, 1891 ....$200.00

Woodcut – 7 x 14", "The Village Depot" from a painting by E. L. Henry, from *Harper's Weekly,* 1868, hand tinted $50.00

Woodcut – 4 x 7", The New United States Railway Post Office – Exterior, showing box for drop letters, from Frank Leslie's *Illustrated* Newspaper, Oct. 8, 1864 ....$15.00

Woodcut – 2¼ x 7", horizontal train masthead of the *American Railway Journal,* 1835. Depicts an early loco and 3 cars — baggage, coach, piggy back, by G. Lansine $20.00

Early Newspaper Engraving

Woodcut – 3¾ x 6½", Bridge over Rock River, Chicago and Rock Island Railroad, from *Ballou's Pictorial Drawing Room Companion,* 1855 ....$15.00

Builder's Lithographs and Photographs

Early builder's lithos and photos, when found in their original antique frames, usually carry a premium price tag. In later years, many came unframed, and some were put in common frames, which are not worth much; in this case, the litho or photo has the real value and is priced accordingly.

LITHOGRAPH – Ch.H. Crosby Litho. 46 Water St., Boston, 22½ x 28½", depicts a 4-4-0 locomotive, Highland Light, CCCRR, built by Wm. Mason, Taunton, MA (ca. 1875). Original frame — ornate 2" raised mahogany molding w/gold lining, 26½ x 32" $1,000.00

LITHOGRAPH – C.H. Crosby & Co. Lith. Boston, 17 x 27", 4-4-0 locomotive depicted inside oval with four HLW monogrammed corners. Title at bottom, THE HINKLEY LOCOMOTIVE WORKS, BOSTON. (ca. 1885) Original frame – 1¼" green finish molding, 19 x 29" $500.00

Framed Locomotive Builder's Photograph, 1926

LITHOGRAPH – lith. & printed in colors, L.N. Rosenthal, Philadelphia, 14 x 19", depicts a 4-4-0 locomotive, Tiger, Pennsylvania RR Company, title at bottom reads, "Engines of this plan weighing from 37,000 to 64,000 lbs., M.W. BALDWIN & CO. LOCOMOTIVE BUILDER'S, PHILADELPHIA," (ca. 1850's) unframed $350.00

PHOTOGRAPH – plate, 13 x 28½", Great Northern 0-6-0 switch engine 27, J. Reid, photographist, mounted on title cardboard w/specs., in original frame, ROGERS LOCOMOTIVE COMPANY, Paterson, New Jersey, 1890.

Frame is 3" ornate acorn leaf oak molding w/gold lining, 27 x 43" $250.00

PHOTOGRAPH – plate, 13½ x 29", 2-10-0 locomotive mounted on titled cardboard in original frame, BALDWIN LOCOMOTIVE WORKS, Burnham, Parry, Williams & Co., Philadelphia, 1885. Frame is 2½" grooved oak molding, 24 x 40" $200.00

PHOTOGRAPH – plate, 11 x 27", C. & E.I., 0-8-0 switch engine #1, mounted on titled cardboard in original frame, Burnham Williams & Co. BALDWIN LOCOMOTIVE WORKS, Philadelphia, 1926. Frame is 2½" mahogany molding w/gold lining, 22 x 37" $125.00

PHOTOGRAPH – plate, 6½ x 10½", Pennsylvania 4-8-2 locomotive #6800, mounted on gray cardboard w/gold title, The BALDWIN LOCOMOTIVE WORKS, Philadelphia, PA, USA, 1926. Frame is narrow black, ½" molding, 10 x 13" $50.00

PHOTOGRAPH – plate, 6½ x 10½", CHICAGO & ILLINOIS MIDLAND 2-10-2 locomotive #602, mounted on grey cardboard w/gold title, The BALDWIN LOCOMOTIVE WORKS, Philadelphia, PA, USA, 1926. Frame is narrow black, ½" molding, 10 x 13" $50.00

PHOTOGRAPH – plate, 7 x 16", M.St.P.&A. 4-4-0 locomotive 2, mounted on titled cardboard, 12" x 20", MANCHESTER LOCOMOTIVE WORKS, Manchester, NH, W.G.C. Kimball, Photographer, Concord, NH (ca. 1890) unframed $100.00

PHOTOGRAPH – plate, 6½ x 10½", 4-8-2 locomotive #132 (unassigned — N&W RY?) mounted on grey cardboard w/ gold title, The BALDWIN LOCOMOTIVE WORKS, Philadelphia, PA, USA, unframed. Mat size 9 x 13" $25.00

PHOTOGRAPH – plate, 4 x 7¼", LEHIGH & NEW ENGLAND, 0-6-0 switch engine, mounted on grey cardboard, locomotive specs. printed on backside of photo, The BALDWIN LOCOMOTIVE WORKS, Built May 1936, unframed. Mat size 6½ x 10½" $15.00

PHOTOGRAPH – plate, 3 x 8", NORTHERN PACIFIC 2-8-8-4 Yellowstone type, unmounted, specs. printed on backside of photo, AMERICAN LOCOMOTIVE COMPANY built December 1928..$10.00

Old Prints and Lithographs

In this category, as with Locomotive Builder's Lithos and Photos, those in their original antique frames are increased in price considerably; however, when an old litho or print is put in a common frame, bear in mind that the real value is placed on the picture. In most cases, the frame should have secondary consideration.

LITHOGRAPH – AMERICAN LITHOGRAPHIC Co. NY, 15 x 24½", excluding margins. "Niagara Falls From Michigan Central Train," scene depicts people getting off passenger train 253 to view the Falls. Copyright 1903, American Lithographic Co. NY, original frame $250.00

LITHOGRAPH – AMERICAN LITHOGRAPHIC Co. NY, 15 x 24½", excluding margins. "Niagara Falls From Michigan Central Train," scene depicts passengers viewing the Falls from waiting train 8317, copyright 1924, The Michigan Central Railroad Co., original frame $200.00

LITHOGRAPH – 16 x 22", no margins, Indian on white horse against dark background holding spear; on his shield is logo, COLORADO MIDLAND RAILWAY, PIKE'S PEAK ROUTE, ca. 1890, rare, framed $500.00

PRINT – (from calendar) 17¼ x 22¾" excluding margins, repro of painting by William Harnden Foster, 1922, showing passenger train rounding river curve entitled "The Twentieth Century Limited of the NEW YORK CENTRAL LINES, The Greatest Train in the World," copyright New York Central RR, Osborne Co. Newark, NJ, original frame $125.00

PRINT – (from calendar) 17¾ x 22¾" excluding margins, repro of painting by Walter L. Greene. Freight and passenger train over/under bridge entitled A NATIONAL INSTITUTION, The Twentieth Century Limited of the NEW YORK CENTRAL LINES, Copyright 1925 NY Central RR Co., printed in USA, original frame $100.00

PRINT – (from calendar) 17¾ x 22¾" excluding margins, repro of painting by Walter L. Greene depicting 3 steam locomotives abreast, entitled THOROUGHBREDS, The Twentieth Century Limited in three sections at LaSalle St. Station, Chicago, NEW YORK CENTRAL LINES, Copyright 1927, NY Central RR Co., printed in USA, original frame $75.00

PRINT – 17½ x 25¾" excluding margins, repro of painting by Grif Teller depicting passenger train (loco 5411) rounding curve under semaphore signals entitled "On Time" Pennsylvania Railroad, ca. 1920's, Osborne Co., Newark, NJ. Copyright The Pennsylvania Railroad System, original frame $100.00

PRINT – 17½ x 25¾" excluding margins, repro of a painting by Grif Teller depicting passenger train (loco 5409) out of city in farm lands entitled SERVANT OF THE NATION'S INDUSTRY, ca. 1925, Osborne Co. Newark, NJ. Copyright the Pennsylvania Railroad System, original frame $85.00

PRINT – (from calendar) 23 x 28¾" including margins, repro of painting by Grif Teller, electric passenger train entitled THE NEW DAY Pennsylvania Railroad, 1933, unframed $45.00

PRINT – 16¼ x 24¼", no margins, repro of painting by Harold Evett showing Pennsylvania RR passenger train (loco 5357) rounding curve on stone arch bridge w/railings, ca. 1926, original frame $35.00

Framed Lithograph –
Niagara Falls from Michigan Central Train, 1903

LITHOGRAPH – 18 x 24" including margins, wood-burning locomotive on display entitled "The Famous War Engine, GENERAL, of the Western & Atlantic RR. Now on Permanent Exhibition in Union Depot, Chattanooga, TN." NASHVILLE, CHATTANOOGA & ST. LOUIS RAILWAY ca. 1920's, framed.....................$95.00

PRINT – 22 x 24", no margins, repro of painting, "The Sunshine Special," "Missouri Pacific Railroad steam passenger train," by William Harnden Foster. Picture on thick cardboard, varnished similar to oil painting. Original frame w/name plate "The Sunshine Special," St. Louis or Memphis and Texas, MISSOURI PACIFIC RAILROAD, ca. 1930....................................$175.00

LITHOGRAPH – 9½ x 13½", including wide margins, b/w shades, depicts girl holding opened wicker basket containing small animals, CHICAGO and NORTH WESTERN Railway in gold letters lower lefthand corner, bottom margin is printed, "Entered according to Act of Congress in the year 1884 by C.H. Zink" (rare) Original antique frame $150.00

LITHOGRAPH – (from Santa Fe calendar) 13 x 13¾" including margins, repro of painting by E. I. Couse showing Indian weaving rug entitled THE WEAVER Copyright 1931, American Lithographic Co. NY, unframed....$20.00

LITHOGRAPH – (from calendar) 13 x 13¾", including margins, repro of painting by Frederic Mizen showing Indian chief beating drum entitled "Indian Chant." Copyright 1952, The Atchison Topeka and Santa Fe Ry. Co. Boston, unframed..$15.00

PRINT – 26 x 32", no margins, repro of painting Mt. St. Helens by Gustav Krollman entitled "Cascade Mountains State of Washington USA" Northern Pacific Railway, ca. 1920's. Picture on thick cardboard and varnished to simulate oil painting. Original frame w/brass nameplate "Mount St. Helens, Washington," NORTHERN PACIFIC RAILWAY, logos....................................$85.00

Currier & Ives Lithographs

"American Express Train," Palmer del., large folio, 1864 ....$3,500.00

"American Railroad Scene — Snowbound," small folio, 1871 ....$900.00

"The Express Train," J. Schutz del, small folio, N. Currier, 1853 ....$800.00

"The Lightning Express Train Leaving the Junction," Palmer del., large folio, 1863 ....$5,500.00

"The Railroad Suspension Bridge near Niagara Falls," small folio, N. Currier, 1856..............................$250.00

"Through to the Pacific," small folio, 1870 ....$500.00

Old Photographs

These are the originals made by commercial Photographic Companies directly from glass plates or negatives – not subsequent copies made from second or third generation prints, etc. The early studio-colored railroad photographs are hard to come by and usually bring a high price whenever offered.

Brown monochrome – 16 x 19½", side view of B.L. & N.R.R. 4-4-0 engine, "Merrimac" on track outside roundhouse, 2 men standing in tender, ca. 1868, unframed (rare) $195.00

Colored – 15 x 19", "Yankee Doodle Lake," Moffat Road, passenger train rounding elevation loop in mountains, copyright 1904, C.L. McClare, Denver, original frame (scarce) $150.00

Colored – 14 x 21", LEHIGH VALLEY RAILROAD, "Black Diamond Express," engine 675 with 4 cars on tracks along river, copyright 1898 by the Photochrome Co., original mat/frame, (rare) $265.00

Colored – 14 x 21", L.S. & M.S. "The Twentieth Century Ltd." engine 604 with 5 cars on tracks along river, copyright 1903, Detroit Photographic Co., mtd. on black cardboard, (rare) $185.00

Colored – 11½ x 12½", Louisville and Nashville RR track along river, "Mountains in Eastern Kentucky," ca. 1920, original mat/frame $50.00

Colored – 15 x 21", Jackson photo, passenger train in Rio Las Animas Canyon, Colorado, copyright 1899, Detroit Photographic Co., original mat/frame $150.00

Photogravure – blue/black etching, 11½ x 20¾" excluding margins with title "The Empire State Express," photo NYC&HR engine 2999 w/5 cars speeding on tracks, ca. 1906, Photogravure & Color Co. NY., unframed $140.00

Sepia – 8 x 10", C.St.P.M. & O. engine No. 157 with engineer and fireman posing at drivewheels, ca. 1900, original mat/frame $50.00

Photogravure, ca. 1906

Sepia – 6 x 8", Chicago Great Western Ry., "cornfield meet," engines 50 and 17 bump head on, train crews posing on roadway, ca. 1895, mtd. on cardboard, unframed $35.00

Sepia – 7½ x 10", NORTHERN PACIFIC and NATIONAL EXPRESS CO. line-up of horse drawn wagons front of delivery depot, Minneapolis, MN, 1900, matted and framed. (rare) $125.00

Sepia – 6 x 8½", SOO LINE RAILROAD, passenger train arriving at EDEN VALLEY depot, people waiting on platform, ca. 1890, matted and framed $75.00

Publicity Photos

These are large framed photographs used by the Railroads in later years for hanging on the walls of ticket offices, stations and other public places. These generally featured streamlined steam and diesel trains up until their demise. Several examples are listed here – those from the steam era are more in demand.

Framed Color Publicity Photo of the 1950's

C&NW – colored, 16 x 22", incl. original yellow mat. Photo shows yellow-green diesel streamliner on stone arch bridge leaving Minneapolis, titled "The '400' on the Stone Arch Bridge crossing the Mississippi." Orig. green frame, ca. 1940's $50.00

FRISCO LINES – colored, 12½ x 25½", "The Firefly" Kansas City-Tulsa-Oklahoma City, blue streamlined locomotive 1026 with 3 cars stationary on track, orig. frame, ca. 1940's..$55.00

ROCK ISLAND – colored, 19 x 26", incl. borders, "The Rocket" streamliner, red diesel 601 w/4 silver cars on track, semaphores at rear, titled below "The Rock Island Rocket," orig. red/silver frame, ca. 1940's $50.00

WABASH-UNION PACIFIC – colored, 24 x 36", "City of St. Louis" streamliner, blue/silver diesel pulling long string silver cars on curve, titled Wabash Streamliner "City of St. Louis" passing through Forest Park, St. Louis, Mo. enroute to Kansas City, Denver, Portland, San Francisco and Los Angeles. Orig. frame, ca. 1950's $75.00

Baggage and Brass Checks

Various brass checks are found that were used years ago to route travelers' baggage and railroad property pouches. Most are rectangular, some have rounded corners, others are irregular in shape. These brass baggage checks came in matched sets on a leather strap. Today the pair is seldom found still intact on the original strap: the duplicate is usually missing, or only a single check is found. Many bear the maker's hallmark. Those from remote or obscure railroads are especially desirable and have the higher value.

Baggage Checks

B&O – B&O RR LOCAL 39590, B&O capitol dome logo, 1½ x 2½", Am. Ry.S.Co. New York $45.00

B&OSW – B&OSW RR, Cincinnati, O. Return To General Baggage Agent, 2¾ x 2⅛", strap, American Ry.S.Co. N.Y. $50.00

B&M – BOSTON & MAINE RAILROAD, 58174 Way, 1⅜ x 1¾" J. Robbins Mfg. Co. Boston $40.00

BCR&N – Property of THE BURLINGTON CEDAR RAPIDS & NORTHERN RY ROUTE inside diamond logo, Cedar Rapids, IA, 2⅛ x 2½", strap, W.W. Wilcox Co. Chicago $95.00

CB&Q – Property of BURLINGTON ROUTE (logo) Chicago, 2⅛ x 2½", strap, Am.Ry.S.Co. New York $50.00

CM&StP – 3138 CM&StPRy, 1910, 1½ x 2", strap, Adams & Co. Mpls...$40.00

C&NW – Property of THE NORTHWESTERN LINE (logo) CStPM&ORy (below) St. Paul, Minn, 2½ x 2¼", strap, W.W. Wilcox & Co. Chicago.....................................$65.00

CRI&P – Chicago RI & Pacific RRD 6101, 1¼ x 1½", Thomas Patent, Feb. 19, 1867..$55.00

FJ&G – return set, two tags, Fonda and Cranberry Creek 6, via FJ&GRR, 1½ x 1⅝", 6 Cranberry CK to Fonda, via FJ&GRR, 1½ x 1⅞" strap, J. Robbins, Boston $135.00

GTRY – The Property of GRAND TRUNK RAILWAY SYSTEM (logo) Please return this Co. as soon as possible, 2¼ x 3", strap $40.00

HVRY – The property of the HOCKING VALLEY RY. CO., Please return this holder with both card checks to this Co. Columbus, O. soon as possible, 2½ x 2¾" $60.00

ICRR – Return this check to Ill. CENT. RR CHICAGO, circle/diamond shape logo below, 2 x 2⅞", strap, W.W. Wilcox Co., Chicago $45.00

LS&M – Return to LS&MSRy, Cleveland, Ohio, 2 x 2⅞" (steel) strap, W.W. Wilcox Co. Chicago $60.00

L&N – Return set, two tags, Cincinnati and Montgomery, M1347, L&NRR, 1¼ x 1½", M1347, Montgomery to Cincinnati, L&NRR, 1½ x 2", strap, Hoole Mfg. Co. New York $140.00

MC – The property of the MICH. CEN.RR.Co. Chicago, IL. Please return to this Co. soon as possible, 1¾ x 2¼", strap, W.W. Wilcox & Co. Chicago..........................$50.00

M&STL – M&StLRy, 307 Local, 1½ x 1¾", strap $55.00

MP – MO.PAC.Ry. 6 24 90 St. Louis to Denver, 1¾ x 2", strap $40.00

NP – Northern Pacific Yellowstone Park Line logo, 2¼ x 2½", strap, Am.Ry.S.Co. New York $55.00

NP – Return to NOR.PAC.RY.Co. St. Paul, Minn., YPL logo at center, 2¼ x 2½", steel $65.00

OSL – OSLRR Local 01881, 1½ x 2", strap, W.W. Wilcox Co. Chicago $75.00

PRR – Please send this check to your Gen. Baggage Office to be returned to Gen. Bag. Agt. PENN. RR, Philadelphia, PA, 1¾ x 2¼" $60.00

P&R – PHIL.& READ. RY. from Chadds Ford Jct., PA. Wilmington BR. LOCAL X23085, 1¼ x 2¼", Am.Ry.S.Co. New York $55.00

SP – 794 So.Pac.RR. To CS&CCRy. 1½ x 2", strap $40.00

TCRR – TEXAS CENTRAL RR LOCAL 2449, 1⅝ x 2", strap, Poole Bros. Chicago $45.00

UP – matched set, two tags, Claim baggage at UN.PAC.RY. depot, Schuyler, Neb. 25, 1⅜ x 1½". Claim Baggage at UN.PAC.RY. depot, Schuyler, Neb. 25, 1⅝ x 2", strap, W.W. Wilcox Co. Chicago....................$150.00

WC – The property of WISCONSIN CENTRAL RY. Milwaukee, Wis. Local, 1⅞ x 2¼", strap, W.W. Wilcox & Co. Chicago $75.00

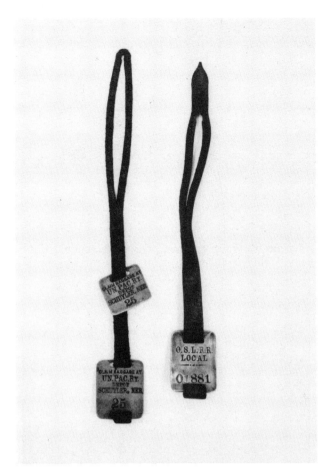

Baggage Checks On Original Leather Straps

Brass Checks

Many types of small brass checks or tags, mostly round with a single hole at the top, can also be found. These were used as time checks, parcel checks, key tags, and so on. Some bear a manufacturer's hallmark. Those from long-gone roads are worth more.

Brass Checks

A ST RR – ASTRR 152, 1 x 1⅜", oval key tag...............$10.00

AT&SF – SANTA FE SYSTEM 616 Topeka on obverse, (1⅛" aluminum) mach. shop stamped on reverse..........$12.00

B&O – B&O RR, fleur-de-lis at top and bottom obverse, 1⅜" dia., reverse side has ORD108 ....$18.00

C&NW – C&NW RR 633 Time Check, 1½ x 1¾", flat top, round bottom $15.00

ERIE – Erie RR 416 J.C. 8-sided, 1" across, Am.Ry.S.Co. NY $12.00

DWP – DW&P RY 110, 1¼" dia. $10.00

FJ&G – FJ&GRR A649, 1½"dia., Am.Ry.S.Co. New York $15.00

FRISCO – COTTON BELT ROUTE logo and diesel loco raised on top side; the back has a serial number stamped, "Finder please return to Public Relations Dept. St.L.S.W.Ry. St. Louis, MO" embossed, ¾ x 1½", rectangular key tag $20.00
GN – GNRY 208, dotted border design, 1¼" dia. $8.00

M&STL – M&StLRR 10, 1⅛" dia. $15.00
NYNH&H – NYNH&H RR, 20433 N H., 1⅝" dia. $18.00
P&R – P&R RY Co. Time Check 1503, 1⅜" dia., Am.Ry.S.Co. New York $18.00
WAB – WABASH RR Co. 4, 1 x 1¼", heart shape $12.00

Books

Poor's Manual of Railroads

Poor's Manual of Railroads have been in publication since the 1860s. They are 6" x 9" hardcover books with title in gold printing on green buckram, varying in thickness from approximately 3" to 5", with hundreds of pages containing the history of all United States railroads with maps, illustrations and great advertisements. Early copies in excellent condition sell for high prices.

1874-1875 – Henry V. Poor (Seventh Series) 2½" thick, 820 pages..$250.00
1886 – 19th Annual Number, 3" thick, 1022 pages $200.00
1892 – 25th Annual Number, 3" thick, 1208 pages (autographed copy Henry V. Poor and bookplate Henry William Poor) $225.00
1896 – 29th Annual Number, 3¼" thick, 1670 pages $175.00
1904 – 37th Annual Number, 3" thick, 1490 pages $150.00
1912 – 45th Annual Number, 5" thick, 3106 pages $125.00

Poor's Manuals

Moody's Manuals

Moody's Steam Railroads, American & Foreign, **John Moody**

Moody's Railroad Manual, a hardcover book, 8½" x 11½", is on the same order as *Poor's*, also published over the years and bring good prices as well.

1925 – 3½" thick, 1915 pages $75.00
1941 – 3¼" thick, 1862 pages $50.00
1945 – 2½" thick, 1565 pages $40.00
1948 – 2¼" thick, 1491 pages $35.00
1950 – 2¼" thick, 1448 pages $30.00

The Official Guide of the Railways

A manual that seems to be more in demand is *The Official Guide of the Railways,* published monthly since 1867. These are soft cardstock cover books, 7 x 10", on the same order as a thick catalog, containing over 1,000 pages, with train schedules, system maps, including an index of railroad stations in the United States and foreign countries. These books are considered a MUST on the railroadiana collector's bookshelf. Copies with clean unmarred covers, pages not soiled or torn, are worth much more than those in a damaged condition.

1921 – January, 1472 pages $85.00
1925 – August, 1664 pages...$80.00
1929 – September, 1760 pages $75.00
1935 – September, 1536 pages $60.00
1937 – August, 1536 pages...$50.00
1940 – October, 1536 pages...$40.00
1943 – January, 1472 pages $35.00
1945 – August, 1440 pages...$30.00
1950 – February, 1504 pages, M&StL Ry copy (property label on cover) $30.00
1956 – January, 1504 pages $20.00
1958 – August, 1416 pages, NP Ry copy (property label on cover) $25.00
1960 – May, 1344 pages $15.00
1965 – June, 1088 pages $10.00
1968 – June, 992 pages, 100th Anniversary Issue, 101st year, No. 1, gold cover.................................$15.00
1969 – June, 944 pages, Golden Spike Centennial Issue, 102nd year, No. 1, gold printing on buff, B&ORR copy, official ink stamp on cover $20.00
1972 – May, 728 pages $10.00

Official Guide of the Railways with property label pasted on cover, 1958

Miscellaneous

Baldwin Locomotive Works, Philadelphia: Exhibit at the Louisiana Purchase Exposition, St. Louis, 1904, 73 pages with illustrations and general description of locomotives on exhibit, 6 x 9", hardcover $35.00

Brotherhood Locomotive Engineers, 27th Grand International Convention at Pittsburg, Penn'a., Wednesday, October, 1890, 192 pages of illustrations and advertisements, 7 x 10", hardcover $45.00

Bullinger's Postal and Shippers Guide for the United States, Canada and Newfoundland, 1930, 1204 pages containing names of all post offices and railroad stations, 7 x 10", hardcover..$30.00

Hotel & Motel Red Book, 1969, The Milwaukee Road, 1360 pages, 5½ x 9", hard red cover $35.00

Lyles' Official Railway Manual for 1869 & 70, published by Lindsay, Walton & Co. New York, 472 pages containing a list of Railroads of North America, 5½ x 9", hardcover $135.00

Pullman's Palace Car Co., The 1897 Official Hotel Directory of the United States (HOTEL RED BOOK) 686 pages, 6 x 9", red hardcover...$50.00

The Mercantile Agency Postal and Shippers Guide for the United States and Canada, 1889, R.G.Dun & Co., 674 pages containing every post office, railroad station and United States' Fort (compiled and published by Edwin W. Bullinger) 7 x 10", hardcover..................................$75.00

The Rector Cook Book, Compliments of the Milwaukee Road, Fifth Edition, 1928, by George Rector, 173 pages, 5 x 8", hard cover..$65.00

Star Head Light & Lantern Co., Catalogue No. 8, 1915, 136 pages, published by S H L & L Co., Rochester, NY, 6 x 9½", hardcover...$135.00

Twentieth Century Manual of Railway Commercial and Wireless Telegraphy by Fred L. Meyer, Ninth Edition, 1925, 287 pages, 4½ x 7", hardcover..................................$35.00

Rule Books

These are small books, approximately 4 x 6", put out by the railroads containing over 100 pages of rules and regulations for employees involved in the movement of their trains. Description of title on the cover is given. All are hardcover unless otherwise noted. Rule books from long-gone roads are especially desirable and worth more.

BURLINGTON ROUTE – logo, BURLINGTON LINES Rules of the OPERATING Department, gold on black, May 1, 1951 ....$12.00

D&IR – The Duluth & Iron Range Railroad Company, Rules and Regulations for the GOVERNMENT OF EMPLOYEES to take effect JANUARY 1, 1907, black on brown $20.00

C&NW – CHICAGO & NORTH-WESTERN RAILWAY Company, Rules & Regulations for the GOVERNMENT OF EMPLOYEES of the OPERATING DEPARTMENT, black on brown, May 1, 1889 ....$25.00

C&NW – CHICAGO & NORTH WESTERN RY CO, RULES for the Government of the OPERATING DEPARTMENT, gold on maroon, January 17, 1928 ....$15.00

C&NW – CHICAGO & NORTH WESTERN SYSTEM, RULES for the Government of the OPERATING DEPARTMENT, effective January 1, 1953, gold on green..................$8.00

C&NW – CHICAGO AND NORTH WESTERN RAILWAY COMPANY, logo, RULES OF THE ENGINEERING DEPARTMENT, effective June 1, 1967, gold on maroon..$5.00

CGW – logo, CHICAGO GREAT WESTERN RAILROAD, BOOK OF RULES of the TRANSPORTATION DEPARTMENT, effective September 1, 1940, black on grey cardboard $20.00

CGW – CHICAGO GREAT WESTERN RAILROAD COMPANY, BOOK OF RULES, effective May 1, 1923, gold on brown $25.00

CSTPM&O – CHICAGO, ST. PAUL, MINNEAPOLIS & OMAHA Railway Company, RULES AND REGULATIONS for the GOVERNMENT OF EMPLOYEES of the OPERATING DEPARTMENT, Revised to Jan. 1, 1920, black on brown cardboard..$15.00

CSTPM&O – CHICAGO, ST. PAUL, MINNEAPOLIS & OMAHA Railway Company, RULES AND REGULATIONS for the GOVERNMENT OF EMPLOYEES of the OPERATING DEPARTMENT, March 1, 1903, gold on black..$30.00

GN – logo, UNITED STATES RAILROAD ADMINISTRATION, W.G. McAdoo, Director General of Railroads, GREAT NORTHERN RAILWAY, GREAT NORTHERN RULES, May 1, 1908, logo, black on grey cardboard $25.00

GN – GREAT NORTHERN RAILWAY COMPANY, RULES AND REGULATIONS of the OPERATING DEPARTMENT, effective May 1, 1921, gold on black..........$15.00

GN – logo, GREAT NORTHERN RAILWAY COMPANY, TRANSPORTATION RULES, 1929, black on maroon..$12.00

IC – logo, RULES AND REGULATIONS of the TRANSPORTATION DEPARTMENT, effective July 1, 1942, black on tan..$10.00

Rule Books

M&StL – The Minneapolis & St. Louis Railroad Company, RULES AND REGULATIONS OF THE OPERATING DEPARTMENT, effective July 14, 1912, gold on black..$25.00

M&StL – logo, THE MINNEAPOLIS & ST. LOUIS RAILWAY COMPANY, Rules and Regulations of the Operating Department, effective May 1, 1953, gold on red........$12.00

MStP&SSM – MINNEAPOLIS, ST. PAUL & SAULT SAINTE MARIE RAILWAY COMPANY Rules and Regulations of the Operating Department, May 1, 1912, gold on dark blue $22.00

MStP&SSM: – MINNEAPOLIS, ST. PAUL & SAULT SAINTE MARIE RAILWAY COMPANY (G.W. Webster and Joseph Chapman, Trustees) TRANSPORTATION RULES, Effective May 1, 1928 (Reprint June 1, 1940) gold on black..$12.00

NP – NORTHERN PACIFIC RAILWAY COMPANY, RULES AND REGULATIONS Operating Department, black on red, June 1, 1899..$27.50

NP – NORTHERN PACIFIC RAILWAY, TRANSPORTATION RULES June 1, 1919, black on red $15.00

NP – NORTHERN PACIFIC RAILWAY, TRANSPORTATION RULES, Effective April 1, 1926, white on brown ..$12.00

ROCK ISLAND – logo, UNIFORM CODE OF OPERATING RULES, Effective May 1, 1950, gold on maroon $8.00

WCF&NR WATERLOO, CEDAR FALLS AND NORTHERN RAILWAY COMPANY, Rules of the OPERATING DEPARTMENT, Effective December 1, 1930, gold on maroon..$18.00

Textbooks

Most of the books in this category pertain to the steam locomotive. Many are profusely illustrated with vocabularies of terms designating all of the railroads' steam power and rolling stock. *Simmons-Boardman's Cyclopedias, Car Builders', Locomotive, Railway Engineering and Maintenance,* published down through the years are highly prized, and early copies from the steam era go for big bucks.

Text Books

Building and Repairing Railways, 1903, Marshall M. Kirkman, 660 pages, 5 x 8", hardcover (Supplement To The Science of Railways) $15.00

Cars – Their Construction, Handling and Supervision, 1911, Marshall M. Kirkman, Book I: *The Railway Car, Its Construction and Handling,* 435 pages; Book II: *The Car Service Department,* 279 pages, 5 x 7¾", hardcover $22.00

Car Builders' Cyclopedia, 19th Edition, 1953, 1280 pages, Simmons-Boardman, 8 x 11¾", red, hardcover.........$175.00

Car Builders' Cyclopedia, 21st Edition, 1961, 955 pages, Simmons-Boardman, 8 x 11¾", blue, hardcover.......$150.00

Catechism of the Locomotive, Revised 1890 Edition, Matthias N. Forney, 709 pages, 6 x 8½", hardcover $45.00

Hoxsie's Pocket Companion For Locomotive Engineers & Firemen, 1875, Weed, Parsons and Company, 104 pages, 4 x 6", hardcover..$15.00

Locomotive Catechism, 13th Edition, 1896, Robert Grimshaw, 437 pages, 5 x 7½", hardcover $25.00

Locomotive Cyclopedia, 10th Edition, 1938, 1232 pages, Simmons-Boardman, 8 x 11¾", black, hardcover $200.00

Locomotive Cyclopedia, 13th Edition, 1947, 1418 pages, Simmons-Boardman, 8 x 11¾", blue, hardcover........$145.00

Modern American Railway Practice (10 volumes) Roundhouse and Shop, Machine Shop Work, L. Elliott Brookes, M.E., 1908, Vol. VIII, 464 pages, 5½ x 9", National Institute of Practical Mechanics, Chicago, Publishers, brown, hardcover...$12.00

Railway Engineering and Maintenance Cyclopedia, Fourth Edition in Series, 1939, 1008 pages, Simmons-Boardman, 8 x 11¾", red, hardcover $175.00

Railway Engineering and Maintenance Cyclopedia, Fifth Edition in Series, 1942, 1224 pages, Simmons-Boardman, 8 x 11¾", red hardcover $150.00

The Car Builder's Dictionary, Third Thousand, 1881, 491 pages, with 84 pages of advertisements in back, published by The Railroad Gazette, New York, 5 x 8", hard maroon cover...$325.00

The Science of Railways, Volume 1 of 12, 1900, Marshall M. Kirkman, 5 x 8", maroon, hardcover.....................$10.00

The Signal Engineer, 21st volume, 1928, 472 pages, Simmons-Boardman, 9 x 12", green canvas/red leatherbound $35.00

Railroad Books — History, Biography, Story

A great many books have been written about the railroads since their beginning and continuing up to the present. Ever since the steam locomotive disappeared from the scene, the interest in railroad books has proliferated and prices on them are on the rise. Listed here are some examples of earlier publications and their estimated values.

A Short History of American Railways, by Slason Thompson, D. Appleton & Co., NY, 1925, 449 pages, 5½ x 8½", hardcover...$12.00

Commodore Vanderbilt, An Epic of the Steam Age, by Wheaton J. Lane, Alfred H. Knoff, NY, 1942, 357 pages, 6 x 8¾", hardcover..$15.00

Daring and Suffering, A History of the Andrews Railroad Raid into Georgia in 1862 by Wm. Pittenger, War Publ. Co., NY, 1887, 416 pages with 52 page supplement, 6 x 9½", hardcover...$55.00

History of the Baldwin Locomotive Works, 1831-1923, The Bingham Company, Philadelphia, 210 pages, 6 x 9", hardcover $45.00

History of the Northern Pacific Railroad, by Eugene V. Smalley, GP Putnam's Sons, NY 1883, 437 pages with fold-out map in back pocket, 5½ x 8½", hardcover..................$185.00

Railroad Avenue, Great Stories and Legends of American Railroading, by Freeman H. Hubbard, Whittlesey House Publs., 1945, 374 pages, 6 x 9", hardcover.........................$15.00

Railroading From The Head End by S. Kip Farrington, Jr., Doubleday, Doran & Co., 1943, 296 pages, 6 x 9¼", hardcover...$15.00

The American Railway, Its Construction, Development, Management and Appliances, Chas. Scribner's Sons, 1889, 456 pages, text and illustrations, 7 x 10", hardcover ..$150.00

The Romance of the Rails by Agnes C. Laut, Volumes I and II, Robert M. McBride & Co., NY, 1929, 307 and 590 pages, 6 x 8¾", hardcover $30.00

The Story of American Railroads by Stewart H. Holbrook, Crown Publishers, Fifth Printing, 1959, 468 pages, 6 x 9", hardcover $12.00

The Story of the Baltimore & Ohio Railroad, 1827-1927, by Edward Hungerford, G.P. Putnam's Sons, NY 1928, (2 vols.) 372 and 365 pages, 6 x 9½", hardcover $65.00

Wonders and Curiosities of the Railway by W. S. Kennedy, 254 pages of stories of the locomotive in every land, publ. 1884 by S.C. Griggs & Co., 5 x 7½", hardcover......$20.00

NPRR History Book, 1883, with map

Children's Books

There is a wide range of children's books – picture books, educational reading material, stories fact or fiction, and many more. The early children's picture books in pristine condition are much in demand, bringing great prices.

Samples of Children's Books

Boy's Book of the Railroad, by Molly Elliot Seawell and others, Harper & Bros., NY, 1909, 245 pages, 5 x 7½", hardcover $10.00

Chuck Malloy, Railroad Detective on the Streamliner, by Thorp McClusky, (Big Little Book) Whitman Pub. Co. 1938, 292 pages, cardstock cover, 2½ x 4½" $15.00

Great Trains of the World by Wyatt Blassingame, Random House, NY, 1953, Pub. Illus. by Jack Coggins w/text, 30 pages, 8 x 11", hardcover $10.00

Iron Horses and the Men Who Rode Them, by Edith McCall, Grosset & Dunlap, Pub. 1960, 125 pages, 6 x 8", hardcover $8.00

My Railroad Book, Sam Gabriel Sons & Co., NY, 1914, illustrated captions and ABC's, 10 pages, 10 x 14", cardstock cover $27.50

On the Railroad by Robert S. Henry, colored illustrations by Otto Kuhler, Saalfield Publ. Co. 1936, photos and text, 10 pages, 10 x 12½", soft cover..............................$10.00

Railroad Picture Book, McLoughlin Bros., NY 1903, boy and girl's journey 1,000 miles by rail, colorful illustrations, 12 pages, 10½ x 13", cardstock cover $37.50

Ralph and the Missing Mail Pouch by Allen Chapman, Grosset & Dunlap, Publ's., (1 of 8 railroad series) 242 pages, 5 x 7½", hardcover....................................$8.00

The Boy's Book of Railroads by Irving Crump, Dodd, Mead & Co., NY, Pub. 1921, 269 pages, 5 x 7½", hardcover $6.00

The Erie Train Boy, by Horatio Alger Jr., Whitman Publishing Co., 1930, 183 pages, 4¾ x 7", cardboard cover $10.00

The Great K & A Train Robbery, by Paul Leicester Ford, pub. International Association of Newspapers and Authors, 1901, 200 pages, 4½ x 7", hardcover $10.00

The Railway that Glue Built, by Clara Andrews Williams, Frederick A. Stokes Co., Pub., 1908 (contains sheets of colored pictures to be cut out and glued on the appropriate background pages) 12 pages, 10½ x 14", cardstock cover $35.00

Trains – Stories and Pictures, by Louis T. Henderson, M.A. Donohue & Co., Pub., 1935, (a children's picture book of trains and stories about them), 20 pages, 10 x 12½", cardstock cover $12.50

Breast Badges

Breast badges were worn by authorized railroad employees and other personnel connected with the railroads – police, deputy sheriffs, watchmen, baggage and railway mail agents, dining car stewards, and the like. Most were star or shield shaped, nickel-plated with indented letters and digits filled in with black enamel. Many have the maker's hallmark on the back side. The badge with an uncommon occupation or from a short-lived railroad generally has a much higher value.

Note: Recent reproduction badges have come on the market, such as brass stars with a railroad name and occupation. These should not be confused with the genuine railroad issues.

Law Enforcement

AT&SF – 810 SPECIAL OFFICER, A.T.&S.F.RY. – six pointed ball-tipped star, 2½", nickel-plated, black letters, hmkd. F.W. Wilcox, Oak Park, Ill.....................................$125.00

B&O – BALTIMORE & OHIO RR RAILWAY POLICE – shield shape, 2¼ x 2½", nickel finish, raised letters, capitol dome embossed low center on pebbled field. Not hmkd $135.00

C&A – C & A RR – SPECIAL POLICE – six-pointed star, 3½", nickel-plated, black letters, hmkd. S.D. Childs & Co., Chicago $145.00

C&O – C & O RY SPECIAL POLICE OFFICER – eagle top, 1½ x 2½" nickel finish, black letters, steam locomotive embossed on center disc. Not hmkd $125.00

D&H – THE DELAWARE AND HUDSON COMPANY PO-LICE PATROLMAN 220 – modified shield shape w/side pillars, 2¼ x 2½", nickel finish, black letters, early locomotive raised inside circle, hmkd. C. G. Braxmar Co., Maiden Lane, N.Y. $165.00

DL&W – D.L. & W.R.R. POLICE – raised letters, shield shape, 2¼ x 2½", nickel-plated, embossed figurals center, cut-out numerals 116 bottom, hmkd. F.G. Clover Co., New York, N.Y...$135.00

DM&IR – SPECIAL OFFICER 254 D.M.&I.R.RY.CO – black letters, six-pointed star, 2½", steel, chromium-plated, not hmkd. $115.00

GM&O – ASST. SPECIAL AGENT, G.M. & O. RR CO. – six-pointed, ball-tipped star, 2½", nickel-plated, black letters, eagle atop shield emblem raised in center, hmkd. W.S. Darley & Co., Chicago 12 ....$150.00

GN – GREAT NORTHERN RAILROAD – shield shape, 2¼ x

Collection of Law Enforcement Breast Badges

2¾", nickel-plated, black letters, SPECIAL OFFICER on cut-out star center, hmkd. St. Paul Stamp Works $145.00

GN – G.N.RY. SPECIAL POLICE – six-pointed ball-tipped star, 2¾", nickel-plated, black letters, hmkd. St. Paul Stamp Works $125.00

IC – LIEUTENANT, CHIEF SPECIAL AGENT'S DEPT. I.C.R.R. – eagle atop sunburst, 1¾ x 2⅛", gold finish, black letters. ILLINOIS CENTRAL R.RD.CO. around shield embossed in center. Pat. No.'s on back....$135.00

IC – POLICE 105 ILL. CENT. R.R. – six-pointed star, 3", nickel finish, black letters, not hmkd. $100.00

IC – I.C.R.R. POLICE – raised letters, six-pointed star 3½", steel, chromium plated, eagle emblem at center, large numbers 5557 in copper finish across bottom, hmkd. H.J. Duckgeischel, Chicago $175.00

K.C. TERMINAL RY. CO. – KANSAS CITY, MO. 1915 – circle, 2¼" dia., nickel finish, black letters, SPECIAL 606 PO-LICE on cut-out star center, hmkd. Allen Stamp & Seal Co., Kansas City $185.00

NYC&STL – NICKEL PLATE PATROLMAN 121, N.Y.C. & ST. L.R.R.CO. – eagle atop shield, 1¾ x 2½", nickel finish, black letters, not hmkd $115.00

NP – DEPUTY SHERIFF N.P.RY. – six-pointed star, 2½", nickel-plated, black letters, hmkd. St. Paul Stamp Works..$110.00

NP – SPECIAL POLICE N.P.RY. – six-pointed star, 2½", nickel finish, black letters, not hmkd $100.00

PRR – P.R.R.CO. SERGEANT RAILWAY POLICE – shield shape, 2¼"x 3", nickel finish, engraved letters, State seal embossed in center, hmkd. S.G. Clover Co., Successor to Am. Ry. S. Co. New York $145.00

REA – RY. EXPRESS AGY. 113 POLICE – six-pointed ball-tipped star with number in center, black indented letters, nickel-plated, 2⅝", hmkd. Meyer & Wenthe, Chicago $125.00

REA – POLICE, RAILWAY EXPRESS AGENCY 20 – black letters, chrome plated shield shape, 1¾ x 2½", eagle atop, raised emblem in center of shield, not hmkd. $200.00

RI – SERGEANT ROCK ISLAND LINES POLICE 657 – six-pointed ball-tipped star, 2½", nickel finish, black letters, not hmkd. $135.00

SAL – CAPTAIN DETECTIVE POLICE – in black enamel letters on seven-pointed gold-plated humped star, 2⅞", SEABOARD AIR LINES RAILROAD in gold on black enamel circle with red heart in center, not hmkd. $175.00

WAB – WABASH RY. 729 POLICE – six-pointed tapered star, 2¾" nickel-plated, black letters, not hmkd..........$100.00

WB&S – PRIVATE DETECTIVE, W.B. & SOU.R.R. – six-pointed star, 2", nickel-plated, black letters, not hmkd. ..$85.00

WP – THE WESTERN PACIFIC R.R.CO. CALIFORNIA, RAILROAD AND STEAMBOAT POLICE 71 – six-pointed star, 3¼, nickel-plated, black letters, not hmkd. $275.00

Misc., Employees, Waiters, Etc.

CMSTP&P – C.M.ST.P.&P.R.R. 4, – black letters, flat top with round bottom, 1⅜ x 1⅝", nickel-plated, not hmkd. dining car waiter badge $18.50

D.M. & N.RY. 1395 EMPLOYEE – black letters on nickel-plated oval, 1⅛ x 2" $30.00

LS&MS – L.S. & M.S. RAILWAY D.C.S. (dining car steward) - - shield shape, 1½ x 1¾", gold finish, black letters, hmkd. J.H. Fleharty, CLEV.D.O. $85.00

NP – RAILROAD WATCHMAN, N.P.RY. – six-pointed star, 2½", nickel-plated, black letters, hmkd. St. Paul Stamp Works $110.00

NP – NORTHERN PACIFIC 594 – disc, 2" dia., black letters, not hmkd. dining car waiter's badge $50.00

NP – RAILROAD WATCHMAN, N.P.RY. – six-pointed star, 2", nickel-plated, black letters, hmkd. St. Paul Stamp Works $90.00

POD – POST OFFICE DEPARTMENT RAILWAY MAIL SERVICE 13415 – embossed designs, oval center with U.S. monogram and stars, eagle at top, laurel leaves at bottom, nickel finish, 2" across oval, hmkd. Am.Ry. Supply Co. Park Place, N.Y. $150.00

STPUD – BAGGAGE & MAILMAN 438 – shield shape, 1¾ x 2⅛", black indented letters, nickel-plated, not hmkd...$55.00

UNION DEPOT 34 – black letters on nickel-plated shield shape, 1½ x 1¾", hmkd. American Stamp Works, St. Paul, Minn. $35.00

UNION PACIFIC 6 – plastic shield shape waiter's badge, red/white stripes with black digit in circle, UNION PACIFIC, white on blue across top, 1½ x 1½", hmkd. Whitehead Hoag $15.00

W.&L.E.RY.935 V – black letters on round brass disc., 1½" dia. $50.00

Employee Breast Badges

Brotherhood Items

Brotherhood items are a segregated specialty that includes badges, celluloid pinback buttons, coat lapel buttons and pins, and other miscellaneous items. Of particular interest are the colorful reversible lodge badges with satin ribbons attached. These were worn at conventions, funerals and in parades. The coat lapel buttons issued to members of the Brotherhood for years of service are also noteworthy; some of these were made of solid gold. Note: Brotherhood magazines are included in the magazine section.

Badges, Lodge

Long wide satin ribbon with red-white-green stripe, having gold or silver printing. Backside is all black with "In Memoriam" printing in silver. Top has an ornate gold finish metal pinclasp, gold fringe at the bottom and ornate gold finish lodge emblem and ornaments hanging down from the top center of ribbon.

Lodge and Convention Badges

B. OF L.F. – Chippewa Valley Lodge No. 425, Abbotsford, Wis. Printing and illus. of engine in gold and red. Ornate gold frame pinclasp with MEMBER in black on white. 2½ x 8", No maker shown $17.50

B. OF L.F. – Chippewa Valley Lodge No. 425, Abbotsford, Wis. Printing and illus. of engine in gold and red. Ornate gold frame pinclasp with SECRETARY in black on white. 2½ x 8", No maker shown $22.50

B. OF L.F. – Chippewa Valley Lodge No. 425, Abbotsford, Wis. Printing and illus. of engine in gold and red. Ornate gold frame pinclasp with VICE MASTER in black on white. 2½ x 8", No maker shown $25.00

B. OF L.F. & E – Taylor Lodge, No. 175, Newark, Ohio. Top pinclasp has "Taylor Lodge No. 175" in black printing on white oval. Gold metal locomotive ornament 175 hangs in center with word MEMBER above. 2¾ x 9". Maker – The M.C. Lilley & Co. Columbus, O $45.00

BROTHERHOOD OF RAILROAD TRAINMEN– top pinclasp reads Killington Lodge No. 297, Rutland, Vt. Two hanging ornaments, one with engine, other is lodge emblem. 2¾ x 8¾". Maker – Hyatt Mf'g. Co. Balto, MD......$45.00

CONDUCTOR – FOND-DU-LAC DIVISION No. 259, O.R.C. Fond-du-Lac, Wis. 2½ x 9¼", ornate pictorial pinclasp at top shows two pass. trains and conductor collecting tickets in coach; Lodge emblem hanging at center of ribbon. Maker – The Whitehead & Hoag Co. Newark, N.J. $50.00

O.R.C. – Fond Du Lac Division No. 259, gold printing on red, top pinclasp is metal likeness of early passenger coach, pair of crossed 2½" metal gavels hang down a bottom. Ribbon is 2½ x 4". No maker shown.....................$30.00

Badges, Convention

The pinclasp bar has the member's name, with or without red-white-green satin ribbon attached. The hanging medallion has raised letters and designs, along with trains, buildings, bridges, etc. Approx. of all measurements are given.

A.R.S.B. & B. – pinclasp has red-green-white enameled emblem, ornate chain linked silver medallion has a train depot and bridge, also "Railway Superintendents of Bridges and Buildings." 1½ x 3¾" hmk'd C.G. Braxmar Co. Maiden Lane, N.Y. $25.00

B.L.E. – pinclasp has name, rectangular silver medallion has front end of passenger train, also "Sixth Triennial Convention, Cleveland, June, 1930." BLE red-white-blue emblem at bottom center, 1¼ x 3". hmkd. Bastian Bros. Rochester, N.Y. $22.00

B.OF R.T. – pinclasp has depot, state seal and "Columbus, May, 1909" embossed. Hanging round silver medallion has BTR on passenger train, two flags criss-crossed and 400. Around the edge is "9th Biennial Convention Brotherhood of Railroad Trainmen." Satin multi-color ribbon has word VISITOR. 1½ x 3¾". Hmkd. Whitehad & Hoag, Newark, N.J. $35.00

B. OF R.T.A. – pinclasp has name, attached multi-color ribbon; hanging gold medallion has three enameled shields at top, pass. train raised in center circle with words "Am. Ass'n of General Passenger and Ticket Agents, St. Paul, Sept. 1911." 1¾ x 4", hmkd. Chas M. Robbins, Attleboro, Mass. $30.00

O.R.C. – pinclasp has name, attached multi-color ribbon has "Guest of Div. 117 O.R.C." hanging silver medallion has enameled Order of Railway Conductor's emblem with two flags, pass. train on stone arch bridge, with words "38th Session Grand Division, Minneapolis, May 1925" around border. 1¾ x 4", hmkd. Greenduck Co., Chgo $35.00

O.R.C. – metal pinclasp is shape of ticket punch with words embossed "Guest of Division 40." Ornate white metal medallion with eagle atop and colorful lodge emblem in center with illus. and words "Grand Division O.R.C. St. Paul, 1901." Multi-color ribbon has black digits imprinted. 2¼ x 5". Maker Whitehead and Hoag Co. Newark, N.J. $42.50

Veteran Ass'n & Misc.

AMERICAN STREET & INTERURBAN RAILWAY ASS'N. ATLANTIC CITY, 1908 – interurban streetcar, eagle raised on ornate bronze 1¼ x 1½" pinclasp with multi-color enamel flags ea. side. Backside has 27th Annual Convention Atlantic City N.J. October 12-17, 1908. Maker – Whitehead & Hoag Co. Newark, N.J. $22.00

B.C.R.&N. – rectangle pinclasp with name, white satin ribbon with yellow printing "First Annual Reunion B.C.R.&N. Cedar Rapids, Iowa, Oct. 1-2, 1915." Blue enamel shield shape medal hanging from ribbon has "The Iowa Route Burlington Cedar Rapids and Northern Ry." in gold. 1½ x 3¾". Maker – The Gustave Fox Co. Cin. O $75.00

GREAT NORTHERN RAILWAY VETERAN'S ASSOCIATION – (memoriam to James J. Hill) organized Feb. 23, 1913. UNITY LOYALTY FRATERNITY, gold printing and gold profile on purple. Pinclasp has VETERAN. 2¾ x 9". No maker shown..$32.50

GREAT NORTHERN RAILWAY – oval pinclasp button, 1¾ x 2¾", with "Veteran's Assn. Great Northern Ry. organized Feb. 23, 1913, incorporated July 30, 1915" on gold. Name of employee in large letters across center. White satin ribbon 2 x 4" hangs down with American and Canadian flags woven in color. Maker – Western Badge & Novelty Co. St. Paul, Minn. $30.00

INTERNATIONAL RAILWAY GENERAL FOREMAN'S ASSN. - narrow rectangular pinclasp top with employee's name written on insert card, red bordered enamel rectangle 1 x 1½" hanging from pinclasp with a steam engine likeness and "Cincinnati, O. May 3-7 1910" in gold on white enamel center. Maker – The Greenduck Co. Chicago $20.00

MILWAUKEE ROAD – Bronze pinclasp rectangle with arched top, 2 x 2¼". Has embossed steam locomotive and insert card below with employee's name. White satin ribbon 1½ x 6" pictures caboose at bottom, 1938 Reunion, C.M.ST.P.&P.R.R. 25 V.E.A. Milwaukee, August 24, 25 printed in brown length of ribbon. No maker shown $22.00

NORTHERN PACIFIC – rectangle pinclasp for name, blue satin ribbon, 1½ x 3" with gold printing "Third Annual Meeting, Veteran's Ass'n. of the NORTHERN PACIFIC RAILWAY St. Paul, Minn. June 15, 1927. Vet's Ass'n. 30 yr." White 1¼" button hangs at bottom. Maker – Western Badge & Novelty Co. St. Paul, Minn. $27.50

Lapel Emblem Pins

These are small decorative emblem pins worn on the coat lapel. They had the Brotherhood ID on them, many with intricate enamel inlay work. Some were real gold or sterling, in most instances gold plated or bronze. Most had a threaded post with a detachable threaded washer to secure them into the coat lapel. Others were made with a straight pin on the back to be pinned to the fabric. The solid gold examples have the higher value. Maker's hallmarks are found on many, also patent dates.

Pinbacks and Coat Lapel Emblem Pins

ARMMA – (American Railroads Master Mechanics Ass'n.) gold letters and side view of steam loco on black enamel, ¾"D. Maker – L. Helwig & Co. Chicago $18.00

B of L E – red-blue-green enamel cut-out letters vertically joined, ¾ x 1¼", sterling. Maker – Pail & Co. Cleveland $20.00

B. of L.F. & E. – (Firemen & Engineers) white letter on gold scroll below cut-out black steam engine above, ⅝ x ¾", No h'mk $25.00

B. of L.F. & E. – gold letters on green-red-blue border, gold steam engine on white enamel center, ⅝"D. 10K gold, Pat. July 21, '14 ....$35.00

B of R R B – (Brakemen) gold letters and brakewheel on black enamel, ¾"D. Pat. Sept. 8, 1883 ....$18.00

B of R R C – (Clerks) gold letters, large black "C," green feather, red pencil, criss-crossed on white enamel, ½"D, J.W. (acorn) h'mk $10.00

B. of R.R.F.H. (Freight Handlers) RAILWAY CLERKS black letters in gold border, 2-wheel cart, hook, ledger, pen & pencil (criss-crossed) inlaid in green enameled center, ½" D. I.U. (acorn) h'mk $12.00

BLE – (Bro. Loco Eng's) intertwined white letters on blue enamel, ⅜"D. Bastian Bros. Co. (shield) h'mk $8.00

BROTHERHOOD OF LOCOMOTIVE ENGINEERS, HONORARY G.I.D. – two steam locomotives raised in center oval, ½ x ¾", 10K gold, Bastian Bros. Co. (shield) h'mk $40.00

BROTHERHOOD RAILROAD TRAINMEN – gold letters in red border, large green letter "T" with gold brakewheel spokes on white enamel center, ⅝", Pat'd Dec. 7, 1909 ....$22.00

BRS of A – (Bro. Railway Signalmen of America) – letters are on cut-out vertical semaphore arm, enamel work on 10K gold, ⅞" long. Maker – Jewel Emblem, Chicago....$25.00

Brotherhood Membership Years of Service

B. of L.E. – LOYAL MEMBER 40 YEARS, gold letters and digits on dark blue enamel; the word YEARS is raised on gold field, ⅝"D. Maker – Josten's, Owatonna, Minn. $20.00

B of RT – (Trainmen) – MEMBERSHIP 45 YEARS, gold digits on dark blue enamel shield within gold wreath, letters in gold on blue on scroll below, ½ x ⅝", ⅒10KGF $30.00

B. of R.T. – 25 YEARS MEMBERSHIP, gold letters on white enamel center within gold wreath, ¾"D. 14K gold, shield h'mk $35.00

B. of R.T. – 10 YEARS OF MEMBERSHIP, letters and digits on all-gold field, ½"D. ⅒ 10KGF, shield hallmark $15.00

B of RT – 30 YEARS MEMBERSHIP, gold letters on light blue enamel disc inside gold wreath, ½"D., 10K gold. Has Union Made h'mk..$40.00

B of RT – 35 YEARS MEMBERSHIP, digits in gold on green enamel within gold wreath, B of RT in gold on green scroll below, MEMBERSHIP YEARS raised on wreath, ½ x ½", 10K gold. H'mkd. Josten's $45.00

B R C A – (Bro. RR Carmen Ass'n) Gold letters, crossed-hammer and wrench on blue enamel, MEMBER 20 YEARS in gold on white enamel scroll below, ½ x ½", 14K gold, BBCo. hm'k $40.00

Pinback Buttons

Some have a history dating back to before the turn of the century. These are rare and have high value. The early pinbacks had a celluloid covering fabricated over the metal. Many are found with the mfr's paper label still intact on the back. In later years, they were made with litho paint over the tin surface, and the more recent were plastic issues. Those with celluloid covering bring the better prices.

B of L.E. of the N.Y.C.S. MCH. 20 1900 – in black around top edge, Empire State Express to the PACIFIC COAST in black around bottom edge; center has b/w photo of the pass. train on tracks and green grass, off-white background, 1¾"D. Celluloid covering. Rare $75.00

B of L F & E – LODGE 814, MAR 1920, BLF&E in center circle, white and black 1"D. Celluloid covering $15.00

B T R R – TWENTY-FIFTH ANNIVERSARY 174, 1883-1908, in black around edge on off-white field; BTRR, brake-wheel, flags, lantern symbol at center, 1¾"D. Celluloid covering, rare...$45.00

INT'R FRT.H. and RY. CLKS. INT. UNION – in blue around edge, DEC. F.H. 1908 in red at center on eggshell color field, 1"D. Celluloid covering, scarce.....................$20.00

O.R.C. – ORDER OF RAILWAY CONDUCTORS in blue on white, O.R.C. is on a line drawing of a caboose at center, 1⅛"D. Litho on tin $12.00

U.S.R.M.S.M.B.ASS'N – in red letters at top edge; a b/w photo of a RR mail car is at center with the word DELEGATE above against an egg-shell background, 24th Annual Convention, St. Louis, Mo. Sept. 26, 1899 is in blue at bottom edge, 1¼"D., rare $65.00

Miscellaneous

ASHTRAY – aluminum, cast, round 5⅝" D. w/3 rests, has track around rim, steam loco front-end raised at center with BLE monogram, S.T.J.M. initials above. Maker – The Nat'l Emblem & Specialty Co. Toledo, Ohio $45.00

CIGARETTE LIGHTER – BLE emblem monogram with crossed U.S. and Canadian flags with slogan "Serving since 1863," printed in red-blue on white card sealed inside clear plastic bottom, metal top, 1½ x 2¾", VU-LIGHTER, by Scripto Inc. $25.00

NECKERCHIEF – cotton, RAILROAD BROTHERHOOD, steam loco within circle of track at center, various Brotherhood logos and motifs printed in white on dark blue field, 20 x 24" $15.00

BLE Aluminum Ashtray

PENCIL CLIP – BROTHERHOOD RAILROAD TRAINMEN red-white emblem w/green "T" on ¾"D., celluloid button at bottom of metal holder..............................$10.00

PROGRAM – colorful cardstock cover illustration depicts passengers at depot platform, train arriving, lanterns, signal flags, Depot Agent, BRT monogram (Brotherhood Railroad Trainmen) FIFTH ANNUAL BALL, Maiden Rock Lodge 791, Tues. Eve. April 21, 1914, Watertown, S.D. Inside pages contains the evening program, 3½" x 5". Scarce $35.00

SHAVING MUG – B of R R T – brakewheel, lantern, crossed signal flags emblem in front, member's name (fancy letters) in gold leaf above, full color floral designs at sides, 3⅜"D. base, 3½" tall, gold rims and handle trim, h'mkd. Vienna, Austria. Supplier – R. H. Hegener, Barber Studios, Mpls. Rare 275.00

SPOON – sterling, souvenir, BLE intertwined monogram and the B.L.E. building, Cleveland, Ohio embossed topside of handle, also "Official BofLE Souvenir" raised on lower portion, backside has "The Ball Watch Co. Cleveland, O." also depicts train & pocket watch with slogan "Safety First" at top. Scarce $75.00

WATCH FOB – nickel-plated over copper, ornate design, 1¼" x 1¾", BRCA blue raised enamel logo at center, BROTHERHOOD RAILWAY CARMEN OF AMERICA raised letters in scrolls ea. side. H'mkd. Bastian Bros. Co. Rochester, N.Y. on backside...................................$55.00

WATCH EMBLEM CHARM – gold filled filagree type, 1⅛ x 1⅜", with inlaid enameled two-sided BRRT logo at center on polished stone disc, worn on gold filled vest chains $50.00

Brotherhood Annual Ball Programs

WATCH CASE – 14K gold filled, Wadsworth – or other Watchcase Co., with raised or engraved gold B of RR ornamented emblem on screw back, approved high-grade railroad movement and standard RR dial, scarce...$500.00

OFFICIAL DESK SEAL STATIONERY EMBOSSER – cast iron instrument, black enamel with red-gold floral decor, weight 5½ lbs., length 6", height 5", with handle down, round brass die imprints – DIXIE LODGE NO. 548, B of L F Commerce, Texas, organized June 8, 1899, likeness of engine in center circle, scarce $185.00

Button and Emblem Pins

Uniform Buttons

These have the name or initials of the railroad embossed on them, and are found in a gold or silver finish with a flat or domed front. They were also made with the occupation designated on them, such as "Conductor," "Brakeman," "Porter," etc. Most were in the standard ⅞"D. (large) coat and ⅝"D. (small) sleeve sizes, but other sizes can also be found. Most had a loop on the back, but they were also made with a patented slide lock-on back to fit over the plain coat or vest button, or, in the case of the cap button, a pronged back to push through the fabric. Prices shown here are for authentic old buttons in very fine condition, with the manufacturer's or supplier's name stamped on the backside. Re-strikes are being made today, so careful study of all buttons is required.

Note: All buttons listed show the actual marking (railroad initials or name) on the front side and the name of the manufacturer or supplier stamped on the backside.

Key to Abbreviations

LGD – Large gold dome
SGD – Small gold dome

LGF – Large gold flat
SGF – Small gold flat

LSD – Large silver dome
SSD – Small silver dome

LSF – Large silver flat
SSF – Small silver flat

Pat'd – Patent slide lock-on back
Prg'd – Pronged back for cap

Uniform Buttons, dome and flat face

"A C & S RR, SHORE FAST LINE" – SSF, Wanamaker & Brown, Phil $3.50

"A C L" – SSF, Superior Quality $2.00

"ATLANTIC & GREAT WESTERN RR" – LGF, D. Evans & Co. Attelboro, Mass. (rare) $35.00

"B&O" – LGF, Scovill Mfg. Co. Waterbury.....................$4.50

"B C E R" – LGF, J.R. Gaunt & Sons, Ltd., Montreal $6.00

"BIG FOUR" – LSF, Scovill Mfg. Co. Waterbury $5.00

"BOSTON ELEVATED RAILWAY" – LGF, Boston Elevated Railway $5.00

"BOSTON & MAINE RR" – LGD, Maltese Cross center, (pat'd) no mfgr's name $6.00

"BOSTON & MAINE RR" – SSD, Maltese cross center, Scovill Mfg. Co. Waterbury.....................................$4.50

"BR" – SGF, (prg'd) Waterbury Co. Conn. $4.50

"BR" – SGF, Waterbury Button Co. $3.00

"CANADIAN PACIFIC RAILWAY LINES" – (shield logo) LSF, W. Scully Ltd. Montreal $5.00

"CANADIAN PACIFIC RAILWAY CO." – (CPR monogram center) SSD, Sword's H'mk. made in England.......$4.50

"CHESAPEAKE & OHIO RAILWAY CO" – (C&O monogram center) LSD, Henderson & Co. Phila. Pa. $8.50

"CHICAGO GREAT WESTERN RY." – (maple leaf in center circle) LGD, Scovill Mfg. Co. Waterbury (scarce) ..$18.00

"C G W" – (script) – LGF, Scovill Mfg. Co. Waterbury ..$7.50

"C I & W" – LGD, J.R. Gaunt & Son Inc. N.Y. – made in England (scarce) $12.50

"C.L.S. & S.B.RY CO." – LSF, Extra Quality $8.00

"CLINTON STREET RY COMPANY" – (script) LSF, Extra Quality $8.00

"C M & ST. P. RY" – LGF, Chas. Rubens & Co., Chgo $6.00

"C M & St. P." – LGF, Browning King & Co. $6.00

"C M & St. P." – SGF, The Royal Tailors, Chgo. USA $4.00

"C M & St. P." – SSF, Cumner Jones & Co., Boston........$4.00

"C M St. P. & P." – LSF, Superior Quality $3.50

"C M St. P. & P." – SSF (prg'd) no mfgr.'s name $4.00

"C N R R" – LSF, Chas. Rubens & Co. Chicago.............$4.00

"C St. P. M. & O" – LSF, Chicago Uniform & Cap. Co...$8.00

"C St. P. M. & O." – LGD, Cumner Jones & Co. Boston $8.50

"C St. P.M. & O." – SGD, (pat'd) no mfgr.'s name $6.00

"C St. P. M. & O." – SSF, Superior Quality $4.00

"C & N W" – LGF, Superior Quality $5.00

"C & W I RR" – SGD (pat'd) no mfgr.'s name...............$4.00

"C U T" – LSF, Pettibone Bros. Mfg. Co. $6.50

"D. P. ELECTRIC LINES" – (Dan Patch) LGF, The Palace, Mpls. (rare) $25.00

"D & H" – LSD, American Button Co., Newark, N.J. $5.00

"D M & V" – LGD, N.Y. Clothing House, Balt. Md $8.00

"D & R G W" – LSD, Superior Quality, Made in England $5.00

"E & T H" – LSF, E.F. Schreimer Bros. & Co., Cincinnati, O...$8.00

"ERIE" – LGD, Scovill Mfg. Co., Waterbury.................$6.00

"ERIE" – LSD, Scovill Mfg. Co., Waterbury $5.00

"GRAND TRUNK RR" – GT monogram center, LGF, Ernest J. Scott, Montreal...$10.00

"GRAND TRUNK RY." – (around circle center,) LGD (pat'd) no mfgr.'s name $8.00

"GRAND RAPIDS RAILWAY CO." – (script) SGF, Waterbury Button Co.; Waterbury, CT......................................$4.00

"GREAT NORTHERN RY LINE" – GN monogram center (pat'd) no Mfgr's name $8.00

"GREAT NORTHER RY LINE" – GN monogram center, LGD, Waterbury Button Co., Waterbury CT $10.00

"G S & F" – SSF, Waterbury Button Co. $4.00

"G T R – CONDUCTOR" – with beaver animal in oval, LGD, Waterbury Button Co., Waterbury, Conn. (scarce) ..$22.50

"HOUSTON & TEXAS CENTRAL RAILWAY" – H&TC monogram in center, LSD, Waterbury Button Co. Waterbury, Conn. $12.00

"H.& B.T.R.R." – SGD, Wannamaker & Brown, Phil......$6.00

"IC" – LSF, Superior Quality $3.00

"I C St. Ry. Co." – LSD, D. Evans & Co., Attleboro, Mass $8.00

"INDIANAPOLIS STREET RAILWAY CO." – LGF, C.A. Bropny, Aurora, Ill $7.50

"I R T Co." – LGD, Superior Quality $6.00

"LACKAWANNA R.R." – monogram center, LSD, Scovill Mfg. Co. $12.00

"L S & M S" – SSD, Scovill Mfg. Co. $5.00

"M & St L" – LGF, Cumner Jones & Co., Boston...........$8.00

"M & St L" – SGD (pat'd) No mfgr.'s name...................$6.00

"M & St L" – LSD (pat'd) No mfgr.'s name $8.00

"M & St L" – SSD (pat'd) No mfgr.'s name $5.00

"MISSOURI KANSAS & TEXAS" – LGD, Steele & Johnson, Waterbury $15.00

"MISSOURI PACIFIC LINES" – buzz-saw edge, LGF, Superior Quality $3.00

"Mo.P." – LGD, Waterbury Button Co............................$4.00

"N.Y.C." – LGF, Scovill Mfg. Co. Waterbury Conn..........$3.00

"N.Y.C. & H R R R" – LGD, Scovill Mfg. Co. Waterbury $7.00

"N.Y.C. & ST. L.R.R. CO." – NICKEL PLATE in center, LSD, Extra Quality $15.00

"N.Y. LAKE ERIE & W.R.R.CO." – BRAKEMAN in center, LGD, Scovill Mfg. Co. Waterbury (scarce) $25.00

"NEW YORK ONTARIO & WESTERN RWY." – O&W monogram center, LGD, Jacob Reed's Sons Phil $20.00

"N P" (monogram) – LSD, (pat'd) Scovill Mfg. Co. $4.00

"N P" (monogram) – LGD, (pat'd) Scovill Mfg. Co.......$4.00

"NORTHERN PACIFIC" – N P center, SGD, Scovill Mfg. Co. $6.00

"NORTHERN PACIFIC" – N P center, LGD, Scovill Mfg. Co. Waterbury $12.00

"N P" (monogram) – SGF (prg'd) Superior Quality......$4.00

"NORTHERN INDIANA RAILWAY CO." – in script, LGF, Superior Quality $9.00

"O W" (logo) – LGF, Scovill Mfg. Co. Waterbury, Conn.$4.00

"O & W" – center, New York Ontario & Western Railway around edge, Jacob Reed's Sons, Phil $12.00

"PORT ARTHUR ROUTE" – (box logo) SSF (prg'd) Superior Quality $6.00

"P & L E" – LGD, Horstmann, Philadelphia $6.00

"P M" – LGD, Marshall Field & Co. $6.00

"P R R" (In Keystone logo) – LSD, S.G. Clover Co. New York $6.00

"P R R" (In Keystone logo) – LGD, Waterbury Button Co. Conn. $5.00

"P R R" – LSD, American Ry. Supply Co. 24 Park Place, N.Y. $7.00

"PENNSYLVANIA CO." – monogram center, LSD, Waterbury Button Co. $8.00

"PORTLAND RAILROAD" – LGF, Scovill Mfg. Co. Waterbury $5.00

"READING LINES" – R Co. in diamond center, LGD, Superior Quality $5.00

"R.F. & P.R.R." – LSD, Superior Quality........................$10.00

"R & I RY." – LSF, Waterbury Button Co. Conn $8.00

"ROCK ISLAND LINES" – star center, LGF, Pettibone Bros. Cinn. O $4.00

"SANTA FE" – (in cross logo) – LGF, Waterbury Co.'s, Waterbury Conn $4.00

"St. J Ry" – (in rectangle) – LGF, F E Cheimer Bros. Co. Cincinnati, O..$8.00

"St L & O R" – CONDUCTOR around edge, car in oval below, LGD, Waterbury Button Co., Waterbury, Conn. (scarce) $25.00

"St P & S.C.R.R." – CONDUCTOR, star center, LGD, Extra Quality (rare) $30.00

"SALT LAKE" – LSD, B. Pasquale Co. S. Fran. Cal $15.00

"S P" – (entwined letters) – LGD, J.M. Litchfield & Co. S. F. Cal. $5.00

"SOUTHERN" – (around center circle) – LGD, Jacob Reed's Sons, Phila $4.00

A Dual Marked Rarity

"SOO LINE" – LSD, (pat'd) no maker's name $6.00

"SOO LINE" – SGD, (pat'd) no maker's name.............$4.00

"S U RyS" – LGD, Superior Quality $6.00

"TOPEKA RAILWAY CO." – TCCo. monogram center, LGF, Waterbury Button Co. Waterbury, CT.....................$6.00

"TORONTO & YORK RADIAL RY." – TYR monogram center, LGD, J.R. Gaunt & Sons Ltd., Montreal $10.00

"TORONTO RAILWAY COMPANY" – beaver animal center, LGD, J.S. Russell, Toronto $8.00

"UNION PACIFIC" – LGD, American Ry. Supply Co. N.Y. $4.00

"UNION PACIFIC" – LSD, F. G. Clover Co. New York....$4.00

"U T C of I N D" – LGF, Supreme Quality.....................$6.00

"VANDALIA LINES" – VL monogram center, LGD, Waterbury Button Co. (scarce) $18.00

"WABASH" – LSD, (pat'd), no maker's name $8.00

"W C RY" – LGD, (pat'd), no maker's name $12.00

"WEST CHICAGO ST. R.R. Co." – WC monogram center, LGD, Waterbury Button Co. $8.00

"YORK ST. RY. CO." – LSF, no maker's name $6.00

Miscellaneous and Express

"AGENT" – LGD, Scovill Mfg. Co. Waterbury $7.00
"AGENT" – SGD, Cumner Jones & Co. Boston..............$5.50
"AGENT" – LSD, Horstmann Bros. & Co. Philada $7.50
"BAGGAGE MAST" – (spokewheel center) LSD, Waterbury Button Co. $8.00
"BRAKEMAN" – (star center) LGD, Scovill Mfg. Co. Waterbury $6.00
"BRAKEMAN" – (spokewheel center) LSD, Chas. Rubens & Co. Chicago $7.00
"BRAKEMAN" – LSF, Fechheimer Bros. Co., Cincinnati, Ohio $6.00
"CONDUCTOR" – LGF, Chas. Rubens & Co. Chicago ..$6.00
"CONDUCTOR" – SSF, Superior Quality $3.00

Express and Palace Car

"CONDUCTOR" – LSD, Charles Rubens & Co. Chicago $5.00
"CONDUCTOR" – (star center) LGD, Pettibone Mfg. Co. Cincinnati $6.00
"CONDUCTOR" – (star center) SSD, Extra Quality......$3.00
"INSPECTOR" – SGF, Superior Quality, Made in England $5.00
"MOTORMAN" – (spokewheel center) LGD, Cumner Jones & Co. Boston $5.00
"MOTORMAN" – LGD, Scovill Mfg. Co. Waterbury......$5.00
"PORTER" – (star center) LSD, Waterbury Button Co. Conn..$4.00
"PORTER" – SGD, Superior Quality............................$2.00
"PULLMAN" – LSF, Superior Quality............................$3.00
"PULLMAN" – LGF, Waterbury Button Co. Conn. $4.00
"PULLMAN" – SSF, Superior Quality............................$2.00
"PULLMAN" – SGF, Waterbury Button Co....................$2.00
"P.P.C.Co." – (within wreath) LSD, Henry V. Allien & Co. N.Y. (scarce) $30.00
"ADAMS EXPRESS COMPANY" – (in rectangle) LGF, Scovill Mfg. Co. Waterbury...$15.00
"AMERICAN EXPRESS CO." – (shield in center) LGD, Waterbury Button Co. $15.00
"NATIONAL EXPRESS CO." – "N" in center circle, LGD, Scovill Mfg. Co. Waterbury...$15.00
"NEW YORK & BOSTON LINE EXPRESS" – LSD, Scovill Mfg. Co. Waterbury...$22.00
"RAILWAY MAIL SERVICE" – "P O D" center, LGD, Scovill $18.00
"WAGNER PALACE CAR CO" – (winged wheel center) LGD, Henry V. Allien & Co. New York $25.00

Railroadmen's Work Clothes Buttons

These work clothes buttons for railroadmen go back to the turn of the century, continuing until about the 1930's. All have a brass shell over a steel back with an eyelet shank for sewing the button to the fabric. The brass shell is embossed with pictures and words. Approximate measurements are given.

"ALRITE BRAND" – with side view of steam engine center, ⅝"D $6.00
"CARHARTT'S" – (heart shape) with railcar in center, ⅞"D $12.00
"CARHARTT'S" – (heart shape) with railcar in center, ⅝"D $8.00
"CARHARTT'S O'ALLS & GLOVES" – With railcar & heart in center, ⅞"D...$12.00
"CONES BOSS" – with lantern in center, ⅞"D $6.00
"CONES BOSS" – with lantern in center, ⅝"D $4.00

"ENGINEER COAT" – ⅞"D $5.00
"FAST LIMITED" – ⅞"D $6.00
"HEAD LIGHT" – ⅞"D $8.00
"LA CRUZ" – with side view of steam engine center, ¾"D..$5.00
"MAIN LINE SPECIAL" – with side view of steam engine in center, ⅞"D...$12.00
"M.E.S.&Co." – with side view of steam engine in center, ⅝"D...$6.00
"OSHKOSH BRAND" – with side view of steam engine in

Work Clothing Button

center, ⅝"D..$8.00
"OSHKOSH BRAND" – with side view of steam engine in center, ¾"D $10.00
"PAYMASTER" – UNION MADE with paycar in center, ⅞"D $15.00

"PIONEER LIMITED" – with UNION MADE across center, ¾"D $6.00
"RAILROAD SIGNAL" – with semaphore signal in center, ⅞"D $10.00
"ROUND HOUSE" – with roundhouse building in center, ⅞"D $16.00
"RAIL ROAD KING" – ⅞"D $5.00
"ROCKFORD" – with steam engine, ⅞"D $8.00
"S.O. CO.N.Y." – with side view of steam engine in center, ¾"D $8.00
"S.O. & CO.N.Y." – with steam engine in center, ⅝"D ..$5.00
"SWOFORD'S MOGUL" – with side view of steam engine center, ⅝"D $6.00
"UNTITLED" – side view of steam locomotive, ¾"D $4.00
"UNTITLED" – side view of steam locomotive, ⅝"D $4.00
"UNTITLED" – Three-quarter view of steam locomotive, ⅞"D $5.00
"UNTITLED" – Three-quarter view of diesel streamliner, ¾"D $4.00
"THE ENGINEER" – with side view of steam engine in center, ⅞"D $12.00
"THE MANCHESTER" – with side view of steam engine in center, ⅝"D $8.00

Coat Lapel Emblem Pins

Most of these small metal objects were made round shape and turned out in a gold-plated finish with color enamel inlaid work. Some were made in sterling or real gold. They came with a threaded post mount or a pin shank on the back for securing to the coat lapel. Manufacturer's hallmarks can be found on many, also patent dates. Those from railroads of years ago are getting harder to come by and realizing good prices now. Those from defunct long gone roads, of course, have a much higher value.

ACL – "Safety Committeeman" around ATLANTIC COAST LINE on white center, pinback shank, ⅝"D $22.00
BURLINGTON ROUTE – "Safety First" around black logo on white center, ⅝"D..$25.00
CMStP&P – CHICAGO MILWAUKEE ST. PAUL & PACIFIC around red "The Milwaukee Road" logo on white center, ½"D...$20.00
C&NW – "Woman's Club" in gold around CHICAGO NORTHWESTERN red/black logo on gold, scallop edge, pinback shank, ⅝"D $18.00
COTTON BELT ROUTE – logo shape, silver and blue, ½" x ½"D...$35.00
D&IRRRCo. – "The Safety Spirit," DULUTH & IRON RANGE R.R. CO. around Indian profile in center circle, hexagon, ¾"D (rare) $75.00
GN – logo pre-1935, GREAT NORTHERN around white goat on red center, ½"D, (scarce) $35.00
GN – GREAT NORTHERN RAILWAY CLUB around white goat & mts. in center, 10K gold, pinback shank, ½"D $22.00
IC – ILLINOIS CENTRAL RAILROAD around "Safety Always First" in yellow/white center, ¾"D $25.00

LS&MS – LAKE SHORE PIONEER "Fast Mail Line" raised letters on gold mail sack emblem, 10K gold, ⅜ x ¾" $50.00
L&N – FRIENDLY SERVICE around white/red L&N logo in center, pinback shank, 1"D..................................$25.00
MP – BOOSTER CLUB around MISSOURI PACIFIC LINES red logo in center, pinback shank, ⅝"D $22.00
M&StL – THE MINNEAPOLIS & ST LOUIS RAILWAY CO. around "The Peoria Gateway" on white center, ⅝"D..$25.00
NYC – oval logo, NEW YORK CENTRAL LINES in gold letters on black, ⅜" x ⅝" $18.00
NP – "Careful Club Bureau of Efficiency" around NORTHERN PACIFIC, white/red/black Monad logo in center, LADIES AUXILIARY on white extended bar each side, pinback shank, ⅝ x 1½" $26.50
OW&N – O W.R.R&N. "Safety First" around Union Pacific System OVERLAND shield logo on white center, ⅝"D..$35.00
SANTA FE – square logo, silver SANTA FE on blue cross in white center, ⅜" x ⅜" $15.00

Coat Lapel Emblem Pins

SOO LINE – SAFETY FIRST around red box logo on white center, ⅝"D $18.00

SP – round logo, SOUTHERN PACIFIC around LINES across track and sunset in center, ⅝"D $22.00

T&P – THE TEXAS PACIFIC RAILWAY on red around T and P in black center, diamond shape 1" x 1¾", Texarkana, Shreveport, El Paso, New Orleans in fine raised gold letters on the edges $45.00

UP – U.P.R.R. "Safety First" around Union Pacific System OVERLAND shield logo on white center, ⅝"D......$30.00

Y&MV – Y.&M.V. RAILROAD around "Always SAFETY First" on yellow/green center, ¾"D $35.00

Veteran's Lapel Pins

These are on the same order as the regular issues except they were made for railroad employees with years of service. Those in solid gold set with mini-gemstones have high value; rarities go on auction.

BN – VETERANS ASSOCIATION raised gold letters on ¹⁄₁₀ 10K gold, ½" square $22.50

B & O – V in blue and a white capitol dome on gold field, ½"D $25.00

BURLINGTON ROUTE – FIFTY YEARS SERVICE raised gold letters around red/black logo in center, 14K ½"D $35.00

C&NW – VETERANS ASSOCIATION C. & N.W.RY.CO around Chicago Northwestern Line logo on white center, ½"D $22.50

CGW – CHICAGO GREAT WESTERN RAILROAD EMPLOYEES around green maple leaf on white center with word VETERAN 1923 across, ⅝"D (scarce) $40.00

CMSTP&P – C.M.ST.P.& P.R.R. V.E.A. around 30 on white center, ½"D $25.00

IC – ILLINOIS CENTRAL across center, Quarter Century Club above and below on green, diamond shape, 10K, ½ x ¾" $35.00

Vet's 35 and 45 Year Service Pins

NYC – N.Y.C. LINES BIG FOUR ROUTE around 21 in gold center headlight, front end steam locomotive shape, word VETERAN on cowcatcher, ½ x ¾" $35.00

NYNH&H The NEW YORK NEW HAVEN and HARTFORD in script, RAILROAD CO. 40 YEARS in black on gold, front end diesel shape with mini-blue gemstone headlight, 10K ½ x ¾" $45.00

NP – NORTHERN PACIFIC white/red/black logo in center with 35 below and mini-ruby gemstone above on rayed gold border, 10K, ½"D $50.00

NP – NORTHERN PACIFIC white/red/black logo in center with 45 below and mini-diamond above on rayed gold border, 10K, ½"D..$75.00

N&WRY – NORFOLK & WESTERN raised letters above detailed steam locomotive on gold with VETERAN on blue stripe below, N&WRY logo at bottom, ornate, 10K, ⅝"D...$35.00

PRR – PENNSYLVANIA RAILROAD "Service 25 Years" raised digits and letters around raised front end of steam locomotive in keystone logo in center on bronze, V shape, ⅝ x ⅝" $27.50

PRR – gold keystone logo, VETERAN PENNA SYSTEM in red center, ½ x ½" $22.50

OMAHA – OMAHA RAILWAY across center, SAFETY VETERAN above and below on red border, "No injury 25 years" on black/silver center, sterling, ¾"D..........$30.00

Official Lapel Insignias (Matched Pairs)

These regulation metal insignias have a single or twin threaded post on the back with nuts for mounting them on top of the fabric. Hallmarks can occasionally be found on some. Gold finish is for the conductor while silver is for brakemen. Most were made in the shape of the railroad's logo, others are in cut-out letters. They came in a set of two, one for each side of the coat lapel or collar. Prices listed here are for a set; the price of a single is generally worth half the value of a pair.

BURLINGTON ROUTE – (box logo) raised silver letters on black field, red enamel border outlined in silver, 1 x 1¼" ....pair $42.00

C & N W – (cut-out "plain" shiny gold letters) on two horizontal bars behind, post mount each end, ½ x 2¼" ......pair $15.00

C M & ST P – (cut-out ornate gold "rope" letters) on two horizontal bars behind, post mount each end, ½ x 2¾" ....pair $40.00

I C – (cut-out "plain shiny" silver letters) joined between, single post mt. on back, ½ x ¾" ....pair $10.00

KCS – (8-sided logo) "KANSAS CITY SOUTHERN Lines" silver inlay letters on shiny dark red enameled surface, silver rims, single post mt. 1 x 1" ....pair $27.50

MILWAUKEE ROAD – (canted box logo) THE MILWAUKEE ROAD silver letters inlaid on shiny baked red enameled surface, white border, twin post mounts, not h'mkd, ¾ x 1"...pair $47.50

MILWAUKEE ROAD – (canted box logo) THE MILWAUKEE ROAD raised gold letters on red enamel finish, white & gold border, twin post mounts, Greenduck Co. h'mk, ¾ x 1"..pair $37.50

MILWAUKEE ROAD – (box logo) "OPENING OUR SECOND CENTURY 1950" black letters on silver circle around silver Hiawatha Indian figure inlaid on shiny red enameled field, silver rim, twin post mounts, ¾ x 1" (scarce)......pair $50.00

O M A H A – (cut-out ornate gold "rope" letters) on two horizontal bars behind, post mount each end, ½ x 2¼" ....pair $40.00

O M A H A – (cut-out ornate silver "rope" letters) on two horizontal bars behind post mount each end, ½ x 2¼" ....pair $38.00

Uniform Lapel Logos

ROCK ISLAND – (cut-out logo shape) blue letters on gold finish surface, twin post mounts, four h'mks, ¾ x 1⅛" ....pair $37.50

ROCK ISLAND – (cut-out logo shape) copper letters inlaid on shiny black enameled flat surface, twin post mounts, Pettibone Mfg. Co., ¾ x 1⅛" (scarce).............pair $60.00

SANTA FE – (cross in round logo) "Santa Fe" in gold on blue cross, shiny enameled surface, gold rim, twin post mounts, 1"D ....pair $35.00

THE NORTH WESTERN LINE – (cut-out logo) with F.E.&M.V.R.R. below, gold letters on shiny blue and black enamel surface, single post mount device, 1 x 1¼" (rare) ....pair $75.00

U P – (cut-out "plain" gold letters) joined between, twin post mounts on back, ½ x ¾".........................pair $10.00

Ornate Cut-Out Letters

Coat Sleeve Service Bars and Stars

These gold and silver gilt metal ornaments were worn by uniformed passenger conductors, brakemen, flagmen, porters, station masters, gatemen and others. The railroads ID are raised letters on an embroidered-like surface, and they have two threaded posts on back with nuts for mounting. Each bar on the sleeve represents five years of service. After five bars, a star would be placed just above the row of bars to represent five additional years of service, and so on.

Coat Sleeve Ornaments

FRISCO LINES – ³⁄₁₆ x ¾" gold bar $20.00
FRISCO LINES – ³⁄₁₆ x ¾" silver bar $18.00
G.N.RY. – ¼ x ¾" gold bar...$22.00
G.N.RY. – ¼ x ¾" silver bar $20.00
ROCK ISLAND – ¼ x ¾" gold bar $18.00
ROCK ISLAND – ¼ x ¾" silver bar................................$16.00
SANTA FE – ⁵⁄₁₆ x ⅞" gold bar $15.00
SANTA FE – ⁵⁄₁₆ x ⅞" silver bar $12.00
UNMARKED – ¼ x ⅞" gold bar $4.00
UNMARKED – ¼ x ⅞" silver bar......................................$4.00
UNMARKED – ¾" gold star...$5.00
UNMARKED – ¾" silver star $5.00

Calendars

Down through the years, the railroads gave away many thousands of calendars which are now being collected. The rarities are the early color-lithographed calendars from the last quarter of the nineteenth century, which bring very high prices. Of special interest are the New York Central and Pennsylvania Railroad's wall calendars illustrating their famous "Name trains" of the steam era. Closely following these are Great Northern's Indian series, done by Winold Reiss in the 1920's and 1930's. Other railroads as well came out with many interesting subjects, all much in demand and selling well. Those that have been kept in their original mint condition, with flyleaf still intact, have the highest value.

AT&SF – 1954, cardstock print 13 x 13¾, entitled "Navajo Shepherdess," all monthly pages (dates/logo) stapled at bottom edge of card..$15.00

AT&SF – 1948, cardstock litho 13 x 13¾", entitled "San Francisco Peaks" along the Santa Fe main line near Flagstaff, Arizona, monthly pages (dates/logo) stapled at bottom edge of card $20.00

AT&SF – 1932, cardstock litho 13 x 13¾", entitled "The Weaver" Indian-detour-Country, monthly pages (dates/logo) stapled at bottom of card. Map of System printed on reverse side $25.00

AT&SF – 1928, cardstock litho 13 x 13¾", entitled "The Blanket" Taos-Puye Indian-detour, New Mexico, monthly pages (dates/logo) stapled at bottom edge of card. Map of System printed on reverse side $30.00

B&O – 1827-1927 Centennial, cardstock color litho 20¾ x 21", depicting laying the first stone of the BALTIMORE and OHIO RAILROAD, monthly pages stapled along bottom edge, scarce $42.00

B&O – 1948, single sheet 21 x 31½", top part has litho depicting map of system, logo/capitol dome and steam diesel trains, bottom has monthly squares printed including tear-off pages at center..$27.50

BN – 1971, single sheet 25½ x 42", photo across center entitled "A Burlington Northern Freight Train Rolls Along the Columbia River in the Cascades, Bound for Portland" $10.00

Early Rare Framed Calendar

BN – 1980, six pages, 12½ x 23", each featuring selected photos from BN employees calendar photo competition......$8.00

BURLINGTON ROUTE – 1934, single sheet 18 x 25" with litho of streamliner entitled "The Pioneer Zephyr – Daddy of 'em All" FIRST DIESEL STREAMLINE TRAIN IN AMERICA 1934 – TENTH ANNIVERSARY – 1944. Monthly pages stapled on bottom..........................$40.00

BURLINGTON ROUTE – 1938, single sheet 18 x 27" with litho depicting steam and diesel trains against a mountain background with vignette of covered wagons in the sky, monthly pages stapled on bottom space $45.00

C&A – Four tri-monthly cardstock lithographed pages, 10 x 15", each, depicting a girl with sword in various fencing positions, entitled "THE ONLY WAY" copyright 1902 by THE CHICAGO & ALTON RAILWAY CO., rare $135.00

C&NW – 1937, 12 pages 15 x 23" with big logo printed across top portion and calendar dates on bottom part ..$20.00

C&NW – 1941, picture of The Famous Streamliner "400" crossing stone arch bridge, 18 x 24", monthly pages stapled below pix $30.00

C&NW – 1945, picture entitled The Twin Cities "400" arriving Milwaukee, Wis. Passenger Station, 18 x 24", monthly pages stapled below pix $25.00

C&NW – 1946, picture entitled SPEEDING THE FREIGHT with NEW "5400" DIESEL Locomotives, scene near Sterling-Rock Falls, Illinois, 18 x 24", monthly pages stapled below pix...$20.00

C&O – 1984 Chessie Calendar 50 Golden Anniversary Edition, 9½ x 16" opened, pages showing various photos of Chessie cat $10.00

C&O – 1960, 7 cardstock pages 10 x 12½" with reproductions of paintings on both sides including calendar months. Front page entitled "Smooth the road – make easy the way" 1960 – One hundred seventy-five years of transportation progress $12.50

CM&StP – 1928, 12 pages, 10¾ x 25¼", each with three months and red logo printed on Yellowstone National Park scenes, scarce $65.00

CK&N RY – ROCK ISLAND ROUTE, 1889, cardstock sheet 14 x 22", top portion has litho depicting portrait of girl in circle and night train with caption Great Vestible & Reclining Chair Car Line. Monthly pages stapled below pix. Jan. Feb. pages torn off, rare $175.00

CRI&P – 1888, cardstock sheet 14 x 22", top portion has litho depicting a man with an umbrella and satchel entitled GREAT ROCK ISLAND ROUTE, all monthly pages Jan-Dec stapled intact below pix, rare $185.00

D&RGW – 1943, single sheet 15 x 25¾", picture depicts three trains passing entitled CASTLE GATE, UTAH Thru The Rockies – Not Around Them. Monthly pages stapled below pix $35.00

D&RGW – 1944, single sheet 15 x 26", picture depicts steam pass. train winding along river in mountains entitled RIO GRANDE Royal Gorge, Colorado, Thru The Rockies – Not Around Them. Monthly pages stapled below pix $30.00

FEC – 1944, single sheet 14 x 24", picture shows speeding freight train, map of Florida and Florida East Coast Railway logo, monthly pages stapled below pix.........$20.00

FEC – 1954, single sheet 14 x 24", picture shows diesel streamliner on bridge over water with caption "Serving an All-Year Vacationland," monthly pages stapled below pix $15.00

FRISCO – 1962, single cardstock sheet 22 x 28", across top is map of System, long diesel freight train and slogan "SHIP IT on the (logo) FRISCO," 12 months, printed below $12.00

Large Wall Calendar

FRISCO – 1980, single cardstock sheet, 20 x 26", top part has 1876 calendar titled "The First Year as St. Louis and San Francisco Ry." with picture of boy and girl seated in depot waiting room, bottom part has calendar mos. printed and photo of diesel frt. at center $8.00

GN – 1928, January, one month cardstock sheet 10 x 22", full-color portrait of Little Plume by W. Langdon Kinn $40.00

GN – 1928, 12 monthly cardstock sheets, 10 x 22" each with full-color Indian portraits by W. Langdon Kinn and Winold Reiss, complete set, hard to come by (12 x $40.00) $480.00

GN – 1929, October, one month cardstock sheet, 10¾ x 20½", full-color scene of Iceberg Lake, Glacier National Park by Adolf Heinze $35.00

GN – 1929, 12 monthly cardstock sheets, 10¾ x 20½", each with full-color moutain scenes of Glacier National Park by Adolf Heinze, complete set hard to come by (12 x $35.00) $420.00

GN – 1930, September, one month cardstock sheet, 10 x 22", full-color portrait of Lazy Boy – Medicine Man by Winold Reiss $30.00

GN – 1930, 12 monthly cardstock sheets, 10 x 22", with full-color Indian portraits by Winold Reiss, complete set, hard to come by (12 x $30.00) $360.00

GN – 1931, July, one month cardstock sheet, 10 x 22", full-color portrait of Yellow Head by Winold Reiss $25.00

GN– 1931, 12 monthly cardstock sheets, 10 x 22", full-color Indian portraits by Winold Reiss, complete set hard to come by (12 x $25.00) $300.00

IC – 1949, single sheet 18 x 27½", picture shows steam and diesel trains going thru farm lands, logo and slogan "Main Line of Mid-America," monthly pages stapled below pix $20.00

IC – 1951, single sheet 18 x 27½", picture depicts two scenes 1851-1951, medallions, entitled "One Hundred Years of Progress," monthly pages stapled below pix $25.00

KCS – 1975, green card 7½ x 12" with red KANSAS CITY SOUTHERN LINES logo at top, pad of tear-off single date pages below $10.00

Perpetual Tin Calendar

M&STL – 1945, single sheet 18 x 24½", color photo of steam locomotive 627 pulling freight entitled "The Minneapolis & St. Louis RAILWAY COMPANY" 12 monthly pages stapled below photo, scarce....................................$65.00

M&StL – 1950, single sheet 18¼ x 24½", color print of Diesel loco 147 on steel bridge, caption reads – CROSSING THE FATHER OF WATERS, M&StL Bridge, Three-Fourths of a Mile Long over the Mississippi at Keithsburg, Illinois, 12 monthly pages stapled below pic.............................$50.00

MP – Perpetual tin wall calendar 13 x 19", green finish with color litho of steam passenger loco 6615 at top and complete set of original removable green date cards below, entitled MISSOURI PACIFIC LINES, Dependable Freight and Passenger Service, scarce $175.00

MP – Perpetual tin wall calendar 12½ x 19", silver finish with color litho of diesel streamliner Eagle 7003 entitled ROUTE OF THE EAGLES. Below picture is complete set of original removable silver date cards, scarce $150.00

NYC – 1923, single sheet, 25 x 26½", reproduction of painting "The Twentieth Century Limited of the NEW YORK CENTRAL LINES 'The Greatest Train in the World'" (passenger train rounding curve) by Wm. Harnden Foster, all monthly pages intact stapled below pic $275.00

NYC – 1924, single sheet, 25 x 26½", reproduction of painting "AS THE CENTURIES PASS IN THE NIGHT" (front and rear of two passenger trains) by Wm. Harnden Foster, monthly pages with flyleaf attached stapled below pic..$250.00

NYC – 1925, single sheet, 25 x 26½", reproduction of painting "When Winter Comes" (passenger train snow scene) by Walter L. Greene, all monthly pages still intact stapled below pic...$225.00

NYC – 1926, single sheet, 25 x 26½", reproduction of painting "A NATIONAL INSTITUTION" (two passenger trains over and under bridge) by Walter L. Greene, all monthly pages still intact stapled below pic $200.00

NP – 1965, single sheet, 25½ x 42", across the top is color photo of NP freight train along the scenic Clark Fork

GN 1931 Indian Series Calendar

River near Missoula, Montana, titled WESTERN WONDERLAND, 12 month calendar printed below pic $10.00

NP – 1970, single sheet, 20½ x 25¾", across top is repro of painting showing diesel freight train coming out of a tunnel out West, 12 months printed below $8.00

PRR – All calendars listed here are single sheets, 28¾ x 28½", with large reproductions of various Pennsy Railroad scenes done by Grif Teller. The year and title of picture is given along with the number of monthly pages still remaining stapled below the picture.

1935 – THE WORLD'S GREATEST HIGHWAY (pass. train rounding Horseshoe Curve) 12 pages $75.00

1936 – SPEED – SAFETY – COMFORT (electric pass. train) 2 pages..$45.00

1941 – THE STEEL KING (bullet-nose locomotive passing steel mill) 6 pages $35.00

1942 – PARTNERS IN NATIONAL DEFENSE (steam locomotives and steel mill) 12 pages $45.00

1943 – SERVING THE NATION (Uncle Sam and trains) 12 pages..$75.00

1947 – WORKING PARTNERS (trains and houses) 12 pages..$65.00

1949 – MAIN LINES – FREIGHT and PASSENGER (freight and passenger train over/under bridge) 2 pages ..$30.00

1953 – CROSSROADS OF COMMERCE (3 trains, bridge, river) 1 page $25.00

1954 – PITTSBURGH PROMOTES PROGRESS (trains and downtown buildings) 4 pages................................$35.00

1955 – MASS TRANSPORTATION (Army-Navy game – people leaving trains lined up at station) 2 pages $30.00

1956 – DYNAMIC PROGRESS (modern streamliner and pig-
gyback freight) 12 pages $40.00
1957 – VITAL LINKS TO WORLD TRADE (train, ferryboat,
dock) 4 pages $25.00
ROCK ISLAND 1939, red cardstock back, 14 x 20", with
black logo at top and black monthly pages stapled below
with flyleaf intact, Map of System under last page $40.00
SR – 1973, single sheet, 12 x 18", photo of diesel freight train
crossing Cumberland River bridge, Kentucky, 6 bi-
monthly pages stapled below pic............................$10.00
UP – 1944, 6 two-sided fold-over sheets, 12½ x 23", each side
has color photo of trains and RR scene, with month
printed below pic $18.50
UP – 1963, 7 two-sided fold-over sheets, 12½ x 23", each side
has color photo of vacation spot reached by train with
month printed below pic $10.00
UP – 1969, 8 two-sided fold-over sheets, 19 x 24", Centennial
1869-1969 issue, each page featuring a full-color RR scene
painted by Fogg with month printed below pic......$20.00

Pennsy 1942 Calendar, Complete

Cans, Torches & Metalware

     Of the large variety of cans used on the railroads, the most popular with the collector seems to be the engineer's classic long-spout oiler. Next are the various types of kerosene cans. Those from the steam era, marked with the name of the railroad, are much in demand. Non-railroad marked, having only the manufacturer's name on them, have less value. Cans badly dented or rusted must be discounted in price. Oil burning torches were used in the old days to provide a light while working around the locomotive and in the roundhouse. They were made of tin or cast iron, with a wick in the spout, and came in a variety of styles, shapes and sizes. Many were not railroad marked; those railroad marked and in fine condition have greater value.

Engineer's Long Spout Oilers

AT&SF RY – marked on bottom, 31" tall, stop flow lever, no
mfr's name $47.50
B&O RR – embossed on front, 30" tall, stop flow lever, J-
Urbana, O $35.00
CMSTP&P RR – raised in front, 27½" tall, no stop flow lever,
J-Urbana, O..$45.00
CRI&P RY – stamped on bottom, 31½" tall, stop flow lever,
Anthes Force Oiler Co., Ft. Madison, IA $55.00
DL&W RY – embossed on side, 29½" tall, stop flow lever, J-
Urbana, O..$42.50
GN RY – incised on handle, 30½" tall, stop flow lever,
Eagle...$47.00

MKT RR raised on front, 26½" tall, no stop flow lever, Main
Metal Prod $45.00
NP RY – embossed on bottom, 30½" tall, stop flow lever,
J-Urbana, O $47.50
PRR – embossed Keystone logo front, 26" tall, no stop flow
lever, J-Urbana, O..$37.50
SOO RR – embossed on bottom, 28½" tall, stop flow lever,
Handlan $42.50
UNMARKED – 26" tall, stop flow lever, no mfr's
name $25.00

Short Spout Oilers

AT&SF RY – raised in front, small long spout engine oil can, 14½"H, 3"D, filler cap, J-Urbana, O........................$30.00

GNR – raised on side tag, oil can, looped handle, spout unscrews, 14½"H, 3¾"D, Pat. Nov. 12, 1912, Eagle...$45.00

PRR – Keystone logo raised in front, small long spout engine oil can, filler cap, 15¾"H 3¼"D, J-Urbana, O $40.00

PRR – Keystone logo raised in front, small oiler can, round top base, 6½"H, 4½"D, filler cap, no mfgrs name $25.00

Kerosene or Signal Oil Cans

Note: Height is measured to top of filler cap, diameter is the base.

AT&SF RY – embossed near bottom, ribbed sides, 10½"H, 7"D, spout on top front, screw filler cap top center, bail, brown, no mfrs name $35.00

C&NW – embossed big at rear, coffee pot shape, 8"H, 4¾"D, spout dome front, screw filler cap top dome center, side grip handle, bail, black, J-Urbana, O......................$30.00

C&NW RY – embossed on side, 13"H, 8"D, spout top front, cork cap top center, finger grip bottom rear, bail, galvanized, Johnson, Urbana, O......................................$40.00

CB&QRR CO ICC 24 – stamped on top rear, ribbed sides, 12"H, 9"D, iron pouring spout top center with screw cap, vent screw cap top rear, wire handle, black, J-Urbana, O...$38.00

Engineer's Long Spout Oilers

CM&StPRY – embossed side of dome, 13½"H, 7½"D, spout dome front, screw filler cap top center, finger grip bottom rear, wood spool on bail, grey, J-Urbana, O ..$45.00

CStPM&O – embossed top rear, 9"H, 6½"D, curved spout top front, screw filler cap top center, wire handle, black, Eagle...$40.00

GN RY – stamped side of dome, 8½"H, 5¼"D, spout dome front, screw filler cap top center, hand grip and bail, galvanized, Eagle $30.00

GN RY – embossed side of dome, 12½"H, 8"D, spout dome front, screw filler cap top center, wood spool on bail, finger grip bottom rear, red, J-Urbana, O $37.50

GN RY – embossed front, 9¼"H, 6"D, spout top front, screw filler cap top center, wire handle, finger grip bottom rear, galvanized, J-Urbana, O $35.00

NPR – embossed on tag rear, 11"H, 8¾"D, spout top front, screw filler cap top center, bail, black, Eagle $36.00

NP RY – embossed on side, teapot shape, 6"H, 7"D, front spout, grip handle, screw filler cap on top peak, bright tin, J-Urbana, O $27.50

PRR – embossed Keystone logo at side, teapot shape, 8"H, oval base 4¾ x 7", front spout, lift-off lid, grip handle, spool on bail, dark tin, no mfrs name $38.00

RI LINES – embossed on side, coffee pot shape, 7¾"H, 5¼"D, front spout, lift-off lid, side grip handle, dark sheet metal, no mfrs name $38.00

Kerosene Can

ROCK ISLAND LINES – embossed on side, coffee pot shape, 7"H, 5"D, front spout, lift-off lid, grip handle, dark tin, no mfrs name $45.00

SOO LINE – embossed on top of screw filler cap, 9"H, 6½"D, spout top front, wood spool handle, dark sheet metal, no mfrs name $37.50

Water Cans, Galvanized

AC&Y RY – embossed on side, 10½"H, 7"D, hinged lid, pouring spout, wood spool on bail, no mfrs name.......$35.00

BURLINGTON ROUTE – embossed logo front, 9½"H, 7½"D, lift-off lid, cap on spout, wire handle, no mfrs name..$35.00

CMSTP&P RR – embossed on side, 9"H, 7¼"D, lift-off lid, pouring spout, wire handle, no mfrs name............$25.00

CMStP&P RR – embossed on front, 9½"H, 7½"D, lift-off lid, no spout, wire handle, S. G. Adams Metalware Co. St. Louis...$30.00

DSS&ARR – embossed on dome, 12"H, 8"D, lift-off lid, no spout, wire handle, no mfrs name $55.00

NP RY – embossed on side, 14"H, 8½"D, pouring spout, hinged lid, wood spool on wire handle, no mfrs name $25.00

NYCS – embossed on side, tea kettle shape, 7"H, 8¼" x 11" oval base, pouring spout, lift-off lid, wire handle, no mfrs name...$30.00

SOO LINE – embossed on dome 12"H, 8"D, lift-off lid, no spout, wire handle, no mfrs name $40.00

Galvanized Water Cans

Torches

B&O RR – embossed on 5" hollow handle, teapot style, 4½"H, 3½"D, front spout, screw filler cap, Peter Gray, Boston $37.50

BURLINGTON ROUTE – embossed side logo, teapot style, 4½"H, 4½"D, front spout with cap, screw filler cap, 9" tubular handle, no mfrs. name $60.00

C&NW RY – embossed on bottom, cone shape, 8½"H, with 2¼" screw on spout, 4½"D, wide grip handle, J-Urbana, O...$35.00

CGW RY – embossed on bottom, cone shape, 7"H, 4½"D, 12" long bail hook, front spout, screw on top filler cap, no mfrs. name $42.50

CM&STP – bottom stamped, teapot style, 6"H, 4¼"D, front spout, grip handle, screw on top filler cap, no mfrs name...$35.00

CMSTP&PRR – bottom stamped, cone shape, 7¼"H, with 2¼",

screw-on spout, 4¼"D, grip handle, no mfrs name ..$30.00

GN RY – bottom stamped, candle type, 13"H, with 3" screw-on spout, 3"D, all brass, no mfrs name..................$65.00

MKT – embossed on top of screw-on cap, teapot style, 6¾"H, 4¼"D, front spout, grip handle, Eagle Pat Nov. 12, 1912 ....$38.00

NPR – embossed on side tag, teapot style, 5¾"H, 4¼"D, front spout, grip handle, screw-on top filler cap, Eagle $32.00

NPR – embossed on side tag, cone shape, 6"H with 2" screw-on spout, grip handle, Eagle $27.50

PRR – raised on side (cast iron torch) cone shape, 5"H, with 4" screw-on spout, 3½"D, grip handle, Dayton Malleable Iron Co..$55.00

SOO LINE – embossed on side tag, teapot style, 5½"H, 4"D, front spout, grip handle, Eagle $40.00

Long-Handled Torch

SOO LINE – embossed side logo, teapot style, 4½"H, 4½"D, front spout, 9" tubular handle, screw filler cap, no mfrs name $75.00

SP&S RY – embossed on bottom, cone shape, 7½"H, with 2¼" screw-on spout, 4½"D, grip handle, Johnson, Urbana, O..$38.00

Tallow Pots

These are teapot-style, round-ended cans with a goose-neck pouring spout, grasping handle at rear, wire bail and screw filler cap on top. Height is measured to top rim and width dimensions are the oval base. Other features are noted.

Tallow Pot – Teapot Style

AT&SF RY – embossed on bottom, 5"H, base 5 x 7¼", no mfgrs. name..$35.00

C&NWRY – embossed on bottom, 5"H, base 5 x 7¼", J. URBANA, O $37.50

C.&N.W.RY.CO. – embossed on side tag, 4¼"H, base 4¼ x 7¼", EAGLE..$35.00

C.B.&QR.R. – embossed on bottom, 7¼"H, base 5 x 8", GEM MF'G CO. PGH.PA $47.50

CMSTP&PRR – embossed on bottom, 5"H, base 5 x 7", grasping handle at side, no mfgrs name $27.50

CSTPM&ORY – embossed on bottom, 4½"H, base 5 x 7", J. URBANA, O..$42.50

GNR – embossed on side tag, 4½"H, base 5¼ x 7½", no bail, EAGLE $38.00

M&STL RR – embossed on side near bottom, 7"H, base 5¼ x 8½", hinged lid, grasping handle at side, no mfgrs name $48.00

NPRY – embossed on bottom, 5"H, base 5 x 7", no mfgrs name $36.00

UNION PACIFIC – embossed on screw cap, 6"H, base 5¼ x 8", no mfgrs name $30.00

Miscellaneous

CASH BOX – AT&SF RY stamped on hg'd cover, 4½ x 6 x 7", with hasp for small padlock, sheet metal, black....$20.00

COAL HOD – ROCK ISLAND LINES embossed exterior side, 12"H, 13" wide at bail loops, rear grasp handle, galv'd $75.00

COAL HOD – C&O RY embossed exterior base rim, 11"H front end, 13" wide at bail loops, rear finger grip, black, J-URBANA, O $50.00

COAL HOD – NPR embossed exterior side, 11½"H front end, 12" wide at bail loops, rear finger grip, galv'd $55.00

COVERED BUCKET – PRR Keystone logo embossed on hinged lid, for sweeping compound, 11"D, height 10", finger grip on lid and at bottom rear, bail, galv'd $50.00

CUP – PRR Keystone logo embossed exterior, 4¼"D, 2¼"H, rounded bottom, tin $27.00

CUP – C&O RY embossed inside of flat bottom, 4½"D top, 3½"D base, height 2", flat loop handle, sheet metal, HANDLAN, ST. LOUIS $25.00

CUP – BN BURLINGTON NORTHERN silk screened in green on exterior, 3½"D, height 2¾", tin $5.00

DIPPER – ST.L.S.F.RWY.CO. embossed inside flat bottom, 4½"D, height 2", tubular handle 7¾" long, tin $35.00

FIRE BUCKET – SOO LINE embossed top front, cone shape, 13½"D, length 19", galv'd, red, J-URBANA, O $65.00

FIRST AID BOX – CB&Q RAILROAD plus logo and Safety First in color on hg'd cover, 4 x 6 x 9", wire handle, mnt'g wall hangers, tin, brown $55.00

FIRST AID KIT – GREAT NORTHERN RAILWAY Goat logo on h'gd. cover, 2½ x 4½ x 8", wire handle, two rear wall mnt'g tabs, sheet steel, green enamel....................$45.00

FLAGMAN'S CASE – CPR stamped on hg'd top compartment, tubular style, 4"D, height 22", attached narrow side tube 1½ x 14" for flag, linked chain for carrying, galv'd., red, H.L. PIPER, MONTREAL.................$35.00

FLAGMAN'S CASE – C&NW RY stamped on hg'd cover of oval top compartment, 4½ x 6½ x 7", round bottom part is 4 x 8", two attached metal loops to hold flag, reg. handle for carrying, tin, black, JOHNSON-URBANA, O..........$50.00

FUNNEL – GNRY embossed exterior of mouth, 4½"D, length 5¾", tin $18.00

FUNNEL – GNRY embossed interior of mouth, 5¼"D, length 6½", tin $22.00

FUNNEL – NPRY embossed exterior of mouth, 5"D, length 6½", tin $25.00

FUSEE BOX – UPRR stamped top front, 3 x 4 x 18", wall mnt'd, to contain sticks of Railway 10 Min. Red Safety Fusees, tin, red...$20.00

GLUE KETTLE – NPR stamped on outside of pail, 6 x 7", for boiling water, inside round container 4½ x 6" to hold glue, both with wire bail, copper (scarce) $65.00

GRADUATED MEASURE – CSTPM&O RY embossed on exterior, marked 1 Pt to 4 Pt, 5"D, height 6", funnel-type spout, side handle, tin $28.00

GRADUATED MEASURE – NP RY embossed inside bottom, unmk'd rings, ½ pt to 1 qt level, 4¼"D, height 4", wide spout, grip handle rear, tin $22.00

MATCH BOX – O.C.R.R. embossed on hg'd. cover, 3 x 4½ x 8½", wire hasp to secure cover, tin, Japanned, (scarce) $45.00

Tin First Aid Box

MEASURER – M.P. LINES embossed exterior front, unmkd., 1 cup (8 oz) 2½"D bottom, 3½"H, wide spout, grip handle rear, tin $27.50

SECURITY BOX – DSS&A RY CO, big letters across front, 10¾ x 13½ x 20", hg'd cover, cyl. key lock, lifting handle each end, tin, maroon, yellow trim, (rare) $150.00

SPRINKLING CAN – CB&Q RR CO embossed on front, round style, 6 x 9", pierced front cover piece, wide metal carrying handle, grip handle at rear, galv'd., green, JOHNSON-URBANA, O $35.00

UTILITY BOX – N.P.R. embossed on front, 3 x 4½ x 8½", hinged cover, back plate with two holes to hang on wall, bright tin...$15.00

WATER PAIL – G.N.RY. embossed big on front, 10"D, 9¼"H, bail, galv'd $35.00
WATER PAIL – NP RY embossed on front, 12"D, height 10", bail, galv'd $30.00

WASTE PAIL – N.P.R. embossed big on front, 12"D, height 10", bail, galv'd $35.00

Cap Badges, Caps Complete

Cap Badges

Cap badges came in a number of styles, from plain narrow rectangular panels to arched and fancy tops. Most had indented letters filled in with black enamel against a nickel-plated or gilt background. Others had raised letters, logos, and colored enamel work on contrasting pebbled silver and gold backgrounds. Manufacturers' hallmarks are found on the back-side of many. Cap badges featuring an unusual occupation or one from a long-gone defunct railroad have a high value. Those not railroad marked, with titles only, such as "Conductor," "Brakeman," "Agent," "Dining Car Steward," or "Sleeping Car Porter," are more moderately priced. Caution: Be on the lookout for repro's in the plain rectangular styles with black letters.

AMTRAK ASSISTANT CONDUCTOR – black letters, red/blue logo on gold finish, 1¾ x 3" $30.00
AMTRAK TRAINMAN – black letters, red/blue logo on gold finish, 1¾ x 3" $25.00
BOSTON & MAINE AGENT – gold finish, curved top, 3⅝ x 1⅛" $35.00
BOSTON & MAINE BAGGAGE MASTER – nickel finish, curved top, 3⅝ x 1⅛" $110.00
BOSTON & MAINE CONDUCTOR – gold finish, curved top, 3⅝ x 1⅛" $45.00
BOSTON & MAINE STATION AGENT – gold finish, curved top, 3⅝ x 1⅛" $40.00
BOSTON & MAINE TRAINMAN – nickel finish, curved top, 3⅝ x 1⅛" $35.00
BUFFALO ROCHESTER AND PITTSBURGH RY "Safety and Service" AGENT – gold finish, blue logo top, 1¾ x 3¾" $85.00
BUFFALO ROCHESTER AND PITTSBURGH RY "Safety and Service" TRAINMAN – silver finish, blue logo top, 1¾ x 3¾" $75.00
C. & O. RY. CONDUCTOR – black enamel and embossed, pebbled gold background, arched top, milled border, 1½ x 4¼" $35.00
C. & O. RY. BRAKEMAN – black enamel and embossed, pebbled silver background, arched top, milled border, 1½ x 4¼" $30.00
C. & O. RY. PORTER – black enamel and embossed, pebbled silver background, arched top, milled border, 1½ x 4¼" $25.00
C.G.W. RY CONDUCTOR – nickel finish, plain rectangle, ¾ x 3½" $75.00
C.M.&St.P.AGENT – embossed, pebbled silver background, fancy pointed top, 1¼ x 3¼" $45.00
C.ST.P.M.& O.RY. BRAKEMAN – nickel finish, plain rectangle, ⅞ x 3¾" $60.00
C.ST.P.M. & O.RY. CONDUCTOR (script) – nickel finish, plain rectangle, ¾ x 3¾" $65.00

C&N.W.RY. FREIGHT CONDUCTOR – nickel finish, plain rectangle, ¾ x 2⅞" $55.00
C.&N.W.RY. FREIGHT BRAKEMAN – nickel finish, plain rectangle, ¾ x 2⅞" $65.00
C.R.I.&P. CONDUCTOR – embossed pebbled gold background, fancy curved top, 1¼ x 3¾" $50.00

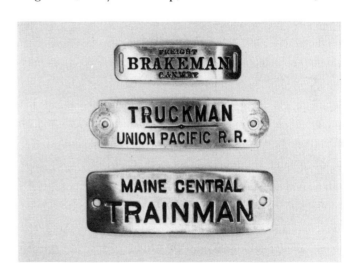

Cap Badges – Rectangular Style

ERIE RAILROAD TRAIN PORTER – nickel finish, plain rectangle, 1 x 4", hmkd. American Ry. Supply Co. New York $100.00
G.N. R.R. U.S. MAIL – nickel finish, fancy pointed top, 1⅜ x 3¼" scarce $95.00
G.N.RY. BRAKEMAN – nickel finish, curved top, 1¼ x 4"..$55.00
G.N.RY. CONDUCTOR – nickel finish, curved top, 1¼ x 4" $60.00
LACKAWANNA RAILROAD BAGGAGEMAN – embossed, silver pebbled field, 1 x 3⅞" $40.00
LACKAWANNA RAILROAD PORTER – embossed, silver pebbled field, 1 x 3⅞" $75.00

Cap Badges With Enamelled and Raised Letters

L.S. & M.S. FREIGHT CONDUCTOR – nickel finish, fancy pointed top, 1⅛ x 3¼", hmkd. Hoole Mfg. Co. 59, 61 Jones St. New York, scarce $75.00

MAINE CENTRAL TRAINMAN – nickel finish, plain rectangle, 1⅜ x 4¼" $30.00

M.C. R.R. CONDUCTOR – embossed, pebbled gold background, NEW YORK CENTRAL LINES – blue enamel logo, arched top, 1½ x 3½" $45.00

M.C. R.R. OPERATOR – embossed, pebbled silver background, NEW YORK CENTRAL LINES – blue enamel logo, arched top, 1½ x 3¾" $45.00

MILWAUKEE ROAD TRAINMAN – silver on black baked enamel rectangle, ¾ x 3", red box logo 1¼" dia. ..$45.00

MINNESOTA AND INTERNATIONAL – Big Fork and International Falls, "Sportsman's Route" Moosehead, 1" dia. logo in red and gold at top, AGENT in gold on black baked enamel ⅝ x 2½" rectangle below, hmkd S.D. Childs & Co. Engravers, Chicago, rare $275.00

M & ST.L.R.R. AGENT – nickel finish, plain rectangle, 1 x 4", Twin City Stamp & Stencil Co. Minneapolis hmkd ..$115.00

M & ST.L.R.R. CONDUCTOR – nickel finish, plain rectangle, 1 x 4", E. R. Williamson & Co. makers, Minneapolis hmkd $125.00

MINNEAPOLIS & ST. LOUIS RAILROAD CO. – "The PEORIA GATEWAY LINE" logo in curved top, CONDUCTOR in gold on black field, 1¼ x 3½", scarce $200.00

MINNEAPOLIS & ST. LOUIS RY. CO. BRAKEMAN – nickel finish, plain rectangle, ⅞ x 3¼" $110.00

M.ST.P.&S.S.M.RY.CO. BAGGAGEMAN – nickel finish, plain rectangle, ¾ x 3¾" $115.00

M.ST.P.&S.S.M.RY.CO. CONDUCTOR – nickel finish, plain rectangle, ⅞ x 3½" $85.00

M.ST.P.&S.S.M.RY.CO. BRAKEMAN – nickel finish, plain rectangle, ⅞ x 3½" $75.00

NEW YORK CENTRAL CONDUCTOR – embossed, pebbled gold field, NEW YORK CENTRAL LINES blue enamel logo, arched top, 1½ x 3½" $30.00

NEW YORK CENTRAL BRAKEMAN – embossed, pebbled silver field, NEW YORK CENTRAL SYSTEM blue enamel logo, arched top, 1½ x 3½" $25.00

NEW YORK CENTRAL GATEMAN – embossed, pebbled silver field, NEW YORK CENTRAL SYSTEM blue enamel logo, arched top, 1½ x 3½" $35.00

N.Y.N.H. & H.R.R. BAGGAGE MASTER – nickel finish, fancy notched top, 1⅛ x 4" $30.00

N.Y.N.H. & H.R.R. TRAINMAN – nickel finish, fancy notched top, 1⅛ x 4" $25.00

NP AGENT – gold on black baked enamel, rectangle, ¾ x 2½", NP logo 1" dia. top, S.D. Childs & Co. Chicago hmk. scarce $95.00

NP BRAKEMAN – silver on black, ¾ x 3½" rectangle, NP logo 1" dia. top $75.00

NP CONDUCTOR – gold on black baked enamel, ¾ x 3⅝", rectangle, NP logo 1" dia. top $85.00

NORTHERN PACIFIC RAILWAY BRAKEMAN – nickel finish, plain rectangle, ⅞ x 4" $55.00

NORTHERN PACIFIC RAILWAY CONDUCTOR – nickel finish, plain rectangle, ⅞ x 4" $65.00

NORTHERN PACIFIC RAILWAY FREIGHT CONDUCTOR – nickel finish, plain rectangle, 1 x 4" $132.00

PC CONDUCTOR – red PC monogram and Conductor in black raised on pebbled gold field, arched top, 1⅝ x 3¼" $30.00

PRR USHER – red Keystone logo at top, Usher in black on pebbled gold rectangle, ¾ x 3⅛", with ornate top, hmkd. EBY Co. Phila. scarce $85.00

PULLMAN CONDUCTOR – black letters raised on pebbled gold background, rectangle with narrow edged borders, 1 x 4" $45.00

PULLMAN PORTER – black letters raised on pebbled silver background, rectangle with narrow edged borders, 1 x 4" $40.00

ROCK ISLAND BRAKEMAN – black enamel logo and title raised on silver background, arched top, 1¼ x 3¾", scarce $65.00

ROCK ISLAND CONDUCTOR – black enamel logo and title raised on gold background, arched top, 1¼ x 3¾", scarce $75.00

SANTA FE BRAKEMAN – black logo, nickel finish, fancy pointed top, 1¾ x 3¼" $40.00

SANTA FE CONDUCTOR – black logo, nickel finish, high curved top, 1⅝ x 3⅞" $45.00

SOO LINE BRAKEMAN – raised blue enamel logo, title raised blue enamel logo, title raised in black on silver pebbled field, high curved top, 1¼ x 3" $175.00

SOO LINE PORTER – raised black enamel logo, title on silver pebbled field, high curved top, 1½ x 3¼", hmkd Wendells Mpls $150.00

SOO LINE STATION AGENT – nickel finish, fancy pointed top, 1⅜ x 3½" rectangle, scarce $200.00

SOUTHERN RY CO. CONDUCTOR – nickel finish, curved top, 1⅛ x 3⅛", hmkd. American Ry. Supply Co. New York $85.00

SOUTHERN RY CO. FLAGMAN – nickel finish, curved top, 1⅛ x 3⅛", hmkd. American Ry. Supply Co. New York $135.00

T.ST.L. & K.C.R.R. BRAKEMAN – nickel finish, curved top, 1⅜ x 3½" scarce $125.00

UNION PACIFIC BRAKEMAN – raised, silver pebbled background, arched top, milled border, 1½ x 4½" $50.00

UNION PACIFIC R.R. BRAKEMAN – silver finish, rectangle with raised borders, hole each end, 1 x 4" $30.00

UNION PACIFIC BRAKEMAN – silver finish, rectangle with raised borders, hole each end, 1⅛ x 4" $35.00

UNION PACIFIC CONDUCTOR – gold finish, rectangle with raised borders, hole each end, 1⅛ x 4"..........$40.00

UNION PACIFIC R.R. ELECTRICIAN – gold finish, rectangle with raised borders, hole each end, 1⅛ x 4"....$65.00

UNION PACIFIC STATION AGENT – raised, pebbled gold background, arched top, milled border, 1½ x 4½" $55.00

UNION PACIFIC STATION BAGGAGE – raised, pebbled gold background, arched top, milled border, 1½ x 4½" $60.00

UNION PACIFIC R.R. TRUCKMAN – nickel finish, plain rectangle, 1 x 4", J.P. Cooke Co. Mfrs. Omaha $55.00

WABASH R.R. BRAKEMAN – nickel finish, plain rectangle, ⅞ x 3¾" $40.00

WABASH R.R. CONDUCTOR – (script) nickel finish, plain rectangle, ⅞ x 3¾"..$45.00

Non-Railroad Marked

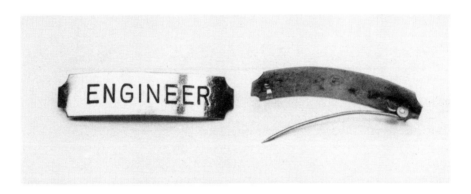

Non-Railroad Marked, Pin Clasp Type

AGENT – nickel finish, plain rectangle, ⅞ x 3", American Ry. Supply Co. New York hmk.....................................$12.50

BAGGAGEMAN – nickel finish, plain rectangle, ⅞ x 3", American Ry. Supply Co. New York hmk $15.00

BRAKEMAN – embossed on pebbled silver background, pointed arched top, 1¼ x 3¾"................................$20.00

CONDUCTOR – gold finish, plain rectangle, ⅞ x 3" $12.50

DINING CAR STEWARD – gold finish, fancy pointed top, 1⅜ x 3¼" $35.00

ENGINEER – nickel finish, plain rectangle, ¾ x 3", American Ry. Supply Co., New York hmk..............................$20.00

FIREMAN – nickel finish, plain rectangle, ¾ x 3", American Ry. Supply Co., New York hmk.............................$20.00

SLEEPING CAR CONDUCTOR – gold finish, fancy pointed top, 1⅜ x 3¼" $35.00

SLEEPING CAR PORTER – silver finish, fancy pointed top, 1⅜ x 3¼"..$30.00

TRAINMAN – nickel finish, plain rectangle, ⅞ x 3", American Ry. Supply Co. New York hmk........................$12.50

Miscellaneous

AMERICAN EXPRESS CO – in red/blue letters with flag shield litho in color on celluloid card inside brass frame, 16038 indented in oval above, brass, irregular shape, 2¾ x 3¼", pin clasp, rare $265.00

AMERICAN RAILWAY EXPRESS – gold on green enamel, square diamond logo, embossed gold floral sides, black No. 296 on gold bottom scroll, pin clasp, 2 x 2", hmkd. Bastian Bros. Co. Rochester, N.Y. $45.00

BARKALOW BROS. NEWS SERVICE – raised on copper pebbled metal, rectangle with narrow raised borders, 1¼ x 4". (train and depot vendor's badge) scarce $125.00

CANADIAN PACIFIC EXPRESS – raised on shiny bronze metal, polished brass digits 1255 on beaver shield at top center, 2¼ x 4¾", hmkd. J.R. Gaunt, Montreal ..$150.00

NORTHERN EXPRESS – black letters on white/red/black Monad logo 1½" dia., black indent 18 on silver tab below, hmkd "The Whitehead & Hoag Co. Newark, N.J." Rare $285.00

REA-X – white on red enamel, square-diamond logo, silver frame, black No.s 81162 on silver bottom, post mount, 1½ x 1⅞", hmkd. Bastian Bros. Co. Rochester, NY. $35.00

RAILWAY EXPRESS AGENCY – white on red enamel, square diamond logo, embossed silver floral sides, black No. 57822 on silver bottom scroll, 2 x 2", post mount $45.00

ST.P.U.D. ATTENDANT 7 – black indented letters, nickel plated, fancy pointed top, 1⅜ x 3¼", hmkd. American Stamp Works, St. Paul, Minn $30.00

TOURIST AGENT B.& M.C.V.G.T. – black indented letters on yellow brass, rectangle with rounded top corners 1½ x 4", hmkd. Mitchell Mfg. Co. Boston (Railroad Travel Agent's badge) scarce $125.00

WELLS FARGO & CO. EXPRESS – white letters, blue/red celluloid litho logo encased in a diamond metal frame at center, with No. C-211 at sides, pebbled aluminum, irregular shape 3⅛ x 2¾", hmkd. N. Stafford, Maker, 67 Fulton, N.Y. Pat. May 22, '06, rare $350.00

WHEELING TRACTION SYSTEM 448 CONDUCTOR – raised silver letters on black enamel, aluminum rectangle, 1½ x 3¾"..$30.00

WHEELING TRACTION SYSTEM 132 MOTORMAN – raised silver letters on black enamel, aluminum rectangle, 1½ x 3¾" $25.00

YONKERS R.R.CO.101 CONDUCTOR – white inlaid letters on black Bakelite, encased in an aluminum rectangle frame with arched top, 2 x 4¾", hmkd. Hesren Bros. & Co. Pittsburg Pa $35.00

YONKERS R.R.CO.682 MOTORMAN – black inlaid letters on white Bakelite, encased in an aluminum rectangle frame with arched top, 2 x 4¾", hmkd. Hesren Bros. & Co. Pittsburg Pa...$30.00

Trainmen's Caps Complete With Badge and Trimmings

Examples listed here are standard uniform caps with badge and specific trimmings, such as cords over the visor, row of lace trim around top of band, and two small railroad-marked side buttons. Caps in fine condition with original badge and trimmings play an important role in determining value. A make-up cap with badge is discounted in price.

Cap With Badge and Trimmings Complete

AMTRAK CONDUCTOR – letters and logo on square shape gold badge affixed to standard royal blue cloth uniform cap. No mfgrs. name..$45.00

BRAKEMAN – rectangle badge, nickel-plated, BRAKEMAN in black enamel, non-railroad marked. Cap – summer, braided brown straw top, black silk band around bottom, white twisted cord above visor, two silver side buttons mkd. B.R. (Burlington Route) Mfr: Hohenadel Bros., Uniform Caps, Chicago $70.00

C.M.ST.P.&P.R.R. – Badge – nickel finish, ornate design, shield at center, eagle atop, two side figures, cut-out RR initials at bottom (police officer badge). Cap is indigo wool, octangular shape, mfr. A.G. Meier & Co., Uniform Caps, Chicago $200.00

CONDUCTOR – Title embroidered in gold on wide black silk band with two stripes of yellow lace trim; band fits around cap with CONDUCTOR showing above visor. Cap – black grosgrain with yellow visor cord and two gold

RR-mkd. side buttons. Mfr: Carlson & Company Uniform Tailors, Chicago $45.00

GREAT NORTHERN RY. PORTER – Badge – rectangular, nickel-plated with fancy pointed top, black letters. Cap – black grosgrain, white knotted rope visor cord, two silver RR-mkd. side buttons. Mfr: Marshall Field & Co., Uniform Division, Chicago $125.00

GREAT NORTHERN RY. TRAIN SALESMAN – Badge – rectangular, nickel-plated, with fancy pointed top, black letters. Cap – black grosgrain, no visor cord, white lace trim around band, two silver RR mkd. side buttons. Mfr: Carlson & Co. Uniform Tailors, Chicago $195.00

MILWAUKEE ROAD CONDUCTOR – Badge – rectangular with red box logo above, title is raised in gold on black enamel. Cap – black grosgrain with silver gilt lace band above visor and yellow lace stripe around crown, two gold side buttons, RR mkd. Mfgr: Carlson & Company Uniform Tailors, Chicago $175.00

MILWAUKEE ROAD TRAINMAN – Badge – rectangular with red box logo above, title is raised in silver on black enamel. Cap – black grosgrain with silver metallic lace band above visor, two silver RR mkd. side buttons. Mfr: A.G. Meier & Co. Uniform Caps, Chicago $95.00

NP CONDUCTOR – Badge – rectangular, gold letters on black, with NP logo above. Cap – black grosgrain with yellow knotted visor cord, yellow lace stripe around crown, two gold NP side buttons. Mfr: Carlson & Company Uniform Tailors, Chicago...........................$150.00

NP BRAKEMAN – Badge – rectangular, silver letters on black with NP logo above. Cap – black grosgrain, white knotted rope visor cord and white lace stripe on black band, two silver NP side buttons. Mfr: Carlson & Company, Uniform Tailors, Chicago $125.00

PULLMAN PORTER – Badge – rectangular, black raised letters on silver pebbled field. Cap – black grosgrain with white knotted cord above visor, two silver Pullman side buttons. Mfr: Ruby's Uniform, Caps, Chicago $95.00

SOO LINE BRAKEMAN – Badge – rectangular, with arched top, title is raised with blue logo above on silver field. Cap – black grosgrain, white knotted visor cord and two silver RR mkd. side buttons. Mfr: Carlson & Company, Uniform Tailors, Chicago $145.00

Cloth Items

In addition to the table linens used in dining car service, a variety of other cloth items were in use over the years by the railroads, most of which are now being collected. This includes towels, pillow cases, sheets and sleeper blankets, passenger car seat headrests, shop cloths or wiping rags, chef's caps, aprons, hot pad holders, etc. All of these bearing authentic railroad markings are being picked up, especially those from roads no longer in business which have become scarce and bring the higher prices. Condition plays an important part in determining value.

Hand Towels, Bath Towels

All white cotton, some have mfrs. name labels, such as Puritan, Niagara, Cannon, etc., still intact.

AT&SF – initials AT&SF RY. 51 woven in white on red stripe, 13 x 17" $15.00

C&O – CHESAPEAKE AND OHIO RY woven in blue across center, blue reversed in white letters on blue stripe on backside, cotton chenille bath towel, 22 x 38"......$25.00

CMSTP&PRR – initials CM&STPRR – 1947 woven in white on orange stripe 16 x 25" $15.00

CMSTP&PRR – initials CMSTP&PRR stamped in black at bottom, 13 x 19"..$10.00

GN – GREAT NORTHERN RAILWAY woven in white on red stripe, 15 x 27" $18.00

NP – initials N.P.RY. stamped in black along side, blue striped borders, 16 x 23" $10.00

NYC – NEW YORK CENTRAL SYSTEM woven in white on orange stripe, 15 x 17"...$12.00

PULLMAN – 1919 PULLMAN woven twice in white on blue stripe, 16 x 24" $20.00

PULLMAN – PROPERTY OF THE PULLMAN COMPANY (undated) woven in white on blue stripe, 16 x 24"..$10.00

PULLMAN – PROPERTY OF THE PULLMAN COMPANY 1929 woven in white on blue stripe, 16 x 24"........$15.00

SOO LINE – SOO LINE 1923 woven in white on blue cross-stripe, 16 x 19½"...$25.00

Cotton Hand Towels

Head Rests

These are rectangular-shaped cloths with the railroad's logo, name trains and advertising on them. They were buttoned over the top portion of the reclining seats in the coaches to keep the upholstery clean and free of hair oil residue. Those in pristine condition and from roads long gone bring the higher prices.

Head Rest Seat Covers

ACL – ATLANTIC COAST LINE RAILROAD, FLORIDA VACATIONLAND at top buttonholes, sunbather beach scene and palms at bottom, 15 x 18" $12.00

CB&Q – Denver Zephyr with dome car and mountains pictured in brown at bottom edge on tan, 15 x 18" ..$12.00

C&NW – "The 400" at bottom, NORTHWESTERN SYSTEM at top, brown on tan, 15 x 19½" $14.00

CMSTP&P – THE MILWAUKEE ROAD at buttonholes, logo and domeliners in script along bottom edge, brown on tan, 13 x 18" $15.00

GN – GREAT NORTHERN and goat in orange at buttonholes on tan, 14 x 19" $18.00

IC – ILLINOIS CENTRAL in script at buttonholes, brown on tan, 15 x 15½" $12.00

IC – Diamond logo at center, slipover double seat type, eggshell white, grey logo, 40½ x 14½" $14.00

MStP&SSM – SOO LINE in red at buttonholes on beige, 15 x 18" $18.00

NP – NORTHERN PACIFIC in black at buttonholes on tan, logo in black/red with four black lines on grey across bottom, 14 x 20½" $22.00

PRR – logo and electric train in brown at bottom edge on tan, 15 x 18" $15.00

SR – southern logo, LOOK AHEAD' LOOK SOUTH at buttonholes, green on pink, 15 x 19" $12.00

UP – winged streamliner motif at bottom, U.P. at buttonholes, red-grey on yellow, 14 x 19" $10.00

Shop Cloths

The roundhouse crew used shop cloths for wiping dirt, oil and grease from tools and machinery and for polishing the brass trim on locomotives, as well as for wiping the soot and grease from their hands. Those in fine clean condition are worth more than those soiled and tattered.

BURLINGTON ROUTE – logo with repeated safety slogans, dark blue on beige, 16½ x 17½" $15.00

C&NW – logo and STAY ALERT, STAY ALIVE, SAFETY FIRST, repeated, blue on orange, 14 x 17" $12.00

EJ&E RY – logo and SAFETY IS YOUR PERSONAL RESPON-SIBILITY, repeated, blue on orange, 13½ x 17½"..$20.00

GN – GREAT NORTHERN RAILWAY goat logo, SAFETY ALL DAY EVERY DAY, repeated, dark blue on white, 15 x 17"..$18.00

IC – diamond logo, TAKE CARE, NOT CHANCES, THINK-WORK-LIVE-SAFELY, repeated, blue on white, 18 x 30" $12.00

MILWAUKEE ROAD – logo and WORK SAFELY, WIPE OUT ACCIDENTS in blue on orange, 14 x 17" $10.00

ROCK ISLAND – logo, "DON'T GET HURT, LOOK-THINK-BE ALERT" repeated, dark blue on olive green, 13 x 15" $15.00

Shop Cloths

Blankets

The earlier sleeping car blankets were very attractive in appearance, with colorful plaids or various overall designs, with the railroad's logo or name worked in. Later, when full-color wool blankets replaced the plaids and ornate patterns, the railroad's identification was imprinted prominently on the material in the center of the piece.

Sleeping Car Blanket

GREAT NORTHERN – full-color rose shade, with the GREAT NORTHERN RAILWAY silhouette goat logo in brown at center, 60 x 83", North Star Woolen Mills Co. label $175.00

GREAT NORTHERN – brown and tan o'all checkered design with GREAT NORTHERN RAILWAY early box logo at top center, 53 x 81", (scarce) $275.00

MILWAUKEE ROAD – beige shade with o'all light brown checkered design, Greek Key top border and C.M.ST.P.&P. 39 in rectangle at top center, 62 x 86", North Star Woolen Mills Co. label........................$150.00

NEW YORK CENTRAL – beige shade with light brown checkered o'all design, Greek Key top border and N.Y.C. Lines in rectangle at top center, 56 x 75".......................$150.00

PULLMAN – full-color rose shade with THE PULLMAN CO. logo in darker color at center, 57 x 79" $75.00

SOO LINE – tan shade with rows of dark brown stripes across top, plaid squares bottom, SOO LINE early style Banner logo at center, 53 x 78" (scarce) $300.00

SOO LINE – grey shade, with rows of beige and black lines across bottom, plaid squares in beige and black at top, SOO LINE box logo in center, 57 x 82".............$200.00

UNION PACIFIC – full dark grey shade, black stripe across top and bottom, UNION PACIFIC the OVERLAND Route early shield logo in black at center, 47 x 75", Pendleton Woolen Mills label (scarce)................$275.00

Pillow Cases

All pillow cases listed here are white cotton with the railroad's ID and where used ink-stamped in black somewhere on the pillow. These are the ones most often found today. Others had a colored embroidered band along the edge showing the railroad's name or name train. This also applies to the sheets.

BN – PILLOW RENTAL 50 CENTS TO DESTINATION ON BURLINGTON NORTHERN stamped inside rectangle, 10½ x 30"..$8.00

GREAT NORTHERN – G.N.RY.CO. also PILLOW RENTAL 50 CENTS TO DESTINATION ON GREAT NORTHERN RAILWAY inside rectangle, 19½ x 30" $10.00

PULLMAN – PROPERTY OF and THE PULLMAN CO. logo, 20 x 28½" $5.00

SOUTHERN RAILWAY – SR SOUTHERN RAILWAY SERVES THE SOUTH LOOK AHEAD – LOOK SOUTH logo, 20 x 28" $6.00

SOUTHERN PACIFIC – SOUTHERN PACIFIC LINES woven in dark blue on pale blue stripe around edge, 18 x 25" $12.00

UNION PACIFIC – UPRR and CHAIR CAR, 18½ x 23" $6.00

UNION PACIFIC – CITY OF SAN FRANCISCO woven in orange on pale orange stripe along edge, 19½ x 28" $10.00

UNION PACIFIC – UPRR, 18½ x 23" (berth pillow) $5.00

Sheet and Pillow Cases

Sheets

PULLMAN – PROPERTY OF and THE PULLMAN CO. logo repeatedly stamped, 63 x 85" $12.00
GREAT NORTHERN – G.N.RY.CO. 1963 stamped on both ends, 63 x 76" $15.00
SOUTHERN RAILWAY – SR SOUTHERN RAILWAY SERVES

THE SOUTH LOOK AHEAD – LOOK SOUTH logo, also Southern Railway System stamped in green, 81 x 64" $18.00
UNION PACIFIC – shield logo repeatedly stamped, 81 x 64" $12.00

Tablecloths

C&NW – THE "400" in green at center on yellow, cotton, 49 x 51" $45.00
C&NW – Chicago & NorthWestern Line logo with C.ST.P.M.& O.RY.CO. woven at top center, fleur-de-lis border design on two sides and bottom, white on white, linen, 53½ x 69½", scarce $125.00
NP – NORTHERN PACIFIC Yellowstone Park Line monad logo center, inner and outer acorn and leaves border, woven in white on white, linen, 54 x 66", scarce $125.00
ROCK ISLAND – logo in center, acorn and leaves border, ROCK ISLAND RAILROAD 11-1-60 at bottom edge,

woven in white on white, linen, 33½ x 53"............$75.00
ROCK ISLAND – logo in center, acorn and leaves border, ROCK ISLAND RAILROAD CO. 7-63 at bottom edge, woven in white on white, linen, 57 x 63½"............$45.00
SOO LINE – box logo woven in center, plain 3" wide border, white on white, cotton, 33 x 33" $55.00
SOO LINE – box logo woven in center, plain 5" wide border, white on white, linen, 54 x 56" $65.00
UNION PACIFIC – UPRR woven in bottom border with two flowers, 3½" wide border in pink on rust, cotton, 42 x 50" $45.00

Cloth Napkins

C&NW – Chicago & NorthWestern Line logo at center, fleur-de-lis border design, A29, woven in white on white, linen, 23 x 23" $22.00
C&NW – Chicago & NorthWestern Line logo with C.ST.P.M.& O.RY.CO. woven in at center, fleur–de-lis border design, white on white, linen, 22 x 23½", scarce $45.00
MILWAUKEE ROAD – the word "Hiawatha" and Indian emblem printed in magenta on tan, narrow magenta border, cotton, 10½ x 16¼" $15.00
NP – NORTHERN PACIFIC Yellowstone Park Line monad logo woven in at center, floral design corners, white on white, linen, 21 x 22" $22.00
NP – NORTHERN PACIFIC RAILWAY monad logo woven in white on tan at center, 1¾" wide border, white on tan, cotton, 20 x 21" $15.00
NP – NORTHERN PACIFIC – Yellowstone Park Line logo in center, wide Greek Key floral design border, dated '38, woven in white on white, linen, 23 x 23", scarce $50.00
NP – NORTHERN PACIFIC YPL red/brown monad logo printed in center on tan, cotton, 12½ x 17½"........$18.00
ROCK ISLAND – logo at center, acorn and leaves design border, ROCK ISLAND RAILROAD dated 3-62 at bottom edge, woven in white on white, linen, 20 x 20" $20.00
ROCK ISLAND – logo with word CALIFORNIAN printed above in arch, 1¼" border with pinstripe in magenta on tan, cotton, 11¾ x 14¾" $18.00
SP – SOUTHERN PACIFIC LINES Sunset logo woven in at center, poppies and wavy design border, dated 1927, white on white, linen, 21 x 21", scarce $45.00

Cloth Napkins

UNION PACIFIC – Winged Streamliner motif printed in corner with 1" wide border in yellow on white, cotton, 11 x 16" $10.00
UNION PACIFIC – UPRR woven in bottom border with two flowers, 1½" wide border in pink on rust, cotton, 17 x 19" $12.00

Miscellaneous Cloth Items

There were a variety of other cloth items manufactured for use by the railroads down through the years. Those bearing authentic railroad markings, especially pieces from long-gone roads, are becoming quite scarce, commanding the higher prices.

C&O – cotton handkerchief, Chessie, Peake and Kittens in corners and at center, multi-color on white, 14 x 14½" ..$35.00

CNS&M – cotton money sack, RETURN TO CHICAGO NORTH SHORE & MILWAUKEE R.R.CO. HIGHWOOD, ILL. $500.00 in black on white, 8½ x 14" $18.00

CStPM&O – cotton money sack, CHICAGO, ST. PAUL, MINNEAPOLIS & OMAHA RAILWAY CO. ST. PAUL, MINN. stamped in black on white, 5½ x 10" $22.00

GN – dining car waiter's three-piece outfit, short style jacket, trousers and apron, white cotton with orange/green braid trim, GREAT NORTHERN goat logo on left sleeve, three large GN silver buttons $150.00

MILWAUKEE ROAD – conductor's three piece uniform, blue wool cloth coat, vest and trousers, three large CMSTP&P gold buttons, two small gold on sleeves, plus pair THE MILWAUKEE ROAD metal coat lapel logos, vest has six small gold buttons.............................$175.00

Dining Car Waiter's Outfit

at center in white, DINING CAR DEP'T in yellow at bottom, 30" long $175.00

NP – shoe bag, string tied, soft cotton, full tan color, "Compliments of THE NORTHERN PACIFIC RAILWAY Dining Car Department," "ROUTE OF THE GREAT BIG BAKED POTATO" and a baked potato illustration printed in black, 14½ x 15½" opened flat $75.00

C&O Chessie Handkerchief

IC – engineer's gauntlet gloves, grey chamois fingers with canvas tops, stamped I.C.R.R. in black on fabric portion, length approx. 15" $25.00

NP – hot pad holder, monad logo at center, SAFETY AT WORK, SAFETY AT HOME, red checkered border, 6 x 6" ..$18.00

NP – felt pennant, green, "Route of the GREAT BIG Baked Potato" at top in color, NORTHERN PACIFIC RAILWAY

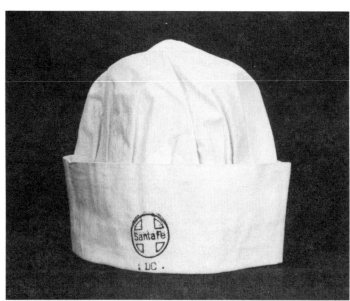

Dining Car Chef's Hat

NP – felt pennant, dark blue, Northern Pacific Yellowstone Park Line logo in red/white, NORTHERN PACIFIC RY. in white, 28" long $150.00

RY EX – cotton money sack, PROPERTY OF RY.EX. AGY.912843 stamped in black on white. $10.00

ROCK ISLAND – jacket, blue serge, SLEEPING CAR PORTER embroidered in silver on breast pocket, blue/silver braid on sleeves, three ROCK ISLAND LINES large silver buttons plus pair ROCK ISLAND metal coat lapel logos $75.00

SANTA FE – chef's cap, logo and "DC" stamped in black on white, 10½ x 8" folded flat $22.00

SP – waiter's jacket, dining car, white cotton twill with orange braid trim, SOUTHERN PACIFIC winged ball logo on upper portion of left sleeve, SOUTHERN PACIFIC LINES red logo label sewn on inside at neck, five large SP silver buttons $50.00

Dining Car Collectibles

China

Most railroads featured their own exclusive designs on their china, while others used a stock pattern. The railroad's logo, name, or initials appeared on the topside, or they were backstamped, along with the manufacturer's name. There is a great variety of patterns and pieces to be found; the earlier patterns or pieces from short-lived railroads bring top prices. The large service plates, such as the two steam and diesel examples from the Missouri Pacific and the complete set of ten Illinois Central's French Quarter service plates, command premium prices; also, demi sets, butter pats, footed egg cups and the like, have skyrocketed in value.

Note: All railroad china must be in excellent condition to warrant the prices listed.

Key to China Manufacturers

BSHR – Bauscher	MIN – Minton
BUFF – Buffalo	MYR – Mayer
IRQ – Iroquois	R-D – Royal Doulton
LAMB – Lamberton	SCM – Scammell
LEX – Lenox	SGO – Shenango
LIM – Limoges	STR – Sterling
MAD – Maddock (N.J.)	SYR – Syracuse
MDK – Maddock (Eng.)	WAR – Warwick

Key to Abbreviations

RRBS – Railroad backstamped
NRRBS – Not railroad backstamped
SM – Side marked
TM – Top marked

China pieces are listed by railroad, then pattern name and description. More extensive dining car china pattern information may be found in Richard Luckin's books, *Dining On Rails (an Encyclopedia of Railroad China)* and *Teapot Treasury (and Related Items)*.

Railroad's Name and China Pattern Descriptions

Alaska Railroad

"McKinley" – white, mustard yellow rim pinstripe, black border band with intricate yellow design and scenic Mt. McKinley Alaska Railroad logo at top/front center.
Saucer – 5¾", NRRBS, SGO $200.00

Atchison Topeka & Santa Fe

"Adobe" – tan, TM with round linear cactus/Indian hut scene at rim. Sometimes backstamped Made Expressly for Santa Fe dining car service.
Salad plate – 7¼", NRRBS, SYR.....................$75.00

"Black Chain" – white, with black link chain and pinstripe border.

Ice cream shell – 5" dia., BS – Made exp. for Santa Fe dining car service – O.P.Co., Syracuse China T-9 ....$125.00

"Bleeding Blue" – white, TM blue Santa Fe logo, double pinstripe border.

Butter pat – 3½", BS – Albert Pick Co. Chicago, Virtrified China A5 ....$150.00

Platter – rectangular, 7 x 11", BS-M-China-L Albert Pick & Co., Chicago $250.00

Double Egg Cups

"California Poppy" – white, yellow poppies with green and tan leaves; earlier pcs were thinner china and RRBS; new pieces made by Syracuse are heavier and sometimes RRBS.

Dinner plate – 9¾", BS – Made expressly for Santa Fe dining car service, O.P.Co. Syracuse China H-9.............$175.00

Cup and saucer – BS – same as above, BSHR..........$165.00

Salad Plate – 7¼", NRRBS, SYR $50.00

"Griffon" – pure white, black mythical Greek half-lion/half-eagle design border

Dinner plate – 10", BS – Made expressly for Santa Fe dining car service, 1930, BSHR.....................................$275.00

"Mimbreno" – ivory china, different Indian stylized animals/birds at center with border designs in brick red and brown. Most pieces have the full Mimbreno Indian and RRBS "Made expressly for Santa Fe dining car service." SYR.

Dinner plate – 10", center without figure, wide cross-hatch border and pinstripes..........................$175.00

Luncheon plate – 7¾" goat center, cross-hatched border, pinstripes $110.00

Sauce dish – 5½", spotted breast bird center, cross-hatched border, pinstripes $75.00

Saucer – crow center in circle, points border design, pinstripes $65.00

Butter pat – flying bird center, pinstripes border........$75.00

Chocolate pot with cover – without figures, stylized borders and design on cover $225.00

Atlantic Coast Line

"Carolina" – ivory china, grey outer band with inner pin-stripe, BS Sterling, East Liverpool, Ohio, Atlantic Coast Line Railroad, dated

Dinner plate – 9", RRBS, 1945 ....$60.00

Oval sauce – 4½ x 5¾", RRBS, 1946.....................$30.00

"Flora of the South" – ivory, green pinstripe border and multiple color flowers in center, Buffalo China.

Luncheon plate – 7¾", BS – Ye Olde Ivory Buffalo China, Flora of the South, Hibiscus, Jessamine, Poinsettia, Made especially for ATLANTIC COAST LINE RAILROAD $75.00

"Palmetto" – white, light green leaf border and red/green logo at top, made by several china companies, sometimes RRBS.

Platter – 8 x 11¾", BS – Warwick knight hallmark, dated 1945, NRRBS $135.00

Baltimore & Ohio

"Capitol" – white, intricate black design on gold band, B&O capitol logo and pinstripes are gold, made by several china companies, NRRBS.

Bowl – 6½", BS – Warwick knight hallmark, dated 1945 ....$45.00

Footed icecream dish $50.00

Plate – 6¼", BS – Shenango China, Newcastle, Pa $75.00

"Centenary" – white, blue picturesque scenes and locomotives. There are three vintages. First issue – BS – 1827-1927, Baltimore & Ohio Railroad capitol dome, Scammell's Lamberton China. Second issue – same BS, but made by Shenango China, Newcastle, Pa. Production in third issue also BS Shenango. Current re-runs are now being sold in the B&O museum.

Dinner plate – 9", Lord Baltimore locomotive 1925 in border, Scammell's, first issue $100.00

Dinner plate – 9", diesel-electric #51 1937 locomotive in border, Shenango, second issue $75.00

Dinner plate – 9", Cincinnatian and diesel-electric #51 in border, Shenango, third issue $65.00

Cup and saucer – coffee, saucer has Thomas Viaduct, cup has Philip E. Thomas loco and horsecart, SCM..$125.00

Cup and saucer – demi, same as above $85.00

Butter pat – 3½", horse-drawn car, SGO $55.00

"Derby" – white, round floral design of blues in center and same applied to border, made by Maddock, Burselm, England, not always RRBS.

Soup plate – 9", BS – Made for B&O, H.P. Chandler Sons Co. Baltimore $85.00

Dinner plate – 9¼", BS – Shenango China, New Castle Pa. NRRBS...........................$75.00

Oval sauce dish – 4¾ x 6", BS – Shenango China, New Castle, Pa. NRRBS $30.00

Boston & Albany

"Berkshire" – white, draped border design with pendants in tan and green with BOSTON & ALBANY RAILROAD

around New York Central Lines tan logo, double top-marked railroad china, sometimes RRBS.
Hot cake cover – 2½"H, 5¾" Dia., finger-hole top, NRRBS $200.00
Compote – footed, 5¾"H, 7" Dia., NRRBS $300.00
Creamer – 4½"H, BS – O.P. Co., Syracuse China $150.00
Rectangular tray – 5½ x 8½", BS – O.P. Co., Syracuse China, D-7, J. McD. & S. Co. Boston, design patented ..$175.00

Boston & Maine

"Minute Man" – white, border has a white floral design on blue band flanked by tan edges with a standing Minute Man figure at top center. Design copyrighted by Kenmoor. NRRBS.
Bowl – 6", BS – O.P.Co., Syracuse China, K-11 ....$150.00

Canadian National

"Algonquin" – (two types)
(a) – white, turquoise blue band border with pinstripes and ornate CNR intertwined light brown initials at top center, BS – Wood & Sons, England, crown h'mk. Not always RRBS.
Salad plate – 5½", NRRBS..$40.00
(b) – white, royal blue band border with black pinstripes and ornate CNR intertwined dark brown initials at top center, BS – T. Eaton Co., Toronto and Winnipeg, made especially for C.N.R.
Salad plate – 5½", RRBS $50.00

"Bonadventure" – (two types) – white, dark blue band with yellow pinstripes border, CANADIAN NATIONAL outlined leaf logo at top center, BS – "Duraline" Grindley Hotelware Co., England, dated, NRRBS.
(a) – Ice cream shell – 5" dia. with tab handle $50.00
Creamer – 5" tall $45.00
(b) – Dinner plate – 9", same as above but with CANADIAN NATIONAL RAILWAYS outlined leaf logo...........$55.00
Salad plate – 6½" $35.00
Vegetable dish – 5¼" $25.00
Cup and saucer – coffee $85.00

"Maritime" – white, sky blue narrow band border with pinstripes and CANADIAN NATIONAL brown outlined Maple Leaf logo at top center. BS – Sovereign Potters h'mk. Sometimes RRBS.
Cup and saucer – coffee, NRRBS...................................$75.00

"Nova Scotian" – white, border is raised gold leaf design with blue band and multi-color "CANADIAN NATIONAL," "NOVA SCOTIAN" crest logo at top center, BS – Wm. Guerin & Co. Limoges France h'mk. NRRBS.
Dinner plate – 8¾" $95.00
Salad plate – 7½" $85.00
Vegetable dish – 5" $45.00
Cup and saucer – coffee $135.00

"Queen Elizabeth" – ivory, brown pinstripe border with CANADIAN NATIONAL SYSTEM brown/yellow maple leaf logo on blue field at top center. BS – Royal Doulton, England h'mk. NRRBS.
Soup dish – 9½"...$50.00
Cup and saucer – demi...$145.00

"Quetico" – eggshell, brown pinstripe border, CANADIAN NATIONAL full color maple leaf logo at top center, BS – Royal Doulton English h'mk. NRRBS.
Dinner plate – 9¾" $55.00

GN's Children's China

"Truro" – (two types) – white, pinstripes and blue band border, brown canted CANADIAN NATIONAL SYSTEM logo at top center.
(a) – Dinner plate, 9", BS – Furnivals (1913) Ltd., Hotelware, Made in England, NRRBS $40.00
(b) – Dinner plate – 9", TM – CANADIAN NATIONAL RAILWAY logo, BS – Barth, Canadian Limited, Vitrified ware, Made in England expressly for Canadian National Railway...$60.00

"Windsor" – white, wide yellow border with brown pinstripes and CANADIAN NATIONAL brown maple leaf logo on the yellow . BS – Made by Medalta, Canada, Vitrified ware, dated. Sometimes RRBS.
Oval plate – 7 x 9¾", NRRBS $35.00

Canadian Pacific

Wide variety of patterns. Those listed are most readily found.

"Bows & Leaves" – white, brown pinstripe and green leaf border design with sprays of bows/leaves in blue, green and brown. RRBS.
Plate – 7", BS, North Staff's, Cobridge Pottery, England, Canadian Pacific Hotels, 1946 ....$50.00

"Blue Maple Leaf" – cream, with wide band maple leaf border

B&O Demi & Coffee

predominately in deep blue/tan and brown pinstripes, CANADIAN PACIFIC is worked in at top center, NRRBS.
Plate – 8", BS, Ridgways, Shelton England, h'mk $55.00

"Brown Maple Leaf" – white, same design as above except browns dominate and lighter blue. NRRBS.
Plate – 9", BS, Minton's England h'mk $75.00

"Crest" – white, green crest design logo at top center reads "Canadian Pacific Dining Car Service," NRRBS.
Plate – 9¾", BS, Soverien Potters, Canada, Hotel China h'mk $85.00

"Green Band" – white, border is a dark green band with pin-stripes and CPR in fancy script at top center, NRRBS.
Plate – 9", BS, made by Medalta, Canada, dated $75.00

Chesapeake & Ohio

"Chessie" – white, with sleepy Chessie kitten insignia, about ½ dozen variations; pieces have different color pinstripes and borders with kitten at center. NRRBS.
Ash tray – 4" dia. with four rests, white, outer blue band, inner yellow pinstripe, black sleepy "Chessie" kitten logo at center, SYR...$85.00

"George Washington" – off-white, gold leaf band and pin-stripe border with oval portrait of George Washington at top center. Not always RRBS.
Oval plate – 6½ x 9", Old Ivory Syracuse China h'mk. RRBS – Made expressly for Chesapeake & Ohio R.R. ..$175.00
Service plate – 10", wide gold leaf intricate design border with oval portrait of George Washington at center, Ye Olde Ivory Buffalo China h'mk. RRBS $700.00

"Silhouette" – white, bust of Washington or Colonial figures and pinstripes in black, sometimes RRBS
Ash tray – rectangular, 3½ x 7½", lettering in front reads "George Washington's Railroad, Chesapeake and Ohio Lines," etc., NRRBS, BUFF $95.00
Plate – square, white, Colonial man and lady standing, pin-

stripe border, RRBS The George Washington, Chesapeake & Ohio Lines, SYR $200.00

"Train Ferry" – white, outer blue band, inner yellow pin-stripe, CHESAPEAKE AND OHIO RAILWAY Train Ferry Service boat insignia at top center, NRRBS.
Dinner plate – 9½", divided, SYR $85.00
Cup and saucer – coffee, cup has boat insignia, saucer does not, SYR $95.00

Chicago Burlington & Quincy

"Aristocrat" – white, black/red/gold pinstripe border with BURLINGTON ROUTE logo at top center, NRRBS.
Bowl – oatmeal, 6¾" dia., 2½" deep, SYR...................$200.00
Dinner plate – 9", SYR $350.00
Double egg cup – 3", SYR $175.00
Platter – oval, 6½ x 9½", SYR.....................................$225.00

"Chuck Wagon" – shaded white to light brown with TM branding iron lgo "C-DZ The Chuck Wagon." Most pieces are squarish. Made by Syracuse. RRBS – Made expressly for the VISTA DOME DENVER ZEPHYR.
Cup and saucer – coffee $250.00
Bouillon cup – 3¼" $135.00

"Violets & Daisies" – white with colorful floral sprays. Made by various China Co's. Earlier pieces are RRBS.
Butter pat – 3⅜", RRBS – Made for C.B.& Q.R.R., BUFF....$135.00
Butter pat – 3⅜", NRRBS, SYR $35.00
Cup and saucer – coffee, NRRBS, SYR.........................$85.00
Cup and saucer – demi, NRRBS, SYR...........................$125.00
Dinner plate – 9" NRRBS, SYR $100.00
Salad plate – 5½", RRBS – Made for C.B.& Q.R.R., BUFF $145.00

Chicago Milwaukee St. Paul & Pacific

"Galatea" – Ivory, classic Greek and Roman design border, figures and scrolls in blue, green, ochre. Made by Syracuse China, not always RRBS.

Dinner plate – 9" – BS Old Ivory Syracuse China, GALATEA design copyrighted, made for C.M.& ST.P.& P.R.R $185.00

Tea plate – 7", BS – same as above, but NRRBS $50.00

"Hiawatha" – white, blue pinstripe border with Hiawatha streamliner going through Bow & Arrow motif at top center. BS-Syracuse China, Designed especially for the Hiawatha.

Plate – 7¼" $285.00

Vegetable dish – 4½" x 1¼" deep $175.00

"Olympian" – bone china, made only in cups and saucers. Cups have gold Greek Key border with RR initials on inside bottom; saucers have gold Greek key border with "The Olympia" in center. Made by several China Co's. NRRBS.

Cup and saucer – CM&StP., Limoges, France h'mk ..$125.00

Cup and saucer – CM&PSRy., Limoges, France h'mk....$150.00

"Peacock" – white, scallop blue design border with elaborate multi-color peacock/floral motif at center. Made by Syracuse China. NRRBS.

Butter pat – 3" $60.00

Hotcake cover – 5¾" dia., 2½" high, with finger hole $75.00

Double egg cup $60.00

Oval platter – 7¾ x 9¾"...$50.00

Plate – 8¼" $125.00

Sauce dish – 4½" dia. $40.00

Vegetable bowl – 6" dia. $45.00

"Traveler" – white, has shaded pink border/tree design and one or more flying geese with touches of black. BS – Syracuse China Econo-Rim trademark patented, the TRAVELER, designed especially for the Milwaukee Road dining car service. Not always RRBS.

Butter pat – 3", NRRBS...$25.00

Cereal bowl – 6¼", RRBS $65.00

Cup and saucer – coffee, saucer RRBS, cup NRRBS..$175.00

Cup and saucer – demi, same as above $150.00

Dinner plate – 9½", NRRBS $175.00

Hotcake cover – 6" dia., 2½"H, finger hole, NRRBS $65.00

Oval plate – 6½" x 8", RRBS $45.00

Soup dish – 7½", RRBS $40.00

Chicago & Northwestern

"Flambeau" – white, border has five pinstripes – two yellow, three red. Some pieces have only three red pinstripes. Nothing in center except service plates have the 400 streamliner pictured in center. The service plate is RRBS, other pieces are not. Made by Shenango China.

Celery tray – 3¾ x 7½" $20.00

Plate – 7" $15.00

Service plate 10½", TM with illus. of the 400 streamliner. BS –history of the famous "400"...............................$950.00

"Patriot" – white, with four groups of red/blue lines on inside of red pinstripe border. RRBS – Made especially for CHICAGO & NORTHWESTERN RY Furnished by Arthur Schiller & Son, Chicago, New York. SGO.

Bowl – 5¾"...$85.00

Dinner plate – 9"..$165.00

"Wild Rose" – white, green band border, a large pink rose with green leaves centered on all pieces. Made by Syracuse China. NRRBS.

Dinner plate – 9¼" $65.00

Oval plate – 7¾ x 9¾" $45.00

Sauce dish – 4½" $30.00

Chicago Rock Island & Pacific

"El Reno" – white, green band border with RI monogram at top center. Shenango China, NRRBS. Also found with pinstripes, no band.

Divided dinner plate – 11¼".....................................$375.00

"Golden Rocket" – ivory, red band border with GOLDEN ROCKET logo at top center. Made by Shenango China. NRRBS.

Plate – 7½" $125.00

"Golden State" – white, green pinstripe with green/white floral border and cluster of oranges with words GOLDEN STATE at top center. Made by various china companies. sometimes RRBS – Made especially for Rock Island Lines.

Creamer – handled, 2¾"H, NRRBS, SGO $275.00

Plate – 7¾", RRBS, BUFF $185.00

Cereal bowl – 6½", RRBS, BUFF $150.00

"LaSalle" – white, sage green intricate border design with red RI worked in at top center, also red outer pinstripe. Some pieces were made without pinstripe and the RI is in sage green. Made by several China Co's. Some pcs RRBS.

Sauce dish – 5¼", red pinstripe border, NRRBS, Albert Pick Co. Chicago, Vitrified China $135.00

Cup and saucer – coffee, same as above, both pcs. NRRBS...$300.00

Dinner plate – 9¾", same as above, NRRBS $200.00

Oval plate – 5¾ x 8¼", has green RI in design, no red pinstripe border, NRRBS, BUFF $250.00

Teapot with lid – 4½" tall, same as above, BUFF $500.00

Delaware & Hudson

"Adirondak" – white, blue wavy edge border with blue the "D&H" logo at top and N.Y. state seal in color at bottom. Center has canal boat and diesel freight scene. Smaller pieces are without scene in center. Made by Syracuse China. NRRBS.

Dinner plate – 9½" $85.00

Platter – 7¾ x 9¾" $55.00

Service plate – 10½" $125.00

Small dish – 5½" $30.00

Delaware Lackawanna & Western

"St. Albans" – white, border – green stripe outer, two inner with green/blue/orange floral sprays spaced around and a larger spray in center. Made by O.P.Co. Syracuse China.

RRBS – St. Albans copyrighted 1915, Syracuse China made expressly for D.L.& W.R.R.Co.
Oval platter – 8 x 11¾" $275.00

Denver & Rio Grande Western

"Prospector" – ivory, blue pinstripe border and RIO GRANDE at top center, made by Syracuse China, NRRBS.
Celery dish – 4½ x 9¾" $65.00
Dinner plate – 9" $125.00
Gravy boat – 6" $150.00
Oval dish – 5¾" x 7" $45.00

Erie

"Gould" – white, border is a line of green leaves and lavendar flowers with ERIE in script centered directly below. Made by several China companies. Sometimes RRBS.
Platter – rectangular, 5¾ x 8½", gold leaf bows at each end, NRRBS, SGO $75.00

"Starucca" – white, cobalt blue outer and inner pinstripes with ERIE on blue diamond logo at top center. Made by various China companies. NRRBS.
Dinner plate – 9¾" (ERIE blue logo) IRQ $165.00
Bowl – 6¼", same as above $50.00
Dinner plate – 9¾" (ERIE outlined logo) Walker China $195.00
Oval sauce dish – 5¼ x 3¾", same as above.................$75.00

"Susquehanna" – white, border – blue and yellow floral design with Erie diamond logo in open space at top center. Made by several China companies. Sometimes RRBS.
Oval celery dish – 4¾ x 10", RRBS – Made especially for Erie Railroad, design patented, Buffalo China, 1928 ..$125.00

Great Northern

"Glacier" – white with black/orange stripe border and an inner black pinstripe. The service plate has a multi-color floral design center. Other pieces only pinstripes. Made by O.P.Co. Syracuse China. RRBS – Great Northern Railway. Some smaller pieces NRRBS.
Large plate – 11" dia., RRBS $125.00
Footed egg cup – 2¼", NRRBS.....................$100.00
Sauce dish – 5¼", RRBS $65.00
Service plate – 10", floral design center, RRBS.........$350.00

"Glory of the West" – white with overall shaded grey mountains and green pine trees scene. The dinner plate and ashtray have a silhouette grey mountain goat in foreground of scene. Made by Syracuse China and RRBS – GREAT NORTHERN RAILROAD. Some pieces are without RRBS.
Ashtray – 4", grey mountain goat in center...............$125.00
Bowl – 6½", wide rim.....................................$60.00

Celery tray – 4½ x 9¾" $75.00
Cup and saucer – coffee $165.00
Cup and saucer – demi $350.00
Dinner plate – 9½", mountain goat in foreground....$200.00
Oval platter – 7 x 8¾" $60.00
Salad plate – 6½" $45.00
Sauce dish – 5", NRRBS..................................$30.00
Teaplate – 7¼" $75.00

"Hill" – (two types)
(a) – all-white with a yellow GNR entwined monogram outlined in red at top center. Early issue.
(b) – all-white with a tan GN monogram outlined in red. Later issue.
Both are old china made by several companies both here and abroad. NRRBS.
(a) – Oval baker – 4¾ x 6¼ x 1¼" deep. BS – Greenwood China, Trenton, N.J. impressed $155.00
(a) – Celery tray – 4¾ x 10", BS – Burley & Co., Made in Germany $185.00
(b) – Oval platter – 8½ x 12½", BS – Shenango China, Newcastle, Pa. $175.00

"Mountains and Flowers" – white, shaded grey mountains/trees/lake scene with different color flowers in foreground. There are variations in the flowers turned out by several China companies. Not always RRBS. Pieces listed are RRBS unless noted.
Ashtray – round, 4" $75.00
Celery tray – 4¾ x 10" $85.00
Cup and saucer – demi, both pieces NRRBS.............$150.00
Cup and saucer – coffee $165.00
Dinner plate – 9½" $175.00
Oval plate – 5½ x 7" $55.00
Oval platter – 7 x 9" $65.00
Salad bowl – 9¼" dia., 3½" deep $375.00
Salad plate – 6½" $55.00
Service plate – (list of the wild flowers and legend on backside) $385.00
Soup dish – 7¼" $110.00
Vegetable dish – 5" dia., 1½" deep $35.00

"Oriental" – tan, with flower pots spaced around near top edge, appear hand painted, BS – Syracuse China – Econo-Rim trademark. Not always RRBS. Pieces listed are RRBS unless noted.
Bouillon cup – NRRBS $40.00
Cup and saucer – coffee $200.00
Cup and saucer – demi, NRRBS $300.00
Footed egg cup – 2½" $135.00
Oval plate – 7 x 9" $125.00
Salad bowl – 10" dia., 2¾" deep $245.00
Tea plate, 7¼" $130.00
Vegetable dish – 5½ x 1½"............................$60.00

"Rocky" – white, blue pinstripe border and logo with animal characters in colorful dress attire spaced around. Three pieces known to exist – mug, bowl and plate. Children's china. Syracuse. Some pieces are RRBS.

Mimbreno Chocolate Pot, B&A Creamer

Mug – 3" tall $600.00
Oatmeal bowl – 5" dia., 1¾" deep................................$550.00
Plate – 8"..$750.00

Gulf Mobile & Ohio

"Rose" – white with shaded pink border and pink GM&O logo at top center. Syracuse China. NRRBS.
Bouillon cup – 3¾"H $65.00
Platter – 9¼ x 12½" $175.00
Sauce dish – 4½" $45.00

Illinois Central

"Coral" – coral pink overall with white border and floral motif in center. Syracuse China, NRRBS.
Cup and saucer – coffee $50.00
Cup and saucer – demi $200.00
Oval platter – 5¾ x 7" $30.00
Salad plate – 5½" $25.00

"French Quarter" – white with wide multi-color floral design border and a New Orleans street scene in center. Series of ten plates, each with a different scene. Made by Bauscher China, furnished by Arthur Schiller & Son. RRBS and dated. Made in service plates only.
Plate – 10¾, Fan Window in Claibourne Court..........$750.00

"Louisane" – white, black/orange/black pinstripe border with black ornate ICRR logo at top center. Old china made by various companies. NRRBS.
Creamer – handled, 3"H, SGO $125.00
Oval dish – 6 x 8½", SGO $85.00

"Panama Limited" – white, wide multi-color floral design border and steam passenger train in center. BS – O.P.Co. Syracuse China with the Illinois Central RR logo. Made in service plate only.

Plate – 10" $450.00

"Pirate" – white, multi-color pirate scene repeated in the wide, nothing in center. Syracuse China. Made in service plate only. NRRBS.
Plate – 10" $175.00

Maine Central

"Kennebec" – white with a black and orange pinstripe border and black MAINE CENTRAL RAILROAD logo at top center. O.P.Co. Syracuse China, NRRBS.
Oval dish – 5¾ x 8¼" $85.00

MINNEAPOLIS ST. PAUL & SAULT STE. MARIE (SOO LINE)

"Citation" – white with red pinstripe border and SOO LINE Banner logo at top center. Early Soo Line RR China. Known pieces found BS – John Maddock & Sons, England, Lion hm'k. NRRBS.
Butter pat – 3¼", very rare $850.00
Oval plate – 5½ x 7¾", rare $500.00

"Logan" – white with brown/yellow sawtooth band border and floral sprays in brown/yellow/blue spaced around. Mayer China, Beaver Falls, Pa. RRBS – Soo Line logo. Some pieces found not RR marked. All listed here are RRBS.
Celery tray – 4¾ x 9¾"..................................$125.00
Cup and saucer – coffee $195.00
Dinner plate – 9¾"..$175.00
Double egg cup – 3" $135.00
Double handled bouillon cup..........................$100.00
Gravy boat $125.00
Oval dish – 5¾ x 8¼"......................................$65.00
Oval vegetable dish – 4½ x 6" $45.00
Plate – 9"..$100.00
Platter – 8 x 11" $95.00
Salad plate – 6¼"..$55.00

Missouri Pacific

"Eagle" – Ivory with lime green band and black pinstripe border with a black flying eagle motif at top center. Mfr. is Syracuse China Co. RRBS – Missouri Pacific Lines. Some pieces found not RR marked.

Cup and saucer – coffee, saucer RRBS, cup NRRBS..$125.00
Cup and saucer – demi, saucer RRBS, cup NRRBS ..$225.00
Dinner plate – 9", RRBS $100.00
Plate – 6½", RRBS $40.00
Platter – 7¼" x 10½", RRBS $60.00

"State Flowers" – (steam plate) white with 11 multi-color panes of state flowers in the border and a passenger train pictured in the center. MISSOURI PACIFIC LINES below. O.P.Co. Syracuse China. NRRBS. Made in service plate only.

Plate – 10½" $250.00

"State Capitols" – (diesel plate) white with 11 multi-color vignettes of state capitols in the border and a passenger train "Route of the Eagles" in center. BS – Syracuse China designed expressly for Missouri Pacific Lines (red buzzsaw logo and blue ribbon.) Service plate only.

Plate – 10½" $350.00

New York Central

"DeWitt Clinton" – white with a floral design border in pale blue and gray with the DeWitt Clinton locomotive 1831 in black worked in the design at top center. Made by Syracuse and Buffalo China. BS – "Design patented, made especially for New York Central Lines." Some pieces found without RRBS.

Bouillon cup – 4", without RRBS...................................$30.00
Cereal bowl – 6¼ x 2" deep, without RRBS $40.00
Celery tray – 4½ x 9¼" $60.00
Dinner plate – 9"..$55.00
Oval platter – 6½ x 9" $45.00
Plate – 7¾"...$35.00
Rectangular platter – 7¼ x 11¼" $65.00
Soup dish – 9", without RRBS $45.00

"Mercury" – ivory with 12 vertical lines and NYC across in brown. Companion pieces have no lines, just NYC. Made by several China companies. RRBS – "Design copyrighted, made especially for New York Central Lines." Some pieces found without RRBS.

Bouillon cup – 3¼"D, 2¼"H, SYR, without RRBS..........$30.00
Celery tray – 4¾" x 10" SYR $45.00
Cup and saucer – coffee, 2¾" tall, SYR, saucer RRBS, cup without RRBS $75.00
Cup and saucer – coffee, 2½" tall, SGO, TM NYC only, both NRRBS $65.00
Dinner plate – 9", SYR $75.00
Double egg cup – 3"H, SYR, NRRBS............................$25.00
Oval dish – 7 x 9", SYR $35.00
Rectangular tray – 6 x 11", BUFF.................................$40.00
Sauce dish – 5¼", NYC Only, SYR $20.00

New York New Haven & Hartford

"Indian Tree" – white with brown geometric border design and pink/green floral sprays around an Indian tree in center. Made by several China companies. RRBS – "Made expressly for the New York New Haven & Hartford Railroad."

Dinner plate – 9"..$100.00
Gravy boat – 6" long...$125.00
Plate – 6¾"...$45.00
Platter – 6½ x 9½"...$55.00
Sauce dish – 5½"...$35.00

"Platinum Blue" – blue grey overall with white pinstripes and a nude kneeling figure cameo spaced around. Made by Buffalo and Lamberton Scammell's China, RRBS – "Made expressly for N-Y-N-H & H-R-R Co." Furnished by Thompson Winchester Co., Boston."

Cereal bowl – 6"...$55.00
Butter pat – 3½"..$125.00

Miscellaneous Vegetable Dishes

Gravy boat – 6" long..$145.00
Plate – 8¼"..$65.00
Platter – 5½ x 8¼" $75.00

Norfolk & Western

"Cavalier" – ivory with tan Roman Key/green leaves border and fancy N W R'y letters at top center. Pieces carry the Lamberton Scammell China crown/wreath h'mk. NRRBS.

Butter pat – 4" $95.00
Cup and saucer – coffee $200.00
Oval platter – 9½ x 13½"..$115.00
Oval platter – 8 x 11½" $75.00
Oval sauce dish – 4¼ x 5½" $45.00
Soup plate – 9" $80.00

Northern Pacific

"Garnet" – white with an outer and inner border of magenta and green leaves, nothing in center. An older china made by several companies. RRBS – Made expressly for No. Pacific RR or Northern Pacific Railway Co. Some pieces found without RR marking.

Cereal bowl – 6¼", SYR, NRRBS $60.00
Celery tray – 4½ x 10", wavy edges, Haviland, Limoges, France, RRBS..$325.00
Dinner plate – 9¾", BUFF, NRRBS $95.00
Oval vegetable dish – 4¼ x 5¾", MYR, RRBS...............$85.00
Salad plate – 7¾", MYR, RRBS $200.00
Soup plate – 8¾", MYR, RRBS.....................................$225.00

"Monad" – ivory, border has light/dark green band with orange pinstripes, and Northern Pacific Railway black/red logo at top center. Made by Shenango, NRRBS.

Dessert plate – 5½"...$50.00
Dinner plate – 9" $200.00
Gravy boat – 6" long...$125.00
Oval platter – 8 x 9½" $75.00
Oval vegetable dish – 4 x 5½" $55.00
Sauce dish – 4¾"..$45.00
Soup dish with wide rim – 7¼" $85.00
Tea plate – 7¼"...$75.00

"Stampede" – white with ornate intwined yellow/brown NP letters at top center. Some pieces have pinstripes. Made by O.P.Co., Syracuse China. NRRBS.

Dinner plate – 9¾"...$300.00
Ice cream shell with tab handle – 5¼" $150.00
Oval platter – 5¾ x 8¼" $200.00
Salad plate – 6¾" $125.00

"Yellowstone" – This is the same pattern as Monad except YELLOWSTONE PARK LINE has been added to the bottom edge of the logo. An older china than Monad, made by Shenango. NRRBS.

Dessert plate – 5½"...$75.00
Dinner plate – 9" $250.00
Dble. handled bouillon cup and saucer.......................$175.00
Oval plate – 5¾ x 7¼" $85.00
Oval platter – 9 x 11¾" $195.00
Shallow soup bowl – 1¼" deep, 7¼" across $90.00
Tea plate – 7¼"...$85.00

Pennsylvania Railroad

"Keystone" – white with border of dark red pinstripes and PRR Keystone logo at top center. An old china with variations in pinstripes, Keystone logo and color. Made by several China companies. Sometimes RRBS.

Butter pat – 3½"..$75.00
Cup and saucer – coffee, LAMB $175.00
Dinner plate – 9", SCM $85.00
Oval platter – 9¼ x 13¼", WAR..................................$100.00
Oval vegetable dish – 4½ x 6", WAR...........................$65.00
Sauce dish – 5¾", LAMB $40.00

Soup plate – 8¾", SCM $65.00

"Mountain Laurel" – ivory with mint green band border and a spray of pink flowers with green leaves in center. Made by Shenango and Syracuse China. Dinner plates are RRBS but smaller pieces are not. Mountain Laurel is the state flower of Pennsylvania.

Cup and saucer – coffee, SYR, NRRBS.........................$75.00
Bouillon cup – 3¾", SYR, NRRBS $25.00
Dinner plate – 9½", SGO, full RRBS $85.00
Small plate – 7¼", SYR, NRRBS $35.00

"Purple Laurel" – white, border has a blue leaf band design with four repeated cross motifs, nothing in center. Made by several China companies. Most pieces are RRBS with PRR logo and China companies name.

Bouillon bowl – 4" dia., 2" deep, STR, RRBS...............$35.00
Butter pat – 3¼", SCM, RRBS $85.00
Butter pat – 3½", SGO, NRRBS...................................$25.00
Cereal bowl – 6½", BUFF, RRBS $40.00
Dinner plate – 9¾", STR, RRBS $65.00
Gravy boat – 6" long, SCM, RRBS...............................$75.00
Platter – 7¾ x 11", SYR, RRBS....................................$50.00
Salad plate – 6¼", WAR, NRRBS $30.00
Sauce dish – 5½", BUFF, RRBS $30.00

Pullman Company

"Calumet" – white with a black/yellow pinstripe and PULLMAN in black letters at top center. Made by several China companies. NRRBS.

Dinner plate – 9", SYR $200.00
Footed egg cup – 2¾" tall, Burley & Co. $75.00
Oval Baker – 4¼ x 5¾" x 1¼", Burley & Co. $45.00
Oval sauce dish – 4½ x 5¼", BSHR.............................$35.00

"Indian Tree" – white with brown geometric band border and orange/green floral sprays spaced around a multi-colored floral Indian Tree in center. Some pieces come without the tree in center. The word PULLMAN is found at top center. Made by several China companies. NRRBS.

Butter pat – floral center...$85.00
Cup and saucer – coffee, saucer without tree, SYR $200.00
Dinner plate – 9", no tree center, SYR $125.00
Divided plate – 12¼", four sections, tree center, SYR..$350.00
Footed egg cup – 3½" high, SYR..................................$50.00
Individual creamer – with handle................................$95.00
Individual creamer – without handle $75.00
Platter – 5¾ x 8½" – tree center, SCM $95.00
Sauce dish – 5¼", no tree center, SYR $65.00

Southern Ry

"Peach Blossom" – white, brown pinstripe border with blue inner strip which has the SR brown logo at top center and a basket/hanging fruit design connected at three places around the blue stripe. Made by several China companies. Some pieces found without the logo. Not always RRBS.

Bowl – 5½", top logo, BUFF, NRRBS $45.00
Bowl – 5¾", no top logo, LAMB, RRBS $35.00
Butter pat – 3¼"D, top logo, BUFF, NRRBS $175.00

Dinner plate – 9", no top logo, BUFF, RRBS............$175.00
Gravy boat – 6" long, side logo, BUFF, NRRBS.........$175.00
Hot food cover – 6" dia., side logo, NRRBS $185.00
Oval sauce dish – 4¾ x 6¼", top logo, LAMB, NRRBS ..$35.00
Platter – 6½ x 9¾", no top logo, BUFF, RRBS.............$65.00
Platter – 8 x 11½", top logo, BUFF, NRRBS $125.00

"Piedmont" – ivory, border has two bluish-green bands and an inner dull yellow pinstripe, nothing in center. Made by several China companies. Usually backstamped with the railroad's name.
Cereal bowl – 6", BUFF......................................$30.00
Cup and saucer – demi, saucer RRBS, cup is not, STR..$65.00
Dinner plate – 9", BUFF.....................................$45.00
Pickle tray – 3¼ x 7¼", octagonal shape, STR.............$25.00
Sauce dish – 4½", BUFF $20.00

Southern Pacific Company

"Prairie Mountain Wildflower" – white with a black pinstripe border and four colorful individual wildflowers spaced around center. Made by Shenango, Syracuse and Onondago Pottery Co. and usually backstamped with the railroad's name and flowers I.D., Azalea, California Poppy, Baby Blue Eyes and Ruby Lily. Smaller pieces have only three flowers. NRRBS pieces sell for less. All pieces listed here are RRBS.
Bouillon cup – 5¾" $30.00
Butter pat – 3" $65.00
Cereal bowl – 6"...$40.00
Cup and saucer – coffee $95.00
Cup and saucer – demi $275.00
Dinner plate – 9½" $150.00
Divided platter – 8 x 12", three compartments.........$165.00
Divided platter – 9 x 13¼", three compartments $195.00
Platter – 8½ x 12½" $125.00
Salad plate – 5½"...$30.00
Sauce dish – 5"...$25.00
Tea plate – 7¼" $75.00

"Sunset" – white, border consists of a green pinstripe and a green/white floral band. A green SOUTHERN PACIFIC LINES Sunset logo is at top center. Some pieces have several larger flowers mixed in the floral band. Made by various China companies. Not always RRBS.
Cup and saucer – coffee, SYR............................$200.00
Dinner plate – 9", SYR $175.00
Individual creamer – 3½" tall $85.00
Oval sauce dish – 5 x 6¼", SYR.........................$55.00
Platter – 8½ x 12¼", larger floral variation, SYR........$225.00
Platter – 8½ x 12¼", SYR................................$135.00
Tea plate – 7¼", larger floral variation, SYR $100.00

Union Pacific Railroad

"Challenger" – tan with "The Challenger" in yellow/brown script lettering across the top, nothing in center. Made by Shenango and Syracuse China. Pieces also RRBS sell for more.
Cereal bowl – 6¼", NRRBS, SYR $25.00
Cup and saucer – coffee, both RRBS, SYR $95.00

Dinner plate – 9½", RRBS, SYR $85.00
Double egg cup – 3" high, RRBS, SYR...................$40.00
Oval platter – 8 x 9¾", RRBS, SYR.....................$60.00
Oval platter – 8 x 9¾", NRRBS, SYR $30.00
Salad plate – 6¼", NRRBS, SYR $30.00
Salad plate – 6¼", RRBS, SYR.........................$50.00
Sauce dish – 5¼", NRRBS, SYR $20.00

"Desert Flower" – white shaded to pea-green with green/brown flowers and leaves in the white area. Most pieces have scalloped edges. Made by Syracuse. Not always RRBS.
Cup and saucer – coffe, both RRBS, SYR $100.00
Cup and saucer – demi, both RRBS, SYR $125.00
Cereal bowl – 6½", RRBS, SYR $35.00
Dinner plate – 9¾", NRRBS, SYR.......................$60.00
Double egg cup – 3¼" tall, RRBS, SYR $35.00
Footed egg cup – 2¼" tall, RRBS, SYR..................$45.00
Oval dish – 6¼ x 8", NRRBS, SYR $30.00
Oval platter – 9¼ x 11½", RRBS, SYR $75.00
Plate – 6½", NRRBS, SYR $25.00
Soup plate – 9", RRBS, SYR $35.00

"Harriman Blue" – white with blue scrollwork design border on scalloped edge. Nothing in center. This is an old china. Pieces found have "SCAMMELL'S TRENTON CHINA" impressed on the back with UNION PACIFIC OVERLAND blue shield logo.
Butter pat – 3" $45.00
Cereal bowl – 6"...$35.00
Cup and saucer – coffee $100.00
Cup and saucer – demi..................................$150.00
Celery tray – 5½ x 12".................................$65.00
Dinner plate – 9¼" $85.00
Oval baker – 5 x 6½" $40.00
Salad plate – 7¼" $50.00

"Historical" – white with a border of repeated series of western scenes depicted in blue curled frames with the UNION PACIFIC shield logo at top center and a buffalo at bottom center. Made by Shenango, Onondago and Syracuse China. Some pieces also RRBS.
Celery tray – 4¾ x 9¾", RRBS, SYR $225.00
Cup and saucer – coffee, both NRRBS, SYR.............$425.00
Dinner plate – 9½", RRBS, SYR $350.00
Platter – 5¾ x 8¼", RRBS, SYR.......................$200.00
Ice cream shell – 4 x 4¾", RRBS, SGO $185.00
Pickle tray – 3½ x 7¼", RRBS, SYR...................$195.00
Salad plate – 6¼", NRRBS, SYR $175.00
Footed sherbet – 3¾" dia. 2½" tall, RRBS, SYR.........$185.00

"Winged Streamliner" – white with a gold leaf band border and motif of a brown winged diesel streamliner going through a green circle in the center. Made by several China companies. Seldom RRBS.
Bouillon cup – 3¾" dia., Homer Laughlin $45.00
Butter pat – 3½", Homer Laughlin $30.00
Cereal bowl – 6¼", STR $35.00
Covered sugar bowl – STR $200.00
Cup and saucer – coffee, STR $50.00

Dinner plate – 10½", STR...$60.00
Footed sherbet – 3¾" dia., 2½" tall, SCM $35.00
Ice cream shell – 4", STR..$75.00
Oval platter – 6¼ x 8¼", Trenton.............................$35.00
Oval platter – 7½ x 9½", SCM $45.00
Salad plate – 6¼", SYR $40.00
Teapot – 7½" long, 4½" tall, STR $250.00

IC's Panama Limited Service Plate

Wabash Railroad

"Banner" – white with grey band border with inner red pinstripe and WABASH flag logo at top center. Slogan reads
"Follow the Flag." Made by Syracuse China. NRRBS.

Bouillon cup – 3¾" tall $75.00
Cereal bowl – 5¾" $85.00
Cup and saucer – coffee $225.00
Cup and saucer – demi $475.00
Dinner plate – 9½" $235.00
Double egg cup – 3" tall $85.00
Oval platter – 5½ x 7¼"..$115.00
Pickle tray – 3½ x 7½"..$120.00
Sauce dish – 5¼"...$65.00
Small plate – 5½"...$100.00
Soup plate – 7¼"...$95.00

Western Pacific R.R.

"Feather River" – tan with red feathers spaced border and a
single red feather off center with these words in black,
"WESTERN PACIFIC FEATHER RIVER ROUTE." Made
by Shenango China. NRRBS.

Bouillon cup – 3¾" dia., 2¼" tall $30.00
Cereal bowl – 6¼" $55.00
Cup and saucer – coffee $200.00
Cup and saucer – demi...$300.00
Dinner plate – 9½"...$195.00
Hot cake cover – 6¼" dia. $145.00
Oval platter – 6 " x 9" $50.00
Salad plate – 5½"...$55.00

Silver Holloware

See Everett Maffett's book, *Silver Banquet,* for year marks.

Key to Abbreviations

BM – Bottom marked
SM – Side marked
TM – Top marked
NRRBM – Not RR bottom marked

Silver Manufacturers

GOR – Gorham
IS – International
MER – Meriden
R&B – Reed & Barton
ROG – Rogers
WAL – Wallace

Atchison Topeka & Santa Fe

All bottom marked pieces are stamped with standard RR initials, unless otherwise noted.

Bread tray – oval, 6¼ x 13¼", BM – Santa Fe Route, R&B
#1610 ....$130.00
Coffee pot – 14 oz., diamond shaped, hinged lid, attached
handle, R&B #3400B...$85.00
Creamer – open, 8 oz., diamond shaped, attached handle,
R&B #3400B $75.00

Serving tray – 6½ x 8½", deep dish style, IS #05002 ....$65.00
Sugar bowl – covered, handles, 12 oz., diamond shaped, R&B
#3400B $75.00
Syrup pitcher – with attached tray, 8 oz., diamond shaped,
R&B #3400B $85.00

Atlantic Coast Line

Coffee pot – 10 oz., BM – ACLRR, IS #05060C............$75.00
Sugar bowl – 14 oz., double handled, SM – logo, BM – Atlantic
Coast Line RR, also A.C.L. 7, ROG $125.00

UP Supreme Set – Unassembled, Assembled

Baltimore & Ohio

Coffee pot – 10 oz., gooseneck spout, BM – B&O, R&B 1400C $125.00
Coffee pot – 10 oz., regular spout, BM – B&O, IS 05097 ....$100.00
Creamer – 8 oz., hinged lid, BM – B&O, R&B 0143H $75.00
Sugar bowl – covered, with handles, 12 oz., BM – B&O, R&B 0143H $85.00

Boston & Maine Railroad

Change tray – 6" square, TM – Boston & Maine RR arrow logo, IS SX0758 ....$75.00
Sugar bowl – 6 oz., covered, handles, SM – Boston & Maine RR arrow logo, IS 03800 ....$95.00

Chicago Burlington & Quincy R.R.

Coffee pot – 14 oz., plain style, reg. spout, SM – BR incised, BM – C.B.& Q.R.R.Co., R&B 3700B3 ....$65.00
Finger bowl – 4¾" dia., footed, SM – BR incised, BM – C.B.& Q.R.R.Co., R&B 3700B3.................................$45.00
Sugar bowl – 6 oz., ornate style, covered, handles, SM – BR raised (B is reversed) NRRBM, R&B 092-H $75.00
Teapot – 18 oz. ornate style, goose neck, SM – BR raised (B is reversed) NRRBM, R&B 0199-H $100.00

Chicago Milwaukee St. Paul & Pacific R.R.
Also *Chicago Milwaukee & St. Paul Ry.* (older name)

Bowl – 5¼" dia., BM – CM&STP, R&B 2580-S.............$50.00
Change tray – 6 x 6", ornate edge, BM – CM&STP, R&B 022-H $65.00
Coffee pot – 8 oz., stylized winged ball finial on lid, SM – The MILWAUKEE Road, IS 05060 ....$75.00

Menu holder – pierced design, holders for two pencils, SM – The MILWAUKEE Road, IS 05060......................$85.00
Syrup pitcher – with attached tray, 8 oz., stylized winged ball finial on lid, SM – The MILWAUKEE Road, IS 05060 ....$75.00

Chicago & Northwestern Railway

Bowl – low footed, 4¼" dia., BM – C&NWRy, IS 05085..$45.00
Coffee pot – 14 oz., pine cone finial, BM – C&NW System, IS 05073, 1949...$85.00
Cream pitcher – 8 oz., w/h'gd. lid, handle, pine cone finial, BM – C&NW System, IS 05073, 1948 ....$65.00
Gravy boat – 4 oz., 6" long, BM – C&NWRy, IS 02850, 1940...$55.00
Sugar bowl – 10 oz., removable lid, pine cone finial, BM – C&NWRy, IS 05073, 1947....................................$75.00

Chicago Rock Island & Pacific Railroad

Coffee pot – 8 oz., goose neck spout, BM – ROCK ISLAND LINES, R. Wallace 0279-10, 1927 ....$150.00
Creamer – 6 oz., hinged lid, handle, BM – ROCK ISLAND LINES, R. Wallace 0279-10, 1924 ....$125.00
Hot cake cover – 5½" dia., pierced holes and acorn finial at top, BM – ROCK ISLAND LINES, GMCo. 08092, 1913...$85.00
Ice cream dish – 4 x 5", shell shaped with three ball feet, BM –ROCK ISLAND LINES, R. Wallace 0721, 1924 ....$50.00
Menu holder – plain style with two pencil holders, SM – winged Golden Rocket logo, BM – ROCK ISLAND LINES, IS 05094 ....$175.00
Salad bowl – 6¾" dia., BM – ROCK ISLAND LINES, GMCo. 02584, 1913...$65.00
Sugar bowl – 11 oz., covered, two handles, BM – ROCK ISLAND, R& B 050-H..............................$135.00

Syrup – with attached tray, 6 oz., BM – ROCK ISLAND LINES, IS SLO986, 1933..............................$95.00

Tray – oval, 7¼ x 9¾" BM – ROCK ISLAND LINES, GMCo. 02251 ....$55.00

Delaware Lackawanna & Western R.R.

Change tray – 6½" square, BM – LACKAWANNA, IS 05082 ....$50.00

Coffee pot – 54 oz., regular spout, ball finial, BM – LACKA-WANNA, IS 05082, 1947............................$125.00

Creamer – 8 oz., with hinged lid and handle, BM – DL&W, IS 05082 ....$75.00

Sugar bowl – 8 oz., with lid and handles, BM – LACKAWAN-NA, IS 05082 ....$85.00

Erie Railroad

Coffee pot – 6½ oz., ornate style, SM – ERIE diamond logo, MER SX0296 ....$150.00

Finger bowl – sloping sides, 4½" dia., BM – ERIE, IS 00296, 1945 ....$75.00

Florida East Coast Railway

Coffee pot – 14 oz., reg. spout, ball finial on lid, SM – FEC incised, BM – FEC Ry., IS 05060C, 1941 ....$135.00

Sugar bowl – 8 oz., with lid, two handles, SM – FEC incised, BM – FEC RY., IS 05060C, 1941 ....$75.00

Great Northern Railway

Bouillon cup frame – 4" dia., open sides, tab handles, SM – GN, BM – GREAT NORTHERN RY. IS 05082, 1964 ......$35.00

Bowl – 7½" dia., beaded edge, SM – ornate intertwined GNR monogram, BM – Rogers Bros. 1847, SX0645, ca. 1900 ....$135.00

Bread tray – oval, deep dish style, 6 x 9¾", TM – GN, BM – GREAT NORTHERN RY., IS 05082, 1951 ....$50.00

Bud vase – candlestick style, 7¼" tall, round base, SM – GN, BM – GREAT NORTHERN RY., IS 05082, 1951 ....$150.00

Butter pat – round, 3½" dia., TM – GN, BM – GREAT NORTHERN RY., IS 041, 1966..........................$30.00

Butter pat – square, 3", BM – GREAT NORTHERN RY., IS GNS20, 1938 ....$40.00

Cake cover – 6" dia., hole at top, SM – GN, BM – GREAT NORTHERN RY., IS 5082, 1951.........................$65.00

Cake stand – footed, oval tray 9 x 12", beaded edge, pierced border, BM – GREAT NORTHERN RY., MER 5006, ca. 1910 ....$300.00

Change tray – 6" square, checkered border, TM – ornate intertwined GN on tab handles, BM – GREAT NORTH-ERN RY., IS – G.N.S.15, 1924 ....$125.00

Coffee pot – 14 oz., hg'd. lid, ball finial, SM – GN, BM – GREAT NORTHERN RY., IS 5082, 1946.................$75.00

Coffee pot – 54 oz., hg'd. lid, ball finial, SM – GN, BM – GREAT NORTHERN RY., IS 05082, 1951 ....$175.00

Coffee pot – ½ pt., beaded edges, regular spout, BM – GREAT NORTHERN RY., Rogers Bros. 02600, ca. 1910 ....$200.00

Coffee pot – ½ pt., beaded edges, gooseneck spout, SM – ornate intertwined GNR monogram, BM – GREAT NORTHERN RY., Meriden 1847 SX0251, ca. 1900 ....$225.00

Creamer – 4 oz., hinged lid, handle, SM – GN, BM – GREAT NORTHERN RY., IS 05082, 1946 ....$85.00

Finger bowl – 4½" dia., sides have narrow openings and stars, BM – GREAT NORTHERN RY., IS – G.N.S.42, 1923 ....$75.00

Finger bowl – 4½" dia., sides have rows of square dots and slits, BM – GREAT NORTHERN RY., ISCo. 00295, 1950 ....$50.00

Menu holder – pierced sides, with two pencil holders, BM – GREAT NORTHERN RY., IS 05060, 1946..............$95.00

Sauce boat – 5oz., 6½" long with handle, SM – GN, BM – GREAT NORTHERN RY., IS 05082, 1950..............$85.00

Sherbet – footed, 3½" tall, for ice cream, SM – GN, BM – GREAT NORTHERN RY., IS 05082, 1946..............$65.00

Sugar bowl – 8 oz., tab handles, removable lid, ball finial, SM – GN, BM – GREAT NORTHERN RY., IS 05082, 1947 ....$75.00

Syrup pitcher – with attached tray, hg'd. lid, ball finial, SM – GN, BM – GREAT NORTHERN RY., IS 05082, 1963 ....$125.00

Syrup pitcher – without attached tray, hg'd. lid over spout, beaded edges, BM – GREAT NORTHERN RY., M.B. Co. S 003...$95.00

Tray for syrup pitcher – oval, 4 x 7", BM – GREAT NORTH-ERN RY., M.B. Co. S 003 ca. 1910 ....$65.00

Tureen – 1 pt., removable lid, handles, beaded edge, SM – ornate intertwined GNR monogram, BM – GREAT NORTHERN RY., Rogers Bros., 1847, SX0248, ca. 1900 ....$135.00

Tray for tureen – 6¼" dia., beaded edge, BM – GREAT NORTH-ERN RY., Rogers Bros., 1847, Sx0248, ca. 1900 ....$85.00

Illinois Central Railroad

Bowl – shallow, 7" dia., Grecian Key mount on wide rim, TM – ornate ICRR monogram, BM – I.C.R.R., R&B 0192-H, ca. 1930 ....$45.00

Menu holder – pierced sides with two pencil holders, BM – ICRR, WAL 01753 ....$65.00

Mustard pot – 3" tall, hg'd. lid with spoon hole, takes glass insert, open bottom, SM – I.C.R.R. in script, GOR A-3-9, 1945 ....$75.00

Sugar bowl – 7 oz., covered, Grecian Key, SM – ornate ICRR monogram, BM – I.C.R.R. script, R&B 0192-H, 1921 ....$150.00

Syrup pitcher – with attached tray, 10 oz., hg'd. lid, SM – diamond/circle logo reading ILLINOIS CENTRAL RAIL-ROAD, MISSISSIPPI VALLEY ROUTE, BM – WAL 0301 ....$175.00

Tray – oval, 9 x 12", plain design, BM – I.C. System, IS 05077, 1941 ....$35.00

Louisville & Nashville R.R.

Butter pat – 3¼" dia., TM – raised L&N in rectangle, BM – IS L&N5 ....$65.00

Coffee pot – 10 oz., gooseneck spout, hg'd lid, blunt handle, SM – raised L&N in rectangle, BM – IS L&N7, 1921 ....$150.00

Finger bowl – with attached tray, 6", TM – raised L&N in rectangle, BM – IS L&N 12 ....$85.00

Mustard pot frame – hg'd. lid with spoon hole, handle, open sides, takes glass insert, BM – L&N, R&B 1716S $125.00

Missouri Pacific Railroad

Bowl – footed, flared rim, 6¼" dia., 2¼" high, BM – MISSOURI PACIFIC, IS 05009, 1926 ....$45.00

Corn on cob holders – matched pair, TM – MISSOURI PACIFIC LINES, Pflegar P1896 ....$50.00

Hot food cover – 6" dia., beaded edge, vent holes and finial at top, BM – Missouri Pacific Ry. in script, R&B 1083, ca. 1915 ....$85.00

Sauce boat – 2 oz., BM – MISSOURI PACIFIC, IS 05009, 1926 ....$50.00

Sugar bowl – 6 oz., covered, handled, ornate style, BM – MISSOURI PACIFIC, Wal 0353 ....$75.00

Minneapolis, St. Paul & Sault Saint Marie (Soo Line)

Bottle holder stand – three prongs/round base, 5" tall, TM – SOO LINE Banner logo, NRRBM, GOR 0155, ca. 1892 ....$200.00

Bread tray – 6 x 13¼", oval, high ended, plain, TM – SOO LINE Banner logo, NRRBM, GMCo.OPT. Ca. 1902........$125.00

Change tray – 6" square, bead & leaf mount, ¾" rim, BM – SOO LINE Dollar logo, GMCo.08025, ca. 1913 ....$85.00

Coffee pot – ⅝ pt., oval base, bead and leaf mount, gooseneck spout, ornate handle, SM – SOO LINE Banner logo, BM – SOO LINE Dollar logo, GMCo.08460, ca. 1911 ....$195.00

Coffee pot – ⅝ pt., oval base, bead and leaf mount, ornate handle, gooseneck spout, BM – SOO LINE Dollar logo, GMCo. 08460, ca. 1910.....................................$185.00

Creamer – ⅝ pt., oval base, bead and leaf mount, ornate hg'd. lid over spout, SM – SOO LINE Banner logo, BM – SOO LINE Dollar logo, GMCo.08679, ca. 1910 ....$175.00

Creamer – 9/16 pt., oval base, bead and leaf mount, ornate hg'd. lid over spout, SM – SOO LINE Banner logo, NRRBM, GMCo. 08679, ca. 1912........................$150.00

Creamer – 8 oz., irregular base, plain, notched hg'd. lid, flat top handle, BM – SOO LINE Dollar logo, R&B 0147-H, ca. 1921 ....$125.00

Finger bowl – 4½" dia., 2" deep, bead and leaf mount, BM – SOO LINE Dollar logo, Gorham Co. OCHL ca. 1912 ....$75.00

Sugar bowl – 10 oz., oval base, plain, lid, rounded handles, BM – SOO LINE Dollar logo, GOR 013502, ca. 1928 ....$125.00

Sugar bowl – 12 oz., irregular base, plain, lid, flat top handles, BM – SOO LINE Dollar logo, R&B 147-H, ca. 1921 ....$135.00

Sugar bowl – oval base, bead and leaf mount, lid, ornate handles, TM – SOO LINE Dollar logo, GMCo. 08792, ca. 1910 ....$175.00

Syrup – with attached oval tray, plain, hg'd. lid, rounded handle, BM – SOO LINE Dollar logo, R&B 1355 ....$150.00

Teapot – ⅞ pt., round base, plain, gooseneck spout, rounded handle, SM – SOO LINE Banner logo, NRRBM, GMCo., 07493, ca. 1907 ....$225.00

Tray – oval, 6 x 8", bead and leaf mount, TM – SOO LINE Banner logo, B/M SOO LINE Dollar logo, GMCo. 08445, ca. 1909 ....$165.00

Tray – round, 7", plain, 1¼" rim, TM – SOO LINE Banner logo, GMCo. 06192, ca. 1902 ....$175.00

Tureen – two pts., round base, plain, lid, small oval handles, SM – SOO LINE Banner logo, NRRBM, GMCo. 06191, ca. 1905 ....$225.00

Tureen – soup, 10 oz., round base, plain, lid, rounded handles, BM – SOO LINE Dollar logo, GOR 013502, ca. 1928.... $125.00

T& P Bowl With Attached Tray

New York Central R.R. Co.

Coffee pot – 8 oz., SM – NYC, BM – NEW YORK CENTRAL, IS 070, 1948 ....$75.00

Creamer – 8 oz., hg'd. lid, handle, TM – NYC on flat top finial, IS 05070, 1948 ....$55.00

Salad bowl – 6" dia., BM – NYC LINES, R&B 6218-S, 1930 ....$50.00

Sugar bowl – 8 oz., regular style lid and handles, BM – NYC LINES, R& B 1400C $75.00

Northern Pacific Railway

Explanations used in describing logos.
MONAD – logo without Yellowstone Park Line
YPL – Yellowstone Park Line added to logo

Bouillon frame – open sides, two tab hand grips, BM – NORTHERN PACIFIC RAILWAY CO. IS 05070A, 1953 ....$65.00

GN Syrup Pitcher and Tray

Bowl – salad, 4" dia., 2" high, BM – NORTHERN PACIFIC RAILWAY CO., IS SE0972, 1960............................$55.00

Bowl – ice, footed, round, 8" dia., 4½" high, SM – NORTHERN PACIFIC YPL logo, BM – NORTHERN PACIFIC RAILWAY CO., IS SF0158, 1930...........................$195.00

Coffee pot – 1 pt., oval base, gooseneck spout, pagoda style lid, ornate handle, 7" tall, SM – NORTHERN PACIFIC Monad logo, BM – N.P.R. script, R&B 441, ca. 1888 (rare) $250.00

Creamer – oval base, hg'd. lid, over spout, ornate handle, BM – N.P.R. script, GMCo. 08097, ca. 1907 ....$75.00

Creamer – 7 oz., oval base, pagoda lid notched, ornate handle, SM – NORTHERN PACIFIC Monad logo, BM – N.P.R. script, R&B 441 ....$150.00

Creamer – ⁹⁄₁₆ pt., oval base, reg. lid, ornate handle, BM – N.P.R. script, GMCo. 08094, ca. 1906 ....$85.00

Finger bowl – 3¾" dia., handled, SM – NORTHERN PACIFIC YPL logo, BM – NORTHERN PACIFIC RAILWAY CO., IS 0812, 1930 ....$75.00

Footed sherbet – 3½" dia., 3½" tall, BM – NORTHERN PACIFIC RAILWAY CO., IS SF0161, 1930..............$50.00

Sugar bowl – 12 oz., oval base, pagoda lid, ornate handles, SM – NORTHERN PACIFIC Monad logo, BM – N.P.R. script R&B 441 ....$150.00

Sugar bowl – oval base, acorn finial lid, ornate handles, BM – N.P.R. script, GMCo.08096, ca. 1907 ....$85.00

Sugar bowl – 12 oz., round base, round lid, flat top finial, handles, SM – NORTHERN PACIFIC YPL logo, BM – NORTHERN PACIFIC RAILWAY CO., IS 091, 1930 ....$185.00

Teapot – 10 oz., oval base, gooseneck spout, reg. lid, ornate handle, BM – N.P.R., R. Wallace, 0333 ....$125.00

Teapot – ¾ pt., diamond shaped bottom, long spout, hg'd. disc lid, round handle, BM – NO.PAC.R.R., Gorham Co. 06582, ca. 1890, (rare) $250.00

Tray – oval, 5¾ x 7¾", BM – N.P.R. script, GMCo. 08098, ca. 1906 ....$65.00

Pennsylvania

Creamer – hinged lid, SM – raised PRR Keystone logo, BM – PL inside outlined Keystone logo, IS 5115, 1912 ....$85.00

Coffee pot – 14 oz., SM – raised PRR Keystone logo, IS 061, 1951 ....$75.00

Finger bowl – 4¾" dia., ornate pierced sides, SM – raised PRR Keystone logo, BM – PRR, IS 903A $65.00

Menu holder – plain rectangular sides with two pencil tubes, SM – raised PRR Keystone logo, IS 05061, 1948 ....$95.00

Sugar bowl – hinged lid, 8 oz., SM – raised PRR Keystone logo, NRRBM, IS 05061A $75.00

Pullman Company

Bowl – 16 oz., BM – THE PULLMAN COMPANY, IS 085, 1932 ....$45.00

Coffee pot – 10 oz., BM – THE PULLMAN CO., WAL 0376, 1927 ....$75.00

Sugar bowl – with cover, 7 oz., BM – THE PULLMAN COMPANY, IS-SLO688, 1939.................................$65.00

Tray – oval, 5½ x 9¾", BM – THE PULLMAN COMPANY, IS-SLO688, 1925 ....$50.00

Southern Pacific

Butter chip tray – 3 x 4", TM – The Southern Pacific's stylized DAYLIGHT Ball & Wing logo, NRRBM, R&B 3300B $50.00

Finger bowl – 4¼" dia., SM – round SOUTHERN PACIFIC SUNSET LINES logo, BM – SPCo., R&B 242 ....$85.00

Sherbet – pedestal style, 3¾" high, 3¼" wide, SM – The Southern Pacific RR's stylized DAYLIGHT Ball & Wing logo, NRRBM, R&B 3300B $75.00

Tip tray – 3¾ x 6¾", TM – etched Southern Pacific passenger train 2401 across entire length, BM – Southern Pacific in script, R&B 1742, 1929 (scarce) $150.00

NP Ornate Coffee Pot

Texas & Pacific

Sauce bowl – with attached tray, 4 oz., S-mkd on bowl – Flying Eagle and streamliner motif with words "The Eagle" below. BM – TEXAS & PACIFIC RAILWAY, IS 05060C, 1946 ....$85.00

Union Pacific

Creamer – open top, 4" tall, 8 oz., BM–UPRR, IS 05045B, 1955 ....$50.00

Hot food cover – 5½" dia., with finger hole at top, TM – stylized Winged Streamliner logo, BM–UPRR, IS 05045A, 1954 ....$55.00

Menu holder – plain half-round style with two pencil tubes, BM–UPRR in script, IS 05070C, 1947 ....$85.00

Sauce boat – 4 oz., 6" long, SM – stylized Winged Streamliner logo, BM–UPRR, IS 0235, 1947 ....$60.00

Supreme Set – five pieces, bottom frame has open sides with two tab handles, liner bowl for the frame; a collar, cone and cover assembles on top, BM–UPRR, IS 05065, 1948. Cover is topmarked with stylized Winged Streamliner logo..$185.00

Tray – oval, 6¼ x 8¾", dulled non-skid surface on bottom, TM – UNION PACIFIC, The Overland Route shield logo, NRRBM, IS-CS 73, 1914 ....$75.00

Wabash

Sugar bowl – covered, 14 oz., shell and leaf design border, SM – fancy engraved letter, W, BM – Wabash in script, R&B 1354, c. 1920 ....$150.00

Western Pacific

Sherbet – pedestal style, 3¼" high, 3¾" wide, BM – Western Pacific Feather logo, IS 05098, 1948 ....$75.00

Silver Flatware

More extensive pattern information may be found in Dominy & Morgenfruh's book, *Silver at Your Service (A Collector's Guide to Railroad Dining Car Flatware Patterns.)*

Flatware pieces are listed here by the way they are railroad marked, either top or bottom, followed by Pattern Name, Silver Company, then the individual item.

Key to Abbreviations

BM – Bottom marked
TM – Top marked
HH – Hollow Handle

Silver Manufacturers

GOR – Gorham
IS – International
MER – Meriden
R&B – Reed & Barton
WAL – Wallace

ACL – TM, ZEPHYR, IS.

Bouillon spoon...$20.00
Table fork $15.00
Teaspoon...$14.00

B&O – (script) – TM, ARLINGTON, R&B

Butter knife...$18.00
Demi spoon $25.00
Table fork $15.00

Tablespoon $15.00

B&O – (script) – TM, CROMWELL, IS.

Cocktail fork $18.00
Iced tea spoon $20.00
Table fork $15.00
Teaspoon..$14.00

BR – (reversed B) – TM, BELMONT, R&B

Table fork $15.00
Tablespoon $18.00
Teaspoon $16.00

C.&N.W..Ry. (script) BM, MODERN ART, R&B

Dessert knife, HH, 4¾", plated blade $30.00
Dinner knife, HH, 5½" plated blade $35.00
Cocktail fork...$25.00
Table fork $22.00
Teaspoon..$20.00

C.& N.W. System (script) BM, AMERICAN, IS.

Dinner knife, HH, 5¾", stainless blade $15.00
Table fork $15.00

C.M.ST.P.& P.R.R. – BM, BROADWAY, IS.

Bouillon spoon..$15.00
Iced tea spoon $18.00
Steak knife, long HH, 3½", stainless blade....................$16.00
Table fork $12.00
Teaspoon..$12.00

C.St.P.M.& O.Ry. (script) BM, MODERN ART, R&B

Dinner knife, HH, 4¾" plated blade $25.00
Table fork $20.00

GN – TM (intertwined) HUTTON, IS.

Bouillon spoon..$16.00
Butter knife, HH, 3½", stainless blade $18.00
Demi spoon $30.00
Dinner knife, HH, 5¾", stainless blade $18.00
Iced tea spoon $22.00
Table fork...$16.00
Tablespoon $15.00
Combination crumbtray & scraper, 12" long, TM – GN
    (intertwined) HH., BM – GREAT NORTHERN RY., IS,
    SFO567, 1947 ....$75.00

GM&O – TM, BROADWAY, IS.

Table fork...$18.00
Table knife $16.00
Tablespoon $22.00

LACKAWANNA – TM, CROMWELL, IS.

Bouillon spoon $16.00
Cocktail fork..$18.00
Iced tea spoon $25.00
Tablespoon $16.00

NYC – BM, CENTURY, IS.

Cocktail fork..$15.00
Demi spoon $22.00
Fruit spoon, pointed tip $18.00
Iced tea spoon, 7¾"...$20.00
Table fork...$16.00
Tablespoon $15.00
Teaspoon $14.00

GN Hutton Pattern Flatware

Northern Pacific – TM – logo, BM – N.P.R. (script) ALDEN, R&B

Demi spoon $35.00
Dinner knife, HH, 5¾" stainless blade $20.00
Soup spoon $22.00
Table fork...$25.00
Combination crumb scraper & tray, 12¾" long $85.00

Northern Pacific – TM – logo, BM – N.P.R. (script) EMBASSY,
    R&B

Dessert knife, HH, 5½" stainless blade $18.00
Fork $18.00
Iced tea spoon $22.00

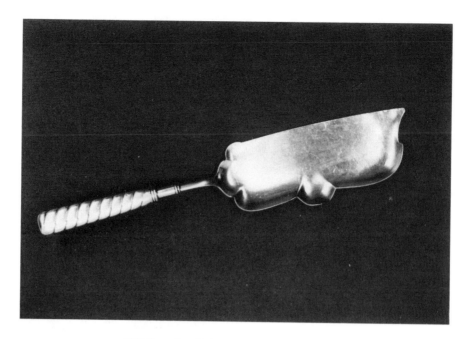

NP Dundee Spiral Pattern Crumber

Soup spoon $20.00
Teaspoon $18.00

Northern Pacific Railway Company – BM, SILHOUETTE, IS.

Butter knife, long HH, 3¼" stainless blade $20.00
Iced teaspoon $22.00
Soup spoon $20.00
Steak knife, long HH handle, serrated 3½" stainless
    blade $25.00
Table fork..$18.00
Sugar tongs $75.00

N.P.R. (script) TM, WINTHROP, GOR.

Dinner knife, HH, 5½" steel blade $25.00
Iced tea spoon $30.00
Soup spoon $22.00
Teaspoon $20.00

N.P.Ry. – (script) BM, DUNDEE (spiral pattern) 1847
    ROGER BROS. Al

Crumber, 12¼" long, 6" HH, with 6¼" scraper..........$125.00

PRR – TM, BROADWAY, IS.

Butter knife, 3½" stainless blade $14.00
Fruit knife, long HH, 3½", serrated stainless blade $16.00
Table fork..$15.00
Teaspoon $12.00

RI – (R over I) TM, ROCK ISLAND LINES – BM,
    CROMWELL, IS.

Dessert knife, 5" straight stainless blade $16.00

Dinner knife, 5¾" curved stainless blade $18.00
Dinner fork $16.00
Teaspoon $15.00

Santa Fe – BM, ALBANY, GOR.

Table fork..$12.00
Table knife..$12.00
Tablespoon $13.00
Teaspoon $10.00

Seaboard – TM, CROMWELL, IS.

Cocktail fork $18.00
Dinner knife, HH, 5½" stainless blade $16.00
Iced tea spoon $25.00
Table fork..$15.00
Tablespoon $15.00
Teaspoon $12.00

Soo Line – TM – Box logo, SUSSEX, IS.

Bouillon spoon $28.00
Dinner knife, HH, 5¾" curved stainless blade $30.00
Iced tea spoon, 7½"..$35.00
Salad knife, HH, 5" curved stainless blade $30.00
Table fork..$25.00
Tablespoon $30.00
Teaspoon $25.00

Southern Pacific – (script) – BM, BROADWAY, IS.

Dinner knife, 5¾" curved stainless blade $20.00
Table fork..$18.00
Tablespoon $16.00
Teaspoon $15.00

S.P. & S. RY. – BM, EMBASSY, R&B

Bouillon spoon $30.00
Fruit knife, 5" curved stainless blade...........................$25.00
Table knife, 5" stainless blade $30.00
Teaspoon $25.00

U.P.R.R. (script) – BM, ZEPHYR, IS.

Bouillon spoon $12.00
Cocktail fork $18.00
Dinner knife $12.00

Iced tea spoon, 8" $15.00
Dinner fork $12.00
Teaspoon $12.00

Western Pacific – BM, Feather logo, HUTTON, IS.

Bouillon spoon $16.00
Cocktail fork $20.00
Iced tea spoon $20.00
Table fork..$18.00
Table knife $18.00
Table spoon $15.00

Glassware With Silverplated Components

CANADIAN PACIFIC – pair salt and pepper shakers, 3½" tall, plain S/P flat tops, cylindrical glass style containers with etched shield logo............................$50.00

GREAT NORTHERN – table water S/P pitcher frame with glass lining, front of frame marked with GN intertwined monogram, BM – Great Northern Ry., IS-28, GNS-60, 1924, scarce $375.00

GREAT NORTHERN – oil and vinegar S/P caster stand, 6½" tall, for two glass bottles with stoppers, SM-GN, BM – GREAT NORTHERN RY. IS-05082, 1947 ....$175.00

ILLINOIS CENTRAL – silverplated mustard pot, 3" tall, hinged lid with spoon hole, has glass lining, SM-ICRR (script) not b'mkd., Gorham A39, 1945 ....$75.00

M&STLRR – table water pitcher, S/P frame with glass lining, mkd. under lid, M&STLRR #04266, Albert Pick & Company, 1928, scarce $350.00

NORTHERN PACIFIC – pair salt and pepper shakers, 3½" tall, heavy glass with panelled sides, SM-NO.PAC.R.R. on ornate silverplated tops, scarce $100.00

ROCK ISLAND LINES – silverplated caster stand, 5¼" tall with three individual glass shakers, 2¾" tall, S/P tops, BM – ROCK ISLAND LINES, IS-SF0790, 1955....$125.00

SOO LINE – pair salt and pepper shakers, 3" tall, ornate, domed S/P tops, thick glass panelled sides, mkd. with etched Banner logo, scarce $200.00

SOO LINE – syrup, cut glass body with cemented ornate S/P hollow handle and finial h'gd. lid, SM SOO LINE logo on lid rim, GMCo.EP 0201, 1911, rare $300.00

M&StL Water Pitcher

Drinking Glassware

Various glassware pieces were used in the railroad's dining cars and club cars, also some in the railroad depot restaurants and lunch counters. The earlier pieces and those from roads long gone are worth more. SM – Side marked.

Canadian National Railways

Sherbert – 4" tall, 3¼" dia., cut glass stem, pinched sides, SM – etched canted box logo. Scarce $50.00

Canadian Pacific

Tumbler – 4" tall, SM – shield shape logo with beaver atop in white enamel $15.00

76

Glassware wtih Frosted Logo

Chesapeake & Ohio

Tumbler – 4¾" tall, SM – "C&O For Progress" in blue...$10.00

Chicago Milwaukee St. Paul & Pacific

Juice – 3¾" tall, 2¼" dia., SM – etched box logo $20.00
Sherbet – footed, 2½" tall, 3¼" dia., SM – etched box logo...$30.00
Tumbler – 4¾" tall, 2½" dia., SM – etched box logo $25.00
Tumbler – 4½" tall, gold rim, The MILWAUKEE road stream-liner HIAWATHA and four lines of poetry all around in maroon and orange enamel....................................$30.00
Wine – 5" tall, 2¼" dia., hollow cut stem, SM – etched box logo (scarce) $65.00

Chicago Rock Island & Pacific

Roly Poly glass – 2¾" high, has ROCK ISLAND logo, 1852, "Route of the Rockets" in red enamel, GOLDEN STATE emblem and "Golden State Route" in gold around sides $25.00

Frisco

Tumbler – 5", SM – blue FRISCO logo $15.00

Great Northern
Claret – knob stem, 4¾" tall, 2¼" dia., SM – frosted GN inter-twined...$45.00
Cocktail – knob stem, 4¼" tall, 2½" dia., SM – frosted GN intertwined...$40.00

Juice – 3½" tall, 2" dia., SM – frosted GN inter twined ..$35.00
Water – 5½" tall, 2½" dia., SM – cut-engraved early GREAT NORTHERN goat logo (rare) $125.00
Wine – knob stem, 5¾" tall, 2" dia., SM – frosted GN inter-twined $35.00

Illinois Central

Bar glass – 3" tall, 3" dia., gold rim, has four vertical ovals, two with diesels, one with map of system, one with ILLINOIS CENTRAL logo in white/black enamel $15.00
Glass, Old Fashion – 4½" high, 3½" dia., has logo, diesel frt. and pass. train, with slogan "Main Line of America" in maroon and yellow around sides.........................$25.00
Roly Poly glass – 2½" tall, has Panama Limited Streamliner and ILLINOIS CENTRAL logo in maroon and yellow around sides $18.00
Tumbler – 5" tall, with vertical grooves, SM – etched ILLINOIS CENTRAL diamond logo.....................$22.00

Lackawanna

Tumbler – 4¾" tall, SM – PHOEBE SNOW (script) in maroon $15.00

New York Central

Claret – knob stem, 4¼" tall, 2½" dia., SM – white frosted 20TH CENTURY LIMITED $35.00
Champagne – knob style stem, 4½" tall, 3½" dia., SM – white frosted NYC $20.00
Champagne – knob style stem, 4½" tall, 3½" dia., SM – white frosted 20th CENTURY LIMITED $35.00

Cordial – knob style stem, 3½" tall, SM – white frosted NYC $25.00
Cordial – plain stem, 4" tall, SM – gold oval NEW YORK CENTRAL SYSTEM logo $42.00
Tumbler – 4½" tall, New York World's Fair 1964-1965, diesel streamliner, world globe, NYCS logo, "Route To The World's Fair" done in black and gold entirely around...........$25.00
Wine – knob style stem, 3½" tall, SM – white frosted NYC..$20.00

Northern Pacific Railway

Cordial – 3¾" tall, SM – etched Yellowstone Park Line logo (rare) $175.00
Juice – 3¾" tall, SM – black/red enamel Monad logo at top, ribbed bottom $30.00
Tumbler – 4" tall, SM – black/red enamel Monad logo at bottom $25.00

Pennsylvania

Glass, highball – 4½" tall, 3½" dia. top. Has PRR logo, passenger train 4902, outlines of clouds and buildings in brown and white around sides..$18.00

Santa Fe

Tumbler – 5½" tall, SM – Santa Fe (script) in white enamel..$15.00
Juice – 4¼" tall, SM – Santa Fe (script) in white enamel..$12.00

Southern Railway

Glass, highball – 4½" tall, 3½" dia., gold rim, has SR logo, diesel 4258, outlined scenes in green and white around sides $20.00

Union Pacific

Goblet – footed, 5½", ball stem, SM – frosted shield logo...$18.00
Martini set – three-piece, pouring pitcher 5¼" tall and two matching Roly Poly glasses 2½" high, each sidemarked frosted shield logo...$45.00
Shot glass – 2½", frosted shield logo $10.00
Tumbler – 4½", SM – frosted shield logo.....................$12.00

Silk-screened Glassware

Misc. Glassware

Burlington Northern

Mug – 5½" tall, "BN Burlington Northern" green, TRANSPORTATION NEEDS YOU black, JA emblem 1972 in black/red on sides $12.00
Tray – rectangular, 4¾ x 11¾", TM – BN logo in green border with white cattle brands, gold/white longhorn motif in clear center..$35.00

Great Northern

Cruet – clear glass, 5½" tall with stopper, SM – cut-etched GREAT NORTHERN old goat logo, rare $750.00
Cruet – clear glass, 6" tall with stopper, SM – cut-etched GREAT NORTHERN RAILWAY silhouette goat logo, rare $500.00

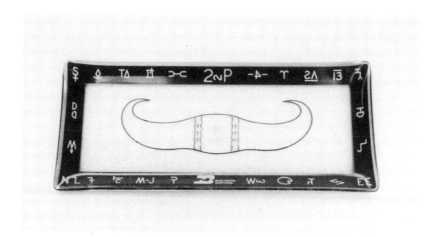

BN Tray with Gold and Enamel Decor

Missouri Pacific Lines

Milk bottle – one quart, 9¾" tall, FM – embossed "Missouri Pacific Lines" buzz saw logo $65.00
Milk bottle – half pint, 4¼" tall, has buzz saw logo in front and Sunnymede Farm Bismark, Missouri in red enamel at rear $30.00

Northern Pacific Railway

Milk bottle – half pint, 5½" tall, FM – "Northern Pacific Railway Dairy & Poultry Farm, Kent., WN." embossed inside circle, rare $150.00

Pennsylvania

Ink well – heavy clear glass, 2 x 2¾ x 2¾", with 1¼" dia. well, raised P.R.R. on bottom; metal cover with ornate PRR intertwined $50.00

Soo Line

Carafe – 9" high, cut glass neck, bulbous bottom, FM – etched SOO LINE Banner logo $175.00

Southern Pacific

Medicine bottle – 5¾" tall, has "Southern Pacific Co. Hospital Department" raised on back side, label on front ..$25.00

The Milwaukee Road

Tobacco jar – clear glass, 5½" high, 4" dia., has canted Box logo 1977 Montana Division, etc., front, map of Montana Division rear, in red enamel $45.00

Half-Pint Milk Bottles

Menus

Early menus were small in size, made of card stock, generally folded in half to make two pages. The covers had fancy letters and colorful illustrations, finely printed on the inside. These are the rarities. Menus from the Golden Era before WWII are also getting hard to come by, while those from the diesel age are more readily available and priced accordingly.

Amtrak

"GOOD MORNING" Club Breakfasts, single card 7 x 11", recent issue $1.50

AT&SF

1939 – The Chief, Table d'Hote Dinner, 5¾" x 9", red monogram on white cover..$12.00
1940 – The Grand Canyon Limited, Table d'Hote Luncheons, 5¾" x 9", gold monogram on white cover $10.00

Political Menu

Burlington Route

1927 – "Seasons Greetings," Dinner, 6¼ x 9", logo, night train and stagecoach on cover. Scarce............................$45.00
1943 – LUNCHEON, 6 x 9", streamliner Zephyr cover $8.00

Chicago Burlington & Quincy Railroad

1876 – Breakfast and Supper, Wine List, 5½ x 7¼" opened flat. Front cover has railroad's name in fancy letters, back cover has a French litho glued on showing children frolicking with a large gold napkin ring. Rare $85.00

Chicago, Milwaukee & St. Paul

c. 1880s – Dinner-Wine List, 5½ x 7½" open flat. Covers show colorful litho woodland scene and RR's name in fancy lettering. Rare..$75.00

Chicago Rock Island & Pacific Railroad

c.1870s – Dinner, Breakfast and Supper, Wine List, 4½ x 5¾" open flat. Front cover has logo with advertising; back cover has dining car scene "Showing the way meals are served on the Overland Trains of the Rock Island Route." Rare..$95.00

Chicago & Northwestern

12-1-09 – supper, 5½ x 6¾", colorful cover depicts couple seated at table, back cover has list of name trains. Rare...$65.00
1913-1914 – HOLIDAY MENU, 5½ x 8", white covers have green holly leaves, RR's logo within a wreath. Scarce $45.00
6-1-54 – "400" Table D'Hote Dinner, 7½ x 10", front cover has color photo of the 400 Streamliner on Stone Arch bridge $8.00

Denver & Rio Grande

10-8-08 – menu and wine list, 5 x 7", engraving of Animas Canon and logo on front cover, back has engraving of Second Tunnel. Rare. $65.00

Great Northern Railway

c. 1914 – menu, wine list, 5½ x 8½", simulated Indian beaded covers in blue and white, with logo and scenes of Tourists' Teepee Camp, Mt. Wilbur, Lake McDermott, New Automobile Highway, Glacier Park, Montana. Scarce $50.00
1928 – Club Breakfast Service, 7 x 10¼", colorful front cover shows couple seated in lobby of Prince of Wales Hotel, and GN goat logo at bottom $18.00
1949 – The Oriental Limited, Luncheon, 6½ x 10", colorful full length Indian Chief, Riding Black Horse, on cover $30.00
1957 – Western Star, Luncheon, 6½ x 10", "Desperate Stand" painting by C.M. Russell on cover, also GN logo........$20.00

Illinois Central

1951 – Luncheon, single card, 8 x 11", Centennial Medallion, 1851-1951, depicted upper right corner $6.00
1963 – Panama Limited, Breakfast, 6 x 9", transition of locomotives, early steam to modern diesel depicted on cover $5.00

Lehigh Valley

c. 1920's – menu, 5½ x 8", front cover shows chef surrounded by culinary served and the Black Diamond Express; back has wine list. Scarce..$45.00

Milwaukee Road

4-6-56 – Olympian Hiawatha, Breakfast, 8"x 10", identical dark red covers, with Hiawatha Indian emblem in cream on orange disc $8.00
11-17-62 – the HIAWATHA, Luncheon, 8 x 10", light red covers, with Thunderbird design in black on yellow disc $7.50

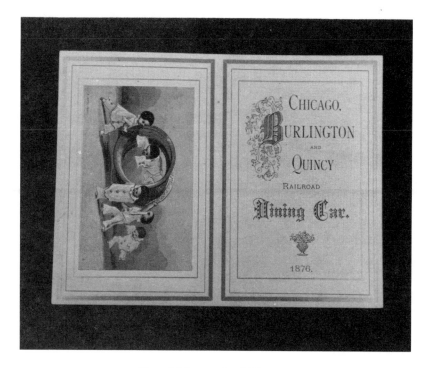

Rare Lithographed Menu

New York Central

c.1939 – Empire State Express, Luncheon, 6 x 9", "The New Streamlined 20th Century Limited" on front cover. Back has map and logo $10.00

Northern Pacific

1885 – dinner, wine list, Special Excursion St. Paul Jobbers' Union, 4¾ x 6¾", litho of Indian maiden front cover, dining car back cover. Rare $115.00

c.1914 – menu, apple shape, 5 x 5", cardstock covers with four pages. Photos of dining car table settings are on the inside and backside of covers. Rare $50.00

c.1914 – menu, baked potato shape, 3½ x 8", cardstock covers with four pages. Photos of bakeshop, dining car table setting and kitchen are on the inside and backside of covers. Rare $75.00

c.1914 – menu, casserole shape, Luncheon, 5½ x 7", cardstock covers with four pages. Photos of dining car table settings are on the inside and backside of covers. Rare $65.00

c. 1920's – breakfast, National Apple Week, Oct. 31st to Nov. 6th, 6¾" x 10", cover has litho of three red apples hanging on a stem, logo in upper left corner. Scarce ..$35.00

1928 – National Egg Week, May 1st to 7th, 6¾ x 10½", Unusual Egg Dishes. Cover shows logo, photos of chickens, inside front cover has photo of chicken farms. Scarce....$25.00

4-53 – menus For Small Travelers, 5 x 7", orange covers, front has logo and illustration of two Teddy bears eating at table, back has animal cartoon scene $6.00

Seaboard

1943 – breakfast, 6 x 9", color illustration of WWII soldier blowing bugle in camp, with waving American flag on pole...$8.00

Soo Line

1929 – luncheon, Enroute Portal to Twin Cities, Sept. 27th. Blue covers, 6¼ x 9¼", cover has word Menu and logo in silver, black/white photo of couple in canoe glued on inside opposite luncheon list $22.00

1943 – menu, Combination Plate Service, 5½ x 8", tan cover with blue logo and floral border design in yellow, brown, blue and black...$18.00

Southern Pacific

June 2-4, 1925 – Special Anzar Temple Pilgrimage Luncheon to Los Angeles, Calif., 5½ x 8½", front cover shows couple seated at table, back has view of San Carlos Borromeo Mission. Rare $75.00

Spokane, Portland & Seattle

1957 – dinner, 7 x 11", front cover has photo of Bonneville Dam Spillway and RR's name across bottom $12.00

Union Pacific

7-26-47 – breakfast, Los Angeles Limited, 7 x 10", white covers, yellow poppies on front cover, San Gabriel Mission on back...$10.00

1969 – dinner, Children's Menu, 7 x 7", opened flat. Covers depict Teddy Bears sitting in tree eating from cereal bowls $6.00

Western Pacific – Rio Grande – Burlington

1940 – dinner, Chicago Democratic Convention, 6 x 9¼", inside pages tied with red/white/blue ribbon. Front cover has cartoon characters of donkey and bear reading menu, back has logos of the three railroads. Scarce $50.00

Paper Napkins

The measurements when folded, as found, are approximately 4¾" square, with either straight or scalloped edges. There are others found folded in rectangular shape, with their measurements noted here.

Napkins and Coasters

AMTRAK – rectangle, 4¼ x 8½", red/white/blue logo, wide crinkled border, straight edge ....$.75

AMTRAK – "We've been working on the RAILROAD!" and logo in blue and red ....$.50

BURLINGTON ROUTE – En Route THE ZEPHYR and The West Wind ZEPHYRUS streamliner logo in blue, pinstripe border ....$.85

GM&O – winged logo, "The Alton Route" in red, royal blue border $1.25

MILWAUKEE ROAD – "The MILWAUKEE ROAD" in grey, speckled red border ....$.50

MILWAUKEE ROAD – Rectangle, 4¼ x 7½", large red logo $1.50

MISSOURI PACIFIC – THE EAGLE streamliner motif in blue, wide red lace effect border with inner blue pinstripe..$.85

MONON – "The Hoosier Line" and border in dark red....$.75

NORFOLK & WESTERN – "N&WRY" circle logo, "The Powhatan Arrow" and border in dark red $1.25

NORTHERN PACIFIC – The Lewis and Clark TRAVELLER'S REST Buffet Lounge, Vista-Dome NORTH COAST LIMITED, rifle, bow & arrows motif in brown $2.00

ROCK ISLAND – black logo, streamliner and slogan "Route Of The Rockets" in red, wide grey lace effect border $2.00

SEABOARD – heart logo, "Silver Meteor" in brown, wide grey lace effect border with brown stripe $1.75

SOO LINE – large box logo and wavy double line border in red $2.50

UNION PACIFIC – rectangle, 4¼ x 8½", red/white/blue shield logo, wide crinkle border, straight edge........$1.50

Stir Sticks

All are plastic unless otherwise noted. The GN sticks, as well as some of the others listed here, are also found in different colors.

AMTRAK – Blue, arrow top $1.00

B&O – Steel, in form of golf club, B. & O. R.R. CO. raised on handle $25.00

BN – White, ball top, BURLINGTON NORTHERN, green, on rod ....$.50

BURLINGTON ROUTE – Light blue, dome car cut-out top $8.00

C&NW – white, spoon tip, NORTH WESTERN, Route of the "400" in gold..$5.00

GN – red, cut-out goat top, GREAT NORTHERN RAILWAY, yellow, on rod..$6.00

GN – blue, cut-out goat top, GREAT NORTHERN'S WESTERN STAR, yellow, on rod...$6.00

GN – green, cut-out goat top, GREAT NORTHERN'S EMPIRE BUILDER, yellow, on rod..$8.00

GN – white, blue goat logo top, THE GROWING GREAT NORTHERN in blue raised on rod $5.00

GN – white, ball top, GREAT NORTHERN RAILWAY, blue, on rod $1.50

GN – black, GN cut-out top, From the ranch of the Empire Builder, yellow, on rod $6.00

GM&O – blue, ball top, GULF, MOBILE AND OHIO R.R., white, on rod $2.00

MILW – yellow, ball top, The MILWAUKEE Road, gold, on rod $2.00

MILW – clear glass, spoon tip, The HIAWATHA, Nothing Faster On Rails, blue, on rod $22.00

NP – clear glass, spoon tip, Route of the NORTH COAST LIMITED, N.P. Railway, red, on rod $22.00

ROCK ISLAND – yellow, fork tip, paddle top, ROCK ISLAND LINES, ROUTE OF THE ROCKETS, gold, on paddle $5.00

SANTA FE – blue, cut-out Indian Chief head top, Santa Fe The Chief Way, yellow, on rod.................................$6.00

SP – green, paddle top, SOUTHERN PACIFIC, Your Friendly Railroad, gold, on paddle $2.50

NH – blue glass, ball ends, THE NEW HAVEN RAILROAD, Dining Car Service $30.00

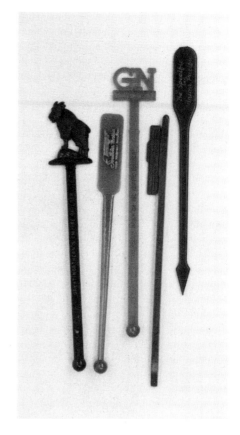

Stir Sticks

UP – red, arrow point, paddle top, Be Specific say "Union Pacific" gold, on paddle $1.50

UP – aqua, entire stick is a streamliner likeness, with "The Domeliners" UPRR raised on it $6.00

UP – red, oval top with gold Union Pacific Railroad shield logo in gold $2.00

UP – red, oval top with two locos 1869-1969 "Golden Spike Centenial" in gold, UNION PACIFIC RAILROAD, gold, on rod $4.00

Miscellaneous

ASH TRAY – cardstock, fold-up edges, triangle shape 3", silver finish, THE MILWAUKEE ROAD logo, Hiawatha's Domeliners copy in black $4.00

ASH TRAY – cardstock, fold-up edges, triangle shape 3", yellow finish CHICAGO NORTHWESTERN logo, "400" Streamliner Fleet copy in green..............................$4.00

DIXIE CUP – for alcoholic beverages, waxed cardboard, yellow, 2½" high, UNION PACIFIC Winged Streamliner logo and "City of Las Vegas" in red $1.50

DRINKING CUP – paper, flat, 4 x 4½", CHICAGO & NORTHWESTERN LINE logo in blue $2.00

DRINKING CUP – paper, flat, 3½ x 3¾", NEW YORK CENTRAL SYSTEM logo, train, "We wish you a pleasant trip and hope you will be with us again" in black ..$1.00

DOILY-COCKTAIL – paper, 5" dia., scalloped edge, NORTHERN PACIFIC RAILWAY logo between two floral sprays, all embossed $5.00

DOILY-COCKTAIL – paper, 6" dia., scalloped edge, N.C.& ST.L.RY. "To and from Dixieland" in red, three embossed floral sprays in border $4.00

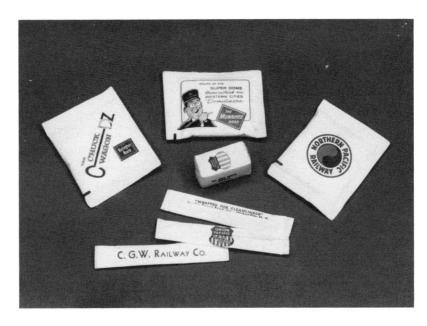

Sugar Packets and Toothpicks

DOILY-COCKTAIL – paper, 6" dia., scalloped edge, ROCK ISLAND logo, streamliner, "Route of the Rockets" in red, three embossed floral sprays in border $3.00

SUGAR LUMP – ½ x ½ x 1¼", wrapped cube, UNION PACIFIC with blue shield logo..................................$4.00

SUGAR PACKET – flat paper packet, 2 x 2½", BURLINGTON ROUTE logo, The Chuckwagon DZ brand in blue and brown $4.00

SUGAR PACKET – flat paper packet, 1¾ x 2½", conductor pointing to THE MILWAUKEE ROAD, logo, "Route of the SUPER DOME Hiawathas and Western Cities Domeliners" in red/black $4.00

SUGAR PACKET – flat paper packet, 2 x 2½", red/black NORTHERN PACIFIC Monad logo $4.00

TOOTHPICK – two quill picks sealed in white paper wrapper marked C.G.W.RAILWAY CO. in red. Scarce $10.00

TOOTHPICK – two wood picks sealed in white paper wrapper marked with blue UNION PACIFIC shield logo ......$.25

WAITER'S CAP – flat white paper 3½ x 11", opens to fit head, blue FRISCO logo and stripe...................................$15.00

WAITER'S CAP – flat white paper 3½ x 11", opens to fit head, NORTHERN PACIFIC logo and "Vista-Dome NORTH COAST LIMITED" in black, red stripe around top ..$18.00

WAITER'S CAP – flat white paper, 5½ x 11", opens to fit head, UNION PACIFIC red/white/blue Shield logo and blue stripe $12.00

COASTERS – paper, disc shape with soft absorbent top and waxed bottom. Some are plain cardstock as noted.

AMTRAK – red/blue logo and blue border on white ....$.50

CHICAGO NORTHWESTERN – cardstock, logo, depicts five "400" streamliners in center and slogan "Pioneer Railroad of Chicago and the West since 1848" on green and yellow border..$2.00

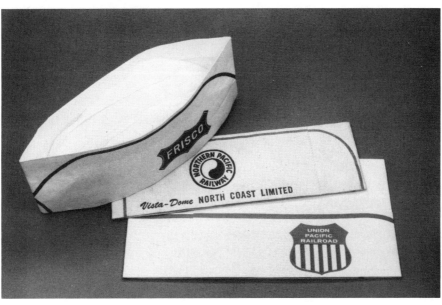

Waiter's Paper Caps

GREAT NORTHERN – comical goat standing and pointing to slogan "You go GREAT when you go Great Northern" green on white $3.00

GREAT NORTHERN – cartoon of goat waiter with tray of drinks, green on white $3.00

SOUTHERN RAILWAY – SR logo Serves The South, "Look Ahead-Look South," green on white $2.00

UNION PACIFIC – cardstock, shows a stemmed cocktail glass and "Always a Favorite" in red on white center, yellow border $1.00

FINGERBOWL LINERS – white paper inserts for silverware bowls, round shape approximately 1¾" high, 4" dia. with expanding crimped sides.

ILLINOIS CENTRAL – PANAMA LIMITED around sides, courtyard scene on bottom, orange $1.75

NEW YORK CENTRAL SYSTEM – logo, "Thank you" on bottom, striped border, brown $1.50

NORFOLK & WESTERN – N&WRY logo, Indian profiles, The Powatan Arrow, The Pocahontas, on bottom, pinstripe border, brown $2.00

SOO LINE – logo and "Thank You" on bottom, striped border in red........................$2.50

Keys

Switch keys have always been popular with the railroadiana collector. Thousands upon thousands of them were made down through the years, of bronze or brass, some of steel or iron. The railroad's name or initials were stamped on the front side of the hilt. The letter S (Switch) or other department letters and a serial number, along with the maker's mark, were generally stamped on the back side. Many collectors suspect that switch keys found without a serial number and maker's hallmark, having only railroad initials stamped on them, are possible fakes. The earlier switch keys, especially from now long gone defunct railroads, with serif letters, tapered barrels with grooved rings around them, nice markings and smooth hand wear, are realizing fabulous prices.

There were many other railroad-marked keys for locks on shanties, coal sheds, signal boxes, cabooses, coaches and so on. These various keys, different in size and shape from the regular switch key, are also being collected. Many recent caboose or coach keys are marked "Adlake" only, and these do not bring the price of those that are railroad marked.

Switch (brass unless otherwise noted) Markings shown are on keys listed here.

A A R R – 479 ADLAKE..$25.00
A C L RR – 19127 FRAIM in banner hm'k $35.00
A T & S F RY – S 13679 ADLAKE $20.00
B & O – C 33498 FRAIM in banner hm'k., long barrel..$18.00
B&ORRCO – S 51566 F-S HDW.CO. diamond hm'k ..$25.00
B & M RR – W. BOHANNAN, BROOKLYN, N.Y. $22.00
B & M R R R IN NEB – (serifs) G 401 S, tapered barrel with ring around $135.00
BELT – 500 ADLAKE..$30.00
BN INC – ADLAKE $10.00
B.R.& P.RR – S 9621 A&W CO. CHICAGO $30.00
BURLINGTON ROUTE – S 8218 A&W CO. CHICAGO (steel key) $22.00
C & A R R – S (serifs) tapered barrel with ring around..$50.00
C&EI – 906 1 ADLAKE unused....................................$22.00
C & I M RR – 634 ADLAKE...$25.00
C & N W – ADLAKE $15.00
C & N W R R – S WILSON BOHANNAN BROOKLYN, N.Y...$30.00
C&N.W.RY – S A&W CO CHICAGO $25.00
C & O – 3393 ADLAKE $15.00
C & S – 4821 ADLAKE...$50.00
C& W C R – 1871 ADLAKE...$15.00
C & W M R R – S A&W CO CHICAGO $50.00
C C & C R R – (serifs) H. C. JONES, NEWARK, N.J. tapered narrow barrel with ring around $95.00

Early Keys with Serif Letters and Tapered Barrels

C.C.C.& I.RY – (serifs) J.L. HOWARD & Co. HARTFORD, CT, tapered narrow barrel......................................$85.00
C.C.C.& ST.L.RR – S X-8782 B A&W CO. CHICAGO..$20.00
C G W – ADLAKE unused $22.00
C G W RR – S ADLAKE $25.00
C G W RY – S A&W CO CHICAGO.............................$30.00
C.I.& S.R.R. – A 945 tapered barrel........................$60.00
C M & P S R R – LOEFFELHOLZ & CO $50.00

CM&STPRY – B steel key..................................$25.00
C M & ST P R R – LOEFFELHOLZ & CO $22.00
C M. ST. P.& P.RR – ADLAKE $15.00
C N R R – S ADLAKE $15.00
C.N.R. – S R.M. Co. (raised letters) $13.00
C R R OF IO – S (serifs) tapered barrel $85.00
C.R.I.& P.RR – S 37860 A & W CO CHICAGO $18.00
C ST P & K C R R – S (serifs) 633 tapered barrel.......$85.00
CSt PM&ORR – S (serifs) E D W. BOHANNAN BROOKLYN
    N.Y. $40.00
CSTPM&ORY – S. R. SLAYMAKER, LANCASTER,
    PA $35.00
C V R R – S WILSON BOHANNAN BROOKLYN N.Y. $30.00
D & H Co. – S (serifs) 1533 big letters...................$25.00
D & I R RR – S (serifs) K 116 tapered barrel with ring
    around $65.00
D & I.R.R. – S 356 steel oiler key $50.00
D & N E R R – S ADLAKE.................................$25.00
D & R G – S (serifs) 475 big letters $45.00
D&TSL – ADLAKE..$25.00
DGH&MRR – S (serifs) 1408 tapered barrel with ring
    around $85.00
D M & I R – 4674 ADLAKE $25.00
D M & N RY – B 839 ADLAKE $50.00
D M V R R – C (serifs) tapered barrel $95.00
DSS&ARY – 4276 F-S HDW.Co. $125.00
D T R R – ADLAKE $22.00
D T & I – 2018 ADLAKE $25.00
D.W. & P.RY – S ADLAKE $30.00
E J & E RY – S 8979 ADLAKE $25.00
E L R R – ADLAKE $15.00
E – (in diamond) ADLAKE................................$12.00
E R R – S (serifs) T. SLAIGHT NEWARK NJ. tapered
    barrel...$35.00
ERIE – FRAIM (in keystone) $18.00
ERIE RR – (serifs) F-S HDW. CO $20.00
E S T L J RR – 15 FRAIM (in keystone) $65.00
E ST L & S RY – S (serifs) HANDLAN-BUCK MFG CO.
    ST. LOUIS tapered barrel $90.00
F & P M R R – (serifs) J. L. HOWARD & CO., tapered
    barrel $65.00
F D D M & S – (serifs) FRAIM (in keystone) $42.00
F E & M V – S (serifs) W. BOHANNAN BROOKLYN,
    N.Y. $75.00
FRISCO – S(big letters) S.R. SLAYMAKER, LANCASTER,
    PA $15.00
F W & D C – ADLAKE $65.00
G & M R R – S (serifs) tapered barrel $50.00
GB&WRR – W 110 ....$40.00
GNRY – C 4603 SLAYMAKER $18.00
G.T.R. – (serifs) steel key..............................$30.00
G T W – ADLAKE $18.00
GR&IRR – S (serifs) $65.00
H & St JO R R – S (serifs) tapered barrel with ring
    around..$175.00
HB&T – 19840 ....$25.00
HBLRR – 968 SLAYMAKER $15.00
I C RR – S 75793 ADLAKE $15.00
ICGRR – ADLAKE unused $12.00
I.H.B. – ADLAKE...$30.00

I U RY CO – S (serifs) HANDLAN-BUCK MFG CO. ST.
    LOUIS (tapered barrel) $85.00
K & I T – 1643 ADLAKE $25.00
K.C.S. – 1531 ....$22.00
KCM&O – S (serifs) 225 ....$160.00
KCP&G – (serifs) W. BOHANNAN, BROOKLYN, N.Y.
    tapered barrel with ring around $100.00
K C S RY – (serifs) 10284 ....$25.00
K.C.S.RY.Co – 17207, steel key $30.00
L & N R.R. – 10638, FRAIM (in keystone) $20.00
L&NE – ADLAKE...$50.00

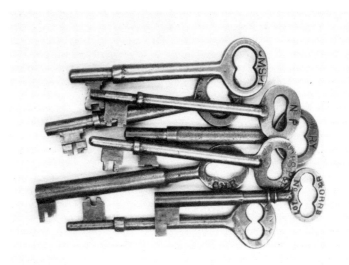

Caboose and Coach Keys

L V R R – S (serifs) big letters, A5913 ....$20.00
M & I – FRAIM (in keystone) $45.00
M&O RR – 4804 F-S HDW. Co $25.00
M & P DU C Ry – S (serifs) tapered barrel with rings
    around $100.00
M & ST L RR – S (serifs) 78 tapered barrel $85.00
M.C.RR. – S A&W Co CHICAGO $30.00
M K & T RY – FRAIM (in banner) short fat barrel......$30.00
M N & S RWY – ADLAKE $35.00
MO.P.R.R. – 26771, steel key...........................$28.00
MO PAC RR – S (serifs) 37325 F-S HDW CHICAGO ..$20.00
MSTP&SSMRR – C D A&W Co. CHICAGO $35.00
M R S – 48 ADLAKE $15.00
M T RY.CO – FRAIM (in banner) tapered barrel.......$35.00
N & W – 7236 ADLAKE....................................$18.00
NP – ADLAKE $15.00
NPRR – (serifs) FRAIM (in keystone) $25.00
NPRY – ADLAKE $18.00
N.Y.C.RR – S A&W Co. CHICAGO........................$20.00
N.Y.C.S. – 42400 steel oiler key, hole in barrel $25.00
NYLE&WRR – S (serifs) T. SLAIGHT, NEWARK, N.J.,
    tapered barrel $65.00
NYO&W – 13760 ADLAKE $45.00
OMAHA RY – ADLAKE....................................$45.00
O.R.& N.Co – R&B 586, A&W Co. CHICAGO $75.00
P&LE – 8628 F-S HDW CO. (diamond hm'k)............$30.00

Miscellaneous Keys – Shanties, Signal Locks, Mail Car, Etc.

P&PU RY – 466 ADLAKE $50.00

PB&NERR – (serifs) 448 SLAYMAKER $55.00

PCC&STL – S (serifs) 2784 big round bow $38.00

PCRR – ADLAKE (unused) $15.00

PMRY – (serifs) F-S HDW.Co. (diamond hm'k) $30.00

P.R.R. – (serifs) 1547 FRAIM (in keystone) knobs around bow $40.00

P T R A – ADLAKE..$45.00

PLANT SYSTEM – (serifs) 2 DIV. W. BOHANNAN, BROOK-LYN, N.Y. $150.00

RDG CO – ADLAKE, unused $20.00

RF&P – TH (serifs) J.H.W.CLIMAX CO. NEWARK, NJ. Two rings around barrel $45.00

R I & P R Y – S (serifs) MM BUCK & CO. ST. LOUIS, MO. tapered barrel $95.00

R.R.I & ST. L R.R. – (serifs) tapered barrel with ring around $125.00

SANTA FE – S 29636 A&W Co. CHICAGO $25.00

SANTA FE ROUTE – A&W Co. CHICAGO (hex. hm'd) $40.00

SCL RR – 205, ADLAKE, unused $15.00

SCT RY CO – S (serifs) F-S HDW.Co. (diamond hm'k) $20.00

SNSY – 104 FRAIM (in keystone) $15.00

SOO LINE – S A&W Co. CHICAGO.............................$25.00

SO. RY. – (serifs) SR $20.00

S.P.CO – FRIEGHT A&W CO. CHICAGO $20.00

S.P.CO. – S 4051 A&W Co. CHICAGO $15.00

S.P.CO. CS-44 SPECIAL 5693 ....$20.00

S.P.CO. CS-24 R&B 6295 A&W Co. CHICAGO $20.00

SP.RY – big letters and bow, long barrel.......................$25.00

SPT CO – C S4S, ADLAKE (unused) $10.00

S T L & C R R – S (serifs) 268 M M BUCK & CO. ST. LOUIS, MO. tapered barrel...$75.00

S T L & S E R W – S (serifs) M M BUCK & CO. ST. LOUIS, MO tapered barrel $80.00

ST.L.& S.F. – S A&W Co. CHICAGO $35.00

ST P M & M RR – S (serifs)tapered barrel $175.00

ST.P.B.& T.RY – S 111 A&W Co. CHICAGO $55.00

SP&S – ADLAKE $42.00

ST P & S C Ry – S (serifs) tapered barrel with ring around $85.00

ST P U S Y CO – 477 ADLAKE $30.00

TAA&NMRR – S 286 tapered barrel with ring around ..$65.00

T&P.RY. – 10414 ADLAKE..$32.00

TRRA – 9918 ADLAKE $30.00

T.RR. A OF ST.L – S 4201, A &W Co. CHICAGO $55.00

U P – 23840 ADLAKE $15.00

U P RR – S 19544 A&W Co. CHICAGO........................$20.00

U.P.SYS. – 228 A&W Co. CHICAGO.............................$20.00

U S T V A – 814 FRAIM (in banner) $18.00

V G N RR – ADLAKE...$38.00

VRR – S 5884 big round bow $35.00

WAB.RR – S (serifs) 2104 M M BUCK & CO. ST. LOUIS, MO. tapered barrel (iron key) $115.00

W C RY – LOEFFELHOLZ CO. $30.00

W M RR – 78 ADLAKE $22.00

W P RR – 11711 ADLAKE $35.00

W&STPRR – S (serifs) WILSON BOHANNAN BROOKLYN, NY, ring around barrel $150.00

Caboose, Coach & Miscellaneous

(Brass unless otherwise noted)

Long Barrel

B&ORR – B No 107, 3⅛" long, hollow barrel, coach, no mfr $22.00
BNINCGN – (dble marked) ADLAKE, 3¾"L, solid barrel, caboose..$20.00
CNR – MITCHELL, Canada, 4"L, solid barrel, caboose..$15.00
CNR – MITCHELL, Canada, 4"L, hollow barrel, coach..$20.00
CMSPR – ADLAKE, 3⅝"L, solid barrel, caboose $18.00
CMSP&P – ADLAKE, 3¾"L, solid barrel, steel, caboose..$12.00
ICRR – ADLAKE, 3¾"L, solid barrel, caboose.............$15.00
L&NR.R. – SPECKMANN, LOU.KY. 3¾"L, solid barrel caboose $22.00
PRR – no mfr's. name, 3¾"L, solid barrel, caboose $18.00
NP – ADLAKE, 3¾"L, solid barrel, steel, coach...........$22.00
NYC – ADLAKE, 3¾"L, solid barrel, steel, coach $15.00
SOO LINE – KELINE, 4¼"L, solid barrel, caboose.....$18.00
WC – ADLAKE, 3½"L, solid barrel, caboose $25.00
UNMARKED – ADLAKE, 3¾"L, solid barrel, caboose ..$8.00
UNMARKED – LOEFFELHOLZ & CO. 3½"L, solid barrel with rings around, coach $10.00

Short Barrel and Flats

C M&S TPRR – BCC (baggage car cellar) hollow barrel, 2"L........$50.00
FRISCO – YALE, flat key, 2¼"L with Cotton Belt Route tag attached $35.00
GNRR – hollow barrel, 1¾"L, shanty key....................$15.00
ICRR – D 380, hollow barrel, 1¾"L, signal box $20.00
GN – solid barrel, 2¾"L, shanty use $12.00
M&STLRR – Road Dept., hollow barrel, 1½"L $45.00
NPRY – US MAIL CAR, hollow barrel, dble. bit, 1⅝"L $85.00
NPR – SIGNAL, flat key, 2"L.......................................$10.00
N.P.S.1 – 36 hollow barrel, 2"L, signal $28.00
P.R.R. – Y65 hollow barrel, 1¾"L, steel, general use $10.00
PRR – GRAND MASTER, flat key, 2¼"L, signal use $10.00
PULLMAN – F315, flat key, locker use.........................$12.00
RY.EX.AGY. – OR253, hollow barrel, 1¾"L, steel, express lock..$20.00
STLSWRY Co. – 4239, solid barrel, 1⅞"L, steel, signal use $25.00
W.F.& Co. – 2881, hollow barrel, 2"L, express lock, JHW CLIMAX CO $135.00

It is recommended that those who are into switch keys subscribe to *Key, Lock & Lantern*, P.O. Box 507, Chatham, NJ 07928-0507 to learn to differentiate between authentic and bogus keys. The buyer should beware when dealing with keys.

Berth and Compartment Keys

Berth Key – T-shape, 3 x 4", two-color brass, unmarked $25.00
Berth and Compartment Key – cross shape, 4 x 6½", iron with brass end, unmarked $35.00

Berth and Compartment Keys

Lamps

The classification lamps displayed at the front of the steam locomotives, the marker lamps that hung on the rear of the caboose or tail end of the passenger trains, the lamps used on switch-stands and signal semaphores, the interior lamps used in the caboose and coaches, and the track-walker's and inspector's lamps, all are being collected today. They bring top prices when found in their all-original condition, especially when bearing a railroad marking.

Classification Lamps, Steam Locomotive Era

A pair of these lamps was displayed on the front end of the locomotive to indicate its running classification at night, such as white (clear) lenses having superiority, green as an extra train, red when locomotive is running backwards. Each lamp has two round clear lenses and a cast iron bracket for mounting the lamp in place on the engine. Several single oil burning and electric models are listed here; a matched pair would have twice the value.

Engine Classification Lamps – Oil and Electric

CM&StPRY – no mfr's name, sheet metal, cyl. body type, flat hg'd. top, cast iron base with mounting bracket, electric, two clear lenses, inside frame contains red/green panes for exterior lenses' color change $275.00

E.J.& E.Ry.Co. – DRESSEL, sheet steel, cyl. body type, high domed top, cast iron base with bracket, oil burning, two exterior clear lenses, inside pocket contains red/green panes to place behind clear lenses for color change, ca. 1900...$325.00

M. SO.R.R. – ADLAKE, sheet metal, cyl. body type, high domed top, cast iron base and mounting bracket, oil burning, two clear ext. lenses, inside slots have removable red/green glass slides for color change, early 1900's $375.00

UNMARKED – PYLE-NATIONAL CO., Chicago, Pat'd. 1924, cast iron, "divers helmet" style, electric, two exterior clear lenses, two flip levers to move inside round green circle for lens color change, two iron brackets extend from base..$250.00

UNMARKED – ADLAKE, steam loco tender classification lamp, "cannon ball" style, cast aluminum, electric model, four lenses, two green, two red, bottom has round knob spring plunger to lock on electric bulb base rear corner of tender $150.00

Marker Lamps – Steam Era

These are made of sheet metal, cylinder style body, generally finished in black, having red, green and amber colored lenses, a cone-shaped or squared-top vent, hinged or sliding door to remove oil fount and burner, and a detachable iron bracket fitted around base for mounting. A pair of these lamps was displayed at the tail end car of passenger trains or on the rear of the caboose of freights to indicate their classification. Prices listed here are for a single lamp, undamaged and complete with colored lenses and oil burning fount. A matched pair marked LEFT and RIGHT would have twice the value.

B.R. – embossed at side of vent, ADLAKE on square top, four lenses – three green 5⅜"d, one red 6⅜"D, black finish $175.00

C&N.W.R.R. – embossed at side of vent ADLAKE on square top, four lenses – 5⅜"D. – two red, two green, black finish $150.00

C.P.R. – PIPER, MONTREAL emb. on sliding door, HLP M on round top, four lenses – 5⅜"D – two red, two green, black finish $145.00

CRI&PRR – embossed on sliding door, HANDLAN on round top, four lenses – 5⅜"D. – two red, two green, black finish $150.00

G.N.RY. – embossed at side of vent, ADLAKE on square top, four lenses 5⅜"D – two red, two green, black finish..$175.00

MSTP&SSTMRR – embossed on sliding door, ADLAKE on round top, four lenses – three green 4⅛"D, one red 5⅜"D, matched pair marked RIGHT on one, LEFT on other, black finish..$500.00

NPRY – embossed at side of vent, ADLAKE on square top, four lenses 5⅜"D – three green, one red, black finish ..$175.00

PRR – embossed Keystone logo on round tag at side near vent, ADLAKE on round top, single lens-style, one red 5⅜"D, bracket at rear, yellow enameled $85.00

SOO LINE – embossed at side near base, DRESSEL on round top, four lenses 5⅜"D – two red, two green, black finish $175.00

Pair of Tail-End Marker Lamps

UNMARKED – ADLAKE on round top, three lens-style, 5⅜"D – one red, two amber, green paint, early 1900 Pat. dates on brass plate of vent cone..........................$130.00

Switch-Stand Lamps – Steam Era

These are on the same order as the marker lamps except they were for switches on the main line or in the yards and mounted on the switch-stand posts. Each lamp has four lenses, a combination of two red and two green or two amber. Some are found equipped with metal discs of matching enameled colors attached around the lens to serve as day signals. Prices listed here are for lamps in their original condition. Those that have cracked lenses, missing parts and in poor shape, have lesser value and must be discounted in price.

CM&StP RY – embossed on hg'd. vent with fluted top, no maker's name. Four lenses – two red 5⅜"D, two green 4½"D, cast iron base with spring socket that locks on square tip of switch-stand post $200.00

DM&IR – embossed on side of vent, ADLAKE on square top, four lenses – two red 4½"D, two green 4⅛"D, four enameled metal discs, two red, two green, 8¾"D, bell bottom base 7"D, with two tubular holes to fit switch-stand fork mount..$185.00

GNRY No.4 – embossed on side of body, ADLAKE on square top, four lenses – two red 5⅜"D, two green 5"D, round flat bottom 6½"D with two holes to fit switch-stand fork mount $165.00

M&STL RWY CO – embossed on sliding door, HANDLAN on round top, four lenses – two blue, two amber, 5⅜"D, four enameled metal discs, two white, two yellow, 9¾"D, round flat bottom 6½"D with two holes to fit switch-stand fork mount, lamp used for repair track switch (scarce) ..$200.00

Switch-Stand Lamps

NP – stamped on bottom, ADLAKE embossed on top, cannon-ball type, hollow "dummy" with four plastic reflective lenses, two red, two green, 5⅜"D, cast iron base with two holes to fit switch-stand fork mount $35.00

ROCK ISLAND LINES – embossed on cyl. body, ADLAKE on round top, four lenses – two amber, two green, 4½"D, bottom is 4"D with attached iron base to fit over square tip of switch-stand post $155.00

SOO LINE – embossed above lens, ARMSPEAR on hg'd vent with round top, four lenses – two red 4½"D, two green 4⅛"D, bottom is 4"D with attached iron base to fit over square tip of switch-stand post $175.00

UNMARKED – ADLAKE on round top, four lenses – two red, two green, 5"D, bottom is 4¼"D with attached iron base to fit over square tip of switch-stand post, numerous Pat. dates on brass plate below lenses, last one is Dec. 18, 1906 ....$100.00

UNMARKED – W.R.R.S.CO. TYPE 1880 ELECTRIC SWITCH LAMP PC. 1880 – 1 raised on top, cast iron cannon ball-type, four glass lenses, two red, two green, 5⅜"D, bottom has attached round pipe base to fit over switch-stand post $65.00

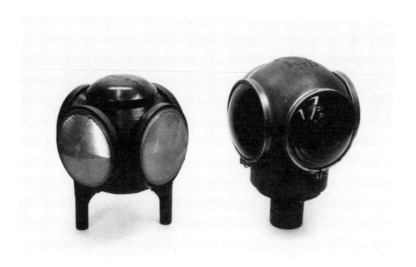

Cannon Ball-Types with Plastic and Glass Lenses

Semaphore Lamps, Steam Era

These were for use on semaphore poles, mounted behind the signal arms to illuminate their colored lenses. They were oil burning at first; many were electrified in later years.

CStPM&ORR – embossed above sliding door, ADLAKE on round top, cyl. body style, 6½"D, equipped with two clear 5⅜"D lenses at right angles, interior oil font, round peek hole glass in sliding door $185.00

GNRR – embossed on body near bottom, ADLAKE on squared top, cyl. body style, 6½"D, equipped with one clear lens 5⅜"D, interior electrified with porcelain socket, small round peek hole glass in sliding door $110.00

NPRR – on body near bottom, ADLAKE on squared top, cyl. body style, 6½"D, equipped with two clear lenses 5⅜"D at right angles, interior oil burning fount peek hole glass at rear $165.00

UNMARKED – ADLAKE on squared top, cyl. body style, 6½"D, equipped with two clear 5⅜" lenses opposite, interior oil burning fount, peek hole glass at side $75.00

Semaphore Lamps, Front and Rear

Inspector's and Track-Walker's Lamps

The inspector's kerosene lamp was used by railroad workers for checking the journal boxes on rolling stock. The lamp was equipped with a clear globe, a bright tin hood about 6" deep, and a 5" silvered glass reflector. The track-walker's lamp is much the same and made especially for inspecting tracks or for use on patrols. The back of the bright tin hood is formed into a reflector having a round opening in which is fitted a clear lens and a circular ruby slide to cover it to show a danger signal when necessary.

AT&SF – mk'd. on handle top, DIETZ ACME INSPECTOR LAMP, kerosene burning, equipped with a bright tin hood and silvered glass reflector at rear of wick $125.00

Track-Walker's Hand Lamp

CMSTP&P – mk'd. on handle top, STAR HEADLIGHT & LANTERN CO., Inspector's lamp, kerosene burning, equipped with a bright tin hood and silvered glass reflector at rear of wick $135.00

GNRY – mk'd. at side of hood, DIETZ ACME INSPECTOR LAMP, kerosene burning, equipped with a bright tin hood and silvered glass reflector at rear of wick.............$145.00

CNR – mk'd side of hood, E.T. WRIGHT CO. LTD. HAMILTON, CANADA, Pat. Feb, 1912, Inspector's lamp, kerosene burning, equipped with bright tin hood and silvered reflector at rear, 15" tall $125.00

UNMARKED – DIETZ ACME INSPECTOR LAMP, kerosene burning, equipped with a bright tin hood and silvered glass reflector rear of wick $50.00

UNMARKED DIETZ PROTECTOR TRACKWALKER LANTERN embossed on handle, pat'd June 26, '09, kerosene burning, equipped with a bright tin finished hood, the back has a 3"D clear lens with a circular ruby glass slide to cover for danger signal....................$130.00

UNMARKED – OXWELD RAILROAD LAMP embossed on top nameplate, Model A Union Carbide Lamp, 11½"H to top of handle, 6½"D base, 5¼" clear glass lens, cast aluminum $75.00

Wall Lamps

There were many special design wall lamps for the caboose, bunk cars, passenger cars, shanties, yard offices, and so on. Some examples are listed here.

D&RGW – raised on cast iron wall mount pot holder, 3½"H, 5"D, with eight oval openings around sides, two rear brackets for wall mounting, D&RGW raised on sheet metal insert fount, complete with chimney, for shanty or bunk car use $95.00

GNRY – embossed front on kerosene burning pot, 5"H, 4"D, flat steel ring to clamp around pot with diamond shape 4" backplate for wall mounting, standard glass chimney on burner, for shanty or bunk car use....................$50.00

NP – raised on cast iron wall plate pot holder bracket, brass adjusting knob on ring holds sheet metal pot intact, special 9"D metal shade fits around top of chimney with wall mount bracket, for interior wall, caboose or yard office $100.00

NP – raised on cast iron wall mount pot holder bracket, circular ring 4¼"D with turn-knob to clamp around kerosene burning fount, complete with cast iron/coil spring wall mounted chimney holder, for bunk car use $65.00

S P C O – embossed on wide tin backplate, V-shaped tin base 2¼"H, backplate top curves forward with round opening for chimney, circular tin smoke deflector at top, wall mount or table use $75.00

Bunk Car Wall Lamp

Caboose Wall Lamp

UPRR – embossed on wide tin backplate, V-shaped tin base 2½"H, backplate top curves forward with round opening for chimney, wall mount or table use $65.00

UNMARKED – brass candle lamp, THE SAFETY CO. NEW YORK, 6½"H, glass chimney 6"L, complete with candle and wall mount bracket, RPO car use $45.00

UNMARKED – caboose wall lamp, ALADDIN, aluminum 3" x 6½"D pot, burner, mantel, tall glass chimney, white 11"D parchment shade, wall mount spring tension bracket with wick and cleaner, complete $95.00

UNMARKED – Pullman compartment lamp, electric, brass wall plate 2 x 7½" with extended brass 3½" light socket and white plastic shade 2¾" high, complete fixture $55.00

UNMARKED – Pullman Co. special electric lamp, white metal, 9"H with half-round milk white glass shade, 5"D with clear round circle, designed for berth $150.00

Miscellaneous Lamp Parts

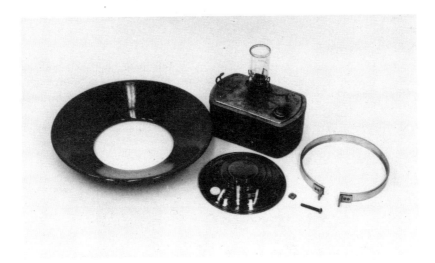

Switch Stand Lamp Parts

SOCKET – cast iron combination lamp and flag mount, 3 x 3 x 3½", front slot for lamp bracket, vertical hole for flag at rear, matched pair $50.00

SOCKET – cast iron mount for lamp only, flat type, 3½"H x 1½"W, matched pair $45.00

SWITCH LAMP FORK – for mounting lamp on switch-stand post, 6½" across, 9"H, incl. squared hole base $20.00

FOUNT – for switch-stand or marker lamp, square type 2½ x 3¾ x 6", with burner and 2½"H glass chimney, DRESSEL, HANDLAN, ADAMS & WESTLAKE or ARMSPEAR, mfgr's $30.00

FOUNT – for switch-stand or marker lamp, round style, 3¾"H, 4¼"H, 4¼"D, with burner and 2½"H glass chimney, same mfgr's as above $25.00

DAY TARGETS – steel discs with enameled colors – red, yellow, green or white, for switch-stand lamps, 9-10" diameter, each $20.00

COUPLING RING – narrow, about ½"W, 5"D, to mount colored glass lens on switch-stand and marker lamps ..$5.00

LENS HOOD RING – fits around lens without nut and bolt, wider at top, narrow at bottom $8.00

Glass Lenses
Unused, specs. as on backs

AMBER – 4½ x 3F CORNING PAT 10-10-05 ....$10.00
AMBER – 4½D x 3 F.S.O. 1935 CORNING $8.00
AMBER – 5⅜D x 3½" F.SO. CORNING $7.00
COBALT – 4½D x 3½ F.S.O. CORNING $18.00
COBALT – 5D x 3½ F.S.O. 1935 CORNING $35.00
GREEN – 4L 2¾F KOPP GLASS $8.00

GREEN – 4½L3½F KOPP GLASS $6.00
GREEN – 5⅜L 3½F KOPP GLASS $7.00
GREEN – 5D x 3½ F.S.O. 1935 CORNING $8.00
RED – 4½L 3F KOPP GLASS $5.00
RED – 5⅜D x 3½ F.S.O. 1935 CORNING $10.00
RED – 6⅜L 3¾F KOPP GLASS $15.00

Lanterns

The earliest lanterns used were the whale-oil type, with no special features. Gradually they were modified to railroad specifications. The railroads identified their lanterns by having their names stamped or embossed somewhere on the frame and also etched or cast on the globe. The manufacturer's name and patent dates are also found on most lanterns. The earlier lanterns came with tall globes; later ones had short globes. An all-original lantern with the railroad's name on both frame and globe brings the higher price. A restored lantern with an unmatched or unmarked globe is priced lower. Battery powered lanterns have replaced these oil-burning lanterns of yesteryear.

Key to Abbreviations

A&W – Adams & Westlake
BB – Bell bottom
P – Last patent date shown
NPD – No patent dates
DWG – Double wire guard
SWG – Single wire guard

Those desiring to learn more about lanterns should subscribe to *Key Lock & Lantern,* P.O. Box 507, Chatham, NJ 07928-0507.

Tall globe lanterns with round tin bottoms are also known as Bell Bottoms. Some have a fixed base with removable oil pot; on others the whole bottom twists off with oil pot intact.

Bell Bottom Lanterns

Bell Bottom and Wire Ring Bottom

AT&SFRY – (on tin bottom) no mfgr., NPD, red 5½" globe, AT&SFRY raised letters, SWG, fixed bottom with insert pot $235.00

B&ARR – (on lid) DIETZ No. 6, BB, NPD, clear 5⅞" globe, B&ARR raised, DWG, fixed bottom, removable pot..$225.00

BR&PRY – (on lid) C.T. HAM, BB, 1889P, clear 5⅜" globe, BR&PRY raised, SWG, fixed bottom, removable pot ..$375.00

CCC&STLRR – (on lid) HANDLAN BUCK "The Handlan" BB, 1909, red 5½" globe, CCC&STL raised, DWG, fixed bottom, insert pot $300.00

CM&StPRY – (on lid) brass top, BB, 1895P, red 5½" globe CM&StPRY etched, SWG, twist-off bottom with pot intact $325.00

CM&StPRY – (on lid) brass top, BB, 1895P, clear 5½" globe, CM&StPRY raised, SWG, twist-off bottom with pot intact $225.00

DM&NRY – (on lid) Armspear Mfg. Co., BB, 1913P, clear 5½" globe, DM&NRY raised, SWG, fixed bottom with insert pot $250.00

DM&NRY – (on lid) A&W, "ADLAKE" RELIABLE, BB, 1913P, red 5⅜" globe, DM&NRY raised, SWG, fixed bottom with insert pot $325.00

FRISCO – (on tin bottom) Handlan-Buck, "THE HAND-LAN," NPD, clear 5½" globe, FRISCO raised, DWG, twist-off bottom with pot intact $375.00

G.T.RY. – (on lid) A&W, "ADLAKE" RELIABLE, BB, 1913P, amber 5½" globe, GTR etched, SWG, fixed bottom with insert pot $350.00

MO.PAC. – (on tin bottom) brass top, HANDLAN-BUCK MFG. CO., NPD, clear 5½" globe, M.P. raised, twist-off bottom with pot intact $225.00

MRR – (on lid) DIETZ VESTA R.R. LANTERN, BB, 1896P, clear 5½" globe, MRR etched, SWG, twist-off bottom with pot intact $150.00

NYC&HRRR HD – (on lid) brass top, BB, no mfr., NPD, red 5¾" globe, NEW YORK CENTRAL raised, DWG, fixed bottom, removable pot $350.00

NEW YORK CENTRAL – (on lid) DIETZ No. 6, BB, clear 5¾" globe, NEW YORK CENTRAL raised, DWG, fixed bottom, removable pot $300.00

PRR – (on tin bottom) brass top, no mfr., NPD, clear 5½" globe, PRR raised, SWG, twist-off bottom with pot intact $225.00

SANTA FE – (on tin bottom) no mfr., NPD, clear 5¼" globe, Santa Fe cross logo raised, SWG, fixed bottom, insert pot $250.00

SANTA FE A – (on lid) A&W, the "ADAMS," BB, 1909P, clear 5½" globe, Santa Fe Route raised, SWG, fixed bottom with insert pot $375.00

Wire Ring Bottom Lanterns

Tall globe lanterns with steel wire ring base. Most have an insert oil pot while others have a twist-off bottom with pot intact. The globes are generally 5½"H in those with twist-off bottom; 5⅜"H in other frames.

B&MRR – (on lid) A&W "ADLAKE" RELIABLE, 1913P, clear 5⅜" globe, B&MRR in panel, SWG $150.00

B&ORR LOCO – (on lid) A&W, "ADLAKE" RELIABLE, 1913P, clear 5⅜" globe, B&ORR, SAFETY FIRST Capitol Dome logo at front, LOCO etched at rear, SWG.............$125.00

B&ORR – (on lid) Keystone Lantern Co., The "CASEY," 1903P, clear 5⅜" globe, B&ORR, SAFETY FIRST Capitol Dome logo, twist-off base with pot, DWG $185.00

BURLINGTON ROUTE – (on lid) A&W, "ADLAKE" RELIABLE, 1913P, clear 5⅜" globe, BURLINGTON ROUTE logo, SWG $225.00

C&NWRy – (on lid) A&W, "ADLAKE" RELIABLE, 1913P, clear 5⅜" globe, C&NWRy in panel, SWG $150.00

C&NWRy – (on lid) A&W, "ADLAKE" RELIABLE, 1913P, clear 5⅜" globe, THE NORTHWESTERN LINE logo and CStPM&ORy below at front, SAFETY FIRST rear, DWG...$375.00

CCC&StLRy – (on lid) A&W, "ADLAKE" RELIABLE, 1912P, clear 5⅜" globe, CCC&StLRy., SWG $125.00

CGWRR – (on lid) A&W, "ADLAKE" RELIABLE, 1913P, red 5⅜" globe, CGWRR in panel, SWG $250.00

CGWRR – (on lid) A&W, The "ADAMS," 1909P, clear 5⅜" globe, CGWRR in rectangle, DWG $165.00

CGWRy – (on lid) Armspear Man'fg. Co. NY, 1905P, clear 5½" globe, CGWRy. in rectangle, twist-off base with pot, DWG $175.00

CH&DRY – (on lid) A&W, "ADLAKE" RELIABLE, 1913P, clear 5⅜" globe, CH&DRY etched, SWG..............$155.00

CM&STPRY – (on lid) Armspear Man'fg. Co. NY, 1912P on base, red 5⅜" globe, CM&StPRy in panel, SWG..$225.00

CM&STPRY – (on dome top) A&W, Adlake RELIABLE, 1923P, clear 5⅜" globe, CM&StPRy. in rect., SWG...........$150.00

CM&STPRY – (on lid) Handlan, St. Louis, Pat. No's. on bottom, clear 5⅜" globe, CM&StPRy etched, SWG....$125.00

CStPM&ORR – (on lid) A&W, Pat. May 28, 1895, clear 5½" globe, CStPM&O in rect., twist-off base with pot, DWG...$175.00

CStPM&ORy – (on lid) A&W, "ADLAKE" Reliable, 1923P, red 5⅜" globe, THE NORTHWESTERN LINE logo and CStPM&ORy below at front, SAFETY FIRST rear, DWG...$525.00

D&H Co. – (on lid) A&W, "ADLAKE" RELIABLE, 1913P, clear 5⅜" globe, "The D&H" logo, DWG $175.00

D&IRRR – (on lid) A&W, "ADLAKE" RELIABLE, 1912P, clear 5⅜" globe, D&IRRR etched, SWG $275.00

D&RGRR – (on lid) A&W, The "ADAMS," 1909P, clear 5⅜" globe, D&RGRR, big, in rectangle, DWG $255.00

DL&WRR – (on lid) DRESSEL MF'G. CORP. NY, 1913P on bottom, clear 5⅜" globe, DL&WRR in panel, DWG ..$165.00

DM&NRY – (on lid) A&W, Pat. May 28, 1895, clear 5⅜" globe, DM&NRy in rectangle, DWG....................$285.00

ERIE RR – (on lid) C.T. HAM Mfg Co., 39 RailRoad, Pat. Dec. 26, '93 on twist-off base with pot, clear 5⅜" globe, ERRCo. in panel, DWG $150.00

GNRy – (on lid) A&W, "ADLAKE" RELIABLE, 1913P, amber 5⅜" globe, GNRy. SAFETY ALWAYS, etched, SWG..$375.00

GNRy – (on lid) A&W, The "ADAMS," 1909P, red 5½" globe, GNRy. in panel front, SAFETY ALWAYS at rear, twist-off base with pot, DWG $275.00

GNRy – (on lid) A&W, "ADLAKE" RELIABLE, 1913P, clear 5⅜" globe, GNRy. in panel front, SAFETY ALWAYS at rear, SWG $175.00

Dietz Vesta Lantern, 1896

GTR – (on lid) E.T. WRIGHT & CO. MFRS., Hamilton, Ont., no pat. date, clear 5½" globe, GTR at center, ETW & Co around top, DWG $130.00

Ia C Ry – (on lid) Armspear Man'fg.Co.NY., 1897P, clear 5¼" globe, Ia C Ry in rectangle, twist-off base with pot, DWG $300.00

ICRR – (on lid) A&W, The "ADAMS," 1889P, clear 5½" globe, ICRR big letters, twist-off base with pot, SWG $150.00

ICRR – (on lid) A&W, "ADLAKE" RELIABLE, 1913P, clear 5⅜" globe, ICRR in rectangle, SWG $115.00

L&NRR – (on lid) Armspear Man'fg.Co.NY., 1913P, clear 5½" globe, L&NRR in panel, twist-off base with pot, DWG...$175.00

LS&MSRy – (on lid) A&W, "ADLAKE" RELIABLE, 1913P, clear 5⅜" globe, LS&MSRy in rectangle, DWG ..$185.00

LVRR – (on lid) RR Signal Lamp & Lantern Co. NY, 1889P, clear 5½" globe, LVRR, twist-off base with pot, DWG...$175.00

M&StLRR – (on lid) Keystone Lantern Co. The "CASEY," 1903P, red 5½" globe, M&StLRy in rectangle, twist-off base with pot, DWG $325.00

M&STLRY – (on lid) Armspear Man'fg. Co. NY, 1905P, clear 5⅜" globe, M&StL Ry in rectangle, DWG $200.00

Lanterns with Fresnel Globes

MCRR – (on lid) Armspear Man'fg. Co. NY, 1897P, clear 5⅜" globe, MCRR in panel, twist-off base with pot, DWG..$175.00

MK&TRR – (on lid) HANDLAN, St. Louis, Pat. Nos. on bottom, clear 5½" globe, MK&TRR in rectangle, SWG $185.00

MO PAC – (on lid) HANDLAN, St. Louis, Pat. Nos. on bottom, clear 5⅜" globe, MP in panel front, SAFETY FIRST at rear, SWG...$165.00

NCRY – (on lid) RR Signal Lamp & Lantern Co. NY, 1897 P, clear 5½" globe, NCR, twist-off base with pot, SWG $225.00

NPRR – (on lid) A&W, The "ADAMS" 1897P, clear 5½" globe, NPRR big letters in rectangle, twist-off base with pot, DWG $250.00

NPRY – (on lid) Armspear Man'fg. Co. NY, 1889P, red 5⅜" globe, NPRR in panel front, SAFETY ALWAYS at rear, twist-off pot with 1910P, DWG $300.00

NYC&StLRR – (on lid) A&W, "ADLAKE" RELIABLE, 1913P, clear 5⅜" globe, NYC&StLRR in rectangle, DWG..$275.00

NYCRR – (on lid) A&W, "ADLAKE" RELIABLE, 1913P, clear 5⅜" globe, NYCRR in panel, SWG.......................$135.00

NYLE&WRR – (on lid) A&W, The "ADAMS," 1889P, clear 5½" globe, NYLE&WRR, twist-off base with pot, SWG $250.00

NYNH&HRR – (on lid) A&W, "ADLAKE" RELIABLE, 1913P, clear 5⅜" globe, NYNH&HRR in panel, DWG $175.00

P&RRY LOCO DEPT. – (on lid) Armspear Man'fg. Co. NY, 1889P, clear 5⅜" globe, P&RRY, twist-off base with pot and 1913P, DWG..$275.00

PERY – (on lid) A&W, "ADLAKE" RELIABLE, 1913P, clear 5⅜" globe, PERY etched front and SAFETY FIRST at rear, SWG $135.00

PRR – (on lid) Keystone Lantern Co., The "CASEY," clear 5⅜" globe, PRR Keystone logo, twist-off base with pot, SWG $225.00

PENNSYLVANIA LINES – (on lid) A&W, "ADLAKE" RELIABLE, 1913P, clear 5⅜" globe, PENNSYLVANIA LINES, SWG $200.00

PENNSYLVANIA LINES – (on lid) A&W, "ADLAKE" RELIABLE, 1913P, red 5⅜" globe, PENNSYLVANIA LINES, SWG $225.00

ROCK ISLAND LINES – (on lid) A&W, "ADLAKE" RELIABLE, 1913P, clear 5⅜" globe, ROCK ISLAND LINES logo, SWG $175.00

ROCK ISLAND LINES – (on lid in curved rectangle) Handlan Buck Mfg. Co. St. Louis, "The HANDLAN" no pat. dates, clear 5⅜" globe, ROCK ISLAND LINES logo on front, SAFETY FIRST at rear, DWG.....................$275.00

SOO LINE – (on lid) Armspear Man'fg. Co. NY, 1905P on base, red 5⅜" globe, SOO LINE in rectangle, twist-off base with pot, DWG $350.00

SOO LINE – (on lid) A&W, The "ADAMS," 1892P, clear 5⅜" globe, SOO LINE in panel front, SAFETY FIRST at rear, twist-off base with pot, SWG................................$200.00

SOUTHERN RY – (on lid) A&W, "ADLAKE" RELIABLE, 1913P, clear 5⅜" globe, SOUTHERN RY in panel, SWG $150.00

T&NORR – (on lid) A&W, "ADLAKE" RELIABLE, 1913P, clear 5⅜" globe, T&NORR in panel, SWG $185.00

UNION PACIFIC – (on lid) A&W, "ADLAKE" RELIABLE, 1913P, clear 5⅜" globe, UNION PACIFIC The OVERLAND Route shield logo, SWG $375.00

Short Globe Lanterns

These have a wire ring base with an insert oil pot. The globes are 3¼" high. Not many short globes were made with cast (raised) RR. initials. Some have etched letters, but most came without any railroad ID, showing only the mfgr's. hm'k. and/or ADLAKE KERO in raised letters. These lanterns are more plentiful than the tall globes and have lesser value. Those with a colored globe, of course, will bring a higher price.

AT&SFRY – (on lid) A&W, pat. dates, No.'s on bottom, clear globe, AT&SFRY raised in front panel, ADLAKE KERO rear $115.00

AT&SFRY – (on lid) HANDLAN, St. Louis, Pat. dates on bottom, red globe, AT&SFRY etched $100.00

B&ORR – (on dome top) ARMSPEAR MFG. CO. NY, "1925" clear globe, B&ORR etched $85.00

5BR – (on lid) ADLAKE KERO, Pat. date 3-59 on bottom, red globe, BR etched, ADLAKE KERO at rear $75.00

C&NWRY – (on dome top) ADLAKE No. 250 KERO, 1923P, clear globe, C&NW etched $85.00

C&O – (on dome top) A&W, Pat. dates, No's on bottom, clear globe, C&O etched $65.00

CB&QRR – (on dome top) A&W, ADLAKE No. 200 KERO, 1923P, clear unmk'd. globe, ADLAKE KERO $55.00

CGWRR – (on lid) A&W, Pat. dates, No's. on bottom, clear unmkd. globe, ADLAKE KERO $75.00

CNR – (on lid) HIRAM L. PIPER CO. LTD., Pat. 3-51 on bottom, clear globe, CNR in front panel, ADLAKE KERO rear $60.00

CPR – (on lid) HIRAM L. PIPER CO. LTD., Pat'd. 3-56 on bottom, clear globe, CPR in front panel, ADLAKE KERO rear $60.00

CMSTPRY – (on lid) A&W, 1923P, red globe, CM&STP etched $100.00

CMSTP&PRR – (on lid) A&W, Pat. dates, No's. on bottom, clear unmkd. globe, ADLAKE KERO $50.00

CMSTP&PRR – (on lid) A&W, Pat. dates, No's. on bottom, green globe, CMStP&PRR etched........................$145.00

CSTPM&ORY – (on dome top) A&W, ADLAKE No. 250 KERO, amber unmkd. globe, ADLAKE KERO $95.00

D&IRRR – (on dome top) A&W, ADLAKE NO. 250 KERO, 1923P, amber globe unmkd., ADLAKE KERO....$115.00

DM&IR – (on lid) ADLAKE KERO, Pat. dates, No's. on bottom, amber unmkd. globe, ADLAKE KERO $85.00

DW&PRY – (on lid) A&W, Pat. dates, No's. on bottom, clear unmkd. globe $75.00

GNRY – (on lid) DRESSEL, ARLINGTON, N.J., no Pat. dates, green globe, unmkd., ADLAKE KERO.................$95.00

GNRY – (on dome top) ADLAKE No. 250 KERO, 1923P, amber globe, GNRY etched, 1925 raised at rear ..$125.00

GNRY – (on lid) ARMSPEAR MFG. CO. NY., "1925," Pat. Feb. 2, 26 on bottom, red globe, GNRY raised, 1925 raised at rear $150.00

GNRY – (on lid) ARMSPEAR MFG. CO. NY., "1925," Pat. Feb. 2, 26 on bottom, clear globe, GNRY raised, 1925 raised at rear $110.00

ICRR – (on dome top) ADLAKE No. 250 KERO, 1923P, red globe, ICRR etched, ADLAKE KERO $100.00

M&STLRR – (on lid) DRESSEL, ARLINGTON, N.J., Pat. No. on bottom, clear globe, M&STLRR etched $105.00

Short Globe Kero and Battery Model

M&STLRR – (on dome top) A&W, ADLAKE No. 250 KERO, red globe, M&STLRR etched, ADLAKE KERO at rear $115.00

NP – (on lid) DRESSEL, ARLINGTON, N.J., Pat. No. on bottom, red globe, NP etched $95.00

NPRY – (on lid) A&W, Pat. dates, No's. on bottom, green globe, NPRY etched $145.00

NPRY – (on lid) A&W, Pat. dates, No.'s on bottom, amber globe, NPRY etched $125.00

NPRY – (on dome top) ADLAKE No. 200 KERO, 1923P, clear globe, unmkd., ADLAKE KERO $85.00

PRR – (logo on dome top) HANDLAN, St. Louis, Pat. dates on bottom, red globe, PRR Keystone logo etched $100.00

ROCK ISLAND – (logo on dome top) A&W, ADLAKE No. 250 KERO, 1923P, clear globe, R.I. LINES raised in panel front, ADLAKE KERO at rear....................$115.00

ROCK ISLAND – (logo on dome top) A&W, Pat. dates, Nos. on bottom, red globe, R.I.LINES raised in panel front, ADLAKE KERO at rear $135.00

SOO LINE – (big on lid) ARMSPEAR MAN'FG CO. NY, "1925," red globe, SOO LINE etched, 1925 raised at rear $125.00

SOO LINE – (on lid) DRESSEL, ARLINGTON, N.J., Pat. No. on bottom, blue globe, unmkd $100.00

SOO LINE – (on dome top) A&W, ADLAKE NO. 250 KERO, 1923P, clear globe, unmkd $85.00

S.P.CO. – (on dome top) A&W, ADLAKE No. 250 KERO, 1923P, green globe, unmkd...................................$90.00

Miscellaneous Lanterns With Uncommon Frames and/or Globes

A&StLRR – raised in rectangle on clear globe, 5½"H, cemented in frame, 12" tall, no wire guard, bottom twists off with glass fount, whale oil burner, tin hoop handle on dome, no mfr's. name, ca. 1850's, rare $1,500.00

B&ORR – on dome top, Armspear Mfg. Co. NY, "1925," no pat. dates, 3¼" blue globe, B&ORR etched, weighted iron ring base, 10"H to dome top $125.00

DW&P – (on lid) HANDLAN, St. Louis, no pat. dates, 4½"H, red (ringed) Fresnel globe, unmk'd., HANDLAN INC raised, round tin oil pot base, 2¼"H, 6"D $85.00

GNRY – big on lid, Armspear Mfg. Co. NY, "1925" red (ringed) Fresnel globe, 3¼"H, unmk'd..................$75.00

GNRY – stamped on side, ADAMS & WESTLAKE, "Adlake" No. 31-D, Pat. No., battery model $22.00

NPRY – stamped on side, CONGER LANTERN CO., Portland, Ore. Pat. No's., battery model $32.00

NYNH&H – on lid, DIETZ VESTA, NY. Pat. dates stamped on lid, 4¼" clear globe, NYNH&H raised in panel, DIETZ VESTA at rear, tubular frame, wire ring base, twist-off bottom with pot intact $100.00

UNMARKED – ADAMS & WESTLAKE, tall globe lantern, "ADLAKE" RELIABLE, 1913P, clear 5⅜" globe, unmk'd ..$50.00

UNMARKED – DIETZ NO 2 BLIZZARD (barn-type lantern) unusual for RR use, Pat. dates to 1934, tall blue globe 6¼"H, CM&STP etched, mfr's hm'k. at rear........$130.00

UNMARKED – DIETZ 39 STANDARD, tin (bell) bottom, 9½"H to dome top, 1910P, clear 5½" globe, unmk'd..$100.00

UNMARKED – C.T. HAM, No. 39 RAIL ROAD, brass top, tin (bell) bottom, 11"H to dome top, 1893P, clear 5½" globe unmkd., twist-off bottom with oil pot $115.00

UNMARKED – F.H. LOVELL & CO NY on dome, all yellow brass lantern, bell bottom-type, 5¾" clear globe, NEW YORK CENTRAL raised, DWG, bottom twists off with fixed fuel pot, whale oil, dble. round wicks, early, rare $500.00

UNMARKED – T.L. MOORE, tin (bell) bottom, 8"H to dome top, 1906P, clear 5½" unmkd. globe, oil pot withdraws from bottom, wood bail handle $75.00

UNMARKED – ADAMS & WESTLAKE "ADLAKE" RELIABLE, tin (bell) bottom, 9"H to dome top, 1913P, clear 5½" globe, unmkd., oil pot withdraws from bottom, wood bail handle $65.00

Conductor's Hand Lanterns

These are nickel plated over brass and generally smaller in size than tall globe lanterns. The globe is clear or sometimes half-colored, such as clear/green or clear/red. They are not railroad marked unless they were presentation pieces, with the name of the railroad and conductor on the globe or frame. Conductor's lanterns are hard to come by.

Conductor's Lanterns

ADAMS & WESTLAKE CO. – pat. Dec. 26, '64 on bottom, nickel plated over brass, closed (bell) bottom, 5¼"H half-colored globe, green/clear, unmkd., oil pot unscrews from bottom, bail attached to dome ..$750.00

ADAMS & WESTLAKE CO., CHICAGO – no pat. date, nickel plated over brass, closed (bell) bottom, clear unmkd. 5" globe, oil pot unscrews from bottom, bail attached to dome $350.00

ADAMS & WESTLAKE CO., CHICAGO – Pat. APR 26, '64 on bottom, nickel plated over brass, closed (bell) bottom, 5"H half-colored globe, green/clear with conductor's name engraved, bail attached to dome $950.00

M.M. BUCK & CO. – Makers, St. Louis, Opposite Post Office, Pat. Dec. 26 '65 on bottom, nickel plated over brass, open (wire ring) bottom, half-colored 5"H globe, green/clear, unmkd., oil pot unscrews from bottom, bail attached to dome $750.00

PULLMAN – raised on base, THE ADAMS & WESTLAKE CO., CHICAGO, Pat Apr. 26, '64 on bottom, nickel plated over brass, 5"H clear globe, PULLMAN etched, oil pot unscrews from bottom, bail attached to dome $450.00

UNMARKED – nickel plated over brass, Pat May 11, 1871 on bottom, closed (bell) bottom, clear 5"H unmkd. globe, twist-off bottom with oil pot, bail attached to dome $300.00

Spare Tall 5⅜" Globes with Raised Railroad Markings

Spare Colored Globes – Tall and Short Styles

BURLINGTON ROUTE – in square panel logo, clear ..$145.00
C.& N.W.RY. – in round ended panel, clear $85.00
C.St.P.M & O.RY. – "The Northwestern Line" logo, clear,
    SAFETY FIRST rear..$225.00
D.L. & W.R.R. – in round ended panel, clear, "CNX" hm'k.
    rear $100.00
G.N.Ry. – in round ended panel, clear, SAFETY ALWAYS
    rear $95.00

I.C.R.R. – in rectangular panel, clear $75.00
NPRR – in rectangular panel, clear, "CNX" hm'k. rear ..$85.00
SANTA FE – cross logo in square, clear "CNX" hm'd. rear ..$175.00
UNMKD – clear, "CNX" hm'k $20.00
UNMKD – green, round ended blank panel, "CNX" hm'k.
    rear, scarce $125.00
UNMKD – half-colored green/clear Conductor's globe,
    unmkd., very scarce $350.00

Spare Short 3¼" Globes, Railroad Marked

C & W.I. – etched, red, "K" hallmark , rear $45.00
N & W – raised in round ended panel, red "K" hallmark,
    rear $55.00
NYC LINES – raised in round ended panel, red, ADLAKE
    KERO, rear $65.00
SOUTHERN RAILWAY – raised, clear, "1925" at rear, "K"
    hallmark $35.00
U.P. – etched in round ended panel, clear, "CNX" hallmark,
    rear $15.00
U.P. – etched, red, "CNX" hallmark, rear $20.00
UNMARKED – clear, ADLAKE KERO $10.00
UNMARKED – red, ADLAKE KERO $20.00
UNMARKED – amber, ADLAKE KERO.......................$25.00
UNMARKED – green, ADLAKE KERO $30.00
UNMARKED – blue, ADLAKE KERO $35.00

Two-Color Conductor's Globe with Engraved Name

Locks

The earlier switch locks were all cast brass; later, they were made of iron or steel. Some were manufactured with a brass case and a steel shackle, or vice-versa. The all-brass, heart-shaped locks with raised railroad markings on them have now gone up in price considerably, especially those from short-lived defunct roads. Also, locks bearing authentic factory stamped railroad markings on the shackle or case from long-gone roads have increased in value. Other letters, such as an S, meaning "Switch," WD – "Western Division," RT – "Rip Track," and stamped digits 4-24 or 1934 for year issued, as examples, along with the maker's name or hallmark, and patent dates, will sometimes appear somewhere on the lock. The cover (metal tab that springs back in place over the keyhole when key is removed) protecting the exposed hole from the elements of the weather, is known as the drop. Some locks are found with a short length of iron chain still intact at the bottom, used for securing the lock to the switch-stand. Locks must be in overall excellent physical condition to warrant top prices. Those that are dented, have deep scratches, defaced or inoperative, are discounted in value. Rarities are exceptions. *Note:* A good source for keeping up to date on locks is to become a member of Key, Lock & Lantern, Inc., P.O. Box 507, Chatham, NJ 07928 – 0507.

Switch Locks (brass, heart-shaped)

B & M R R – stamped on shackle rear, Wilson Bohannan Co. Marion, Ohio, U.S.A. on shackle front \$55.00

B C R & M R R – incised on shackle front, ILLS MFG. CO., ADRIAN MICH. stamped next to key drop. (very rare) ..\$450.00

C & N W – stamped on shackle front, SLAYMAKER, LANCASTER, PA. on shackle rear..................................\$75.00

C.A.& C.R.R. – cast on back panel, A&W Co., CHICAGO, hex. h'mk on key drop. (rare) \$300.00

CM&ST.P.R.R. – cast on back panel, LOEFFELHOLZ & CO. on shackle front \$100.00

C.M.&ST.P.R.R. – cast on back panel, S.B. Co. diamond h'mk on shackle \$125.00

C M & St P Ry – stamped on back panel, LOEFFELHOLZ & CO. MILWAUKE on shackle \$80.00

C M ST P & P R R – stamped on shackle front, 4-56 HANSL MFG CO stamped on shackle rear.........................\$65.00

C ST P M & O RY – stamped on shackle rear, SLAYMAKER, LANCASTER, PA. on shackle front \$85.00

C R I & P R R – stamped on shackle front, UNION BRASS MFG. CO. CHICAGO on key drop \$175.00

D&SF – stamped on shackle rear, Eagle Lock Co. Terryville, Conn. U.S.A. on shackle front \$200.00

DL&W – stamped on shackle front, FRAIM on rear of the iron shackle \$85.00

G.N. R'Y. – cast ornately on backside, UL&K CO. LANC.PA. h'mk on shackle front. (rare) \$300.00

H & St J RR – stamped on pack panel, R.M. WOODWARD on the key drop, Pat. Aug. 23, 1853 on shackle front. (very rare) \$475.00

M R R. CO. – cast in back panel, MILLER LOCK CO. PHILA, U.S.A. on shackle, MILLER in script on key drop ..\$150.00

M & P Du C Ry – stamped on back panel, LOEFFELHOLZ & CO. MILWAUKEE on shackle \$130.00

M & I – stamped on shackle rear, SLAYMAKER, LANCASTER, PA. on shackle front..................................\$100.00

M & ST L R R – stamped on shackle front, A&W CO CHICAGO hex. h'mk on key drop \$125.00

M H C & W R R – incised on shackle rear, W. BOHANNAN, BROOKLYN, N.Y. Pat. June 25, 79 stamped on shackle front (very rare) \$485.00

MISSOURI PACIFIC LINES MAINTENANCE WAY – cast on entire backside, has iron shackle, 1927, no mfr....\$115.00

MStP&SSM RR – cast ornate over back, T.S. LOCK & M. CO. NEWARK, N.J. on shackle front. (scarce) \$275.00

M ST P R & D E T Co – stamped on shackle front, A&W CO, Chicago, hex. h'mk on key drop. (very rare) \$500.00

N&W R'Y Co – cast ornate over back, 1924, F S HDW CO. diamond h'mk on shackle \$100.00

Cast Brass Heart-Shaped Locks

N.P.R. – cast on back panel, FRAIM 1911 Keystone h'mk on shackle front \$165.00

N P R R – cast on back panel, no mfr \$150.00

N P R R – stamped on back panel, LOEFFELHOLZ & CO. on shackle front \$85.00

NORTHERN PACIFIC – cast in back panel, SWITCH raised each side of back panel, ADLAKE cast on key drop \$175.00

NORTHERN PACIFIC – cast on back panel with SWITCH raised each side of panel, M & I RY stamped on shackle front. ADLAKE cast on key drop (rare - double RR mk'd) ..$250.00

NYB&MRR – stamped on back panel, T. SLATGH, Pat. Dec. 29, 65, Newark, N.J. stamped next to key drop ..$175.00

P R R Co. – cast ornately on backside, FRAIM 1911, Keystone h'mk on shackle $100.00

S T L & S F – stamped on shackle front, no mfr $75.00

St.P.M&M – cast in back panel, Dayton Mfg. Co. stamped on key drop (very rare) $950.00

ST P M & M R R – stamped on shackle front, UNION BRASS MFG. CO. CHICAGO on key drop (rare) $450.00

ST P & P R R – stamped on shackle front, UNION BRASS MFG. CO. CHICAGO on key drop (rare) $500.00

St P & S C Ry – stamped on back panel, LOEFFELHOLZ 26 PRIER, MILWAUKEE on shackle (rare) $375.00

ST P USY CO– stamped on shackle front, A&W CO CHICA-GO hex. h'mk on key drop $65.00

SOO – cast on back panel, SLAYMAKER, LANCASTER, PA. on shackle front....................................$100.00

SO.PAC.CO. – cast on the key drop and on back panel, no mfr $125.00

SWIFT & CO – cast on back panel, MANF'D BY NATIONAL BRASS MFG CO. KANSAS CITY, USA stamped on key drop $75.00

U P R R SWITCH – raised on back, 1951 stamped on shackle, no mfr $125.00

UNIONPACIFIC – cast in back panel with SWITCH CS1 raised each side of panel, ADLAKE stamped on key drop..$125.00

UNION PACIFIC – cast in back panel, CLOSE THE LOCK TO GET KEY OUT cast on key drop, A&W CHICAGO hmk on shackle $125.00

W N R R – stamped on shackle rear, THE O.M. EDWARDS CO. SYRACUSE, N.Y. U.S.A. on shackle front, RAOWNYC trademark on key drop (rare) $250.00

Switch Locks (all steel, except as noted)

These are big round-bottomed steel clad standard type that have been continuously in production since the early 1900's and up to the present. Railroad markings are either stamped on the back or on the shackle, sometimes embossed on the key drop. Older styles have an extended steel swivel at bottom center with a chain attached. Later ones have a chain attached through two holes of the lock at bottom right. Patent dates, such as "Patented August 31, 1915" can be found on the backs of earlier locks, or a year date, such as 323, decoded as Mar 1923, stamped under the key drop. The more recent issues just have a row of digits, like Pat. 2040482, stamped on the back, or the year of issue, 1966 or 75, along with the letter S.

AT&SF S – on shackle front, 1965 on shackle rear, Slaymaker S-diamond h'mk on key drop, brass rivets $12.00

B&O – on shackle front, 1946 on shackle rear, Slaymaker S-diamond h'mk on key drop, brass rivets $14.00

BURLINGTON ROUTE – on shackle front, A&W CO CHICAGO h'mk on shackle rear, brass rivets $22.00

C & N W – Pat 2040482 on back, 154 under key drop, ADLAKE raised on drop $12.00

C & W I – Pat 2040482 on back, 77 on shackle rivet, ADLAKE raised on key drop $15.00

C B & Q RR – PAT SEPT. 24, 1912 on back, ADLAKE raised on key drop..$25.00

C G W – Pat 204082 on back, ADLAKE raised on key drop $20.00

C M ST P & P – Pat 2040482 on back, has brass shackle, ADLAKE raised on key drop $16.00

CMSTP&PRR – on back, KEYLINE raised on key drop, brass shackle...$15.00

C N R – raised on key drop, MITCHELL, CANADA h'mk. stamped adj. drop, AA340 on shackle rear $12.00

C ST P M & O RY – on shackle front, 1948 on shackle rear, Slaymaker S-diamond h'mk on key drop, brass rivets $25.00

D& R G W – Pat 2040482 on back, ADLAKE raised on key drop...$18.00

DSS&A RY – on shackle front, Patented August 31, 1915 on back, F S HDWE CO, Lanc. Pa. USA h'mk on key drop, brass rivets...$85.00

ERIE RR – on shackle front, 1966 on shackle rear, Slaymaker S-diamond h'mk on key drop, brass rivets $15.00

F E C RY – Pat 2040482 on back, 80 on shackle rivet, ADLAKE raised on key drop $12.00

FRISCO – Pat 2040482 on back, ADLAKE raised on key drop...$12.00

G M & O – on shackle front, 1966 on shackle rear, Slaymaker S-diamond h'mk on key drop, brass rivets........$15.00

G M & O R R – on shackle front, Made by the Yale & Towne Mfg. Co. USA on back, YALE h'mk incised below key drop, brass rivets, figure 8 style $36.00

G N RY – on shackle front, 1939 on shackle rear, F S HDWE CO. Lanc. Pa. USA diamond h'mk on key drop ..$22.00

G T W – PAT MAR 20, 1920 on back, 434 under key drop, ADLAKE raised on drop $16.00

I C R R – Pat 2040482 on back, 75 on shackle rivet, ADLAKE raised on key drop $12.00

I C G RR – Pat 2040482 on back, 75 on shackle rivet, ADLAKE raised on key drop $15.00

I H B RR – Pat 2040482 on back, 78 on shackle rivet, ADLAKE raised on key drop $18.00

L & A R R – on back, 76 on shackle rivet, ADLAKE raised on

key drop $15.00

L&NRR – on shackle front, 1967 on shackle rear, Slaymaker S-diamond h'mk on key drop, brass rivets $20.00

MO PAC LINES – Pat 2040482 on back, ADLAKE raised on key drop $18.00

MK&T – on shackle front, 1948 on shackle rear, Slaymaker S-diamond h'mk on key drop, brass rivets $20.00

M N & S RY – Pat 2040482 on back, ADLAKE raised on key drop...$35.00

M ST P & SSM RY – on brass shackle front, WC (Wisconsin Central) on shackle rear, FRAIM h'mk on back, brass rivets, double RR marked...$75.00

N & W – Pat 2040482 on back, 79 on shackle rivet, ADLAKE raised on key drop $12.00

N K P – Pat 2040482 on back, 364 under key drop, ADLAKE raised on key drop $12.00

N P SWITCH – Pat 2040482 on back, ADLAKE raised on key drop...$15.00

NORTHERN PACIFIC SWITCH – Pat 2040482 on back, ADLAKE raised on key drop $20.00

N.Y.C.S.MOON – incised on each side of key drop, CORBIN h'mk on drop, brass rivets $30.00

P R R – SLAYMAKER raised on key drop, brass rivets..$12.00

SOO LINE – on brass shackle front, FRAIM h'mk on back, brass rivets..$22.00

SOO LINE – Pat 2040482 on back, 75 on shackle rivet, AD-LAKE raised on drop $15.00

SOO SW – on shackle front, PATENTED AUGUST 31, 1915 on back, F S HDW CO. Lanc. Pa. USA h'mk on key drop and case, brass rivets $25.00

SO RY – on shackle front, Made By The Yale & Towne Mfg. Co. USA on back, YALE h'mk incised below key drop, brass rivets, figure 8 style $36.00

Standard Steel-Clad Switch Lock

SP CO– on shackle front, 1955 on shackle rear, Slaymaker S-diamond h'mk. on key drop, brass rivets..............$12.00

S S C S Y – on shackle front, Patented August 31, 1915 on back, F-S HDW.CO. Lanc. Pa USA h'mk on key drop and case, brass rivets $20.00

T P & W – Pat 2040482 on back, ADLAKE raised on key drop...$15.00

W P RR – on back, 323 under key drop, ADLAKE raised on key drop $18.00

Signal Locks

There are a variety of small padlocks classified as Signal Locks used to secure the electrical boxes on semaphores and for other purposes in the railroad's block system operating department. Most of these locks have a cylinder mechanism requiring a flat key to open them while others need a hollow barrel (HB) type key. All listed here are brass unless otherwise noted.

Brass Raco Signal Lock

AT&SF RY – stamped on bottom edge, EAGLE LOCK CO. TERRVILLE CONN. U.S.A. on shackle, EAGLE cast in rectangle on front and back, square shape $30.00

B&O – cast in circle on front, SIGNAL DEPT. incised, YALE cast in circle on back, THE YALE & TOWNE MFG CO. stamped on shackle, square type............................$25.00

B&ORR – stamped on front, RACO raised at side, white metal, takes hexagon wrench type key $15.00

BR&PRY – cast intertwined in circle front, SIGNAL DEPT. stamped below, YALE cast in circle on back, square shape $35.00

C & A SIGNAL – stamped on shackle, MILLER in script on key drop, small heart-shape, takes HB key...........$30.00

C. & E.I.R.R. – stamped on front, also XLCR trademark, no mfgr., square type...$32.00

C B & Q – stamped on front, RACO raised on side, white metal, takes hexagon wrench type key $15.00

CB&QRR – stamped on shackle, no mfr., small heart-shape, takes HB key $22.00

CB&QRR – embossed on key drop, Made in U.S.A. stamped on back, steel, brass rivets, round bottom shape, no mfr, takes HB key $16.00

CCC&STLRY SIGNAL DEPT – stamped in circle on front, YALE cast in circle backside, square type...............$30.00

C.R.I.& P. Signal – stamped on front, also XLCR through arrow trademark and "Use No Oil" at bottom edge, square type $25.00

C.ST.P.M.& O – stamped on shackle frontside, SIGNAL on shackle backside, MADE IN U.S.A. on back, no mfr, steel, brass rivets, round bottom shape, takes HB key $22.00

THE D&H – incised in script on front, SIGNAL stamped at bottom, YALE cast in circle on rear, THE YALE & TOWNE MFG. CO. on shackle, square type $25.00

DL&WRR – cast in back panel, REMOVE KEY WHEN LOCK-ING cast on key drop, no mfr., round bottom style, takes HB key...$35.00

D.M.& N. – cast on both sides of steel case, SARGENT, NEW HAVEN, CT. U.S.A. cast on front/rear of brass shackle, square shape $95.00

Brass Signal Locks

GNRY – stamped on front, RACO raised at side, brass, with brass hexagon wrench type key to open – both lock and key $30.00

G.N.RY. SIGNAL – cast in back panel, REMOVE KEY WHEN LOCKING cast on key drop, S (Slaymaker) h'mk., round bottom style, steel shackle, takes HB key $32.00

I.C.RR SIGNAL – raised on back panel, no mfr., small heart-shape, takes HB key $18.00

ILLINOIS CENTRAL SIGNAL – cast in back panel, REMOVE KEY WHEN LOCKING cast on key drop, S (Slaymaker) h'mk round bottom style, takes HB key $25.00

NEW JERSEY CENTRAL – stamped within circle on front, HARDENED on steel shackle, no mfr., square shape $20.00

NEW YORK NEW HAVEN AND HARTFORD RAILROAD – incised in script within circle, SIGNAL DEPT. above and below on front side, YALE cast in circle back side, square shape $30.00

NICKEL PLATE R.R. – cast in circle on front, SIGNAL DEPT. stamped around, YALE cast in back circle, The Yale & Towne Mfg. Co. on shackle, square shape $25.00

N.K.P. – stamped at top front, YALE cast in circle, THE YALE & TOWNE MFG. CO. on shackle, square shape ..$15.00

N.P.S.1 – stamped on shackle, MADE IN USA on back, no mfr., steel, brass rivets, round bottom shape, takes HB key $18.00

NYCS – stamped on front, RACO raised at side, brass, takes hexagon wrench type key $10.00

PENNA. LINES SIGNAL – stamped on frontside circle, YALE cast in back circle, square shape $25.00

P.& L.E.R.R. – cast in front circle with SIGNAL DEPT. stamped around, YALE cast in back circle, square shape......$30.00

ROCK ISLAND LINES Signal – incised on frontside, Mfr'd. by Corbin Cabinet Lock Co. New Britain, Conn. U.S.A. with patent No. 1849775 on backside, square shape $25.00

SOO LINE SIG – stamped on steel shackle, REMOVE KEY WHEN LOCKING cast on key drop, no mfr., small heart shape, takes HB key $38.00

SO. RY. SIGNAL – cast in back panel, A&W CO. CHICAGO, hexagon h'mk on key drop, large heart shape, takes HB key $55.00

U.P.R.R. CS-61 Use No Oil – incised on entire front, no mfr., small square shape $20.00

WABASH – flag logo cast in circle on front with SIGNAL DEPT. stamped around, YALE cast in back circle, THE YALE & TOWNE MFG. CO. on shackle, square shape..........$35.00

Miscellaneous

The railroads used many types of padlocks – Maintenance of Way, Road & Bridge Department, shanties, shops, depots, baggage or mail cars, and for other general purpose use. They came in a variety of shapes and sizes, made of all-brass, iron or steel, some a combination of brass and steel. Some required a flat key to open them, others needed a hollow barrel-type (HB) key. All of these old discarded railroad-marked padlocks have collector value now, and some are bringing very high prices.

AM.RY.EX – incised big on back, AM.RY.EX. stamped on shackle front, Pat 1-25-05 no mfr., steel, round bottom shape, chain, takes HB key $37.50

B & O R R – Pat. Jan. 31, 99 stamped on front, small round steel type, with brass rivets, shanty use, no mfr., takes flat key $15.00

Cast Iron General Purpose Lock

C&NW GENERAL PURPOSE – stamped on drop, steel, round bottom shape, brass rivets, EAGLE LOCK CO. TERRYVILLE, CONN. stamped on shackle rear, takes HB key $30.00

CB&QRR – embossed on drop, steel, square type with brass rivets, chain attached, shanty use, no mfr., takes HB key $35.00

CM&STPRR – cast in back panel, BAGGAGE CAR CELLAR cast on drop, brass, heart shape, chain at bottom, takes HB key $250.00

CM&STPRR – cast in back panel, REPAIR TRACK cast on drop, brass heart shape, chain at bottom, no mfr., takes HB key...$185.00

C ST P M & O RY – stamped on shackle, E.T. FRAIM LOCK CO. Lancaster, PA. stamped on drop, steel, round bottom shape, chain attached, gen'l use, takes HB key $30.00

CSTPM&ORR, PROPERTY OF COMPANY – cast on entire front above/below keyhole, W. Bohannan, Brooklyn, N.Y. on shackle, iron, heart shape, chain attached, takes flat key $85.00

D.M.& I.R. – cast on both sides of iron case, SARGENT, NEW HAVEN CT. USA raised on both sides of brass shackle, square shape, takes flat key $95.00

FRISCO – logo cast on front, DON'T USE OIL BUT PLENTY OF GRAPHITE incised on back, brass, square shape with pointed bottom, gen'l use, takes flat key $175.00

G.N.RY. – stamped on shackle rear, MILLER embossed on drop, MILLER LOCK CO. PHILA. USA on shackle front, steel, shield shape, shanty use, takes HB key $30.00

G.N.Ry. – stamped on back, U.S. MAIL CAR stamped on shackle front, Loeffelholz Co. Milw. on drop, small brass heart shape, takes HB key $75.00

G.N.RY – stamped on back panel, A&W Co. CHICAGO hex. h'mk on drop, brass, heart shape with over-sized steel shackle, box car door use, takes HB key $100.00

M & ST L RY – stamped on shackle front, F S HDW Co dia. h'mk on drop, steel, round bottom shape, takes HB key..$35.00

M & ST L R R – stamped on shackle front, B&B DEPT and FRAIM keystone h'mk on shackle back, brass heart shape, no mfr., takes small HB key $85.00

MSTP&SSM – stamped on shackle front, SHOREHAM SHOPS on drop, 1930 and F-S Hdw Co. diamond h'mk on shackle back, brass heart shape, takes HB key $150.00

N.P.R.R. – stamped on back, CORBIN on drop, brass, round bottom shape, chain attached, no mfr., gen'l use, takes HB key $55.00

PRR – Keystone logo raised on front, 2604F incised on back, heavy cast iron bulbous body with chain attached, keyhole on bottom within raised star $75.00

RY.EX.AGY. – incised big on back, RY.EX.AGY. stamped on shackle front, Pat 11-21-05, steel, round bottom shape, chain, no mfr., takes HB key.................................$37.50

SO. PACIFIC CO CS-44 ROADWAY & BRIDGE DEPARTMENT – cast on entire backside, ADLAKE stamped on drop, brass, round bottom shape, takes HB key $125.00

SOUTHERN PACIFIC – Sunset logo cast on front, brass, round bottom shape, no mfr., gen'l use, takes flat key...$115.00

Brass Baggage Car Cellar Lock

ST L & S F – stamped on shackle front, Slaymaker S-diamond hallmark on drop, 1954 on shackle rear, steel, round bottom shape, chain attached, maintenance shed, takes HB key $30.00

UNION PACIFIC CS-21 ROADWAY & BRIDGE DEPARTMENT – cast on entire backside, ADLAKE stamped on drop, brass, heart shape, takes HB key $125.00

W.F. CO.EX – cast in back panel, 2881 stamped on shackle front, steel, heart shape with brass drop, chain at bottom, no mfr., takes HB key $275.00

WESTERN UNION TEL. CO. – cast on back, PUSH SHACKLE IN TO GET KEY OUT incised on drop, 1946 stamped on shackle, brass heart shape, chain at bottom, takes HB key $75.00

Locomotive Builder's Plates

Locomotives have always been identified with the name of their builders by means of a metal plate mounted on each side of the smokebox. They were cast in all shapes and sizes, in various types of metals, with the name of the locomotive builder, serial number, location of the company, and year date of completion. Builder's plates from the steam era have now become scarce and have high value. Early diesel plates are starting to bring good prices, too. A few examples of plates from the more common producers are listed here. Reproductions have come on the market, so be wary.

Steam Era

Cast Bronze Steam Locomotive Plate

AMERICAN – AMERICAN LOCOMOTIVE COMPANY – serial no., Schenectady Works, July 1912, cast bronze rectangle, 7½ x 14" $300.00

BALDWIN – THE BALDWIN LOCOMOTIVE WORKS, curved at top, Serial No., Philadelphia U.S.A. across center, August 1914 at bottom, cast bronze disc, 9¼" dia.......$275.00

BALDWIN – BALDWIN LOCOMOTIVE WORKS curved at top, Burnham Williams & Co., Serial No. across center, November 1904, Philadelphia, U.S.A. at bottom, cast brass disc, 16½" dia $325.00

BALDWIN – built by THE BALDWIN LOCOMOTIVE WORKS Philadelphia, Pa., Serial No., August 1913, cast bronze rectangle, 3½ x 9", scarce $350.00

JUNIATA – JUNIATA SHOPS at top, B.6.SB across center, 9-1917 3316 at bottom, cast brass oval, 7½ x 11¾"..$400.00

LIMA – LIMA LOCOMOTIVE WORKS, Incorporated, December, 1939, cast brass, diamond shape, 9¼ x 16"..$375.00

PORTER – H.K. PORTER COMPANY, Pittsburgh U.S.A. 1750, cast brass, shield shape, 7⅞ x 8⅜".............$250.00

SHOREHAM – SHOREHAM SHOPS – M.ST.P. & S.STE.M.RY., Serial No., Built at SHOREHAM SHOPS, Jan. 1930, cast brass rectangle, 7 x 15½" $500.00

Diesel

ALCO-GE – AMERICAN LOCOMOTIVE CO. GENERAL ELECTRIC CO., Schenectady, N.Y. Serial No., May 1948, Alco & GE logos, cast iron rectangle, 6 x 12" $150.00

BLW – THE BALDWIN LOCOMOTIVE WORKS, 5-sided cast brass plate, pointed top shape, 14¾ x 10¼", Serial No., Baldwin-Westinghouse, Phila, U.S.A. Mar 1947, scarce......$300.00

GM-EMD – DIESEL LOCOMOTIVE built by ELECTRO-MOTIVE DIVISION, General Motors, Corporation, LA GRANGE, ILLINOIS U.S.A. CLASS 0-4-4-0, Serial No., 1-16-42, stainless steel rectangle, 4¾ x 14¾", silver printing on black...$100.00

GM-EMD – GENERAL MOTORS LOCOMOTIVES, DATE MAR 54 CLASS 0-4-4-0, Tons, Serial No. Electro-Motive EMD Division in center circle, stainless steel, elongated oval plate 4⅛ x 15", original red/blue colors on silver finish $75.00

Luggage Stickers

During the Golden Years of the passenger train, when travel by train was the way to go, colorful paper labels with a gummed back were handed out at the ticket counters to be pasted on suitcases and valises. It was a common sight to see these stickers on luggage everywhere, toted by tourists, advertising that they were riding the popular "name trains," and had been or were going to the many vacation spots throughout the country. These unused luggage stickers are now being sought after. Those from the steam era are harder to find and are worth more than those issued during the waning years of rail travel.

ALASKA RR – large oval shape, 4¼ x 5½", pictures Mt. McKinley in center with slogan "The ALASKA RAILROAD Mt. McKinley National Park Route" in red on black border (scarce) $27.50

BURLINGTON ROUTE – yellow/violet cut-out profile of Buffalo Bill with slogan, "Yellowstone Park via Cody Road," 3 x 4" $22.50

BURLINGTON ROUTE – round sticker, 3¼", aluminum foil type in blue, depicting the silver streamlined diesel-powered ZEPHYR built of stainless steel at center $10.00

BURLINGTON ROUTE – large rectangle, 3¼ x 5", logo on waterfall/canyon scene with slogan "CODY ROAD To Yellowstone Park" in yellow border $15.00

C&O – round red/white sticker, 2½", showing sleepy kitten within a heart entitled "Sleep like a Kitten," "THE GEORGE WASHINGTON, CHESAPEAKE and OHIO LINES" around border $8.00

C&NW – large round 4" red/blue sticker with "400" yellow streamliner pictured in center and slogan "The train that set the pace for the world between Chicago-Milwaukee-St.Paul-Minneapolis" around border $10.00

CHICAGO & NORTH WESTERN UNION PACIFIC – large red/black hexagon style sticker, 3 x 4", showing yellow streamliner, CITY OF DENVER, and slogan "World's Fastest Long Distance Train" $12.00

GN RY – large round sticker, 4½", side view of white mountain goat atop box logo encircled with red on yellow slogan, "SEE AMERICA FIRST, GLACIER NATIONAL PARK" ca. 1914 (rare)...$45.00

GN RY – large round sticker, 4½", front view of white mountain goat atop box logo encircled with black on yellow slogan, "SEE AMERICA FIRST, GLACIER NATIONAL PARK" ca. 1914 (rare)...$45.00

GN RY – multi-color rectangular sticker, 3½ x 4¾", logo centered on mt. scenery with slogan "GLACIER NATIONAL PARK, Route of the Empire Builder." $6.00

MILWAUKEE ROAD – round orange black sticker, 3¾", depicting HIAWATHA streamlined steam train No. 1 at center, with "Nothing Faster On Rails" below........$12.00

MILWAUKEE ROAD – round sticker, purple/orange colors, 3½", depicting the electric train, "OLYMPIAN" in black $14.00

MILWAUKEE ROAD – orange/maroon round sticker, 3½", picturing streamlined steam train with slogan "The HIAWATHAS 2 a day each way"...............................$12.00

MILWAUKEE ROAD – round sticker, 3¼", pictures orange diesel OLYMPIAN HIAWATHA in mtns. with words Chicago Milwaukee Twin Cities Spokane Seattle Tacoma Speedliner Service in border $10.00

Three Early Luggage Stickers

MO-PAC – cut-out sticker, 2¾ x 3¼", of black steam engine with red buzz-saw logo entitled "THE SUNSHINE SPECIAL" with ad copy below $22.50

MO-PAC – cut-out sticker, 2¾ x 3¼", of black steam engine with red buzz-saw logo entitled "THE SCENIC LIMITED" with ad copy below $22.50

MO-PAC – large red and white buzz-saw logo, 2¾"D $4.00

NORTH WESTERN UNION PACIFIC – round label type sticker, 3¼"D, with wavy border entitled "The Streamliner CITY OF DENVER," tourist ID label and streamliner pictured in center $5.00

NORTH WESTERN UNION PACIFIC – round label type sticker, 3¼"D, with wavy border entitled "The Streamliner CITY OF LOS ANGELES," tourist ID label and streamliner pictured in center $5.00

PRR – Keystone logo shape, 2 x 2", "Travel By Train" PENNSYLVANIA RAILROAD, white letters on burgundy $4.00

SANTA FE – square type 3 x 3¾", blue and silver field with red Indian and silver logo at center, entitled "SUPER CHIEF" $6.00

SANTA FE – round sticker, 3", red logo on yellow at upper right, entitled "EL CAPITAN" in white on black $4.00

SANTA FE – round blue sticker, 3", with Indian and logo, entitled "TEXAS CHIEF"...$6.00

SANTA FE – round Indian motif sticker, 3½" white/orange/blue, "THE CALIFORNIA LIMITED" around logo in center $10.00

SANTA FE – blue/silver rectangle, 3 x 3¾", aluminum foil type, logo at top, Indian motif below, "SUPER CHIEF" in red across center $8.00

SP – yellow rectangle, 4 x 4", stylized orange/black locomotive front with slogan above "Southern Pacific DAYLIGHT Los Angeles San Francisco," tourist's ID label at bottom..$15.00

SP – round logo, 2¼"D, "SOUTHERN PACIFIC LINES" in blue, white and gold $4.00

WP&YR – round red/blue sticker, 3¼"D, showing pass. train on trestle in mtns. with WHITE PASS & YUKON ROUTE in white letters around (scarce) $37.50

WP&YR – round red sticker, 3¼"D, with photo of Lake Atlin in center, ATLIN INN "White Pass & Yukon Route" in white letters around (scarce)..................................$27.50

Magazines

Literally thousands of railroad magazines were published over the years for both trainmen and the general public. Many were put out by the Brotherhoods for the engineer, fireman, carman and other members. The railroads themselves also published various inter-company magazines for their employees. Railroad magazines for the public, both pulp and slick paper, have been in publication from the turn of the century up to the present. The earlier issues containing interesting articles and ads in them are most in demand, bringing the highest prices.

Brotherhood and Railway Service Magazines

Early Brotherhood Magazines

FREIGHT-HANDLER'S AND RAILWAY CLERK'S JOURNAL, Vol. 4, No. 9, Sept. 1912 ....$6.00

BROTHERHOOD OF LOCOMOTIVE ENGINEERS JOURNAL, Vol. XXX. No. 4, April, 1896 ....$8.00

LOCOMOTIVE ENGINEERS JOURNAL, Vol. 54, No. 9, September, 1920 ....$5.00

LOCOMOTIVE ENGINEERS JOURNAL, September, 1923 ....$4.50

LOCOMOTIVE ENGINEERS JOURNAL, September 1930 ....$3.50

LOCOMOTIVE ENGINEERS JOURNAL, March 1940 $2.00

BROTHERHOOD OF LOCOMOTIVE FIREMEN'S MAGAZINE, June, 1905...$6.50

BROTHERHOOD OF LOCOMOTIVE FIREMEN AND ENGINEMEN'S MAGAZINE, October, 1911 ....$6.00

BROTHERHOOD OF LOCOMOTIVE FIREMEN AND ENGINEMEN'S MAGAZINE, August, 1912 ....$5.00

THE RAILWAY AGE MONTHLY AND RAILWAY SERVICE MAGAZINE, Vol. 111, No. 3, Mar. 1882 ....$12.00

THE RAILWAY AGE WEEKLY, Vol. X, No. 29, July 16, 1885 ....$10.00

RAILWAY CARMEN'S JOURNAL, May, 1908 ....$7.50

THE RAILWAY CLERK, Vol. X1X, No. 7, June 1, 1920 ....$4.50

RAILROAD TRAINMEN'S JOURNAL, Vol. x1, No. 120, February, 1894...$10.00

RAILROAD TRAINMEN'S JOURNAL, Vol. XX, No. 5, May, 1903 ....$6.00

RAILROAD TRAINMEN'S JOURNAL, Vol. XX1, No. 3, March, 1904..$5.00

THE RAILROAD TRAINMAN, Vol. 47, No. 2, February, 1930 ....$3.00

THE RAILROAD TRAINMAN, Vol. 57, No. 1, January, 1940 ....$2.50

Inter-Company

BALTIMORE & OHIO MAGAZINE – Dec. 1941, Christmas issue $5.00

CHICAGO GREAT WESTERN RAILWAY SAFETY NEWS – Vol. 6, Nos. 11 and 12, Nov. Dec. 1960 ....$4.00

GREAT NORTHERN GOAT – Vol. 7, No. 4, April 1930, Special Edition $6.00

GREAT NORTHERN GOAT – Vol. 8, No. 10, Summer, 1937...$5.00

GREAT NORTHERN GOAT, Vol. 11, No. 7, December-January, 1940-1941 ....$4.00

GREAT NORTHERN GOAT – Vol. 15, No. 12, December, 1945...$3.00

GREAT NORTHERN GOAT – Vol. 20, No. 12, December, 1950...$2.50

MAINE-CENTRAL RAILROAD EMPLOYEES MAGAZINE – Vol. 3, No.'s 1-12, Oct. 1946-Sept. 1947, complete set $15.00

THE MILWAUKEE RAILWAY SYSTEM EMPLOYEES' MAGAZINE – Vol. V, No. 9, Dec. 1917 ....$5.00

THE MILWAUKEE ROAD MAGAZINE – Vol. 45, No. 4, July-August 1957 ....$3.00

THE MILWAUKEE ROAD MAGAZINE – Vol. 58, No. 4, Sept-Oct. 1970..$2.00

NORTH WESTERN RAILWAY MAGAZINE – C&NW RR, Vol. 1, No. 10, October, 1923 ....$5.00

NORTH WESTERN RAILWAY MAGAZINE – C&NW RR, Vol. II, No. 10, October, 1924 ....$4.00

ROCK ISLAND EMPLOYEES' MAGAZINE – CRI&P RR, December 1908 ....$8.00

Railway Employee Magazines

ROCK ISLAND EMPLOYEES' MAGAZINE – CRI&P RR, June 1909 ....$6.00

ROCK ISLAND EMPLOYEES' MAGAZINE – CRI&P RR, 70th Anniversary number, Oct. 1922 ....$30.00

THE FOUR-TRACK NEWS – NYC&HR RR, Vol. 111, No. 3, September, 1902..$5.00

THE FOUR-TRACK NEWS – NYC&HR RR, Vol. IV, No. 4, April, 1903 ....$4.00

Public

MODERN RAILROAD – March, 1955 ....$3.00

RAILROAD MAGAZINE (pulp) – May, 1942 ....$5.00

RAILROAD MAGAZINE (pulp) – complete set, Jan.-Dec., 12 x $6.00 = $72.00, 1938 ....$72.00

RAILROADMAN'S MAGAZINE (pulp) – March,1939 ..$6.00

RAILROAD STORIES (pulp) – May, 1932....................$7.00

RAILROAD STORIES – 12 copies, complete, 12 x $7.00 = $84.00, 1934 ....$84.00

RAILWAY PROGRESS – complete set, Jan-Dec., 1954 ..$12.00

TRAINS MAGAZINE – (small) February, 1944 ....$5.00

TRAINS MAGAZINE – (large) January, 1952...............$3.00

TRAINS MAGAZINE – (small) 9 copies, bound, Vol. I, Nov. 1940-July 1941..$50.00

TRAINS MAGAZINE – (large) 12 copies, bound, Vol. 27, Nov. 1966-Oct. 1967 ....$30.00

Boy's Weeklys

A series of nickel and dime novels, published weekly for the American youth, were issued around the turn of the century, with names such as PLUCK AND LUCK, WORK AND WIN, BRAVE AND BOLD, to name a few. These early pulps had eye-catching front covers with illustrations of exciting railroad scenes, and are being picked up, too. Copies of all these various magazines in fine condition are bringing good prices today.

Boy's Weeklys

BUFFALO BILL WEEKLY – "Buffalo Bill At Canon Diablo," No. 246, May 26, 1917...............................$10.00

BUFFALO BILL WEEKLY – "Buffalo Bill's Transfer," NO. 247, June 2, 1917.......................................$10.00

FAME AND FORTUNE WEEKLY – "Striking His Gait," or "The Perils of a Boy Engineer," No. 570, September 1, 1916 ....$12.00

PLUCK AND LUCK – "Sam Strap, The Young Engineer," or "The Luckiest Boy On The Road," No. 393, December 13, 1905 ....$15.00

PLUCK AND LUCK – "Dick, The Apprentice Boy," or "Bound To Be An Engineer," No. 405, March 7, 1906 ....$15.00

PLUCK AND LUCK – "True As Steel," or "Ben Bright, The Boy Engineer," No. 423, July 11, 1906....................$15.00

THE GEM LIBRARY – "Dick, The Boy Engineer," or "On The Right Track," Vol. 111, No. 2, April 11, 1896 ....$20.00

TIP TOP WEEKLY – "Frank Merriwell's Advancement," or "Engineer Of The Mountain Express," No. 124, August 27, 1898 ....$18.00

WORK AND WIN – "Fred Fearnot's New Trouble," or "Up Against A Monopoly," No. 211, December 19, 1902 ....$15.00

Maps

Roll-down maps were issued by the railroads for use in classrooms, libraries, offices, wherever. Large system maps hung on the walls of railroad ticket offices and depots. Tourist travel brochure maps were handed out freely by the railroads. Private firms also published railroad maps for the public's use. You will also find railroad commissioner's state maps and a wide variety of other railroad maps issued down through the years. Some examples and prices are listed here. The early rare maps, of course, bring the higher prices.

Roll-Down Wall Type

BN – Roll-down map of the United States showing Road's system in red, 39" x 62", logo and BURLINGTON NORTHERN in lower right corner, Rand McNally, 1971, grey metal rods $15.00

MP – roll-down Rand McNally Co.'s Cosmopolitan World Map, 38 x 51", has Missouri Pacific Lines logo at bottom center with slogan – Now More Than Ever "A Service Institution," wood rods $30.00

PRR – roll-down map of the U.S. showing The Pennsylvania Railroad and Connections in red, logo, 56 x 34", canvas-backed paper, wood rods, J.W. Clement Co. Matthews-Northrup Works, Buffalo, N.Y. $35.00

SP – roll-down map of the U.S. showing routes in red, 40 x 51", SOUTHERN PACIFIC LINES across top and logo at right-hand side, Rand McNally, Chicago, 1952, wood rods...$37.50

UP – roll-down map of the U.S. showing Road's system in red, 40 x 62", UNION PACIFIC RAILROAD across top and logo in right-hand side, Rand McNally, grey metal rods, recent $20.00

Tourist's Travel Brochure Maps

Tourist Maps

BURLINGTON ROUTE – tourist's MAP of the United States and Vacation Guide, unfolds 19 x 37", dated 1938, The National Park Line, Everywhere West....................$10.00

C&NW – tourist's MAP of the United States issued by the Chicago and North Western System, unfolds 19 x 32", dated 2-'53 ....$8.00

GN – tourist's MAP of the United States "showing how GREAT NORTHERN RAILWAY serves the Great Northwest," unfolds 18 x 32", dated 1935, Route of the Air-Conditioned EMPIRE BUILDER and other fine trains $15.00

GN – tourist's GREAT NORTHERN RAILWAY Map of the United States, "You go GREAT when you go GREAT NORTHERN," unfolds 18 x 31", dated 1957 ....$6.00

GN – tourist's GREAT NORTHERN RAILWAY AEROPLANE MAP Glacier National Park, Waterton Lakes Park, "The Route of the Empire Builder," unfolds 18 x 31½", dated 3-38 ....$10.00

L&N – tourist's MAP of Florida and the GULF COAST, Including the territory from NEW ORLEANS to Havana, Louisville & Nashville RR. booklet, 23 pages, opens flat 8 x 9", dated 1926..$12.00

ROCK ISLAND – tourist's A MAP that talks – First Aid in Planning Trips Anywhere in the U.S.A., unfolds 18 x 23", dated 1923 ....$12.00

SP – tourist's MAP OF CALIFORNIA, with a brief description of its RESOURCES ATTRACTIONS TOPOGRAPHY AND CLIMATE, SOUTHERN PACIFIC, unfolds 21½ x 27" dated 1924 ....$10.00

UP – tourist's MAP of the UNITED STATES, UNION PACIFIC SYSTEM, unfolds 18 x 32", dated 1922, dark blue covers with logo in center $12.00

UP – tourist's MILITARY MAP of the UNITED STATES, Union Pacific Railroad, unfolds 18½ x 32", dated 1950, olive covers with logo in center................................$8.00

Sectional and/or Complete U.S. Map

C&NW – sectional Map of the Lakes and Resorts of Central Wisconsin reached by the Chicago & North-Western Railway, 20 x 22", dated 1904 ....$25.00

CRI&P – small map, 7 x 9½", showing routes of Chicago Rock Island & Pacific Railway Lines, EAST & WEST of Missouri River, copyright 1889 by E. St. John......................$12.00

M&S – section map of the MILWAUKEE & SUPERIOR RAILROAD and CONNECTIONS, It Being an Extension of the GREAT AMERICAN LAKE SHORE ROUTE to LAKE SUPERIOR, 1856, thin translucent paper, 33 x 39", rare $85.00

MKT – sectional Map of Texas traversed by the Missouri, Kansas & Texas Lines, Compliments of Jackson-Verrland Securities Co. Kansas City, Mo. 22¼ x 21½", dated 1908 ....$15.00

NP – small U.S. map, 5½ x 9" with a hunting dog pictured showing route of the Northern Pacific Railway starting from the dog's tail going along the back and ending at the nose, titled "MARK! When you want a Pointer regarding your western trip," copyrighted 1896 by Chas. S. Fee $18.00

Sectional Map, Dated 1904

NP – sectional land map of Eastern Washington and Northern Idaho, Traversed by the NORTHERN PACIFIC RAILROAD, unfolds 35 x 37", back side has advertising "Lands for Sale to Settlers," dated 1891 ....$30.00

SOO LINE – two logos, SOO LINE MAP OF MINNESOTA, "A Home For Everyone" across top, at bottom of map is "The Land of Opportunity," unfolds 18 x 32", backside has GOVERNMENT STATISTICS, dated 1914 ....$20.00

SOO LINE – two logos, SOO LINE MAP OF NORTH DAKOTA across top, at bottom of map is "The Land of Opportunity," unfolds 23 x 27", backside has "Facts about North Dakota Farm Lands," dated 1914 ....$20.00

RAILROAD COMMISSION MAP OF OHIO – steam railroads operating in Ohio, canvas backed, 30 x 34", copyrighted 1909 by Columbus Lithograph Co. $25.00

Soft/Hard Cover Book Types

Book Type – CLASON'S WYOMING GREEN GUIDE with Road and Railway Maps, unfolds to 17½ x 21" from soft cover, Publ. The Clason Map Co. Denver, ca. 1920.............$12.00

Book Type – CRAM'S TOWNSHIP and RAIL ROAD MAP OF WISCONSIN, 1885, unfolds to 19 x 24" from soft cover, Pub. by George F. Cram, Chicago (scarce) $30.00

Book Type – GOLDTHWAIT'S RAIL ROAD MAP of the NEW ENGLAND STATES, CANADA and EASTERN NEW YORK, unfolds to 18 x 24" from hard cover, Boston Redding & Co., 1850 (rare) $75.00

Book Type – topographic map of Glacier National Park, Montana, unfolds to 31 x 34" from hard cover, cloth backed, GREAT NORTHERN goat logo on cover, dated 1922 ....$25.00

Book Type – RAILROAD COMMISSIONERS' Official Map of Minnesota, May 1916, unfolds to 30½ x 47" from soft cover..$10.00

Hard Cover Unfolded Map, 1850

Medallions, Medals and Tokens

Railroads issued medallions, medals and tokens down through the years to commemorate special events in their history, anniversaries, advertising and World's Fair events. Most of the larger ones were made of bronze, smaller in brass, and in various diameters, few rectangular in shape, depicting locomotives and historical data. Special medallions were also issued to railroads for their safety efforts and prevention of accidents, also memorials. Prices are based on the scarcity of the medallion, medal or token. *Note:* Some of the large heavy medallions were also used as paperweights.

B&O – 100th Anniversary medallion, bronze, 2¾"D. Obverse: THE BALTIMORE AND OHIO RAILROAD COMPANY 1827-1927 around likeness of Peter Cooper's "Tom Thumb" locomotive in center. Reverse: ONE HUNDRED YEARS SAFETY STRENGTH SPEED around steam passenger train and flying nude figure above train in center. Maker: Medallic Art Co. N.Y. $125.00

B&O – aluminum token, 1¼"D, with Lincoln penny inserted in center. Obverse: BALTIMORE & OHIO RAILROAD "Century of Progress, Chicago, 1933" and two locomotives.

Reverse: B&ORR advertising....................................$18.00

BCR&N – advertising medallion, pewter, 2¾"D. Obverse: "Albert Lea Route" THE BURLINGTON CEDAR RAPIDS AND NORTHERN RAILWAY within wreath. Reverse: listing of cities served, North, South, East, West. Maker: S.D. Childs & Co. Chicago.......................$130.00

Centennial Medallion

C&NW – EDWARD H. HARRIMAN MEMORIAL MEDAL (medallion) 2¾"D. Obverse: Awarded by the American Museum of Safety to CHICAGO and NORTH WESTERN RAILWAY COMPANY, Harriman profile and torch in center. Reverse: trainman carrying lanterns and flag walking on RR track. Maker: Medallic Art Co. N.Y. $85.00

CM&StP – bronze medallion 3"D. with rimmed ½" edge. Obverse: box logo, THE CHICAGO MILWAUKEE AND ST. PAUL RAILWAY, "To Puget Sound" above, "Electrified" below. Reverse: SPECIAL APPRENTICES STAFF MEETING, MILWAUKEE around "1925 Courage, Character, Courtesy" in center. No maker's name......$125.00

D&H – 100th Anniversary medallion, bronze, 2½ x 4", round cornered rectangle; obverse: 1829-1929 and likeness of early locomotive across center, "The Stourbridge Lion" above, THE DELAWARE AND HUDSON COMPANY below. Reverse: The D&H logo and history of the locomotive's first run. Maker: Metal Arts Co. N.Y. $150.00

DM&IR – EDWARD H. HARRIMAN MEMORIAL MEDAL, bronze, 1¼"D. Obverse: Awarded by American Museum of Safety to DULUTH, MISSABE and IRON RANGE RAILWAY CO. Reverse: trainman carrying lanterns and flag walking on RR track. No maker's name (pocket piece) $25.00

GN RY – memorial medallion, bronze, 3"D., Obverse: MEMORIAL JAMES JEROME HILL around profile in center. Reverse: September 16, 1838 – May 29, 1916, "One of the World's Greatest Builders" within a wreath. Maker: Whitehead & Hoag...$160.00

IC – 100 Year's Centennial medallion, bronze, 3"D. Obverse: FOR 100 YEARS MAINLINE OF MID-AMERICA 1851-1951 around ILLINOIS CENTRAL diamond logo in center. Reverse: map of system inside wreath border. Maker: Robbins Co. Attleboro $65.00

IC – 100 Year's Centennial token, bronze, 1⅜"D. Obverse: FOR 100 YEARS MAINLINE OF MID-AMERICA 1851-1951 around ILLINOIS CENTRAL diamond logo in center. Reverse: map of system inside wreath border. No h'mk (pocket piece) $25.00

MILWAUKEE ROAD – souvenir medallion, die cast metal with copper finish, 3"D. Obverse: two streamlined steam locomotives abreast, "HIAWATHA NOTHING FASTER ON RAILS" above and below. Reverse: LUCKY SOUVENIR PENNY around running Indian figure in center. No maker's name $55.00

MILWAUKEE ROAD – bronze token, 1½"D. Obverse: CHICAGO MILWAUKEE, ST. PAUL & PACIFIC R.R. established 1850 around detailed streamlined steam locomotive in center. Reverse: box logo in center $15.00

NH – aluminum token, 1¼"D. Obverse: NEW HAVEN RAILROAD around streamlined steam locomotive in center. Reverse: "Compliments of the dining service" across horn of plenty motif in center. (scarce) $30.00

ROCK ISLAND – 70th Anniversary medal, bronze, 1¼"D. Obverse: 70th ANNIVERSARY 1852-1922 around logo in center. Reverse: Lincoln profile between two locomotives, RR bridge across center, "First bridge Mississippi river Rock Island Lines 70 Years of Service" at bottom, red/white/blue satin ribbon pinback intact in top slot $45.00

Aluminum Token – Obverse and Reverse

SANTA FE – progress token, coin-like with milled edge, brass, 1½"D. Obverse: 1868-1968 "Always on the move towards a better way," modes of transportation depicted. Reverse: 1968-2068 "Our second century of progress" around cross logo in center...................................$15.00

StLSW – advertising medallion, bronze, 3"D. Obverse: ST. LOUIS SOUTHWESTERN RAILWAY LINES in border, COTTON BELT ROUTE logo, diesel train, floral spray, lightening bolt and words "Blue Streak – Fast Freight" are arranged in center area. Reverse: blank. No maker's name $75.00

Front and Back of Anniversary Medal

UP – centennial medallion, bronze, 2½"D. Obverse: "Golden Spike Centennial Celebration Commission – The Oceans United By Railway" around likeness of golden spike, 1869-1969 in center. Reverse: two locomotives meeting on track and history of completion of line. No maker's name..$30.00

UP – centennial token, bronze, 1⅜"D, obverse and reverse same as above large medallion. (pocket piece) ..$10.00

UP – sourvenir token, aluminum, 1¼"D. Obverse: UNION PACIFIC 1934 Lucky Piece around diesel streamliner in center. Reverse: history data. Maker: Greenduck, Chgo..$15.00

UP – souvenir token, aluminum, 1¼"D. Obverse: GOLDEN GATE INTERNATIONAL EXPOSITION 1939, San Francisco Bay. Reverse: UP logo, two trains, advertising, name trains, etc. $12.00

UP – souvenir token, aluminum, 1¼"D, 1940 Luckey Piece. UNION PACIFIC logos, trains, slogans and advertising on both sides $10.00

UP – aluminum token, 1¼"D, front has CECIL B. DE MILLES MOTION PICTURE "UNION PACIFIC" around old-time loco. depicted in center; backside has logo between two locos., slogans and advertising $15.00

Passes

Passes were issued by the railroads down through the years to officials of railroads, newspapermen, politicians, clergymen, and other favored persons. The earlier passes having a picture of a locomotive, passenger train, picturesque scene, vignette, ornate designs and fancy lettering are highly desirable, and generally bring the most money. However, some of the plain less attractive passes from obscure, short-lived and now defunct roads sometimes turn out to be the real finds, and are priced according to their rarity. This is where research comes in when determining value. *Note:* All passes listed here are standard white cards, otherwise color will be noted.

ALABAMA CENTRAL RAILROAD – 1873, plain $25.00

ALBANY & SUSQUEHANNA R.R. – 1867, plain $75.00

ALLEGHENY VALLEY RAILROAD – 1873, ornate, loco pic $60.00

ATCHISON, TOPEKA & SANTA FE RAILROAD and Leased Lines – 1877 ....$20.00

ATLANTIC & PACIFIC RAILROAD CO. Lessee MISSOURI PACIFIC R.R. – 1876, Exchange Ticket, (tan) bridge vignette $75.00

ATLANTIC MISSISSIPPI and OHIO RAILROAD CO. Virginia & Tennessee Division – 1873 (blue) ornate corner designs, vignette center $65.00

AVON, GENESEO & MT. MORRIS R.R. – 1868, plain $40.00

BALTIMORE & OHIO RAIL ROAD – 1873, ornate with train vig in brown $50.00

BUFFALO, ROCHESTER & PITTSBURGH RAILWAY CO. – 1894, (shaded orange)...$20.00

BURLINGTON & LAMOILLE RAILROAD – 1884 (blue) $45.00

BURLINGTON, CEDAR RAPIDS and MINNESOTA RAILWAY – 1871, map back (rare) $125.00

BURLINGTON, CEDAR RAPIDS & NORTHERN RAILWAY – 1900 (blue) $35.00

BURLINGTON, CEDAR RAPIDS AND NORTHERN RY – 1894, Editorial Pass with photo of bearer, lt. blue double-hinged cards (rare) $135.00

BUFFALO, NEW YORK & PHILADELPHIA RAILROAD COMPANY– 1883 (green) Clergyman's Half-Fare Order $40.00

CAIRO & VINCENNES RAILROAD – 1876 (grey) map back $45.00

CENTRAL IOWA RAILWAY CO. – 1884 (blue) Exchange $20.00
CHESAPEAKE and OHIO R.R. – 1873 (pink) $15.00
CHESHIRE and ASHUELUT RAILROADS – 1873, ornate monogram green logo $35.00
CHICAGO & ALTON RAILROAD – 1865, eagle and flags vignette, pic on back $85.00
CHICAGO & ALTON R.R. – 1895, Exchange Pass., full-length passenger train........................$50.00
CHICAGO AND ALTON R.R. – 1896, Exchange Pass., color litho of locomotive $60.00
CHICAGO & NORTH WESTERN RAILWAY – 1873, ornate...$20.00
CHICAGO & NORTH-WESTERN RAILWAY – 1897 (tan) Exchange ticket $15.00
CHICAGO & NORTH-WESTERN RAILWAY – 1902, Exchange Ticket, logo $10.00
CHICAGO & ROCK ISLAND R.R. LINE – 1865, vig train on bridge and steamboat $75.00
CHICAGO GREAT WESTERN RAILWAY – 1898 (yellow) colorful maple leaf emblem $25.00
CHICAGO GREAT WESTERN RAILWAY – 1909 (blue) shaded maple leaf emblem................$12.00
CHICAGO MILWAUKEE & ST. PAUL RAILWAY – 1875 (brown stripes) $22.00
CHICAGO, MILWAUKEE & ST. PAUL RAILWAY – 1892 (lt. grey) $15.00
CHICAGO, MILWAUKEE & ST. PAUL RAILWAY – 1906 (tan) $10.00
CHICAGO, ST. PAUL and KANSAS CITY railway Co. – 1891 (lt. blue) Clergyman's Half-fare Permit................$45.00
CHICAGO, ST. PAUL, MINNEAPOLIS and OMAHA RAILWAY – 1885, ornate, Annual Exchange Pass $25.00
CHICAGO, ST. PAUL, MINNEAPOLIS & OMAHA RAILWAY – 1899 (lt. green) Annual Exchange Pass................$20.00
CHICAGO, ST. PAUL, MINNEAPOLIS & OMAHA RAILWAY COMPANY – 1902 (lt. blue) logo $15.00
CINCINNATI & ZANESVILLE – 1869 (lt. blue) $40.00
CLEVELAND & PITTSBURGH RAILROAD CO. – 1865, ornate...$60.00
CONNECTICUT RIVER RAILROAD – 1868, ornate ..$45.00
CORNING, COWANESQUE & ANTRIM RAILWAY – 1876, with two brown vignettes, map back $50.00
DAYTON and UNION RAILROAD – 1868, ornate with train in fancy letter D........................$55.00
DELAWARE, LACKAWANNA & WESTERN RAILROAD CO. – 1869 (pink) Annual Ticket...................$40.00
DEL. & HUDSON CANAL CO'S RAILROAD – 1869 (tan) ornate $45.00
DES MOINES VALLEY RAILROAD – 1873, with two blk vignettes, train on back........................$50.00
DETROIT LANSING and LAKE MICHIGAN RAILROAD – 1872 (rare) $75.00
DETROIT & MILWAUKEE RAILROAD – 1873 (pink) Free Pass, vignette $45.00
DULUTH, SOUTH SHORE & ATLANTIC – 1891 (blue) picturesque harbor scene........................$30.00
EASTERN RAILROAD – 1873, map back light green ..$30.00
ELGIN, JOLIET & EASTERN RY – 1895, logo; black/white map on back $20.00

ERIE RAILWAY – 1874, ornate, grey picturesque scene..$25.00
ERIE & PITTSBURGH RAIL ROAD From Erie to New Castle – 1869, ornate...............................$40.00
EVANSVILLE & CRAWFORDSVILLE RAILROAD – 1876, ornate $40.00
EVANSVILLE & TERRE HAUTE RAILROAD COMPANY – 1897 (green)......................................$15.00

Civil War Era Passes

FARMVILLE & POWHATAN RAILROAD CO. – 1895 (yellow) plain $25.00
FLINT & PERE MARQUETTE RAILWAY and BAY CITY & EAST SAGINAW R.R. – 1872, picturesque scene of train on bridge, map back $60.00
FLINT & PERE MARQUETTE RAILWAY and Branches – 1873, pic of train on covered bridge $50.00
FLORIDA CENTRAL and PENINSULAR RAILROAD – 1896 (shaded blue) map back $15.00
FLORIDA EAST COAST RY. – 1899 (yellow) map back ..$10.00
FOREST CITY and SIOUX CITY RAILROAD – 1895, Exchange Ticket, ornate $45.00
GEORGIA SOUTHERN and FLORIDA RAILWAY CO. – 1899, shield emblem at center $18.00
GRAND TRUNK RAILWAY SYSTEM – 1897, oval pic train on bridge $20.00
GREAT NORTHERN RAILWAY – 1902 (green) Annual Exchange $12.00
GREAT NORTHERN RAILWAY Co. – 1950 (yellow) goat logo $8.00
GREAT WESTERN RAILWAY OF CANADA – 1865 (lt. green) vig train on Suspension bridge $65.00

Picturesque Passes

GREEN BAY & MINNESOTA RAILROAD – 1875 (gray) plain $45.00
GREEN BAY, WINONA & ST. PAUL RAILROAD CO. – 1884, plain $40.00
GULF & SHIP ISLAND RAILROAD CO. – 1889 (pale green) $15.00
HANNIBAL & ST. JOSEPH R.R. – 1865, plain $70.00
HOUSTON and TEXAS CENTRAL RAILWAY – 1873, ornate $25.00
ILLINOIS & ST. LOUIS R.R. – 1876 (lt. brown) plain $25.00
ILLINOIS CENTRAL RAILROAD – 1865, Complimentary Ticket, pink picturesque depot scene...................$65.00
INDIANA DECATUR and WESTERN RAILWAY – 1896 (pink) plain $20.00
INDIANAPOLIS CINCINNATI & LAFAYETTE RAILROAD & BRANCHES – 1869, ornate.....................................$45.00
INTERNATIONAL and GREAT NORTHERN RAILROAD COMPANY – 1899 (pink) American & Mexican crossed flags $20.00
IOWA CENTRAL RAILWAY CO. – 1898, vig. of farming and industry scene..$30.00
JACKSONVILLE LOUISVILLE & ST. LOUIS – 1895 (pink) $20.00
JACKSONVILLE PENSACOLA & MOBILE RAILROAD – 1872 (grey) ornate, map back...............................$25.00
KANSAS CITY FORT SCOTT & MEMPHIS RAILROAD COMPANY – 1899 (tan) blue star logo $12.00
KANSAS CITY ST. JOSEPH & COUNCIL BLUFFS RAILROAD – 1885 (pink) plain $30.00
KANSAS CITY ST. LOUIS & NORTHERN RAILWAY – 1876 (tan) ornate $35.00
KANSAS CITY SOUTHERN RAILWAY COMPANY – 1909 (grey) Port Arthur Route logo $18.00
KANSAS PACIFIC RAILWAY – 1873 (pink) with two round state emblems..$25.00
LA CROSSE & MILWAUKEE R.R. – 1863, plain..........$55.00

LAKE ERIE & WESTERN RAILWAY – 1882, Editor's Pass with photo of bearer, pale green, double-hinged cards (rare) $125.00
LAKE SHORE and MICHIGAN SOUTHERN RAILWAY – 1895, plain $18.00
LEHIGH VALLEY RAILROAD – 1942 (violet) plain $8.00
LITTLE ROCK & MEMPHIS RAILROAD CO. – 1895 (pink) plain...$20.00
LOUISVILLE and NASHVILLE RAILROAD COMPANY – 1899, L&N logo $12.00
LOUISVILLE CINCINNATI and LEXINGTON RAIL ROAD – 1873, SHORT LINE (red letters) pic of train on bridge at Cincinnati, ornate back $37.50
LOUISVILLE NEW ALBANY and CHICAGO RAIL ROAD – 1865, ornate $60.00
MAINESTEE & NORTH EASTERN RAILROAD – 1896 (violet) pics of train/lake steamer.............................$35.00
MANITOBA and NORTH WESTERN RAILWAY of Canada – 1895 (grey) locomotive pic $30.00
MICHIGAN CENTRAL RAILROAD – 1865, Complimentary ticket not transferable, violet vig of Great Central Union Depot..$70.00
MICHIGAN CENTRAL RAIL ROAD – 1870 (lt. blue) with three vigs eagle, train, State seal $45.00
MICHIGAN CENTRAL RAILROAD and Branches – 1873 (pink) with two vigs, eagle and State seal.............$35.00
MILWAUKEE LAKE SHORE and WESTERN RAILWAY – 1892, loco pic in circle......................................$25.00
MINNEAPOLIS & ST. LOUIS RAILWAY – 1884 (tan) two vignettes $27.50
MINNEAPOLIS and ST. LOUIS RAILWAY and Operated Lines – 1887, pic of train on bridge $30.00
MINNEAPOLIS & ST. LOUIS RAILROAD COMPANY – 1911 (yellow) plain $15.00
MINNEAPOLIS SAULT STE MARIE & ATLANTIC RY – 1885 (tan) vig of train $50.00

MINNEAPOLIS ST. PAUL & SAULT STE MARIE RAILWAY–1892 (lt. brown) logo..$25.00

MINNEAPOLIS ST. PAUL and SAULT STE MARIE RY –1899 (blue) red logo $15.00

MINNEAPOLIS, ST. PAUL & SAULT STE. MARIE RAILWAY COMPANY – 1917 (yellow) plain $10.00

MINNESOTA and NORTHWESTERN RAILROAD – 1887 (shaded blue) $37.50

MISSOURI KANSAS & TEXAS RAILWAY – 1876 (grey) ornate $20.00

MISSOURI-KANSAS-TEXAS LINES – 1924 (yellow) logo $6.00

MOBILE & BIRMINGHAM R.R. – 1897 (tan pic of passenger train) $20.00

MOBILE & OHIO RAILROAD Controlled & Operated Lines – 1899 (yellow) logo $8.00

NASHVILLE CHATTANOOGA and ST.LOUIS RAILWAY – 1897 (pink) blue vig at center $12.00

NEWPORT and WICKLORD RAILROAD and Steamboat Co. – 1884, plain $35.00

N.Y. CENTRAL & HUDSON RIVER R.R. – 1874, Legislative Pass, ornate...$20.00

NEW YORK PENNSYLVANIA and OHIO RAILROAD CO. – 1883 (yellow) Clergyman's Certificate, picturesque scene of sailing boats on back...............................$25.00

NEW YORK & OSWEGO MIDLAND RAILROAD COMPANY – 1874, plain, fancy monogram $30.00

NORTH MISSOURI RAILROAD – 1865, Complimentary Pass, ornate, vig 4-4-0 locomotive $85.00

NORTHERN ALABAMA RAILWAY COMPANY– 1899 (blue) plain $10.00

NORTHERN CENTRAL RAILWAY – 1866 (pink) fancy letters...$45.00

NORTHERN CENTRAL RAILWAY COMPANY – 1873, blue monogram logo $25.00

NORTHERN PACIFIC RAILROAD And Leased Lines – 1880, two wheat sheaf vigs (rare) $85.00

NORTHERN PACIFIC RAILROAD – 1883 (yellow) pic of train on bridge $65.00

NORTHERN PACIFIC RAILWAY COMPANY – 1903 (green) logo $12.00

OGDENSBURG and LAKE CHAMPLAIN RAIL ROAD – 1870 (pink shaded) ornate $35.00

OHIO RIVER RAILROAD COMPANY – 1895 (yellow) pic of loco in circle $25.00

OHIO RIVER & CHARLESTON RAILWAY COMPANY – 1896 (green/pink) fancy..................................$20.00

OHIO VALLEY RAILWAY – 1897 (green) plain $22.00

OIL CREEK and ALLEGHENY RIVER RAILWAY – 1873 (pink) oil well derrick vig $30.00

PAINESVILLE & YOUNGSTOWN RAILROAD – 1876, plain $25.00

PENNSYLVANIA RAILROAD – 1868, Editorial ornate $35.00

PENNSYLVANIA RAILROAD – 1873, brown, horses vignette $25.00

PEORIA AND PEKIN UNION RAILWAY – 1918 (blue) plain..$15.00

PEORIA DECATUR and EVANSVILLE RAILWAY – 1896 (grey) plain..$20.00

PHILADELPHIA WILMINGTON & BALTIMORE RAIL ROAD – 1868, plain...$37.50

PITTSBURGH & CONNELLSVILLE R.R. – 1870 (tan) plain..$25.00

PITTSBURGH COLUMBUS & CINCINNATI R.R. – 1865, Complimentary, fancy $55.00

PLANT SYSTEM RAILWAYS – 1895 (yellow) fancy brown motif across center $20.00

PONTIAC OXFORD AND NORTHERN RAILROAD COMPANY – 1899, Pontiac Indian logo $22.00

PORT EDWARDS CENTRALIA & NORTHERN RAILROAD – 1892 (blue) plain...$27.50

QUEEN & CRESCENT ROUTE – 1895 (lt. blue) plain$16.00

QUINCY, MISSOURI & PACIFIC RAILROAD COMPANY – 1876 (grey) fancy $30.00

Passes Picturing Locomotives

QUINCY, OMAHA & KANSAS CITY RAILWAY – 1895 (shaded brown) Quincy Route logo $20.00

QUINCY, ALTON & ST. LOUIS RAILROAD – 1873, plain $45.00

RACINE & MISSISSIPPI and NORTHERN ILLINOIS RAILROADS – 1865 (lt. green) ornate $65.00

RALEIGH WESTERN RAILWAY COMPANY – 1895 (tan) ornate $22.00

READING & COLUMBIA RAILROAD – 1870 (yellow) ornate $50.00

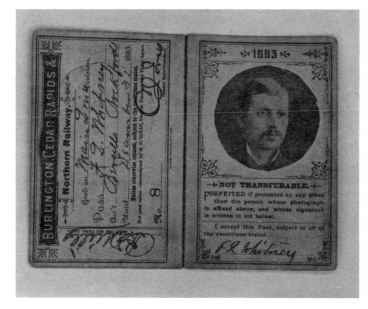

Pass With Photo of Bearer

ROCK ISLAND & PEORIA RAILWAY – 1895 (grey) train vignette...$22.00

ROCKFORD, ROCK ISLAND and ST. LOUIS RAILROAD – 1876 (lt. green) ornate $30.00

ROME, WATERTOWN & OGDENSBURGH R.R. – 1868, plain $35.00

ST. LOUIS & IRON MOUNTAIN R.R. – 1865 (tan) pic of primitive train $70.00

ST. LOUIS & IRON MOUNTAIN R.R. – 1873 (grey) pic of train and mountain $45.00

ST. LOUIS & SAN FRANCISCO RAILWAY COMPANY – 1881 (green) ornate, loco vig $35.00

ST. LOUIS, CAPE GIRARDEAU and FORT SMITH RAILWAY – 1895 (tan) loco vig circle $42.50

ST. LOUIS, KANSAS CITY and NORTHERN RY. and Leased Lines – 1873, ornate, map bk. $40.00

ST. LOUIS, VANDALIA, TERRE HAUTE & INDIANAPOLIS RAILROAD, VANDALIA LINE – 1873, (grey) ornate, two round vigs, fancy blue monogram back $42.00

SAINT PAUL & DULUTH RAILROAD – 1892 (shaded brown) Duluth Shore Line logo............................$30.00

ST. PAUL & PACIFIC RAILROAD, First Division – 1866 (tan) plain $60.00

ST. PAUL AND PACIFIC RAILROAD – 1876 (gold digits) plain $45.00

ST. PAUL and PACIFIC RAIL ROAD The First Division – 1877, ornate...$35.00

ST. PAUL, MINNEAPOLIS & MANITOBA RAILWAY COMPANY – 1881, Jas. J. Hill signature $75.00

ST. PAUL, MINNEAPOLIS & MANITOBA RAILWAY – 1887 (green) plain $30.00

SAINT PAUL and SIOUX CITY and SIOUX CITY and ST. PAUL R.R. – 1876, plain $37.50

SOUTH CAROLINA and GEORGIA RAILROAD COMPANY – 1896, green border and masthead $15.00

SOUTHERN RAILWAY CO. – 1898 (lt. blue) SR monogram..$12.00

SOUTHERN RAILWAY COMPANY – 1925 (green logos repeated) $10.00

SOUTHERN MINNESOTA RAILWAY – 1876 (lt. green) ornate..$37.50

SUFFOLK AND CAROLINA RAILWAY – 1895 (grey) plain $22.50

TALLAHASSEE & MONTGOMERY RAILWAY Co. – 1896 (pale blue) plain $27.50

TAUARES AND GULF RAILROAD CO. – 1895 (blue) train vignette...$25.00

TERRE HAUTE & INDIANAPOLIS RAILROAD COMPANY, Vandalia Line – 1894 (tan) plain $20.00

TEXAS & PACIFIC RAILWAY – 1876 (lt. blue) Complimentary, ornate...$25.00

TOLEDO & OHIO CENTRAL, KANAWHA & MICHIGAN RAILWAYS – 1895, plain $18.50

TOLEDO, PEORIA & WARSAW RAILWAY – 1869, plain $37.50

TOLEDO, ST. LOUIS and KANSAS CITY R.R. – 1897 (shaded tan) three-leaf clover $18.00

TOLEDO, WABASH & WESTERN RAILWAY and Leased Lines – 1873 (pink) ornate...................................$35.00

TROY & BOSTON RAILROAD – 1874, plain.............$28.00

UTAH CENTRAL RAILROAD – 1876, plain (rare) $75.00

UTAH NORTHERN RAIL ROAD – 1876 (shaded brown) ornate (rare) $85.00

UTAH SOUTHERN RAILROAD – 1876, plain (rare) $95.00

VERMONT CENTRAL RAILROAD, Including Leased Lines – 1873, plain, pic RR depot bk $27.50

VERMONT CENTRAL and Vt. & CANADA R. ROADS – 1870, depot vignette (ornate) $37.50

VICKSBURG & MERIDIAN R.R. – 1873, plain...........$30.00

WABASH RAILROAD COMPANY – 1896, red flag logo, map back $18.00

WABASH, CHESTER & WESTERN RAILROAD COMPANY – 1895 (lt. blue) plain $20.00

WABASH, ST. LOUIS and PACIFIC RY. – 1887, fancy black masthead logo $27.50

WASHINGTON CITY VIRGINIA MIDLAND AND GREAT SOUTHERN RAILROAD CO. – 1876, (lt. brown) ornate...$37.50

WEST WISCONSIN RAILWAY – 1873 (lt. green) ornate...$32.50

WESTERN RAIL ROAD COMPANY OF ALABAMA – 1873 (tan) green vignette center $35.00

WESTERN UNION RAIL ROAD – 1869, Complimentary (grey) ornate $47.50

WILMINGTON and WELDON, WILMINGTON, COLUMBIA & AUGUSTA RAILROADS, Consolidated Line – 1873 (lt. grey) ornate $37.50

WINONA & St. PETER RAIL ROAD – 1868 (shaded pink) ornate $55.00

WISCONSIN CENTRAL MILWAUKEE & NORTHERN, Wisconsin & Minnesota Railroads – 1882 (shaded blue) with two vignettes in corners (rare) $65.00

WISCONSIN CENTRAL – 1889, Annual Exchange Ticket (grey) red logo, three corner vignettes, pic of train on bridge (rare)..$75.00

WISCONSIN CENTRAL LINES, NORTHERN PACIFIC R.R. Co. Lessee – 1892 (shaded brown) $40.00

WISCONSIN CENTRAL RAILWAY – 1903 (blue) plain $25.00

WRIGHTSVILLE & TENNILLE RAILROAD COMPANY – 1897 (tan) plain $18.00

YAZOO & MISSISSIPPI VALLEY RAILROAD – 1898 (blue) plain $25.00

Employee

Railroads also issued passes to their employees and their families. These were either annual passes or were good for one trip only. They were usually made of cardstock, but a great many were made of paper stock, larger than the standard size pass. Employee passes are generally priced lower, exceptions being the uncommon and long-gone railroads.

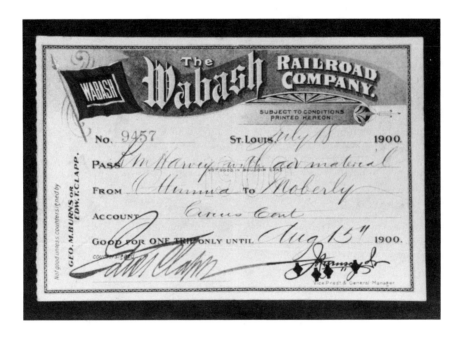

Employee Trip Pass

BUFFALO, ROCHESTER & PITTSBURGH RAILWAY COMPANY– 1920, Trip Pass, lt. blue paper stock, 3½ x 5"..$17.50

CHICAGO, MILWAUKEE & ST. PAUL RAILWAY – 1894, Employee's Time Ticket, yellow card, 2¼ x 4" $10.00

CHICAGO, MILWAUKEE & ST. PAUL RAILWAY – 1887, Annual, pink card, 2½ x 3¾" $12.50

CHICAGO & NORTH-WESTERN RAILWAY CO. – 1884, Employee's 30 Day Pass, pink paper stock, 3 x 4¼" $15.00

CHICAGO GREAT WESTERN RAILROAD CO. – 1924, Exchange Trip Pass, orange paper stock, 3 x 5" $12.00

COLORADO MIDLAND – 1916, Annual Pass, grey card, 2½" x 4" (scarce)...$35.00

DELAWARE & HUDSON CANAL CO. – 1875, One Trip Only, lt. grey paper stock, 2¾ x 4¼" $17.50

DULUTH IRON RANGE R.R. – 1892, Trip Pass, pink paper stock, 2½ x 4½"..$15.00

GREAT NORTHERN RAILWAY COMPANY – 1937, Trip Pass, grey paper stock, 3¼ x 5" $10.00

GREEN BAY, WINONA & ST. PAUL R.R. – 1889, Trip, grey paper stock, 3¾ x 6¾" $22.50

HOCKING VALLEY RAILWAY CO. – 1908, Time Pass, tan paper stock, 3 x 4¾" $12.00

ILLINOIS CENTRAL RAILROAD CO. – 1892, One Trip Only, grey paper stock, 2½ x 8" including Pass Check $10.00

MICHIGAN CENTRAL R.R. – 1872, Ten rides during the month of December, white card, 2½ x 4".............$15.00

MINNEAPOLIS & ST. LOUIS RAILROAD COMPANY – 1930, Annual, blue paper stock, 2½ x 4" $7.50

MINNEAPOLIS, ST. PAUL & SAULT STE. MARIE RAILROAD COMPANY– 1951, Trip Pass, orange paper stock, 3¼ x 5"..$6.00

MISSOURI PACIFIC RAILWAY CO. – 1899, Trip Pass, green paper stock, 3 x 4¾".................................$12.50

MISSOURI, KANSAS & TEXAS RAILWAY SYSTEM – 1906, One Trip Only, tan paper stock, 3 x 5"..................$10.00

NORTHERN PACIFIC RAILROAD COMPANY – 1882, Engineer's Time Pass, tan card stock, 2¾ x 4½" $15.00

NORTHERN PACIFIC RAILWAY – 1904, Exchange Trip Pass, lt. brown paper stock, 3 x 5¼" $10.00

PHILADELPHIA, BALTIMORE and WASHINGTON RAILROAD CO. – 1904, Annual, blue card stock, 2½ x 3¾" $8.00

PHILADELPHIA, WILMINGTON and BALTIMORE RAILROAD CO. – 1899, Annual, blue card stock, 2½ x 3¾" $12.00

RENSSELAER & SARATOGA R.R. – 1874, Trip Pass, lt. grey paper stock, 2¼ x 3½" $18.00

SOUTHERN RAILWAY COMPANY – 1914, Annual, yellow card, 2½ x 4" $8.00

SOUTH EASTERN RAILWAY – 1884, 30 Days, blue paper stock, 2¾ x 5" $20.00

TOLEDO & OHIO CENTRAL RAILWAY, ZANESVILLE & WESTERN RAILWAY – 1910, Annual, yellow card, 2½ x 4" $12.00

TOLEDO & OHIO CENTRAL RAILWAY, KANAWHA & MICHIGAN RAILWAY – 1906, Time Pass, pink card, 2½ x 4" $10.00

TOLEDO, CINCINNATI & ST. LOUIS RAILROAD CO. – 1883, One Trip Only, pink card, 3 x 4½" $12.00

WABASH RAILROAD COMPANY – 1900 Trip Pass, lt. green, paper stock, 3½ x 5"....................................$10.00

WINONA & SOUTH WESTERN – 1891, Trip Pass, grey, paper stock, 2¾" x 4½"..................................$15.00

WISCONSIN CENTRAL LINES – 1891, Employee's Time Ticket, lt. blue card, 2¾ x 4" $17.50

Miscellaneous

There were also passes issued by Express Companies, Telegraph Companies, Omnibus Lines, The Pullman Company, etc., in connection with the railroads, allowing the holder to occupy a Pullman seat or berth, transport packages, send telegrams, cross a river on a toll bridge or ferryboat, get transportation between depots and hotels, and so on, without charge. Value on these various railroad-related passes are based according to their rarity. *Note:* Passes listed here are cardstock, in the standard size, 2½ x 4" unless otherwise noted.

ADAMS EXPRESS COMPANY – 1895, blue..................$22.50

AMERICAN EXPRESS COMPANY – 1895, blue, pic of watchdog in circle $20.00

AMERICAN EXPRESS COMPANY – 1899, blue, flag shield logo $15.00

CHEQUAMEGON BAY TRANSPORTATION CO. – 1904, STEAMERS: Chequamegon, Mary Scott, Skater, tan, 2 x 3½" $45.00

COOK'S OMNIBUS LINE – (St. Paul) 1904, blue $12.00

DOMINION EXPRESS COMPANY – 1894, tan, Express emblem top left corner..$10.00

EAST ST. LOUIS TRANSFER COMPANY – 1873, white, 2¼ x 3½"...$12.00

ILLINOIS & ST. LOUIS BRIDGE – 1876, grey, bridge and river scene, 2½ x 3½" $30.00

MINNEAPOLIS OMNIBUS LINE – 1903, pink, horses pulling stagecoach & wagon $17.50

MONTREAL TELEGRAPH COMPANY – 1873, tan, 2¼ x 3½"...$20.00

NATIONAL EXPRESS COMPANY – 1902, pink $12.00

NATIONAL MAIL COMPANY – 1895, grey, stagecoach scene $50.00

PACIFIC & ATLANTIC TELEGRAPH CO. – 1873, yellow, 2¼ x 3¾"..$20.00

PARMELEE CO. CHICAGO OMNIBUS LINE – 1903, blue $12.00

PITTSBURGH & CINCINNATI PACKET LINE – 1895, pink, river packet scene..$30.00

Steamboat and Stagecoach Passes

POSTAL TELEGRAPH CABLE COMPANY – 1902, tan $12.00

PULLMAN'S PALACE CAR CO. – 1873, Geo. M. Pullman signature, 2¼" x 3¾" (rare) $100.00

PULLMAN'S PALACE CAR CO. – 1897, lt. green $15.00

SENECA LAKE STEAM NAVIGATION CO. – 1895, yellow, pics steamboat and train..$50.00

UNION DEPOT CO. and UNION RAILWAY & TRANSIT CO. ST. LOUIS – 1876, tan $18.00

UNITED STATES EXPRESS CO. – 1897, yellow, winged safe/horseshoe logo $15.00

UNITED STATES EXPRESS CO. – 1899, white, safe/horseshoe/flag logo $15.00

WESTERN EXPRESS CO. – 1900, tan, express car and wreath motif..$12.00

WESTERN UNION TELEGRAPH COMPANY – 1873, white, 2½" X 3¾" $25.00

WESTERN UNION TELEGRAPH COMPANY – 1895, brown $15.00

WESTERN UNION TELEGRAPH COMPANY – 1902, blue...$10.00

WIGGINS FERRY COMPANY – 1876, pink, 2¼" x 3½" $27.50

WOODRUFF SLEEPING AND PARLOR COACH CO. – 1873, blue checkered, Jonah Woodruff signature (rare) $85.00

Pinback Buttons

Railroad pinback buttons can be found dating back prior to the turn of the century. The earlier ones were made with color designs printed on paper with a celluloid covering fabricated over the shell. Occasionally the manufacturer's paper label is still glued on the backside of the shell. In later years, many pinbacks were made with a lithographed paint coating over the tin surface, and in more recent years most were turned out in plastic and are not worth much. The earlier examples, especially from railroads advertising homesteads to immigrants are rare, and bring a good price as well as those from roads long gone; they are getting scarce, with prices steadily on the increase.

Railroad-related pinback buttons are also included in this category, and a representative group of them are listed at the end. Prices on these, of course, are also based on rarity.

AMTRAK – with blue-red logo, "Tracks are Back!" in black on white, 2¼"D $8.00

AMTRAK – 1973 RIDE THE TURBO! white on aqua, turbo train at center, 1¾"D $10.00

ACL – ATLANTIC COAST LINE (script) 100% Safety 1931, white on purple, ⅞"D $12.00

BCR&N – "The Burlington Cedar Rapids & Northern Ry Route," white in red diamond on off-white field, ⅞"D., rare $35.00

BN – logo, white on green, ⅞"D $4.00

BN – BURLINGTON NORTHERN CLOWNS, white on green, black/white cartoon clown in black on white center circle, 1½"D $10.00

BN – 1975 A year for SAFETY Chicago region, logo, white on green, 1½"D $5.00

BURLINGTON ROUTE – logo in center, tracks, 1850-1940 in black on off-white, 11/16"D $8.00

BURLINGTON ROUTE – silver streamliner and word Zephyr above on dark blue, 1¼"D $12.00

CPR – black beaver atop red CANADIAN PACIFIC RAILWAY shield logo at center, "Get Your Canadian HOME from the Canadian Pacific," black on off-white, 1"D, scarce ..$25.00

C&O RY – Chessie sleeping kitten in color on white, 1½"D..$18.00

C&O RY – CHESAPEAKE AND OHIO RAILWAY 1951 Conference Freight Traffic Department, blue on off-white field, rep's name in window card across center, 3"D $10.00

CC&L – (logo) CHICAGO CINCINNATI black on off-white field, "The Straight Line" in red diagonally through logo, ¾"D $15.00

CM&StP RY – canted red box logo at center, SAFETY FIRST in black around logo with red pinstripes on off-white field, 1"D $10.00

CM&StP RY – red logo at top and bottom, OPPORTUNITY in red band on white center, ORCHARD HOMES GOVERNMENT HOMESTEADS on yellow border, 1½"D scarce $35.00

C&NW LINE – black and red logo, PASSENGER AGENT black on off-white field, 2¼"D $12.00

C&NW LINE – black and red logo at center, ALFALFA The Great Wealth Producer in black on yellow, 1¼"D..$15.00

CSTPM&O – C.ST.P.M & O Woman's Club BOOSTER in red around blue/red logo at center on off-white field, blue border, 1¼"D $20.00

GN – GREAT NORTHERN RAILWAY b/w box logo on shock of yellow wheat in center with "Farms Free" in red on off-white field either side, MONTANA FOR ME 320 acres in white on black border, 1¾"D, rare.........................$85.00

GN – GREAT NORTHERN RAILWAY box logo at top, waving American flag, farm home, with words in red under the stars and stripes "Ask Leedy" on off-white field, FREE HOMES IN CENTRAL OREGON in white on blue border, 1¾"D., rare $85.00

GN – GREAT NORTHERN RAILWAY, mountain goat atop logo at center, SEE AMERICA FIRST GLACIER NATIONAL PARK red on yellow border, 1½"D., scarce $35.00

GN – GREAT NORTHERN RAILWAY, blue/white box logo with gold border, P.P.I.E. 1915 above and below on grey, gold rim, blue and gold satin ribbons attached, 1¾"D., scarce $45.00

Railroad Homestead Pinbacks

GN – GREAT NORTHERN RAILWAY green letters, white goat on orange/white top half, diesel streamliner and "the Red River 1950" on green bottom, 1¾"D $20.00

GN – GREAT NORTHERN RAILWAY goat logo front diesel, goat waving from cab "You're on the right track with GREAT NORTHERN," multi-colors on yellow, 2¼"D $15.00

GN – GREAT NORTHERN RAILWAY goat logo, comic goat passenger running holding travel bag and camera with slogan at top, "A GREAT WAY TO TRAVEL," red-white-black on blue rectangle, 1¾ x 2¾".........................$25.00

GN – white silhouette goat on red center, 1953 SAFETY CAMPAIGN black on white border, 1¼"D $12.00

GN – white silhouette goat on red center, "BE INJURY FREE IN 63, SAFETY COURTESY" blue on white border, 1¼"D..$10.00

GN – white modern silhouette goat on gold center, "PACE YOUR LIFE TO LIVE" 1969, white on blue border, 1¼"D..$7.00

L&N – logo, "We'll shine in '69," red on white field, 1¼"D ..$3.00

LV – red/black flag logo in center within green wreath, "Black Diamond Express" above, LEHIGH VALLEY RAILROAD below, black letters on off-white field, ⅞"D $20.00

MILWAUKEE ROAD – red logo at center and CHICAGO RAILROAD FAIR #24348 in black on off-white field, 1¾"D..$15.00

MILWAUKEE ROAD – white Indian figure on black center, HIAWATHA TRIBE MEMBER in black on yellow, 1¼"D $8.00

NP – NORTHERN PACIFIC Yellowstone Park Line logo in red/black on off-white field, 1¾"D $12.00

NP – NORTHERN PACIFIC Yellowstone Park Line logo in red/black on off-white field, 1¼"D $8.00

NP – red/black logo in center, NORTHERN PACIFIC Picnic "Let's Go," July 24, 1926, Big Lake, Minn. black on off-white field, 1¼"D, scarce $30.00

NP – NORTHERN PACIFIC RAILWAY monad logo at center, SAFETY 1964 Harriman Gold Medal, dark blue on gold field, 1¾"D...$15.00

NP – NORTHERN PACIFIC Yellowstone Park Line logo at center, N.P. Junction Jubilee, Carlton, Minnesota, 1870-1948, Sept. 4-5-6 in red and black on off-white field, 2¼"D..$20.00

SANTA FE – blue/white cross logo in center, and "Get the Safety HABIT" blue letters on off-white, ⅞"D..........$8.00

SOO LINE – SOO LINE RAILROAD Anniversary around circle of track with wheat spray and 75, 1883-1958 in center, red on off-white field, 2¼"D $22.50

SP – S.P.R.R. EMPLOYEES PICNIC around Sunset, Ogden & Shasta Routes logo at center, red on off-white, 1¼"D $12.50

UP – UNION PACIFIC EMPLOYEE white around dark blue edge, BOOSTERS LEAGUE white letters on red center, oval, ⅝ x 1"...$5.00

UP – UNION PACIFIC FAMILY war SERVICE club in white on red/white/blue shield logo, ⅞"D $10.00

UP – BE SPECIFIC SAY "UNION PACIFIC" around shield logo at center, red/white/blue on off-white field, 1¾"D $8.50

Railroad-Related

ART – "Ship your Perishable Freight care AMERICAN RE-FRIGERATOR TRANSIT CO. General Offices, St. Louis, Mo.," red letters on off-white field, full-color refrigerator car across center, red/white/blue satin adv. ribbons with brass bells attached, 2⅛"D., scarce..........................$50.00

AM.RY.EX. – AMERICAN RAILWAY EXPRESS COMPANY white on grey around red diamond logo center with words RIGHT WAY COMMITTEE, 1¼"D $10.00

CHICAGO-RAILROAD-FAIR-1848-1948 WHEELS A ROLL-ING and b/w photo of diesel streamliner across center in red/blue on white, red/white/blue ribbon attached, 1¾"D...$20.00

KEYSTONE OVERALLS – "27 Years The Best" white on blue border, B of RT keystone multi-color emblem at center, 1¼"D...$12.00

NYD – NEW YORK DESPATCH REFRIGERATOR LINES, National Despatch in black letters on off-white field, black/yellow detailed reefer car at center, 1½"D ..$22.50

NORFOLK – large 5-pt. red star with NORFOLK in center black circle, pass. trains departing between points of star to various cities, multi-color scenes, 1½"D $18.00

RAILROAD CENTENNIAL – 1848-1948 CHICAGO, ILL. with illustration of trains and people around edge in black/red/tan on white, 1⅝"D................................$15.00

Railroad-Related Pinbacks

READING LINES – diamond logo and steam engine with words above, "Schuylkill Haven Science Club" in black on yellow, 1¼"D...$8.00

SHIP BY RAIL – white letters on black, 1"D $5.00

Playing Cards

Railroad playing cards go back to before the turn of the century. Top prices are paid for the early souvenir decks having 52 different photographic views on their faces, which came in an original two-piece slipcase box. Next are the sealed mint decks and/or in VF unused condition in their original cardstock cases or covered boxes featuring advertising, trains, logos and intricate designs issued during the Golden Years of rail travel. Subsequently, railroads came out with less extravagant decks which were just cello wrapped or put in plastic covered boxes, not worth too much. Physical condition plays an important role in determining value. Used decks with damaged or missing cards are usually discounted. Those from uncommon or long-gone defunct roads are now bringing big bucks. Rarities are going on the auction block realizing incredible prices. *Note:* A detailed description is given to readily ID a deck and its value. A duplicate card is usually glued on the case to show what the backs look like.

AMTRAK – two logos on white, blue or red border, cardstock case $8.00

ACL – diesel pass. train 525 and palm trees, yellow border, blue cardstock case $25.00

B&A – logo and "Bangor and Aroostock Railroad Company" on white, blue or red border, gold cardstock case..........$18.00

B&O – double deck, original grey slipcase, map of System, logo, two trains, slogan "11,000 miles of track serving the heart of industrial America," red/blue borders, 1943........$45.00

B&O – Pass. train and canal scene, "The Line of The Capitol Limited, New York Washington Chicago" on blue border, 1926, blue cardboard slipcase $50.00

B&O – pass. train and river scene, "The Line of the National Limited, New York Washington St. Louis" on red border, 1926, red cardboard slipcase $50.00

B&O – pass. train scene, "Liberty Limited" Washington – Chicago" on maroon border, 1922, green cardboard slipcase $65.00

BN – double deck, logo and BURLINGTON NORTHERN green/white, white/green, clear plastic cov. box ..$12.00

BURLINGTON ROUTE – double deck, two red box logos on black backs with gold x's in border, dated 1925, 7½" long red slipcase box $75.00

BURLINGTON ROUTE – color photo of diesel streamliner on blue, "America's Distinctive Trains," orig. silver box, glued on card, 1943 ....$30.00

BURLINGTON ROUTE – two horseback riders watching BURLINGTON Vista-Dome Zephyr going by, silver box, glued on card $25.00

BURLINGTON ROUTE – line up of five locomotives, ghost riders in the sky, yellow border, clear plastic box ..$20.00

C&A – photo of "Cow Boy Girl" on red backs with slogan CHICAGO & ALTON RAILROAD "THE ONLY WAY" orig. case with CB girl and slogans, dated 1903, rare......$135.00

C&EI – oval logo at top center and SOUTH – SOUTHEAST – SOUTHWEST in red on yellow, orig. cardstock case with same ID $45.00

C&NW – logo and gladiator figure on blue, also on purple back, gold border, orig. case with gladiator, 1935...............$30.00

C&NW – logo and yellow streamliner across "400" on brown, slipcase box has card glued on.................$75.00

C&NW – double deck, orig. green slipcase box with cards glued on, yellow diesel in white circle on green/yellow back with white logos $70.00

C&O – Souvenir, 53 scenes, C & O F.F. V. "EAST-WEST VIA WASHINGTON" on filagree design backs of yellow/brown, ca. 1897, orig. orange slipcase box, ca. 1897 (rare) $125.00

C&O – double deck, orig. blue box with red figure, Chessie and two kittens sleeping, grey border, Chessie sleeping alone, pink border, "Sleep like a Kitten"................$40.00

C&O – double deck, orig. grey/blk box with heart, cat sitting, "Peake – Chessie's Old Man" red border and CO in corner, "Chessie and the Kittens" grey border and CO in corner $50.00

C&O – double deck, orig. clear plastic box, "Chessie" sleeping, blue line border, head of "Peake" brown line border, both with "Chessie System, Purr-fect Transportation"......$30.00

C&O – double deck, orig. box with boat pix, RR cars and S.S. Badger boat at loading dock, ferry boat S.S. Spartan en-route on lake $35.00

CGW – white round logo with engine protruding on blue, white border, orig. cardstock case has same ID $45.00

CGW – gold logo on black with gold border, also on red backs, orig. cardstock case has same ID $25.00

CM&StP – souvenir, 53 views, snow-capped mtns. and pines on backs, orig. maroon slip box with glued card, ca. 1915 ....$50.00

CMStP&P – souvenir, 53 views, ELECTRIC locomotive on orange backs, orig. orange slip box with glued card, ca. 1930 ....$45.00

CMStP&P – souvenir, 53 views, red logo and Old Faithful Geyser on backs, orig. blue slip box with glued card, 1928....$40.00

CMStP&P – logo, streamliner, slogan "HIAWATHA Nothing Faster On Rails" in black on orange/yellow/gold backs, orig. covered box has glued card...................$20.00

CO&G – Rookwood Indian portrait on backs, orig. red slip box has glued card one side, other The CHOCTAW Route logo, ca. 1899 (rare) $150.00

D&RG – souvenir, 53 views, train in Royal Gorge without Suspension Bridge on backs with State seal in corners, orig. blue slip box with glued card, ca. 1922 ....$45.00

D&RGW – souvenir, 53 views, train in Royal Gorge with Suspension Bridge, orig. maroon slip box with glued card, ca. 1930's $35.00

DM&IR – Safety First, red logo and gold Armed Forces insignia on tan/blue backs with gold stripes, orig. blue box, 1943 ....$40.00

ERIE – Dia. Ship and Travel logo in center, "Route of the ERIE LIMITED" at top, ERIE RAILROAD SYSTEM at bottom in white on blue, gold border, orig. slip box with glued card..................$45.00

ERIE – double deck, 100th Anniversary 1851-1951, Great Lakes to the Sea, ERIE RAILROAD dark blue on yellow, yellow on dark blue, orig. blue slip box has same ID $50.00

FRISCO – double deck, gold logo centered on red/blue backs, gold border, orig. blue slip box has glued on cards $20.00

GN – two GREAT NORTHERN white goat logos on red backs with diamond gold border, orig. red cardstock case having same ID, ca. 1930's...........................$45.00

GN – two large round red/gold circles with mountain goat in center atop black logo on blue backs, orig. blue cardstock case has same ID, ca. 1915 ....$85.00

GN – portrait of Water Black Bird Indian squaw on backs, orig. cardstock case has glued-on card, 1943 ....$20.00

GN – double deck, two standing Indian children, First-Stabber, red bdr., Singing-For-Nothing, blue bdr., green covered box with glued on cards, 1935 ....$70.00

GN – double deck, two Indians, Julia-Wades-In-The-Water, blue bdr., Chief Wades-In-The-Water, red bdr., red slip box with logo and glued on cards, 1947...............$40.00

GN – double deck, two Indians, Buckskin Pinto Woman, red bdr., Chief Middle Rider, blue bdr., blue slip box with logo and glued cards, 1951 ....$40.00

Souvenir Pack With 53 Different Views

GN – standing Indian girl, Singing-For-Nothing, blue bdr., orig. cardstock case has glued-on card and photo of lady waving from Empire Builder car $30.00

GN – Indian portrait Chief Wades-In-The-Water, red bdr., orig. cardstock case has glued-on card and photo of streamlined EMPIRE BUILDER $30.00

GTP – souvenir, 52 views, girl with hat, gold filagree with four logos on black, orig. red slip box has glued-on card and gold printing, mfr'd by Chas. Goodall & Sons, Ltd., ca. 1913 (scarce) $85.00

GTR – souvenir, 52 views, bonnet girl with roses, and gold filagree border on blue, orig. blue slip box has glued-on card and gold printing, mfr'd by Chas. Goodall & Sons, Ltd. ca. 1913 (scarce) $110.00

IC – The Floridan, black steam train against orange sky, with slogan – Chicago-St. Louis and all Florida Cuba-Nassau, cardstock case has same ID printing, 1935...........$65.00

IC – Panama Limited, black steam train against blue sky with slogan – Chicago, St. Louis and New Orleans Mississippi Gulf Coast, cardstock case has same ID printing, 1935 ....$65.00

IC – church steeple and trees on backs and ILLINOIS CENTRAL, white border, cardstock case with same ID printing $15.00

L&N – double deck, diesel streamliner and bridge scene entitled "Tunkhannock Viaduct on the route of Phoebe Snow," red/blue bdrs., plain red covered box $30.00

L&N – double deck, six different shipping scenes one, other has diesels pulling string gondola cars along river. L&N logo, blue slip box with gold logo $15.00

MP – double deck, red logo and diesel streamliner "Eagle" against mountain background, gold/red bdr., silver/blue bdr., red cov. box with two glued cards, 1948 ....$40.00

MP – double deck, stylized Mo-Pac Eagle logo on each, blue/white on red, white/red on blue, slipcase box has same ID cards glued $20.00

MP – buzz-saw logo, "WEST SOUTHWEST, a Service Institution" in white on blue, blue cardstock case with same ID printing, 1932 ....$55.00

NYC – double deck, one has train/river scene entitled "Morning on the Hudson," other has Niagara Falls scene entitled "Majestic Niagara Falls," grey box has logo and "Niagara Falls – Hudson River Edition" in gold printing, bottom has two ID cards glued on $45.00

NYC – the Twentieth Century Limited pictured and Morning on the Mohawk, New York Central Lines in white printing on red bdrs., red cov. box has gold logo imprinted, 1932 ....$45.00

NYC – sailing boats river scene pictured and The Palisades of the Hudson, New York Central Lines in white print on blue bdrs., blue cov. box has gold logo imprinted, 1926 ....$30.00

NYNH&H – double deck, round logo joined with four diesels on each, gold/maroon, gold/blue, blue slipbox has same cards glued on and logo in gold $50.00

NICKEL PLATE – double deck, logo, silver on red, silver on blue, silver bdrs., silver cov. box has blue logo......$25.00

N&W – double deck, logo, gold on blue, gold on black, gold bdrs., black slipcase box has gold logo and RR's name.........$25.00

NP – logo and gold vertical lines on black, red/gold bdr., black slipcase box has same ID card glued on and logo imprint in gold, also came in red backs with same ID, 1932 ....$30.00

NP – two logos and gold vertical lines on red, black bdr., red cardstock case has same ID printing, also came in tan backs, 1935 ....$25.00

NP – logo and gold diagonal lines on black, gold bdr., black cardstock case has same ID card glued on, also came in red backs $15.00

PRR – double deck, logo, gold on red, red on white, gold bdrs., red box has logo and Pennsylvania Railroad in gold on cover, two ID cards glued on bottom $25.00

PRR – double deck, one has illustration of pass. train on bridge titled Pennsylvania Railroad on blue bdr., other has illus. of pass. train against background of bldgs.

Two Early Rock Island Decks

titled Pennsylvania Railroad on red bdr., orig. red cov. box has gold logo, box has compartment with score pad and pencil, 1926, scarce $130.00

PRR – pass. train on bridge, logo and Liberty Limited Chicago-Washington on gold/blue border, orig. maroon slipcase has same ID card glued on, 1922..................$50.00

PRR – line-up of locomotives and 1846 One Hundred Years 1946, Pennsylvania Railroad, on red border, cardstock case has 1846-1946 symbol $35.00

ROCK ISLAND – souvenir, 53 views, orange/black backs, globe map in center with logo-train above and below, "Best Service West" at each side, orig. yellow slipcase box has same ID card glued on. ca. 1910, rare...........$135.00

ROCK ISLAND – two logos on red/white filagree design backs, white bdr., orig. red cardstock case has same ID card printed plus list of 14 states, ca. 1912 . Also came in blue with same ID $45.00

ROCK ISLAND – double deck, one has black backs with diesel streamliner in center, "Route of the Rocket" above, red logo below; other deck has maroon backs with same ID, orig. blk/red box has black logo on cover $70.00

ROCK ISLAND – double deck, red/black backs, logo in center, "Route of the Rockets" below, gold bdrs., orig. box has logo, two diesels on cover, two ID cards glued on bottom $20.00

ROCK ISLAND – white logo on front of stylized diesel in black on red, gold border, cardstock case with ID glued card, logo suit symbols on white $12.00

StLSW – black girl eating watermelon within cotton oval frame at center on green backs, Cotton Belt Route logo in corners, wide white bdr., orig. red slipcase has same ID card glued and logo/RR's name in gold, rare $250.00

SANTA FE – double deck, picture of two diesel streamliners abreast on track in mountains, one with blue bdr. other with red bdr., slipcase box has same ID cards glued on...$35.00

SANTA FE – double deck, one shows picture of trains going over and under a bridge, other shows trains going above and below embankment, desert scenes, orig. clear plastic cov. box has logo/Indian boy face, "SANTA FE ALL THE WAY" in white printing $20.00

SANTA FE – double deck, front end of yellow diesel loco 5695 and 5696 on red/blue backs with yellow borders, clear plastic cov. box has logo/Indian kids and slogan "Always on the move towards a better way" in white printing $20.00

SAL – souvenir, 53 views, logo centered on white flowers with green leaves on tan field, no border, orig. green slipcase has same ID card glued on and logo in gold $95.00

SCL – picture of diesel frt. train along curved highway with cars, blue cardstock case has same ID card glued on and printed logo $10.00

SP – souvenir, 53 views, photo of snow-capped mountains in West, no bdr., blue slipcase box has same ID card glued on plus gold printing, ca. 1915 ....$60.00

SP – souvenir, 53 views, photo of steam train on bridge crossing Great Salt Lake, blue slipcase box has same ID card glued on and gold logo, ca. 1926 ....$50.00

GN Indian Double Decks

SP – souvenir, 53 views, picture of yellow diesel pass. train on bridge crossing Great Salt Lake, blue slipcase box has same ID card glued on and gold logo, ca. 1939 ....$60.00

SP – souvenir, 53 views, picture of Daylight streamliner steam pass. train at Mission, maroon slipcase box has same ID card glued on and gold logo, ca. 1943 ....$40.00

SP – souvenir, 53 views, picture of cotton field and diesel streamliner on bridge crossing river, no bdr., yellow slipcase box has same card glued on and gold logo, ca. 1951 ....$30.00

SR – double deck, one has photo of steam engine on display in museum, other has photo of diesel frt. on white bridge, orig. green slipbox has logo in gold..........$25.00

SOO LINE – two white logos and vertical gold lines on red inside white border, orig. red cardstock case has logos, "THE WINNIPEGER," and names of cities printed, also came in blue with same ID $75.00

SOO LINE – white logo centered on pink field inside red line borders, orig. cardstock case has same ID card printed and picture of steam locomotive and two logos, also came in blue with same ID $40.00

SOO LINE – picture of fish jumping after fly with bear watching titled "Whose Breakfast?" blue bdr., cardstock case has same ID card glued on....................................$45.00

SOO LINE – gold logo on green backs, gold bdr., orig. cardstock case has same ID card glued on and picture of steam locomotive and two logos, also came in tan with same ID $35.00

SOO LINE – double deck, gold logo inside curlicue gold frame on maroon/green backs, red box has gold logo imprinted..$25.00

SOO LINE – double deck, gold logo inside gold filagree design on maroon/blue backs, red box has gold logo imprinted..$30.00

SOO LINE – double deck, one has blue logo centered in grey scallop oval on blue with gold lines, other is same but in maroon, orig. hinged box has same ID printed in gray/gold on maroon $40.00

SOO LINE – double deck, one has photo of ore boat going thru locks, other has aerial photo of locks, red logo on ea., plastic cov. box has gold logo on red bottom $30.00

SOO LINE – 75th anniversary 1883-1958, round yellow symbol on maroon, white logo in corner, orig. cardstock case has same ID glued-on card, diesel and two logos printed on other side, also came in blue with same ID card $20.00

SOO LINE – double deck, one has photo of wooded trail in woods, other has photo of Copper Falls in Wisc., red logo on ea., orig. red slipbox has gold logo on cover ..$30.00

SOO LINE – double deck, one has photo of Aerial Bridge, Duluth, Minn., other has photo of Duluth, Minn., red logo on ea., red box has gold logo $40.00

SOO LINE – Limited Edition Centennial, 1883-1983 logo, in gold on maroon, white bdr., orig. gold cardstock case has same ID card glued on, also came in maroon 1883-1983 logo on tan $15.00

SOO LINE – modern SOO logo in red/white on white with red horiz. stripe, orig. gold cardstock case has same ID card glued on, also came in red backs $10.00

SOO LINE – photo of frt. train on high trestle over river, gold cardstock case has same ID card glued on, SOO LINE RAILROAD on other side $15.00

SOO LINE – double deck, black sketch of Engine No. 1 Built For Soo Line Railroad in 1884 on silver/gold backs, plastic clear cov. black box $20.00

UP – shield logo, yellow streamliner, white smoke and green cars, The Challenger on blue backs with gold border, cardstock case has same ID printed and slogan "Road of the Streamliners and the Challengers" on grey $30.00

UP – picture of yellow streamliner 103 against background of mountains/sunset out West, cardstock case has same ID card glued one side, other has logo, 1869 Centennial 1969 Driving of the Golden Spike on blue $25.00

UP – picture of two engines meeting at Driving of the Golden Spike, cardstock case has same ID card glued one side, other has logo, 1869 Centennial 1969 Driving of the Golden Spike on blue $20.00

UP – picture of Jackson Lake and the Teton Range, Wyoming with logo and slogan "Be Specific ... say UNION PACIFIC," cardstock case has same ID card glued one side, other has logo and slogan "Road of the Domeliners" on blue $15.00

UP – UNION PACIFIC shield logo on bottom corner on red backs with yellow/white strip bdr., orig. cardstock case has opening one side to show card's back, other side has black printed panel on silver, also came with blue backs, same ID $15.00

WCF&N – double deck, photo of locomotive 207 and W.C.F.&N. RAILROAD, WATERLOO, IOWA on white, red/gold and green/gold bdrs., orig. brown box has gold ID imprinting on cover $45.00

WP&Y – souvenir, 53 views, red backs have colorful ornate design and borders in red/blue/gold, at center is WHITE PASS & YUKON ROUTE blue logo with rear of train extending through inner circle, orig. green slipcase box has same ID card glued on and logo printed in gold, rare $125.00

WP&Y – souvenir, 53 views, blue backs with similar ornate design and borders with red logo at center and rear of pass. train is inside inner circle, orig. tan slipcase box has same ID card glued and gold logo, rare $110.00

Postcards, Stereo View Cards

Railroad postcards have become one of the fastest growing collectibles in this field. There were millions printed, starting from around the turn of the century. Many collect them by categories, such as locomotives, passenger trains, depots, bridges, train wrecks, various scenes, and so on. In addition to the single card, folders, booklets and sets of postcards were turned out. Besides those put out by the railroads themselves, carrying their logos, thousands were made by commercial card manufacturers, both here and abroad. Most collectors prefer only the official railroad cards that have gone through the mail, as the cancellation dates them, while others want unused cards and will pay a higher price for these.

AT&SF – shops, Topeka, Kansas, Pub. by Hall Stationery, Topeka, Kans., mint $15.00

B&O – locomotive No. 5320, "President Cleveland," at Century of Progress, Chicago, canc. 1933 ....$8.00

B&O – Century of Progress, 1933, set of 15 cards picturing early railroad scenes from paintings, original envelope, mint $45.00

B&O – Centenary Pageant, 1827-1927, Baltimore, set of 15 cards picturing locomotives, early to modern, original envelope, mint..$60.00

B&M – R.R. Station, Salem, Mass., Hugh C. Leighton Co., Mfr's, Portland Me. canc. 1910 ....$12.00

BURLINGTON ROUTE – Thousand Island Dressing recipe, interior view of dining car, logo back, mint $10.00

BURLINGTON ROUTE – 50 Years of Progress in Burlington (2) Locomotives, exhibited at Century of Progress, 1934, logo back mint..$8.00

C&NW – interior view of "Ultra-modern parlor cars on the famous '400,'" logo back, mint $8.00

C&NW – railway station, Des Moines, Iowa, Pub. by Des Moines Post Card Co., Des Moines, Iowa, canc. 1912............$15.00

C&O – wreck of train No. 3 near Hinton, W. Va., Mar. 12, 1907, unused $18.00

CB&Q – depot, Hinsdale, Ill., pub. by H.C. Kammayer, Hinsdale, Ill., canc. 1909 ....$12.00

CGW – interior view of a Standard Steel Sleeping Car, logo back, unused $10.00

CGW – repair shops, Oelwein, Iowa, Pub. A.C. Bosselman & Co., N.Y. canc. 1910 ....$15.00

CM&STP – The Overland Limited – Chicago, Omaha, San Francisco, PRIVATE MAILING CARD authorized by Act of Congress of May 19, 1898, canc. 1905 (rare) $35.00

CM&STP – depot, Aberdeen, S.D., cancellation date 1909 ....$12.00

CM&STP – souvenir folder No. 1 of scenes along the Chicago, Milwaukee & St. Paul Railway, Pub. by Van Noy-Inter-state Co., (pic – elec. loco on cover) mint $18.00

CM&STP – souvenir booklet No. 2 of 12 cards of scenes along the Chicago, Milwaukee & St. Paul Railway, Made by Curt Teich & Co., Chicago, (pic – elec. loco on cover) mint.........$20.00

CPR – yards, Winnipeg, pub. by E.P. Charleton & Co., Winnipeg, canc. 1909 ....$8.00

CRI&P – passenger station, Davenport, Iowa, The Royal Series, mint $15.00

D&RG – souvenir folder, Over Soldiers Summit on the line of the Denver & Rio Grande RR., Pub. by the Inter-state Co., unused $18.00

D&SL – looping the loop, Denver & Salt Lake Railroad, Colorado, "Moffat Road" unused $15.00

ERIE – view of Erie Railroad Yards, Hornell, N.Y., Pub. by The Union News Co., N.Y., canc. 1910 ....$12.00

GH&SA – Sunset Route On Causeway, Galveston, Texas, mammoth structure connecting Galveston To The Mainland, 3-part folding postcard, Pub. by J.M. Maurer, Galveston, Texas, 1910 (scarce)................................$47.50

Complete Set of 1933 B&O Century of Progress postcards

GN – set of 10 cards picturing Blackfeet Indians from paintings by Winold Reiss, original envelope, mint $50.00

GN – set of 10 cards, Views of Scenic and Historical Interest along the Great Northern Railway, Pub. by GN RY., orig. blue mailing envelope, mint $27.50

GN – souvenir folder, Scenes of Great Northern Railway from the Oriental Limited, Pub. by C.H. Shaver, St. Paul, Minn., unused, dated 1906 ....$18.00

GN – Lake McDonald, Montana, reached only by the Great Northern Railway, logo on back, postmarked 1910 ..$6.00

GN – depot, Devils Lake, N.Dak., Pub. by American Import Co., Mpls. canc. 1909 ....$10.00

IC – streamliner, Panama Ltd., against Michigan Ave. skyline, Chicago, mint $8.00

L&N – R.R. bridge across Ohio River between Evansville, Ind. and Henderson, KY., Loge News Co., Evansville, Ind., canc. 1952..$6.00

LV – Black Diamond Express between New York, Philadelphia and Buffalo, "PHOSTINT"card, made only by Detroit Publishing Co., mint $22.50

LV – RR shops and round house, Sayre, Pa., Pub. by Wm. Erk, Athens, Pa. cancelled 1910 ....$10.00

MC – Niagara Falls From Michigan Central Train, Pub. by Metrocraft, Everett, Mass., mint..............................$15.00

MK&T – depot, Chanute, Kans., Pub. by E.C. Kropp Co., Milwaukee, canc. 1921 ....$6.00

NP – A CANDY TRAIN, model of the North Coast Limited made entirely of sugar, made in the dining car bakeshop, logo upper corner, mint........................$22.50

NP – "A Delicious Northern Pacific Breakfast" (pictures a table setting), menu and logo below, mint............$25.00

NP – diesel locomotive 6000 against mountain background, logo back, mint..$5.00

NP – souvenir folder of Scenes Along The Northern Pacific Railroad, Pub. by J.L. Robbins Co., Spokane, Wash., unused $18.00

NYC – N.Y. Central's "Empire State Express," The fastest long distance train in the world, embossed gold card, S. Langsdorf & Co., N.Y., canc. 1908 ....$15.00

NYC – New York Central's 20th Century Limited in the Hudson Highlands, Pub. by Bryant Union Publ. New York City, canc. 1905 ....$17.50

D&RG Souvenir Folder

Postcards With Official Railroad Logos

NYNH&H – depot, Hartford, Conn., canc. 1911 ....$8.00

PRR – Broadway Limited speeding on stone arch bridge entitled "Speed and Security," canc. 1926..................$10.00

PRR – Horse Shoe Curve on Pennsylvania R.R., Publ. by Union News Company, New York & Pittsburg, canc. 1908 ..$8.00

RI – Rock Island wreck at Gowrie, Ia. Aug. 15, 1910 (photo) canc. 1910 ....$18.00

RI – Rock Island Passenger Station, Des Moines, Ia., canc. 1912 ....$10.00

RI – ROCKY MOUNTAIN ROCKET At the Foot of Famous Pikes Peak, logo back, mint $5.00

SANTA FE – set of six cards in natural colors featuring streamlined trains, pub. by Fred Harvey, orig. mailing envelope, mint $25.00

SEABOARD – Silver Meteors pass in the scenic highlands of Florida, mint $8.00

SOO LINE – A Modern Railway (pic of Passenger train) Twin Cities To Winnipeg, Fifteen Hours, logo, canc. 1906 ....$17.50

SOO LINE – "Soo Depot," Duluth, Minn. E.C. Kropp, Pub. Milwaukee, No. 1518, canc. 1915.....................$10.00

SP – souvenir folder, The CASCADE and SHASTA Routes, Scenes Along The Southern Pacific From San Francisco to Portland, Made by Curt Teich & Co., Chicago, 1934, unused $18.00

SP – Album of Views (18 cards) THE SHASTA ROUTE, Scenes Along the Southern Pacific from San Francisco to Portland, pub. by Van Noy-Interstate, mint $25.00

SP – depot, Eugene, Ore., pub. E.C. Kropp Co., Milwaukee, canc. 1910 ....$8.00

UP – Union Pacific Depot and Park, Rawlins, Wyo., Pub. by Barkalow Bros., Omaha, Neb., mint $15.00

UP – Union Pacific Streamliner "City of Denver," logo on back, canc. 1937 ....$6.00

UP – Union Pacific Limited Train Crossing Great Salt Lake, Utah, logo on back, mint $5.00

WABASH – The Wabash Banner Limited – operated between St. Louis and Chicago, logo in upper corner, canc. 1915 ....$15.00

Stereo View Cards

These cards were for use with the steroscopic hand viewer, popular years ago. Two identical photos, aligned side by side, came mounted on a 3½ x 7" card, and when looked at through the viewer, gave a three-dimensional effect. Many railroad shots were taken by photographers to be made into these cards. Some of these views are the only known photographs of various railroad scenes now long gone, making them of historical value today.

BCR&N – passenger train wreck near Waterloo, Iowa, May 28, 1899. J.P. King, photographer, Waterloo, Iowa $25.00

CM&STP – passenger depot, LaCrosse, Wisconsin, 1879, photographed and published by Elmer & Tenney, Winona, Minn...$15.00

D&RG – passenger train in the Royal Gorge Grand Canyon of the Arkansas, near Canyon City, Colo., 1879, Keystone View Company, Mgrs.-Publishers.........................$20.00

F&PM – express train at Clare Station, ca. 1875, Goodridge Brothers, Publishers of Stereoscopic Views, East Sagnaw, Mich. $30.00

M&STP – "The Snowed-in Engine," No. 127 of SNOW-BOUND Series of nine cards put out after the great storm of Jan. 7 and 8, 1873. Photographed and published by A.L. McKay, Decorah, Iowa (rare set) $135.00

M&STP – "The Dead Engines," No. 126 of SNOW-BOUND Series of McKay's Views taken on the Iowa Division of the M&StP between Conover and Ridgway, Iowa after the great storm of Jan. 7 and 8, 1873 ....$15.00

LV – "Mt. Jefferson Plane," No. 179 of a Series of Views on the Line of the Lehigh Valley R.R., Photographed and Published by M.A. Kleckner, Bethlehem, Pa $15.00

Stereo View Card

MW RY – "The Great Trestle," No. 1825 of a Series of Views on the Mt. Washiongton Railway, ca. 1885. Photographed and published by Kilburn Brothers, Littleton, N.H. $18.00

MW RY – "Summit of Mt. Washington," No. 1245 of a Series of Views on the Mt. Washington Railway, ca. 1885. Photographed and published by Kilburn Brothers, Littleton, N.H. $18.00

NYNH&HRR – railroad depot, Springfield, Mass., ca. 1891. Published by E. & H.T. Anthony & Co., 591 Broadway, New York $20.00

PRR – engine on "NEWPORT BRIDGE" No. 158 of a series of Scenery of the Pennsylvania Railroad, ca. 1870, Purviance, Philadelphia, photographer and publisher $30.00

PRR – Train Rounding the Famous Horseshoe Curve, Allegheny Mountains, in Pennsylvania, ca. 1897, Keystone View Company, Meadville, Pa $20.00

P&O – passenger train at Gates of Crawford Notch and P&O RR, No. 2088. Photographed and published by Kilburn Brothers, Littleton, N.H. $15.00

P&O – passenger train on bridge, Portland & Ogdensburg Railroad, Crawford Notch, N.H., No. 2117. Photographed and published by Kilburn Brothers, Littleton, N.H. $15.00

WM – Western Maryland passenger train in moutains, ca. 1885, United States Views by W. M. Chase $18.00

W&StP – view of roundhouse at Waseca, Minnesota, ca. 1881, Elmer & Tenney, photographers, Winona, Minnesota $35.00

Pullman Company Collectibles

George Mortimor Pullman, a businessman riding the train one night in the 1850's, came upon the idea of a coach with seats which could be converted into sleeping berths. He experimented with several old day coaches, making them into sleeping cars, and thus The Pullman Company became a reality in 1859, continuing into the late 1970's, when the remaining railroads still running passenger trains took over the operations from The Pullman Company, the end of an era.

Collectors are now busily searching for Pullman Company memorabilia in use down through the years. This takes in a host of things, such as blankets, sheets and pillow cases from the sleeping cars, china and silverware from the diners, ashtrays, cuspidors and playing cards from the smoking cars, signs, wall shelves and lighting fixtures from the compartments and berths, caps, buttons and badges worn by the Conductors and Porters, stepstools, lanterns, and much, much more. A representative listing with their tentative values are listed here.

ADVERTISING POSTER – cardboard, horiz. type, 23 x 29", Travel in PULLMAN SAFETY and COMFORT to Your Favorite Winter Resort, 1936 ....$45.00

ASH TRAY – brown Bakelite, round, 5½"D, THE PULLMAN COMPANY raised on rim between rests $22.00

ASHTRAY – brown Bakelite, round, deep dish type, 4¼"D, THE PULLMAN COMPANY in white on exterior $18.00

BED SHEET – white cotton with PROPERTY OF THE PULLMAN CO. logo stamped in black............................$10.00

BLANKET – full color rose shade with THE PULLMAN CO. logo in darker color at center $75.00

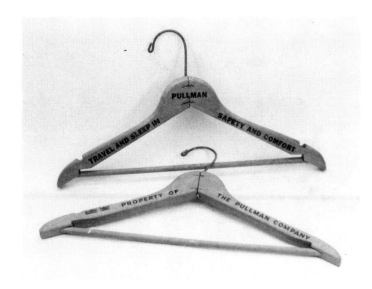

Wooden Clothes Hangers

BOOK – hard cover, PULLMAN'S PALACE CAR CO. 1897 Official Hotel Directory of the U.S. (Hotel Red Book) $45.00

BOOKLETS – series of 12, PULLMAN FACTS, 3½ x 6", illustrated, ca. 1930's, complete set $25.00

BRASS LOCK – ½ x 1¼ x 1¼", stamped PULLMAN CO. (curved) on front, keyhole on bottom $15.00

BROCHURE – black covers, " x 9", Go PULLMAN for travel at its best by day-by night, 23P, 1950's $5.00

CAP BADGE – rectangular 1 x 4", PULLMAN CONDUCTOR, black letters on pebbled gold field $50.00

CAP BADGE – rectangular, 1 x 4", PULLMAN PORTER, black letters on pebbled silver field........................$45.00

CAP – PULLMAN PORTER, complete with badge, visor cord and two side buttons...$125.00

CASTOR STAND – silverplate stand with three glass bottles, 4¾"H, PULLMAN CAR COMPANY LTD. round crest on front of stand, Sheffield $95.00

CHINA – oval platter, 8 x 13", PULLMAN in black/yellow pinstripe border $115.00

CHINA – tea plate 7½"D, PULLMAN in black/yellow pinstripe border $75.00

CHINA – oval dish, 4¼ x 5¾", PULLMAN in black/yellow pinstripe border $35.00

CHINA – dinner plate, 9"D, PULLMAN in multi-color floral design border with Indian tree center $85.00

CHINA – individual creamer with handle, 2¾" tall, PULLMAN, brown geometric border and orange flower $95.00

CHINA – individual creamer without handle, 2¾ tall, PULLMAN, brown geometric border and orange flower $75.00

CLOTHES HANGER – wood, standard type with crossbar, mkd PULLMAN, Travel and Sleep in Safety and Comfort $12.00

CLOTHES HANGER – wood, standard type with crossbar, mkd Property of the PULLMAN COMPANY $12.00

CONDUCTOR'S LANTERN – nickel plated, PULLMAN on base and on clear globe $450.00

CUSPIDOR – nickel finish, PULLMAN incised on cast iron bottom, 8¼"D, flared top $100.00

DOUBLE SHOT GLASS – heavy, 3" tall, 2½"D, PULLMAN COMPANY raised letters on bottom $45.00

DRINK STAND ASH TRAY – floor type, 26"H, chrome finish, two-tier round tray, PULLMAN on black cast iron circular base 13"D $350.00

FIRE EXTINGUISHER – white brass in wall mount bracket, 3"D, 14"L, mkd THE PULLMAN CO. near top $40.00

FOLDER – two sided, 11 x 47", PULLMAN PROGRESS, illustrated history of the Pullman car, 1859-1942, pub. by Pullman Co. 1945 ....$10.00

HAND TOWEL – 1918 PULLMAN-PULLMAN 1918 on blue center stripe across towel $22.00

HAND TOWEL – PROPERTY OF THE PULLMAN COMPANY 1929 on blue center stripe $15.00

HAND TOWEL – PROPERTY OF THE PULLMAN COMPANY (undated) woven in white on blue stripe $10.00

MECHANICAL PENCIL – hexagon, 6"L, PULLMAN-STANDARD CAR MFG. CO., "World's Largest Builders of Railroad Cars," white on brown, Autopoint $15.00

NAPKIN – white linen, PULLMAN woven in center and corners, floral design, 21 x 22" $10.00

Ash Tray and Box of Matches

PASS – cardstock, Pullman's Palace Car Co., 1873, Geo. M. Pullman's signature in ink $100.00

PASS – cardstock, Pullman's Palace Car Co., 1897, light green $15.00

PENCIL – blue lead, hexagon, THE PULLMAN COMPANY in gold on blue, 7"L, unsharpened $4.00

PILLOW CASE – white cotton with PROPERTY OF THE PULLMAN CO. logo stamped in black...................$5.00

PLAYING CARDS – intertwined "P" in center of oriental design on green backs, original case.....................$20.00

SAFETY MATCHES – cardboard slipbox, ⅝ x 1⅜ x 2¼", dark blue, PULLMAN logo both sides, Diamond Match Co.........$10.00

SERVICE PIN – coat lapel, gold, 30 years, PULLMAN across car at top $45.00

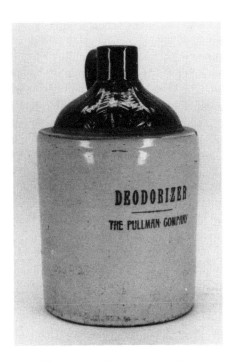

Stoneware Deodorizer Jug

STEP STOOL – cast aluminum, PULLMAN on cross-hatched square top, Utica $300.00
STONEWARE JUG – 9" tall, brown top, DEODORIZER, THE PULLMAN COMPANY, blue letters on light grey $75.00
SWIZZLE STICK – THE PULLMAN COMPANY in gold on blue, square rod with ball tip, 5½"L...........................$1.00
THERMOS BOTTLE – chromium, 11" tall, PULLMAN etched in front, made by Stanley $75.00
TICKET PUNCH – nickel finish, mk'd. PULLMAN on side, punches circle design $45.00
UNIFORM BUTTON – P.P.C.Co. within wreath on large silver dome, Henry V. Allen Co. NY (scarce) $30.00
UNIFORM BUTTON – PULLMAN across large gold flat, Waterbury Button Co., Conn....................................$4.00
UNIFORM BUTTON – PULLMAN across small silver flat, Superior Quality $2.00
WALL LAMP – compartment, electric, brass back plate, light socket and white shade, 9"H..............................$75.00
WALL LAMP – berth, electric, chrome metal, round white globe with clear spot, 9" long $150.00
WALL SHELF – washroom, for hand towels, brass, rectangular 6½ x 27", railing with rounded front corners $95.00

SHEET MUSIC – "PULLMAN PORTER'S PARADE," Maurice Abrahams Music Co. NY, 1913.........................$20.00
SIGN – cardstock, 5 x 7", DINING CAR IN OPPOSITE DIRECTION, white on dark blue $35.00
SIGN – cardstock, two-sided, 6 x 9", QUIET is requested for the benefit of those who have retired, "Have you forgotten any personal property?" white/dark blue $45.00
SIGN – stainless steel, 1¼ x 3¼", FOR PULLMAN PASSENGERS ONLY, black letters $15.00
SILVERWARE – sugar bowl with lid, 10 oz., PULLMAN CO. stamped on bottom $65.00
SILVERWARE – coffee pot, 10 oz., THE PULLMAN CO. stamped on bottom $75.00
SILVERWARE – oval tray, 5½ x 9¾", THE PULLMAN COMPANY stamped on bottom $50.00
SILVERWARE – tablespoon, THE PULLMAN COMPANY stamped on backside, Int'l. Silver $18.00
SILVERWARE – table fork, THE PULLMAN COMPANY stamped on backside, Int'l. Silver $16.00
SOAP – individual small bar wrapped in blue/white paper, PULLMAN both sides $5.00
SPITTOON – nickel finish, THE PULLMAN CO. stamped on bottom, 6"D, twist-off top $65.00

Silverplate Caster Stand With Three Bottles

Railroad Postmarks, RPO's

Covers bearing railroad postmarks are of interest to both the philatelist and the railroadiana collector. Early envelopes were postmarked with the name of the railroad on which they were carried, and these are rare. When railway post office cars were instituted to sort mail enroute, the envelopes bore R.P.O. postmarks. In more recent years, anniversary, first day and last trip covers were issued to collectors. Many of these had special art work and commemorative railroad postage stamps, known as "cachet covers." There are some who make a specialty of railroad-mail collectibles.

Special Note: Many early covers bearing railroad postmarks have high catalog value postage stamps affixed, increasing the price of the cover considerably. Those listed here bear the more common stamps on them, with only nominal catalog value.

Covers Bearing Early Railroad Postmarks

BOSTON & ALBANY R.R. – Dec. 10, in black circle on three-cent red envelope stamp, (1853-55) $45.00

BOSTON & FITCHBURG R.R. – Oct. 29 in blue circle on three-cent red glued-on stamp (1851-56) $45.00

MIC. CENTRAL R.R. – Jan. 9, in black circle on three-cent red envelope stamp (1853-55) $100.00

N.Y. & BOSTON STMB & R.R. – Aug. 28, in black circle on three cent-red envelope stamp (1853-55) $85.00

N.Y. & ERIE R.R. – May 6, in black circle on three cent-red glued-on stamp, (1851-56) $100.00

PENNSYLVANIA R.R. – Aug. 2, in blue circle on three-cent red glued-on stamp (1851-56) $50.00

PROV. & STONGINGTON R.R. – Oct. 19, in black circle on three-cent red glued-on stamp (1857-61) $40.00

PROV. & WOR.R.R. – Aug. 1 in blue circle on three-cent red glued-on stamp, (1851-56) $35.00

ST.P.&SIOUX CITY R.R. – Mar. 16, in black circle on three-cent green glued-on stamp (1870-73) $40.00

SOUTH MINN. R.R. – Feb. 11, in black circle on three-cent red envelope stamp (1871) $50.00

WASHINGTON & PHILA R.R. – Feb. 18, in black circle on three-cent red envelope stamp (1853-55) $85.00

WI & ST. PETER R.R – in blue circle on one-cent brown postal card, 1873 ....$45.00

Cover With Early Railroad Postmark

Covers Bearing R.P.O. Postmarks

R.P.O. cancellations can be found on various postal cards as well as on all types of business, tourist and common correspondence. When found on post cards picturing trains and on railroad-marked covers, an extra charge is generally put on them.

ALAMOSA & DURANGO – R.P.O. TR 216, JAN 31, 1951 (cachet cover, last trip San Juan narrow gauge passenger train in U.S.A.) $7.50

BROOKINGS & GETTYS – R.P.O. DEC. 28 EAST 1891 (reg. business cover) $12.00

CHI. & FREEPORT – R.P.O. TR703, Oct. 25, 1948 (cachet cover, 100th Anniversary Chicago and North-Western System) $8.50

CO. BLUFFS & K.C. – R.P.O. TR 20, NOV. 11, 1934 (cachet cover, first trip Burlington Route Zephyr streamliner) $9.50

DAYTON & PASCO – R.P.O. DEC. 25, 1906 West (tourist post card) $6.00

ELROY & TRACY – R.P.O. T 517, JUL. 11, 1910 (tourist post card) $5.00

GLENWOOD & ST.P. – R.P.O. T 110, MAY 18, 1910 (Soo Line tourist cover) $8.00

HASTINGS & COLOGNE – R.P.O. East AUG 27, 1913 (reg. business post card) $5.00

MILES CITY & SPOK. – R.P.O. TR 4, JAN 31, 1912 (Railroad Co. cover) $12.00

N.Y. & CHI – R.P.O. TR51, DEC. 7, 1941 (cachet cover, first trip new streamlined Empire State Express, New York Central System) $10.00

OMAHA & K.C. – R.P.O. T 109, MAY 4, 1936 (reg. business cover) $3.50

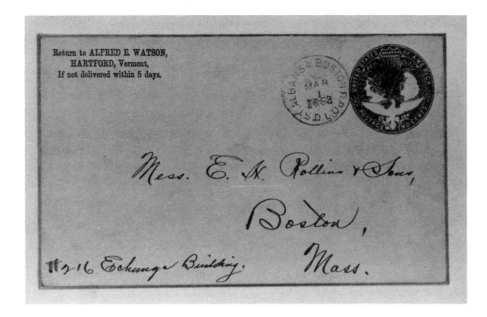

RPO Cover, 1893

PITTS. & ST. LOUIS – R.P.O. TR 7, DEC. 15, 1909 (tourist cover) $7.50

ST. ALBANS & BOSTON – R.P.O. TR 53, MAR 1 (1893 Columbian Exp. cover) $22.00

ST. P. & MILES CY – R.P.O. TR 8, OCT 22, 1927 (reg. business cover) $5.00

ST. PAUL & HAVRE – R.P.O. TR 4, OCT. 21, 1915 (post card with train) $15.00

ST. PAUL & JAMESTOWN – R.P.O. TR 8, APR. 23, 1911 (Railroad Co. post card) $10.00

Rolling Stock Relics

Since the demise of the Iron Horse, and soon after the railroads dropped their passenger trains, there has been an increasing interest among rail buffs in preserving relics from the steam locomotive and discontinued passenger cars. Engine bells, headlights, whistles, builder's plates and other items from the locomotive are now bringing high prices, along with furnishings and hardware from old coaches, such as brass door handle sets, fancy brass luggage racks, wall shelves, ceiling and wall lamps, step stools, plaques and so on. Many of these items from the vanished steam engine and rolling stock of yesteryear still can be found today by the diligent collector.

AIR BRAKE CONTROL HANDLE – locomotive cab, removable, cast brass with steel tension bar, 9½" long, square end opening $20.00

AIR GAUGE – locomotive, all brass, 3⅜" diameter, C.M.& St.P.Ry. on dial, The Ashton Valve Co. $85.00

BELL – steam locomotive, cast bronze, iron yoke and stand, unmarked $950.00

BRAKE WHEEL – cast iron, curved spoke type, 16" diameter, mk'd. C&NW, pre-1900 ....$75.00

BUILDER'S PLATE – steam engine era, round, 9¼" diameter, BALDWIN LOCOMOTIVE WORKS, AUG. 1915......$275.00

BUILDER'S PLATE – steam engine era, rectangular, 7½" x 14", AMERICAN LOCOMOTIVE CO., July 1912 ....$300.00

CABOOSE LAMP – wall mount, aluminum, kerosene burning, ALADDIN, complete with shade $95.00

CANDLE LAMP – RPO car, brass, tubular style, 10" tall with glass chimney, THE SAFETY CO. NY $65.00

CLASSIFICATION LAMP – steam locomotive, cast iron, round ball type, electric, exterior lever for lens color change, PYLE NATIONAL CO., pair $500.00

Steam Locomotive Headlight, Electric

Locomotive Steam Whistle

DEODORIZER JUG – Pullman car, stoneware, 9" tall, brown top, THE PULLMAN COMPANY in blue letters on light grey $75.00

DINNER CHIME – dining car, DEAGAN, Model 206, bronze, mint set in orig. box $250.00

DISPOSAL PLATE – washroom, wall mt'd., FOR USED RAZOR BLADES, brass, 1½ x 3¼", with slot opening $25.00

DOOR HANDLE SET – coach, two pieces, cast brass, ornate design, early 1900s..$50.00

DOOR HANDLE – box car, sliding door, cast iron, 10" long, three bolt holes ea. end mk'd C&NW M8805, early 1900s..$25.00

DOOR LATCH – box car, two-piece set, cast iron, hinged latch and eye for padlock, early 1900's................$18.00

DRINK STAND ASHTRAY – Pullman car, metal, chrome, 26" high, double round tray top, PULLMAN on base $325.00

DRINKING WATER JUG – locomotive cab, stoneware, 10" high, brown top, ROCK ISLAND LINES blue letters on light gray $185.00

DRUMHEAD – rear observation car, CHICAGO & NORTH-WESTERN LINE logo at center, NORTHWESTERN LIMITED around, 26" dia., electric lighted $500.00

DRUMHEAD – rear observation car, NORTHERN PACIFIC, NORTH COAST LTD., rectangular, 28¼ x 20½", electric lighted $450.00

FIRE EXTINGUISHER – railroad car, wall mt'd, brass, Pyrene, 14" long with hanger, mk'd NP RY $65.00

FIRST AID KIT – caboose, sheet steel, 2¾ x 4½ x 7½", wall mt'd, removable, GREAT NORTHERN RAILWAY goat logo on olive green enamel $85.00

FIRST AID KIT – coach, sheet steel, 2½ x 4½ x 7½", wall mt'd, removable, NORTHERN PACIFIC RAILWAY logo on brown enamel $75.00

HAND HOLD – coach, exterior entrance, brass bar, 32" length $25.00

HEADLIGHT – locomotive, early, box type, oil burning, made by M.M. Buck & Co., St. Louis, ca. 1860s..$950.00

HEADLIGHT – steam locomotive, round style with engine number, electric, not railroad marked, Pyle National, ca. 1920's...$750.00

HERALD – locomotive, sheet metal, round, 24" diameter, GREAT NORTHERN RAILWAY with goat at center, red/black/white, reflective enamel $325.00

HERALD – locomotive, sheet metal, rectangle, 17 x 23", THE MILWAUKEE ROAD, white letters on red, reflex finish $185.00

JOURNAL BOX COVER – box car, cast iron, 9 x 11", CB&Q RY, mfr. Gunite Foundries, Rockford, Illinois $40.00

LAMP – locomotive cab, kerosene type, complete with fount and globe, NYC EAST, Dietz, early 1900's $95.00

Name Train Logo From Rear Passenger Car

LAMP – coach, ceiling, center aisle type, oil burning, brass, ornate design, pre-1900...$750.00

LAMP – coach, side wall, oil burning, complete with fancy holders, lamp chimney and bracket, pre-1900 ..$150.00

LAMP – roomette, corner mt'd, electric, all cast metal including bell-shape shade, 1940's...........................$75.00

LAMP MOUNT BRACKET – caboose, for marker lamps, cast iron, 3½" high GN, pr $65.00

LAMP MOUNT BRACKET – front engine classification, combination, cast iron, with hole for flag mount, 4" high, mk'd ACL, pair...$75.00

LETTER DROP CHUTE – mail car, exterior, cast iron with hinged cover, 4 x 7"...$75.00

LINK & PIN COUPLING SET – two pieces, heavy cast iron, oval link 4½ x 13", coupling pin 13¾" long, UPRR, ca. 1880's $65.00

LUGGAGE RACK – coach, fancy cast brass ends with steel bottom grill, 12 x 36"..$175.00

Ornate Brass Door Handle Set

Passenger Car Step Stool

LUGGAGE RACK – coach, brass, fancy cast design ends with interwoven wire, mesh bottom, 10½ x 48"..........$250.00

MAIL POUCH – express car, canvas and leather trim, black stencilled letters RAILWAY EXPRESS AGENCY, with serial number $40.00

MARKER LAMPS – caboose, oil burning, four lenses, green/red, ADLAKE, square tops, mk'd GN RY, pair $400.00

MARKER LAMPS – passenger train, tail end car, oil burning, four lenses, green/red, ADLAKE, round tops, mk'd MStP&SSMRR, pair $600.00

MATCH BOX HOLDER – smoking car, for stick matches, wall mt'd, brass, open sides, 2½ x 4¼", back plate........$55.00

MATCH STRIKING PLATE – smoking car, for stick matches, wall mt'd, brass, 1¾ x 4½" $30.00

NAME TRAIN LOGO – rear passenger car, red metal, rectangle 24 x 24", GREAT NORTHERN RAILWAY logo and train name BADGER, electric lighted..........$375.00

NUMBER PLATE – front of steam engine, cast brass, round, 8½", BALDWIN LOCOMOTIVE WORKS, PHILADELPHIA, U.S.A., digits in center $300.00

OIL LEVEL CUP – locomotive, brass, round with clear glass liner, 5" tall, Lunkenheimer No. 3 Sentinel.........$25.00

PLACARD HOLDER – baggage car, cast iron, rectangular, 8¼ x 11¼", mk'd. GN....................................$15.00

PLAQUE – coach, brass, rectangle, 4 x 12", raised letters PASSENGERS NOT ALLOWED TO STAND ON THE PLATFORM $35.00

PLAQUE – passenger car wall decor, MILWAUKEE ROAD, Hiawatha Indian figure cut-out, aluminum, 11½ x 19", oval, ½" thick $175.00

RUG – parlor car, wool, green and black floral design on red, large G. N. RY. goat logo in center, 27 x 46" $200.00

SEAL – express car, metal strip 8¼" long with ball end, embossed "REA EXP." and serial number, unused $2.00

SEAL – box car, metal strip 8¼" long with ball and embossed with CMStP&P initial and serial number, unused ..$4.00

SIGN – coach, PASSENGERS ARE PROHIBITED FROM STANDING ON PLATFORM WHILE TRAIN IS IN MOTION, 3 x 10½", white letters on blue porcelainized steel $35.00

SIGN – passenger car entrance, WATCH YOUR STEP, 3½ x 21", porcelainized steel, white letters on black $45.00

SIGN – sleeping car, stainless, rectangle, 3¼ x 5", white letters on black, TO GET IN OR OUT OF UPPER BERTH PLEASE USE THE LADDER.................................$55.00

SOAP HOLDER – coach, wall type, brass, ornate, early ..$20.00

SPEED RESTRICTION PLAQUE – locomotive, brass, 1¾ x 5¼", cast letters, 70 MPH MAXIMUM PERMISSIBLE LOCOMOTIVE SPEED $35.00

SPITTOON – smoking car, nickeled finish brass, round, 2¾" high, stamped THE PULLMAN CO $65.00

STEP STOOL – passenger car, metal, embossed GREAT NORTHERN front side, Morton Mfg. Co. Chgo....$285.00

STEP STOOL – passenger car, metal, embossed with NORTHERN PACIFIC Monad logo front and back..........$385.00

STEP STOOL – passenger car, metal, embossed with SOO LINE logo front, Morton Mfg. Co., Chgo $350.00

STEP STOOL – passenger car, metal, embossed UNION PACIFIC across front, Morton Mfg. Co., Chgo $275.00

Roomette Electric Wall Lamp

STEP STOOL – Pullman car, metal, embossed PULLMAN both sides, made by Utica $300.00

STEP STOOL – passenger car, metal, embossed NYC SYSTEM both sides, Morton Mfg. Co., Chgo $250.00

STEP LADDER – sleeping car, wood, height 36", hinged back, carpeted treads, marked NPR.....................$95.00

TENDER PLATE – steam locomotive, cast iron, rectangular, 3¼ x 6", Tender No., Class, Lt. Weight, mk'd C.M. & St.P.Ry...$75.00

TICKET HOLDER – coach, wall mount type, brass, ornate shape, 1⅜ x 2", incised TICKET and C&NW $15.00

TRUST PLATE – rolling stock, cast aluminum, 5 x 12", NORTHERN PACIFIC RAILWAY EQUIPMENT TRUST OF 1966, FIRST NATIONAL CITY BANK, TRUSTEE, OWNER, LESSOR $40.00

TRUST PLATE – rolling stock, cast iron, 6½ x 16", THE NORTHERN TRUST COMPANY, TRUSTEE, OWNER AND LESSOR, CHICAGO AND NORTHWESTERN RY. CO. THIRD EQUIP. TRUST OF 1953..................$50.00

TRUST PLATE – rolling stock, cast aluminum, 5¼ x 13½", CHICAGO BURLINGTON & QUINCY RAILROAD EQUIPMENT TRUST NO. 3 OF 1965, THE NORTHERN TRUST COMPANY, TRUSTEE, OWNER AND LESSOR $45.00

WALL LAMP – Pullman berth, electric, brass, complete with white shade $75.00

WALL SHELF – Pullman compartment, open rectangular railing design with rounded front corners, 6½ x 27"..$95.00

WALL SHELF – coach washroom, brass, overall ornate design, mk'd Nor Pac Ry Co., 3½ x 10½" $150.00

WALL SHELF – coach washroom, brass, narrow railing openings with rounded corners, 2½ x 8½" $65.00

WHISTLE – caboose, back-up, all cast brass, whistle in lever, 8" tall, Sherburne Co., Boston, Mass $75.00

WHISTLE – steam locomotive, brass, triple chamber chime, 14" tall to acorn finial, Buckeye Brass Works, Dayton, Ohio $275.00

WHISTLE – steam locomotive, brass, single chamber chime, 15" tall to finial, Powell's....................................$200.00

WHISTLE – locomotive cab, cast brass, "peanut" whistle, 3" tall, air operated, engineer overspeed warning ..$22.00

WHISTLE – steam locomotive, brass, triple chamber, 13" tall, rounded top, Mocking Bird whistle Lunkenheimer $375.00

Locomotive Cab Air Gauge

WINDOW SASH LOCK – coach, brass, spring action type with finger grips...$10.00

WOODEN CLOTHES HANGER – sleeping car, standard type with crossbar, mk'd N.Y. CENTRAL, Sleeping Car Service $20.00

Cast Brass Plaque

Cast Aluminum Trust Plate

WOODEN CLOTHES HANGER – sleeping car, standard type with crossbar, mk'd PULLMAN, Travel and Sleep in Safety and Comfort $18.00

WOODEN CLOTHES HANGER – sleeping car, curved top, 18" long with wire crossbar, mk'd CANADIAN PACIFIC Sleeping Car Service $15.00

Sheet Music

Many pieces of sheet music have been published pertaining to the railroads over the years. "Casey Jones, The Brave Engineer," "I've Been Working On the Railroad," and "The Wabash Cannon Ball" to name a few. Especially desirable are those picturing the train on their colorful covers. Fine copies from the early 1900s are in demand, steadily increasing in price. Some sheet music was published exclusively for the railroad or dedicated to the Brotherhoods, and these are worth more than those that are railroad-related.

Sheet Music Published For Railroads or Dedicated to Brotherhoods

"HAIL THE BALTIMORE & OHIO" – centenary march, pub. for the B&O by Walter Goodwin, Inc., N.Y. 1927. Cover shows an artist's rendering of a side view of the steam loco "The President Washington" $35.00

"MY DAD'S THE ENGINEER" – descriptive song and chorus by Chas. Graham, Henry J. Wehman publisher, New York, Chgo. 1895, dedicated to the Brotherhood of Locomotive Engineers. Cover depicts a speeding passenger train and girl seated inside of coach without worry 'cause her Dad's the engineer $40.00

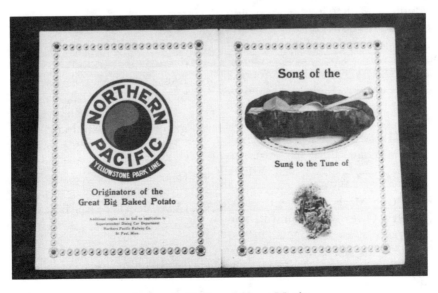

Authentic Railroad Sheet Music

"THE MIDNIGHT FLYER" – march two-step by Frederick W. Hager, arranged by E.T. Paull, pub. by E.T. Paull Music Co., N.Y. 1903, specially composed, arranged and dedicated to the Brotherhood of Locomotive Engineers of America. Lithographed cover of express train leaving depot at night $30.00

"THE NEW STEEL TRAIL" – march and two-step, lyrics and music by Charles E. Hunt, Railroad Editor Seattle Post-Intelligencer, published by the Passenger Department Chicago, Milwaukee & St. Paul Railway, Seattle, 1913. Front cover has colorful art work of "The Olympian" passenger train crossing a bridge in the mountains. Back cover has the Chicago Milwaukee and St. Paul Railway logo $40.00

"THE PENNSYLVANIA SPECIAL" – two-step march by Bandmaster F.N. Innes, dedicated to Samuel Moody, Gen'l Pass. Agent, Pennsylvania Lines, published by The Pennsylvania Company, 1905. Front cover has photo of F.N. Innes, back cover-photo of "The Pennsylvania Special" pass. train $35.00

"SONG OF THE GREAT BIG BAKED POTATO" – words by Geo. D. Emery, to be sung to the tune of "The Old Oaken Bucket," pub. for the Northern Pacific Railway Co. Dining Car Dept., 1912. Covers picture the baked potato and logo $55.00

Sheet Music – Railroad-Related

"CASEY JONES, THE BRAVE ENGINEER" – words and music by Seibert and Newton, Southern California Music Co., Los Angeles, 1909. Cover shows front end of locomotive with two men in cab $25.00

"DREAM TRAIN" – song, words by Charles Newman, music by Billy Baskette, Milton Weil Music Co. Inc., Chicago, 1928. Cover depicts passenger train and portrait of Guy Lombardo $5.00

"FARE-THEE-WELL" – words and music by Tell Taylor and Geo. Fairman, Tell Taylor Music Publisher, Chicago, 1911. Cover has illustration of passenger train leaving depot and girl waving goodbye to her boyfriend $6.00

"GUNGL'S RAILROAD GALOP" – as played by Willis' Band at the Mechanics' Industrial Fair, arranged for the piano by H.M. Bosworth, published by M. Gray, 609-613 Clay Street San Francisco, 1869. Cover has engraving of wood burning funnel stack locomotive (rare) $45.00

"I'M GOING BACK TO CAROLINA" – "Here comes my train, ding dong, toot toot, farewell, so long" – words and music by Billy Downs and Ernie Erdman, Harold Rossiter Music Co. Chgo., N.Y., 1913. Stylized front end sketch of steam locomotive on cover $6.50

"IN THE BAGGAGE COACH AHEAD" – song and refrain, written and composed by Gussie L. Davis, published by Howley Haviland & Co., N.Y. 1896, "Empire State Express" on cover $35.00

"I'VE BEEN WORKING ON THE RAILROAD" – words and music, Calumet Music Co., Chicago, 1935. Man waving to train on cover $12.00

"MAKE THAT ENGINE STOP AT LOUISVILLE" – words and music by Sam Lewis and Geo. Meyer, publ. by Geo. W. Meyer Music Co., N.Y. 1914. Cover has a Louisville and Nashville RR train speeding on track......................$10.00

"MY HAN IN LOUSIAN" – "I hear that engine whistle blowing, toot-toot, farewell, I'm going to" – words and music by C.E. Olson, Up-To-Date Music Publishers, Chicago, 1914. Cover has nice drawing of passenger train rolling along $7.50

Public Railroad Sheet Music

"OH! MISTER RAILROAD MAN WON'T YOU TAKE ME BACK TO ALABAM?" – words by Stanley Murphy, music by Henry I. Marshall, Jerome H. Remick & Co., Detroit, 1914. Framed moonlight scene on cover with wash drawing of passenger train below $8.00

"ON THE 5.15" – song, lyric by Stanley Murphy, music by Henry I. Marshall, Jerome H. Remick & Co. N.Y. Detroit. Front of engine 5.15 depicted with photo of Miss Con Farber of Farber Sisters on cover.............................$8.50

"PULLMAN PORTER'S PARADE" – words by Ren. G. My, music by Maurice Abrahams, Maurice Abrahams Music Co., N.Y. 1913. Cover shows porters marching $18.00

"SUNSET LIMITED" – march, two-step by Harry J. Lincoln, Vandersloot Music Pub. Co. Williamsport, Pa., 1910. Color cover of puffing train heading into the setting sun; group of passengers standing on rear car platform waving $12.50

"SUNSET LIMITED" – march by Henry Bartell, pub. by McKinley Music Co. Chicago, 1910. Cover has pass. train speeding into the setting sun $6.00

"THAT RAILROAD RAG" – words by Nat Vincent, music by Ed Bimberg, Head Music Pub. Co. New York, 1911. Cover depicts front of steam locomotive entering ragged opening in burlap screen $8.00

"THE BUFFALO FLYER" – march, two step, by Harry Lincoln, publ. Vandersloot Music Co., Williamsport, Pa. 1904. Speeding pass. train at night pictured on cover $12.50

"THE CHICAGO EXPRESS" – march, two-step by Percy Wenrich, McKinley Music Co. Chicago, 1905. Passenger train on cover..............................$8.50

"THE WESTERN FLYER" – march two-step by Paul Morton, pub. McKinely Music Co. Chgo. 1919. Pass. train rounding curve of track on cover $5.00

"WABASH CANNON BALL" – by Wm. Kindt, with guitar chords and special Hawaiian guitar chorus, Calumet Music Co., Chgo. 1939. Black/white drawing of speeding pass. train and photo of cowboy singer, Rex Griffin $15.00

"WHEN THAT MIDNIGHT CHOO-CHOO LEAVES FOR ALABAM" – by Irving Berlin, Ted Snyder Co. Music Publishers, N.y. 1912. Cover depicts passenger train at night..............................$10.00

"WHERE DO YOU WORK-A JOHN?- DELAWARE LACKA-WAN" – by Mortimer Weinberg, Charley Marks and Harry Warren, Shapiro, Bernstein & Co. Publishers,N.Y. 1926. Cover depicts two men on hand-car $18.00

Signs

Ever since the railroads got out of the passenger train business, the collecting of all the various signs and placards that once adorned the walls or depots and passenger coaches has proliferated. Of special interest are the Express and Telephone Company blue and white porcelainized steel signs that hung on the exterior walls of small town depots. Many were two-sided so they could be read from both ends of the station platform. Express Companies also used signs on their baggage carts and delivery trucks and distributed call cards to local merchants for displaying in their store front windows alerting the driver to stop and make a parcel pick-up. All of these miscellaneous signs and placards from the vanished depots and long-gone passenger coaches are bringing high prices today. Reproductions are being made, so be wary!

Porcelainized Steel Signs

ADAMS EXPRESS COMPANY, MONEY ORDERS SOLD HERE – depot exterior, one sided 3 x 30", red herald one end, white letters on green, ca. 1900 ....$150.00

AIR EXPRESS, DIVISION RAILWAY EXPRESS AGENCY, INC. – delivery trucks, one-sided diamond shape, 8 x 8", white wings and letters on red $125.00

Porcelainized Steel Signs

AMERICAN EXPRESS CO., Money Orders, Foreign Drafts, Travelers Cheques, Letters of Credit, Telegraphic Transfers – depot exterior, two-sided, 13 x 17", white on blue, dated 1914 ....$250.00

PUBLIC TELEPHONE – blue bell inside white circle with blue letters around, depot exterior, hanging, two-sided, 18 x 18" $125.00

PUBLIC TELEPHONE – blue bell inside white circle with blue letters around, depot exterior, hanging, two-sided, 11 x 11" $75.00

RAILWAY EXPRESS AGENCY, PACKAGES RECEIVED HERE – depot exterior, hanging, two-sided, 15 x 18", red diamond on white, black letters at bottom $185.00

RAILWAY EXPRESS AGENCY – depot exterior, mounted flush, one-sided, 11½ x 72" long, yellow letters and border on black..............................$225.00

RAILWAY EXPRESS AGENCY – baggage cart, one-sided, diamond shape, 14 x 14", black outlined white letters on red, white border $75.00

RAILWAY EXPRESS AGENCY – baggage cart, one-sided, diamond shape, 8 x 8", black outlined white letters on red, white border $65.00

RAILWAY EXPRESS – baggage cart, one-sided, two pieces, 4 x 30¼", red/cream letters on olive green, three grommet holes on each..............................$145.00

RAILWAY EXPRESS – two piece hanging, each panel 5¾ x 20", with round bottom corners, red/cream letters on olive green, two grommet holes at top $135.00

Cardboard Call Card Signs

REA EXPRESS – depot exterior, 3¾ x 60", long ribbon sign, white letters on green $50.00

REA EXPRESS – baggage cart, one-sided, diamond shape, 12 x 12", white letters on red, two grommet holes $75.00

REA EXPRESS – baggage cart, one-sided, diamond shape, 8 x 8", white letters on red, two grommet holes $50.00

Rare Tin Sign, 1914

UNION PACIFIC SYSTEM – TICKETS FOR CHILDREN Under the Law, children 5 years old and under 12 must pay Half Fare: 12 years or over, Full Fare, depot interior, 8 x 10", white letters on dk blue, 1930s $135.00

WESTERN UNION, TELEGRAPH here, white on blue, WESTERN UNION in black on yellow slanting below, depot exterior, two-sided, 16¾ x 25".....................$145.00

WESTERN UNION, TELEGRAPH here, white on blue, WESTERN UNION in black on yellow slanting below, depot exterior, two-sided, 11 x 17" $125.00

WESTERN UNION TELEGRAPH AND CABLE OFFICE – depot exterior, hanging, two-sided, 12 x 24", white on blue $225.00

WESTERN UNION TELEGRAPH AND CABLE – blue cross-hatched globe inside circle with letters around and through center, depot exterior, hanging, two-sided, 11 x 16" $275.00

WESTERN UNION TELEGRAPH & CABLE OFFICE – depot exterior, hanging, two-sided, 12 x 24", white letters on dark blue (note use of "&," early version) Maker-Ing-Rich Beaver Falls Pa $275.00

WESTERN UNION TELEGRAPH & CABLE OFFICE – depot exterior, hanging, two-sided, 12 x 24", white letters on royal blue (note use of "&," early version) Maker – B.S. Co., 52 State St. Chi $275.00

WESTERN UNION TELEGRAMS – depot exterior, hanging, two-sided, 10 x 17", white on dark blue $125.00

WESTERN UNION TELEGRAPH AND CABLE BLANKS – depot exterior door, mounted flush, one-sided, 4 x 9", white letters on blue, 1930's $75.00

WESTERN UNION TELEGRAPH AND CABLE BLANKS – depot exterior door, mounted flush, one-sided, 3 x 9½", white letters on blue, 1930's $55.00

WATCH YOUR STEP – passenger coach entrance, 3¼ x 21", white letters on black $40.00

WATCH YOUR STEP – passenger coach entrance, 3¼ x 21", white letters on blue, later issue, more scarce $50.00

PASSENGERS ARE PROHIBITED FROM STANDING ON PLATFORM WHILE TRAIN IS IN MOTION, interior coach, 3 x 10½", white letters on blue $30.00

Miscellaneous – Metal, Cardboard, Fiberglass

AMERICAN EXPRESS CO. – (name around stars and stripes shield logo) established 1841. MONEY ORDERS, FOREIGN DRAFTS, TRAVELERS CHEQUES, etc., white/blue letters on orange, Letters of Credit (in rectangle), two round white circles in bottom corners, depot sign, tin, 19½ x 27½", dated Feb. '04 (rare) $400.00

AMERICAN RAILWAY EXPRESS – call card, diamond shape, two-sided, 14 x 14", red/white letters on green, heavy cardboard with red metal rims, grommet hole at top, ca. 1920's $185.00

Built by PULLMAN – STANDARD Car Manufacturing Company – interior car, 2¾ x 8¼", black letters on stainless steel $25.00

BURLINGTON ROUTE – white, black and red logo, depot exterior, mounted flush, rectangular, 21 x 27", heavy steel, stamped CB&QRR on back $150.00

CAUTION! Avoid Fires, Do not throw lighted matches, cigars, cigarettes, etc. from cars, Northern Pacific Railway Co., 6¼ x 9¾", framed placard.................................$37.50

DEER CREEK – depot exterior, station name sign, heavy steel, 12 x 66", mounted flush, black letters on white......$35.00

DINING CAR IN OPPOSITE DIRECTION – 5 x 7", cardboard, white on dark blue, Pullman Co. $35.00

FOR PULLMAN PASSENGERS ONLY – interior car, 1¼ x 3¼", black letters on stainless..................................$15.00

MISSOURI PACIFIC LINES – buzz saw logo, interior depot wall, 12 x 12", fiberglass, white letters on red $65.00

NORTHERN PACIFIC RAILWAY COMPANY – NOTICE! Baggage Tariff require that the value of all baggage must be declared in writing, depot interior, 10 x 13", cardboard, dated 1948 ....$15.00

QUIET – is requested for the benefit of those who have retired, 6 x 9", cardboard, white on sky blue; other side reads Have you forgotten any personal property? Great Northern Ry $10.00

RAILWAY EXPRESS AGENCY – call card, diamond shape, two-sided, 14 x 14", white letters on red, heavy cardboard with metal rims, grommet hole at top, 1950's $150.00

RAILWAY EXPRESS AGENCY – depot interior, 13¼ x 19¼", lithographed tin, depicts locomotive, men unloading Express car, truck arriving. Black letters FAST DEPENDABLE THROUGH SERVICE on white background, 1930's...$325.00

REA X – call card, two-sided, diamond shape, 14 x 14", fiberglass, white on red, brass grommet hanging hole at top. Final issue $45.00

ROCK ISLAND – depot exterior logo, mounted flush, rectangular, 13½ x 18", white, black and red enamel on sheet metal $100.00

SOO LINE – exterior shanty, 4 x 33", metal, embossed enameled black letters on white $45.00

TO GET IN OR OUT OF UPPER BERTH, PLEASE USE THE LADDER – interior sleeping car, aluminum, 3¼ x 5", silver letters on black $35.00

TO SEND MONEY anywhere, at any time, for any purpose use – AMERICAN EXPRESS MONEY ORDERS for sale by AGENT, C.ST.P.M.& O. DEPOT, red/white letters on blue, 12 x 16", cardboard, interior depot wall, dated 1916.......$45.00

Railway Express Signs

Misc. Cardboard and Metal Signs

WELLS FARGO & CO EXPRESS – call card, diamond shape, two-sided, 14 x 14", white letters on dark blue circle, red background, heavy cardboard with black metal rim, grommet hole at top, ca. 1920's $375.00

WESTERN UNION TELEGRAMS – for depot counter, 5½ x 9", easel back, white letters on dark blue enameled tin $55.00

Smoking Accessories

Millions of book matches having their logos, name trains and colorful advertising featured on them have been freely handed out by the railroads over the years. Those from the steam era are especially sought after and worth more than those from the diesel era. Countless thousands of ashtrays were used on the smoking and parlor cars, diners, depots and in the railroad's ticket offices. Most were made of glass, others in china, ceramic and metal, in a variety of shapes and sizes, with the railroad's name or logo prominently displayed. Older ashtrays from merged roads are bringing the better prices. *Note:* Reproduction heavy glass ashtrays with authentic railroad heralds on them are being made for the hobby trade, and these are not to be confused with the genuine railroad issued ashtrays.

The small, pocket-type cigarette lighters with the railroad's name or logo on them are collectible and moderately priced. Those from several decades past sell for a lot more. The railroad-marked spittoons or cuspidors from the early days are also sought after by collectors. The all-brass cuspidor is the most popular and generally realizes a top dollar price. A number of miscellaneous items are listed at the end.

Ashtrays (BS – backstamped)

ALTON – glass, 3½" square, four rests, triangle logo "The Only Way" with THE ALTON RAILROAD COMPANY in red on white bottom $20.00

BN – glass, eight-sided, 5 x 5", six rests, BN BURLINGTON NORTHERN in green on clear bottom $10.00

BURLINGTON ROUTE – cast metal, nickel plated, shape of cowboy spur, 4 x 5½ x 1¾" with a red/black logo between two rests at front $95.00

C&NW – glass, 3½" square, two rests, CHICAGO and NORTH WESTERN LINE logo on clear bottom ..$15.00

C&NW – plaster, 4½ x 5", irreg. base, two rests with standing figure of owl character with lantern at rear, inscribed "Freight Wise" CHICAGO & NORTHWESTERN LINES between rests (scarce) $115.00

C&NW – PLASTER, 4½ x 4½", irreg. base, two rests with standing figure of owl character at rear with luggage, inscribed "Travel Wise" CHICAGO & NORTHWEST-ERN LINES between rests (scarce) $115.00

C&O – china, Syracuse, round, 4"D, four rests, blue/yellow pinstripes with sleeping Chessie kitten on white bottom...$95.00

C&O – china, Buffalo, rectangular 3¼ x 7¼", no rests, Geo. Washington silhouette profile on back tab, "CHESAPEAKE and OHIO Lines" with black pinstripes frontside $95.00

CGW – glass, round, 3¼"D, with five protruding rests, fluted sides, Chicago GREAT WESTERN Railway in blue on clear bottom $25.00

CGW – ceramic, white, round, 6"D with four rests, 1¾"H, Chicago Great Western Railway Company, CORN BELT ROUTE black logo on raised center.....................$50.00

CGW – ceramic, white, oblong, 3¾ x 6½" with three rests, 1"H, Chicago Great Western Railway Company, CORN BELT ROUTE black logo on raised end $45.00

CN – china, Hall's, round base 5½"D with 3½"H match box holder in center, dark green glaze with gold CANADIAN NATIONAL RAILWAYS logo and pinstripes $65.00

CLINCHFIELD – china, no BS, white, round 5"D with three rests, double end steam locomotive logo on bottom, CLINCHFIELD RAILROAD CO. and ad copy in gold around edges $40.00

CLINCHFIELD – china, Royal, white, round 5¼"D with three rests, double end diesel locomotive logo in brown on bottom..$35.00

D&RGW – porcelain, BS-SNUFF-A-RETTE, 4¼ x 4¼ x ³⁄₁₆" square, two rests, four snuf holes, slot for bookmatches at rear, DENVER Rio Grande WESTERN RAILROAD in gold on cream...$50.00

Copper Ashtray

DT&I – china, BS – The "SABINA" Line, round, 7¾"D with 12 rests, gold pinstripe border, black-red-blue DETROIT TOLEDO IRONTON RAILROAD logo on white in center $60.00

FRISCO – glass, 3½" square, two corner rests, black/white FRISCO LINES logo on clear bottom $12.00

FRISCO – glass, orange iridescent, 4" squarish, four rests, black FRISCO LINES logo on red bottom............$16.00

GN – BS Genuine P&S Porcelain, black glaze, round, 4"D with fluted edge, three rests, gold GREAT NORTHERN goat logo in center.................................$50.00

GN – glass, round, 4"D with fluted sides, two rests, white GN monogram on clear bottom $20.00

GN – glass, round 4"D, 1½" sides with two extended rests, white GN monogram on clear bottom $25.00

GN – porcelain, maroon glaze, BS-SNUF-A-RETTE, round 4¼"D, 1"H sides, seven triangle snuf-holes and slot for bookmatches at rear, white GREAT NORTHERN RAILWAY goat logo on bottom front $50.00

GN – molded black plastic, BS – The DERBY No. 925, round, 4¾"D with 1¾" sides, four rests, four white GREAT NORTHERN RAILWAY goat logos around sides $22.00

GN – china, Syracuse, white, round 4"D silhouette goat on mtn. top with evergreens border, four rests, BS – GREAT NORTHERN RAILROAD $125.00

GN – china, Syracuse, white, round 4"D, three colorful flowers in center, four rests, BS – GREAT NORTHERN RY $75.00

GN – china, Syracuse, white, 4" square with 1½" sides, four corner rests, three flowers around center, BS – GREAT NORTHERN RY...$75.00

LACKAWANNA – china, BS-M.B.Co. Trenton, N.J., 3¾ x 3¾ x ⁵⁄₁₆" square, blue Lackawanna Railroad logo in center on cream glaze $55.00

M&STL – glass, 3½" square, four corner rests, red/black MINNEAPOLIS & ST. LOUIS RAILWAY "The Peoria Gateway Line" logo on clear bottom $20.00

M&STL – ceramic, green glaze, round 5½"D, THE MINNEAPOLIS & ST. LOUIS RAILROAD raised on 1" sides, single rest, The PEORIA GATEWAY Line logo raised in center $65.00

M&STL – ceramic, blue glaze, round 5½"D, same as above with white letters and logo $65.00

MILWAUKEE ROAD – glass, 2½" square with 1" extended rest tab, HIAWATHA streamliner bow and arrow motif in blue on gray bottom...$35.00

NP – glass, 3½" square, two corner rests, red/black NORTHERN PACIFIC Yellowstone Park Line logo on clear bottom $15.00

NP – glass, 4½" square, 1¼"H with four corner rests, red/black NORTHERN PACIFIC Yellowstone Park Line logo on clear bottom $22.00

NP – glass, 4½" square, 1¼"H with four corner rests, red/black NORTHERN PACIFIC RAILWAY logo on clear bottom $20.00

NP – glass, 8-sided, 5 x 5", rect. tray center with two rows of rests, red/black NORTHERN PACIFIC logo on clear bottom..$18.00

PRR – glass, 3½" square with two corner rests, red/white PRR Keystone logo on clear bottom $12.00

PULLMAN – dark brown Bakelite, BS – Samuel Lewis Co. N.Y., round, 5½"D, with three rests. THE PULLMAN COMPANY raised between two rests $22.00

PULLMAN – dark brown Bakelite, BS – deep-dish ashtray, 4¼"D with six rests around edge, THE PULLMAN COMPANY in white on exterior $18.00

REA EXPRESS – ceramic, gray glaze, no rests, 3½" square, "Loss & Damage Prevention Means Job Protection" impressed on bottom $15.00

REA EXPRESS – white plastic, BS – ORNAMIN 4135, round, 5¼"D, three rests, red diamond AIR EXPRESS logo on bottom center, PRIORITY AIR EXPRESS white on blue around inside edge $25.00

Glass Ashtrays

ROCK ISLAND – glass, 3½"D, round base with 4¼" square top, four angled rests, red logo on clear bottom $15.00

ROCK ISLAND – glass, smoky, 3¼" round base with 4" squarish top, four corner rests, grey/black logo on bottom ..$18.00

ROCK ISLAND – glass, six-sided, 4½ x 4½" with six rests around 1" sides, center depicts a diesel and slogan RIDE THE ROCKETS, 20 Great Streamlined Trains, in red/maroon on white round bottom $20.00

SANTA FE – black glass, rectangular, 3¾ x 4¾", no rests, TURQUOISE ROOM with design in center, logo and "Super Chief" at bottom, white on blue $22.00

SOO LINE – glass, 3½" square, two corner rests, red/white logo on clear bottom $12.00

SOO LINE – glass, 4 x 4" square top with four corner rests, red/white logo on clear square bottom $15.00

SOO LINE – glass, blue, BS-NOMESSER PATT. APPLIED FOR, round, 4½"D, two rests on raised center knob, three red/white logos spaced around 1"H sides (also found in clear, green & amber) $35.00

SOO LINE – metal, black finish, round 6"D, four rests, red logo on pearlized round center disc $30.00

SOO – glass, 3¾ x 3¾" square, 1"H sides with four corner rests, red SOO logo on clear bottom $10.00

SP – porcelain, HALL, cobalt blue glaze, oval, 3¾ x 5¾", with 2½"H center holder for matches and two snuff-out holes, gold SOUTHERN PACIFIC LINES logo and pin stripes $75.00

SR – copper, round, 5¼"D with two rests, SR logo raised on bottom center, SOUTHERN RAILWAY SYSTEM, THE SOUTHERN SERVES THE SOUTH impressed in border $35.00

SR – ceramic, white, 6½"D with four rests in gold pinstripe edge, green SR logo with LOOK AHEAD – LOOK SOUTH on bottom center.....................................$30.00

T&P – porcelain, HALL, cobalt blue glaze, oval, 3¾ x 5¾" with 2½"H center holder for matches, and two snuff-out holes, gold TEXAS PACIFIC RAILWAY logo and pin stripes $75.00

UP – glass, blue, round, 4¼"D, 1¼"H, ribbed sides, three rests, Sun Valley, Idaho, UNION PACIFIC RAILROAD, Utah Parks Co. in red on white bottom (also found in clear, green & amber)..$18.00

UP – glass, blue, round, 4¼"D, 1¼"H, ribbed sides, three rests, red-white-blue UNION PACIFIC RAILROAD shield logo on white bottom (also found in clear & smoky glass) $15.00

UP – porcelain, white, BS – Ashtray Specialty Co. Chicago, round, 4⅜"D, 1¼"H sides with three rests, red-white-blue shield logo on bottom center $10.00

Book Matches
(Complete with Matches Unless Otherwise Noted.)

Book matches were produced in abundance and have been a common railroad giveaway over the years. Those dating from the named passenger train era, picturing famous trains on their covers, both steam and diesel, are especially sought after. Some collectors prefer only the mint books with all the matches still intact while others try to accumulate the empty covers from as many different railroads as possible. Not too many matchbook covers, either mint or empty, representing railroads from the early years, are to be found today.

ACL – logo, list of name trains, silver printing on purple $3.00

ANN ARBOR – flag logo, "Dependable DOUBLE A Service," red/white printing on blue $3.50

B&O – gold logo on blue, list of name trains, map inside (cover only) $3.00

BURLINGTON ROUTE – pic of Zephyr, list of name trains on blue, logo on inside................................$4.00

CGW – gold logo front, map backside on red background $5.00

CMStP&P – red logo, Hiawatha streamliner #1, black/grey with orange stripe $3.50

CPR – beaver atop red shield logo on gold background, hotel listing inside.....................................$2.00

ERIE – logo & diesel streamliner, yellow on blue, map inside (cover only) $3.50

C&NW – logo, two yellow diesel streamliners on green, map inside $3.00

FRISCO LINES – two black logos on yellow against red stripes, map inside.....................................$3.00

FRISCO – red logo, two diesel locomotives on white background, map inside..................................$2.00

GB&W – red logo and diesel on black with six yellow stripes (cover only) $4.00

GN – logo, Indian, "Route of the EMPIRE BUILDER" on white, "FAST" Freight inside $5.00

GN – logo, four named streamliners on green, "PROGRESS" with streamliner inside, orange................$4.00

IC – Circle/Diamond logo and black steam locomotive on green and gold $4.50

IC – gold centennial medallion on royal blue, map inside...$3.50

LACKAWANNA – gold logo, "The Route of PHOEBE SNOW" on maroon background............................$3.00

M&StL – cartoon showing brakeman catching boxcar ladder with slogan "Get A Grip on SAFETY," red/black printing on white $4.75

MILWAUKEE ROAD – pic of "Hiawathas" Super Dome car on maroon, logo on inside.......................$2.75

MOPAC – hound dog, "Route of the EAGLES," logos, on yellow background.....................................$3.50

MOPAC – red logo, list of three name trains on royal blue (cover only) $3.00

NYCS – red logo frontside, two trains, "TRAVEL & SHIP by Dependable Rail" backside, on grey, map on inside $2.75

NYCS – black logo with train frontside, pic of the 20th CENTURY LIMITED backside on gold (cover only) $2.00

NYO&W – W logo, "Ship via N-Y-O & W" white printing on royal blue (cover only) $3.25

NICKEL PLATE ROAD – logo, "N K P" across map, blue printing on cream $3.00

NP – two Yellowstone Park Line logos on red background, "MAIN STREET OF THE NORTHWEST" $3.25

NP – two Monad logos on red background, "The Vista-Dome NORTH COAST LIMITED" $3.00

N&W – "The Pocahontas and the Cavalier" frontside, streamlined steam train backside on blue, map inside $3.50

N&WRY – "The SCENIC ROUTE North-South" frontside, logo backside on maroon, map inside................$3.00

PRR – PENNSYLVANIA RAILROAD 1846-1946, 100 Year Emblem, gold on maroon $3.50

PRR – pic of two trains "Ready To Go" frontside, advertising backside, maroon (cover only) $2.25

QUANAH ROUTE – logo, Indian chief, purple/white, map inside (cover only) $8.00

RIO GRANDE – logo and advertising, black printing on red (cover only) $3.00

ROCK ISLAND – two black logos on red background, white logo inside...$2.75

SOO LINE – red logo on royal blue both sides, map inside...$4.00

SOO LINE – logo, "The BEST of Freight and Passenger Service" frontside, TRAINS OF STEEL and list of cities backside on light blue $5.00

Book Matches

SP – Southern Pacific STREAMLINED Daylights on frontside, pic of stylized Daylight streamliner backside on yellow, advertising inside $3.25

T&P – two red diamond logos on green background (cover only) $2.50

UP – logo and pic of Zion National Park frontside, list of National Parks backside on yellow, advertising inside $2.50

WABASH – two red flag logos on royal blue, map inside (cover only) $3.00

Pax of Four and Six, Boxed or Cello Wrapped

B&O – four pax, boxed – diesel freight frontside, map backside; book matches – diesel locomotive and three symbols on white, map inside $15.00

C&O – six pax, boxed – diesel freight frontside, map backside; book matches – sleeping Chessie kitten frontside on white background $22.00

FRISCO – six pax, boxed – pix of two diesel trains frontside, advertising backside; book matches – red logo and two diesel locos on white, map inside $25.00

GN – six pax, cello wrapped, red/black goat logo, "Great For Freight/Travel," black printing on white, ROCKY goat cartoon inside..$15.00

GN – six pax, cello wrapped, modern white goat logo and GREAT NORTHERN on blue $12.00

MILWAUKEE ROAD – six pax, cello wrapped, cartoon character holding red logo frontside, advertising backside on yellow, black telephone on red inside.............$15.00

NYCS – six pax, boxed – open door boxcar frontside, freight train backside; book matches – pic of steam freight and advertising copy on red, map inside $25.00

NYCS – six pax, boxed – Pacemaker freight train frontside, boxcar backside; book matches – red logo, "Travel & Ship by Dependable Rail" on grey, map inside $20.00

NP – six pax, cello wrapped, VISTA DOME North Coast Limited and logo frontside, big logo, "Main Street of the Northwest" backside, red covers $18.00

NP – four pax, cello wrapped, two logos, "The Vista-Dome North Coast Limited" on red covers......................$10.00

RIO GRANDE – four pax, cello wrapped, black diesel sketch, "Where the short, fast train was invented" frontside, pic of diesel train backside, orange covers....................$8.00

ROCK ISLAND – six pax, cello wrapped, two black logos on red covers, logo inside $10.00

SANTA FE – six pax, boxed – dark blue with three cut-out windows to show white logos on dark blue book match covers inside $12.00

SOO LINE – six pax, cello wrapped, red logos on royal blue covers, map inside $22.00

UNION PACIFIC – six pax, cello wrapped, "Union Pacific Railroad" and shield logo in gold on red covers $8.00

WABASH – six pax, cello wrapped, red flag logos, "When freight can't wait ship Wabash" in white on purple covers...$18.00

WM – six pax, cello wrapped, red Western Maryland Railway logo on white; backside has pic of red diesel loco #7447, map inside..$15.00

Cardboard Boxes of Book Matches (Full Count)

BN – 50 books, BN BURLINGTON NORTHERN in white on green covers, recent (50 @ 25¢ ea) $12.50

C&NW – 28 books, green covers, "Route of the '400' Streamliner Fleet and Western Streamliners" with two diesels on front cover; back has colored logo, 1940's, (28 @ 2.50 ea.) $70.00

NYC – 50 books, red/white/blue covers, logo and Mercury figure on front cover. Back has the "James Whitcomb Riley" streamliner pictured, 1940's. (50 @ 1.75 ea.) $87.50

NYC – 50 books, white covers, logo and "Empire State Express" on front cover. Back has picture of the new steam Empire State Express. 1940's (50 @ 1.75 ea.) $87.50

ROCK ISLAND – 25 books, red covers, black/white logo both sides, 1940s. (25 @ 1.00 ea.) $25.00

SANTA FE – 50 books, white covers, Indian boy holding black Santa Fe logo both sides. 1970's (50 @ 35¢ ea.) $17.50

UNION PACIFIC – 25 books, "Union Pacific Ralroad" and shield logo on red covers. 1950's. (25 @ 50¢ ea.) $12.50

UNION PACIFIC – 50 books, white covers, shield logo and "the Union Pacific railroad people" on front cover. "We can handle it" in blue on back cover. 1960's (50 @ 75¢ ea.) $37.50

Cigarette Lighters

A&S – "St. Louis Gateway Service Line," A&S logo and locomotive on front, Agent's name, ALTON AND SOUTHERN RAILROAD backside on silver, Rolex............$50.00

BN – BN BURLINGTON NORTHERN in green on stainless steel, ZIPPO..$15.00

C&NW – red/black logo, 1964 Safety Award Dakota Division on stainless steel ZIPPO $25.00

FRISCO – logo, ship and travel SOUTHEAST-SOUTHWEST front side, map of System in gold on red, Vulcan ..$35.00

GN – goat logo front side, Ship ... travel GREAT NORTHERN, diesel train in red& black on pale gold, "GN" $40.00

MILWAUKEE ROAD – logo frontside, Hiawatha Indian figure backside, white on red, Warren......................$30.00

M&STL – The Peoria Gateway black/red logo on stainless steel, ZIPPO..$45.00

M&NS – raised red diamond logo on stainless steel, Halco $55.00

SANTA FE – Chico Indian boy holding logo, Santa Fe all the way, blue on chromium, ZIPPO $20.00

SOO LINE – logo both sides, white on maroon, Warren $22.00

SOO LINE – logo both sides, white on red, WARCO ..$25.00

UP – raised flag shield logo on stainless steel, BARLOW $20.00

Frisco Cigarette Lighter – Front and Back

Cuspidors and Spittoons

MKT – porcelainized steel, dark blue exterior, M.K. & T. in light blue on white flared rim, 8¼"D across top, 5"H $85.00

N&W – cast iron, "N & W" raised on exterior, 8¼"D white porcelainized flared rim, 4¾"H $100.00

PULLMAN – nickel finish on brass, "THE PULLMAN CO." stamped on bottom, 6"D twist-off top, 2¾"H $65.00

PULLMAN – nickel finish on brass, "PULLMAN" incised on cast iron bottom, 8¼"D across flared top, 7¼"H $125.00

SP – white porcelainized steel with blue "S.P.CO." on inside flared rim, 8"D across top, 5"H $75.00

SOO LINE – brass, raised logo on cast iron bottom, 9"D across top, 7½"H $175.00

SOO LINE – dark blue porcelainized steel with "SOO LINE" in light blue on inside white flared rim, 8¼"D across top, 5"H $95.00

UP – green porcelainized steel, black "UNION PACIFIC" on inside flared rim, 8"D across top, 3¾"H $85.00

Soo Line Brass Cuspidor and Porcelain Spittoon

Miscellaneous (YPL – Yellowstone Park Lines)

CIGAR BAND – M-K-T logo with two trains on red-black-gold $6.00

CIGAR BAND – Northern Pacific, YPL logo on ornate red-white-gold..$7.50

CIGAR BAND – Pennsylvania Special around PRR logo on maroon-white-gold $5.00

CIGAR BAND – Southern Pacific Lines logo on red-black-gold $8.00

CIGAR BAND – Union Pacific flag/shield logo on red-white-gold $4.00

CIGAR – mint, cello wrapped in tube 6¼" long with UNION PACIFIC cigar band $8.00

CIGAR BOX LABEL – (from inside cover) The NORTHWESTERN Line, red/black logo on white smooth paper $15.00

CIGAR BOX – BURLINGTON ROUTE, wood, 2½ x 5½ x 8½", HAND MADE brand, logos around sides, on top, and inside of cover, ca. 1930s..................................$45.00

CIGAR BOX – NORTHERN PACIFIC, wood, 1½ x 6¼ x 8½", CARABANA brand, YPL logo on white smooth paper inside of cover, ca. 1930s $40.00

CIGAR BOX – UNION PACIFIC, wood, 1½ x 5¾ x 8¼", Sun Valley Special, The Challenger, red-white-blue shield logo on cover inside and out, ca. 1940's $30.00

CIGARETTE CASE – Northern Pacific, tin, black enamel, 1 x 2 x 3", YPL logo and "Route of the North Coast Limited" and "First of the Northern Transcontinentals" in white around sides $45.00

FLOOR STAND ASH TRAY – C&NW, cast iron and steel, 26"H, black/chrome finish, round top 15"D tray, chrome logo on base..$350.00

FLOOR DRINK STAND ASH TRAY – PULLMAN, cast iron and steel, 26"H, black chrome finish, two-tier round tray

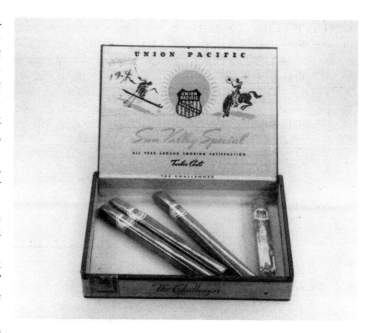

Cigar Boxes and Cigars

15"D, top has four cut-out holes around center ashtray, PULLMAN on 13"D base $325.00

MATCH BOX HOLDER – cast brass, railroad coach wall mount type, 2½ x 4¼" back $55.00

MATCH STRIKING PLATE – cast brass, railroad coach type, for stick matches, 1¾ x 4½" $30.00

SAFETY MATCHES – MKT, four gold boxes with 100 YEARS 1870-1970 and red KATY logo, cello wrapped in gold cardboard tray with slogan "Count on KATY" $6.00

SAFETY MATCHES – UNION PACIFIC, yellow cardboard boxcar 1 x 1½ x 4¼" with four boxes safety matches inside... $8.00

SAFETY MATCHES – UNION PACIFIC, grey cardboard hopper car 1 x 1½ x 4¼" with four boxes safety matches inside $8.00

SAFETY MATCH CASE – BURLINGTON ZEPHYR, stainless steel, ½ x 1 x 1¾", etched black ZEPHYRUS logo on topside, adv. on back, dated 1934 ....$75.00

BOOK MATCHES – FRISCO, yellow cardboard boxcar, 1½ x 2 x 6½" with 25 book matches inside......................$18.75

BOOK MATCHES – FRISCO, red cardboard boxcar, 1½ x 2 x 6½" with 25 book matches inside $18.75

Brass Match Holder and Striking Plate

Stationery Items

There are numerous items in this category, such as pencils and pens carrying railroad logos and slogans, blotters featuring vacation spots and name passenger trains, rulers with interesting advertising copy, scratch pads, letterheads, envelopes and so on. All were once produced in large quantities and widely distributed. All railroad marked stationery items from the heyday of rail travel are now getting scarce and prices on them are on the rise.

Ball Point Pens

BN – green/white, logo, BURLINGTON NORTHERN and slogan "The right way to ship, safety begins with you" in green on white, Tucker, USA $5.00

BN – white, logo, BURLINGTON NORTHERN and diesel loco 6465 coupled to BN box car, green, Sheaffer ..$8.00

DM&IR – gold/maroon, D.M.&I.R. "Marshalling Yard, Keenan 10/23/76" in maroon on gold, Readyriter$15.00

GN – chromium plated top, orange plastic bottom half, goat logo and slogan "Safety-Courtesy GREAT NORTHERN RAILWAY" in green printing, Douglas Kennedy....$12.00

GN – chromium plated top two-thirds, black plastic bottom one-third, goat profile and logo with slogan "GREAT FOR FREIGHT GREAT FOR TRAVEL – GREAT NORTHERN RAILWAY" in black on chromium, Autopoint, USA $20.00

MILWAUKEE ROAD – gold plated top-half, black plastic bottom-half, canted box logo in yellow on black, Readyriter $12.00

MKT – blue/white "100 YEARS 1870-1970 KATY logo" within gold circle, slogan "Our Centennial Year, Count on Katy" in gold on white, Silverline, USA $15.00

NP – sky blue, logo and slogan "The Right Way to Ship, NORTHERN PACIFIC RAILWAY Safety Begins With YOU" in black printing, Rite-O-Graph USA............$5.00

NP – dark green/light green, logo in red/black and "NORTHERN PACIFIC RAILWAY COMPANY St. Paul, Minn." in black, Readyriter, USA $6.00

SOO LINE – black with four gold stripes at clip, box logo and SOO LINE RAILROAD in gold, Wings, USA $10.00

SOO LINE – royal blue with four silver stripes below clip, SOO LINE RAILROAD in silver letters, US Pencil Co. NYC $8.00

UP – chromium plated top-half, black plastic bottom-half, tiny UNION PACIFIC shield logo on clip, Paper Mate USA $10.00

Steel Pen Points for Wood Holders

Note: Exact markings as stamped on the points.

C.M. & ST.P.RY STUB PEN No. 3 (straight shape) 1¼" L..$5.00

M & ST.L.R.R. (arrow shape) 1⅝" length $6.00

N & W RY CO E-10 (arrow shape) 1⅝" length $3.50

NORTHERN PAC. RAILWAY CO. STUB 312 (straight shape) 1½" length $5.00

NORTHERN PAC. RAILWAY CO PROFESSIONAL, No A1 (straight shape) 1¼" length $4.00

NORTHERN PAC. RAILWAY CO. MANIFOLD No 1 (straight shape) 1⅜" length $3.00

PENNA. R.R. MEDIUM (straight shape) 1⅝" length......$3.00

PENNA. R.R. CO. FINE STUB (straight shape) 1⅜" length $2.50

PENNA R.R. FINE (arrow shape) 1⅝" length $4.00

PROPERTY OF THE NORTHERN PACIFIC RAILWAY CO. (arrow shape) 1⅝" length..$6.00

STANDARD RAILROAD PEN No. 5 (bowl shape) 1⅝" length $2.00

STANDARD RAILROAD No. 2 (arrow shape) 1⅝" length $2.00

U.S.R.R. ADMINISTRATION No. 1 (straight shape) 1¼" length $2.00

U.S.R.R. ADMINISTRATION No. 5 (bowl shape) 1¾" length $2.00

THE N.Y.N.H. & H.R.R. No. 1 (arrow shape) 1⅝" length ..$4.00

RR Marked Wood Penholder

LOUISIANA RAILWAY & NAVIGATION COMPANY and LOUISIANA RAILWAY & NAVIGATION COMPANY OF TEXAS, black printing on brown enamel, round type, length 6" $25.00

Pencils (Wood with Graphite Leads – Unsharpened)

ACL – ATLANTIC COAST LINE, gold printing on dark brown, round, No. 2, eraser $3.00

ALTON – "THE ALTON RAILROAD" Dependable Freight Service BETWEEN Kansas City-St. Louis-Peoria-Chicago, red printing on yellow, round, fat pencil, eraser $15.00

BN – BURLINGTON NORTHERN – SAFETY & COURTESY PAYS, white printing on green, hexagon, No. 1, eraser $1.50

CB&Q – "BURLINGTON LINES – EVERYWHERE WEST," black printing on yellow, hexagon, No. 2, eraser $3.00

C&EI – BE GOOD TO YOURSELF: TRAVEL – TO YOUR FREIGHT: ROUTE – "Cool Travel & Hot Schedules," two logos, black printing on green, round fat pencil, no eraser $15.00

CGW – C.G.W.RY., gold printing on green, hexagon, No. 2 "Bondexed lead," eraser $5.00

C&NW – C & N W RY CO., white printing on maroon, round, No. 2, no eraser $3.00

C&NW – CHICAGO AND NORTH WESTERN SYSTEM SAFETY FIRST, gold printing on black, round, No. 1, no eraser $4.00

C&O – THE CHESAPEAKE AND OHIO RAILWAY COMPANY, black printing on chrome yellow, hexagon, no eraser $1.50

CSTPM&O – C.ST.P.M.&O.RY., gold printing on maroon, round, No. 2, no eraser $5.00

CStPM&O – C.St.P.M.& O.Ry. Official, fancy gold printing on dark brown, hexagon, No. 3, no eraser $6.00

GN – GREAT NORTHERN RAILWAY, black printing on green, round, no eraser..$5.00

GN – GREAT NORTHERN RAILWAY COMPANY ROUTE OF THE STREAMLINED EMPIRE BUILDER, orange printing on green, No. 1, round, no eraser $4.00

GN – GREAT NORTHERN RAILWAY COMPANY SERVES THE BEST OF THE GREAT NORTHWEST, green printing on orange, No. 2, round, no eraser $3.00

IC – ILLINOIS CENTRAL GULF RAILROAD "SERVICE WITH SAFETY" gold printing on black, hexagon, No. 3, eraser $2.00

KCS – KANSAS CITY SOUTHERN LINES "Work in Safety," silver printing on tan, round, No. 1, no eraser $2.00

M&StL – M.&St.L.Ry Co., gold printing on black, round, No. 1, no eraser $6.00

MILWAUKEE ROAD – red logo, "SAFETY FIRST, Always Be Careful, Prevent Accidents" black printing on yellow, round, eraser $4.00

MILWAUKEE ROAD – red logo, "SAFETY ALWAYS!" "Think about your Safety, on and off the job," black printing on yellow, round, eraser $4.00

MILWAUKEE ROAD – "Friendliness is a Milwaukee Road Tradition," black printing on yellow, round, No. 2, no eraser $3.00

MILWAUKEE ROAD – red box logo, "SAFETY FIRST Always be Careful Prevent Accidents," 1950 red round logo, black/red printing on off-white, round, eraser $5.00

MKT – M-K-T KATY LINES – "The Bluebonnet, The Texas Special," red/blue printing on yellow, hexagon, eraser...$3.50

MP – MISSOURI PACIFIC LINES, white printing on brown, hexagon, No. 2, eraser.....................................$2.50

NC&StL – N. C. & ST. L. RWY. "TO AND FROM Dixieland," green printing on yellow, hexagon, No. 2, eraser ..$3.50

NP – "NORTHERN PACIFIC RY. – Courteous-Friendly," silver printing on maroon, round, No. 1, no eraser ..$3.00

NP – NORTHERN PACIFIC RY. – SAFETY & COURTESY PAYS, black printing on red, hexagon, No. 2, eraser...$5.00

RI – ROCK ISLAND LINES, black printing on red, round, No. 2, no eraser $2.50

SOO LINE – FRIENDLINESS IS A (logo) TRADITION, white printing on black, round, No. 2, no eraser ..$3.50

SOO LINE – SOO LINE Copying, VENUS, American Pencil Co. Made in U.S.A. (T'mkd.) gold printing on mottled blue/black finish, round, 165 Medium, no eraser....$5.00

SP – SOUTHERN PACIFIC YOUR FRIENDLY RAILROAD, red printing on orange, round, No. 2, no eraser ..$2.50

SR – Southern Railway gives a Green Light to Innovations, Aware-Alert-Never Hurt, gold printing on green, hexagon, No. 2¾, eraser $3.00

SANTA FE – SANTA FE Friendliness is a Tradition, gold printing on maroon, round, No. 2, no eraser $2.50

UP – UNION PACIFIC RAILROAD, "If Damage Is Low Business Will Grow," red printing on yellow, hexagon, No. 3, eraser..$2.00

WABASH – "Follow the Flag" above flag logo, WABASH RAILROAD, blue letters on white, round, fat pencil, eraser...$15.00

Miscellaneous Pens and Pencils

Pencils, Mechanical

C&NW – CHICAGO AND NORTH WESTERN LINE – Route of THE "400," THE CHALLENGERS, THE STREAMLINERS, green printing on yellow, green ends, Redi-point $15.00

DSS&A – You Will Make No Mistake When You Route Via DULUTH, SOUTH SHORE & ATLANTIC RY. "The Line of Service And Attention," blue printing on white, red/blue ends, Redipoint, eraser (scarce) $45.00

FRISCO – logo and slogan "Serving the SOUTHEAST AND SOUTHWEST" gold printing on black, gold ends, Ritepoint..$18.00

GN – GREAT NORTHERN RAILWAY goat logo in red/blue on pearlized finish, black ends, no mfgr's name on clip ..$20.00

GN – goat logo and "SHIP and TRAVEL GREAT NORTHERN Route of THE New EMPIRE BUILDER" in green/red printing on white, black ends, Redipoint...............$15.00

GREEN BAY ROUTE – red box logo, "Green Bay & Western R.R.," KEWAUNEE, GREEN BAY & WESTERN R.R., in black printing on grey, silver ends, eraser, SCRIPTO Atlanta USA (scarce) $35.00

MILWAUKEE ROAD – likeness of steam train streamliner and red box logo with slogans "Route of the HIAWATHAS," "Friendliness is a MILWAUKEE ROAD Tradition," in red/black printing on pearlized, silver point, Quickpoint, St. Louis, (scarce) $30.00

MILWAUKEE ROAD – same as above, except short 4" ladies styles with eyelet at top for use with a chain $18.00

MILWAUKEE ROAD – likeness of electric train and red box logo with slogans "Friendliness is a MILWAUKEE ROAD Tradition," "Electrified Over the Mountains To the Sea," in black printing on pearlized, silver point, eraser, Quickpoint, St. Louis, (scarce) $30.00

MILWAUKEE ROAD – same as above, except short 4" ladies style with eyelet at top for use with a chain............$18.00

M&STL – likeness of diesel freight train, "The Minneapolis & St. Louis Railway" in red/black printing on white, black ends, Redipoint (scarce) $30.00

MO-PAC – red logo with black steam engine, with slogans "It's 70 in the SUNSHINE when it's 100 in the SHADE," "AIR CONDITIONED" "A Service Institution," black printing on pearlized, silver point, Quickpoint, St. Louis (scarce)..$35.00

PULLMAN – PULLMAN-STANDARD CAR MFG. CO. "World's Largest Builders of Railroad Cars," white printing on brown, black ends, Autopoint $15.00

RIO GRANDE – logo, Rio Grande, "The Direct Central Transcontinental Route," black printing on red arrow, with slogan "Thru The Rockies – Not around them," black printing on pearlized, silver point, no mfgr's name on clip....$20.00

ROCK ISLAND – rocket diesel streamliner, two red logos, "TRAVEL and SHIP Route of the ROCKETS," red/black printing on pearlized, silver tip, no mfgr's name on clip $22.00

SAL – SEABOARD AIR LINE RAILWAY and slogan "Completely Air-Conditioned Trains," black printing on cream, black ends, Scripto $15.00

SOO LINE – red box logo and slogan "SOO LINE SATISFIES," red printing on pearlized, silver point, Quickpoint, St. Louis $22.00

SOO LINE – red box logo and slogan Ship and Travel "SOO LINE" on steel tires, blue printing on off-white, blue/red ends, Spotswood $15.00

SOO LINE – box logo and SOO LINE RAILROAD in gold printing on black, gold ends, SAF-T-RITE $12.00

SOO LINE – SHIP & TRAVEL VIA SOO LINE in white printing on maroon, black point, eraser, REALITE (hexagon shape) $7.50

UP – chromium plated top-half, black plastic bottom half, tiny UNION PACIFIC shield logo on clip, Paper Mate USA $8.00

Rulers

A&S – 6" aluminum, black printing, ALTON AND SOUTHERN RAILROAD "The St. Louis Gateway's Speed Belt" across center, Always Specify A&S and R.M. Hill, G.A. Kansas City, Mo. at both ends. Back side has 1937 calendar months (scarce) $25.00

BN – 7" white plastic, black printing, logo – BURLINGTON NORTHERN RAILROAD and "WHERE GOOD NEIGHBORS WORK," also freight train pictured length of ruler. Back side has metric system conversion table $5.00

BURLINGTON ROUTE – 12" enameled tin, red/black printing, logo and diesel freight, and slogans "STRAIGHT AS A RULER BURLINGTON'S new KANSAS CITY SHORTCUT Between CHICAGO and KANSAS CITY."......$15.00

C&NW – 15" wood, front – 2 logos and slogans "A Good RULE TO FOLLOW" SHIP and TRAVEL via CHICAGO and NORTH WESTERN RAILWAY SYSTEM, back – logo, two diesel trains and slogan "Ship and Travel via CHICAGO and NORTH WESTERN RAILWAY SYSTEM".........$22.00

CGW – 12" plastic, Chicago GREAT WESTERN Railway logo in center, black printing on white $15.00

CGW – 12" wood, front – TRAVEL AND SHIP VIA THE CHICAGO GREAT WESTERN RAILROAD, R.W. GOODELL, Gen'l. Frt. Agt., CHAS D. FISHER, City Pass. & Ticket Agt. Mpls., back has names of cities served, etc (scarce) ..$30.00

D&RGW – 12" clear plastic, orange route map in center with DENVER & RIO GRANDE WESTERN RAILROAD – THE KANSAS CITY CONNECTION in black printing each end..$8.00

GM&O – 12" white plastic, red/black printing shows two logos, diesel freight train and map of system $15.00

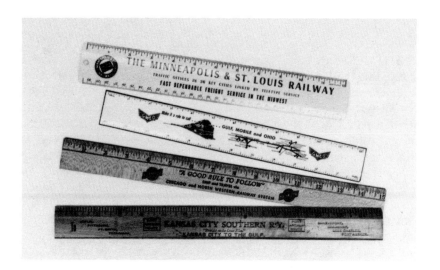

Rulers – Wood, Tin and Plastic

GN – 8" celluloid on tin, logo, 1931 calendar and slogans, "Route of the EMPIRE BUILDER, The ORIENTAL LIMITED Luxurious, Clean, Cinderless, Scenic," black printing on white, back side has ink blotter strips $25.00

KCS – 15" wood, front – two PORT ARTHUR ROUTE box logos, KANSAS CITY SOUTHERN R'Y. "Straight as the Crow Flies." KANSAS CITY TO THE GULF., and eight cities printed in black. Back – map of System and names of RR President and two Agents (ca. 1903) rare ..$50.00

M&StL – 12" white enameled tin, red/black printing, THE PEORIA GATEWAY logo, THE MINNEAPOLIS & ST. LOUIS RAILWAY Traffic Offices in 36 Key Cities Linked By Teletype Service FAST DEPENDABLE FREIGHT SERVICE IN THE NORTHWEST..................................$18.00

MONON – 12" white plastic, black printing, two logos, MONON RAILROAD and steam locomotive pictured at right end..$12.00

NP – 12" white plastic, red/black printing, map of system across length with slogan, "Route of the Vista Dome NORTH COAST LIMITED" and logo each end ..$15.00

ROCK ISLAND – 12" white plastic, ROCK ISLAND LINES and logo in red, slogan "Route of the ROCKETS and the ROCKET FREIGHTS Serving 14 Mid-Continent States"and freight train depicted in black printing $15.00

ROCK ISLAND – 6" white plastic, red/black printing, two logos, ROCK ISLAND LINES and slogan "striving to make good transportation better." Back side pictures string of freight cars $8.00

SOO LINE – 12" enameled tin, box logo, map of System and slogans SHIP AND TRAVEL, "A Good Rule To Follow," red printing on white $15.00

Ink Blotters

AC&Y – large map of System and advertising – When routing shipments to and from AKRON and BARBERTON specify "A C & Y" the "Road of Service." Black printing on white, 4 x 9" $6.00

BURLINGTON ROUTE – logo – 100th Anniversary 1849-1949, pictures a vintage pass. train and diesel streamliner with slogan "Way of the Zephyrs and Vista-Domes," black/maroon/blue/white, 4 x 9" $8.50

C&G – map of COLUMBUS AND GREENVILLE RAILWAY and DELTA ROUTE logo in red/yellow/brown/white, 4 x 8½" $5.00

C&NW – logo, semaphore blades and advertising – The Train for Comfort is the NORTH-WESTERN LIMITED, etc., red/brown/green on yellow, 4 x 9" $20.00

CGW – logo/steam train with much advertising copy – Chances are even we can save money for you, etc., CHICAGO GREAT WESTERN. Dated Mar. 1931, 3¾ x 8½" (scarce) $22.00

CSS&SB – route of CHICAGO SOUTH SHORE and SOUTH BEND RAILROAD from SOUTH BEND to CHICAGO and Chicago Switching District, red/black printing on white, 4 x 9" $6.00

CStP&KC – picturesque – Iron Horse with wings galloping down track and lavish ads with slogans – CHICAGO, ST. PAUL and KANSAS CITY RY., Time Reduced to 13½ Hours, The Fast Line, New and Modern Equipment, etc., 4 x 9", ca. 1889 (rare) $50.00

CSTPM&O – picturesque – fireman shoveling coal in engine cab, THE NORTH-WESTERN LINE logo, CHICAGO, ST. PAUL, MINNEAPOLIS & OMAHA RY. plus more ad copy in blue on white, 4 x 9", ca. 1895 (rare)........$45.00

GN – left side – Indian girl standing beside photo of bridge over river, right side – A LAND OF FISH AND GAME, SPOKANE advertisement and GREAT NORTHERN RAILWAY box logo, dated 1915, 3 x 8" (rare) $25.00

GN – multi-color litho of Indian Chief Little Plume at left, remaining space has EMPIRE BUILDER – ORIENTAL LIMITED schedules and GREAT NORTHERN logo printed in green on tan, dated 3-31, 4 x 9".........$15.00

KCS – logo/three diesel trains abreast, advertising THREE TOP TRAINS – "Southern Belle," "FLYING CROW," "Trains NINE and TEN," purple printing on white, 4 x 9"....$6.00

MILWAUKEE ROAD – 1933 A CENTURY OF PROGRESS motif at left, remaining space has logo, ad copy – CHICAGO! Travel by Train, The MILWAUKEE Road, etc. blue/red printing on white, 3¼ x 6¼"..................$12.00

MILWAUKEE ROAD – logo and steam locomotive at left, rest of space has ad copy, "The Pioneer Limited" and other name trains, etc., red/blue printing on white, 3¼ x 6¼"..$8.00

MILWAUKEE ROAD – red logo, advertising "To Chicago – THE SIOUX" in red with black steam train, plus add'l adv. copy in blue on white, 3¼ x 6¼"...................$10.00

MKT – red/yellow logo in lower right corner and slogan "call KATY For Your Transportation Needs" in blue printing on white, 3 x 6"..$4.00

MP – MISSOURI PACIFIC LINES red buzz-saw logo with black steam train and slogan "A Service Institution" in black print on white, 3¼ x 6"..................................$8.00

NYC – three circles across center picturing CHICAGO LaSalle Street Station, TWENTIETH CENTURY LIMITED and the NEW YORK Grand Central Terminal. Remaining space consists of ad copy plus logos, black printing on white, 4 x 9½"....................................$15.00

N&W – multi-color wharf scene on tan, "1838 – A CENTURY OF SERVICE – 1938" NORFOLK and WESTERN Railway, three yellow calendar months 1938, 3¾ x 9"..........$10.00

NP – color photo of baked potato on plate at right, logo and ad copy in red, FAMOUS FOR GOOD FOOD ... The Streamlined NORTH COAST LIMITED, etc. on white space at left. ca. 1930's, 3¼ x 8½".........................$18.00

NP – cut-out baked potato on plate showing butter pat and spoon in potato opening, white card in front has logo and GREAT BIG BAKED POTATO advertising, 3¾ x 8½" (scarce) $30.00

PM – PERE MARQUETTE RAILWAY, map and TIME-SAVING CONNECTIONS listed at right hand side, red/blue printing on white, 4 x 9"..........................$5.00

ROCK ISLAND – logo/steam train at top center, remaining is advertising copy to HOT SPRINGS National Park Arkansas, etc., red/black printing on white, 1930's, 4 x 9" $10.00

ROCK ISLAND – TRAVEL and SHIP Via ROCK ISLAND (logo) and showing diesel/steam locomotives abreast,

red/black printing on white, 3¼ x 6¼" $6.00

SOO LINE – logo, system map, slogan "For Dependable Service ROUTE SOO LINE" An International Railroad System, red/black printing on white, 3 x 7"...............$5.00

SP – SOUTHERN PACIFIC LINES map with two logos, three calendar mos. 1926, green printing on tan, 4 x 9" $12.00

SR – WE WANT YOUR FREIGHT IN '58 and VP's testimony, logo and freight train at bottom with caption THIS YEAR – SHIP VIA SOUTHERN AND SEE! multi-color on white, 3¾ x 8¾" $8.00

UP – three National Park pictures – Grand Canyon, Zion National and Bryce Canyon in color and ad copy, 3 NATIONAL PARKS IN ONE FIVE-DAY MOTOR-BUS TRIP reached from Cedar City, Utah via UNION PACIFIC, black printing on yellow, 4 x 9" $10.00

Two Rare Ink Blotters

WABASH – flag logo, lady seated in coach and adv. copy "The Luxurious Way to CHICAGO," 6½ Hour Service Lv. St. Louis 12:20 p.m. Wabash "BANNER BLUE LIMITED" blue/orange printing, ca. 1920's, 3½ x 6½" $18.00

WABASH – map of System on big red heart, flag logo, freight train along bottom, slogan – "SERVING THE HEART OF AMERICA" Wabash Railroad, red/blue printing on white, 4 x 9" $8.00

Stationery – Tourist

During the Golden Years of rail travel in this country, passenger trains were equipped with a writing desk in the parlor car filled with stationery for tourist use, especially designed for each train. The railroad's ID and name of train was usually featured across the top of the sheet of paper, approximately 5 x 7" and small envelope about 3½ x 5½" in size. Depots also had stationery in the waiting room. Examples listed here are matched sheet and envelope, unused.

BURLINGTON ROUTE – sheet and envelope, logo, "Aboard the Vista-Dome, AK-SAR-BEN ZEPHYR" grey printing on white, CHICAGO-OMAHA-LINCOLN on sheet bottom $3.00

BURLINGTON ROUTE – sheet and envelope, logo, "Aboard the Vista-Dome, DENVER ZEPHYR" brown printing on cream, CHICAGO-DENVER-COLORADO SPRINGS on sheet bottom $3.00

Tourist's Stationery

GN – sheet and envelope, two logos – GREAT NORTHERN RAILWAY goat, BURLINGTON ROUTE box logo, "The ORIENTAL LIMITED via Glacier National Park," brown printing on tan, envelope has VIA AIR MAIL between red/blue stripe $5.00

GN – sheet and envelope, engraving of the GREAT NORTHERN RAILWAY Passenger Station Minneapolis Minnesota at left top corner in dark green on light green, goat logo at left, envelope is without logo (scarce) $15.00

GN – sheet and envelope, goat logo, "GREAT NORTHERN RAILWAY Cafe and Parlor Car Service," dark green printing on light green, envelope without logo $8.00

MILWAUKEE ROAD – sheet and envelope, "THE MILWAUKEE ROAD, Route of the Hiawathas" in black printing on white, also a red Indian figure logo between the words, envelope without logo...................................$5.00

ROCK ISLAND – sheet and envelope, red diesel streamliner, logo and "Route of the Rockets" in black printing on white, ROCK ISLAND LINES on sheet bottom $5.00

SANTA FE – sheet and envelope, logo, likeness of Indian Chief & slogan, "the Chief Way," brown printing on white....$4.00

UP – winged streamliner motif at upper left in red, "Domeliners, City of Los Angeles, Denver, Portland, St. Louis and San Francisco" printed below motif in blue on white. "Enroute" in red $4.00

Stationery – Railroad Business

Envelopes – R.R.B. legal size – 4 x 9½", regular – 3½ x 6"

BCR&N – manila, regular, Form 111, return in three days to BURLINGTON, CEDAR RAPIDS & NORTHERN R'y Co. (rare) $15.00

BN – white, legal, BN BURLINGTON NORTHERN, "This envelope is exclusively for railway business" in stamp box $1.00

CGW – manila, regular, CHICAGO GREAT WESTERN RAILWAY COMPANY, Form 6003 Rev 55, (scarce) $6.00

CGW – manila, legal, CHICAGO GREAT WESTERN RAILWAY COMPANY, Form 6004-Rev. 3-300M, scarce ..$8.00

CRI&P – manila, regular, Return Postage Guaranteed, Chicago, Rock Island and Pacific Railroad Co., OFFICE OF, slogan is in lower corner – Ship and Travel "Rock Island" Route of the Rockets..$2.00

CRI&P – manila, legal, Chicago Rock Island and Pacific Railroad Company, office of $3.00

GN – manila, regular, goat logo atop GREAT NORTHERN RAILWAY Co..$2.00

GN – white, regular, GREAT NORTHERN and modern goat logo in dark blue..$1.50

GN – white, legal, GREAT NORTHERN and modern goat logo in sky blue $2.50

GN – manila, 5 x 11½", goat logo atop GREAT NORTHERN RAILWAY CO $3.00

IC – white, regular, ILLINOIS CENTRAL diamond logo, If not delivered in five days return to 135 EAST ELEVENTH PLACE Chicago 5, Illinois, Return postage guaranteed..$1.50

LV – white, legal, Lehigh Valley Railroad Co. Form 1083 ....$2.00
MILWAUKEE ROAD – white, legal, red box logo, Chicago, Milwaukee, St. Paul and Pacific Railroad Company........$3.00
MILWAUKEE ROAD – manila, legal, black box logo, Form 1510 W 10-79 200M $2.00
NP – manila, regular, NORTHERN PACIFIC RAILWAY COMPANY Form 320, R'Y.B. $1.50

NP – manila, legal, logo, NORTHERN PACIFIC RAILWAY COMPANY Form 321, R'Y.B. $2.00
WC – manila, regular, Office of Superindent, WISCONSIN CENTRAL RAILWAY Abbotsford, Wisconsin, Railway business only, Penalty $100.00 printed in stamp box, rare $15.00

Sheets – white paper, 8½ x 11" or less

BN – green BN logo and BURLINGTON NORTHERN in black ....$.50
CB&Q – CHICAGO, BURLINGTON & QUINCY RAILROAD COMPANY, logo, Operating Department, Galesburg, Illinois in black printing................$1.00
CRI&P – CHICAGO, ROCK ISLAND AND PACIFIC RAILROAD COMPANY in black printing................$.75
FRISCO LINES – logo at top, ST. LOUIS AND SAN FRANCISCO RAILROAD COMPANY CHICAGO AND EASTERN ILLINOIS RAILROAD COMPANY in black printing (scarce)................$10.00
GN – GREAT NORTHERN RAILWAY in green printing across top, map of System, goat logo, stylized streamliners and slogan "Route of the World Famous Empire Builder" in green printing along bottom................$3.00

LV – LEHIGH VALLEY RAILROAD COMPANY Traffic Department in black printing $1.00
MILWAUKEE ROAD – red box logo, Chicago, Milwaukee, St. Paul and Pacific Railroad Company, City Ticket Office, Minneapolis, Minnesota in black printing $2.00
MRL&M – MINNEAPOLIS, RED LAKE AND MANITOBA RAILWAY COMPANY, Bemidji, Minnesota (scarce) $12.00
NP – red/black logo, NORTHERN PACIFIC RAILWAY COMPANY in black printing, "Route of the Vista-Dome NORTH COAST LIMITED" in white on red horiz. stripe $2.00
ROCK ISLAND – red ROCK ISLAND LINES, logo, horiz. line across top, Chicago, Rock Island and Pacific Railroad Company, Milwaukee Station, 3rd Ave. So. & Washington, Minneapolis, Minn. in black printing $3.00

Scratch Pads – Memo Pads – Pad Holders

All are white paper unless otherwise noted. The scratch are pads with cardboard back intact; Memo are pocket size with a stapled bound cover; Holders have a felt-backed metal base with spring clip at top for securing pad in place. Another type is a foam back plastic with a slit for inserting the pad.

Scratch Pads

BN – pad 5 x 7", BN logo BURLINGTON NORTHERN, green printing $1.00
BN – memo 2½ x 5", BN logo BURLINGTON NORTHERN in white/green, calendar (1974) cover $3.00
BN – pad and holder, BN logo BURLINGTON NORTHERN, holder 5½ x 9" white plastic with green printing, pad 5 x 7" with green map of System on flyleaf, mint $10.00
BN – pad and holder, BN logo BURLINGTON NORTHERN, holder 5½ x 9" white plastic with green printing, pad 5 x 7" without flyleaf intact $8.00
BURLINGTON ROUTE – pad 4 x 7¼", red/black printing, logo, two diesel trains depicted side by side, slogan "Freight and Passenger Dependable Service" $4.00
BURLINGTON ROUTE – pad, 4¾ x 7½", intermittent pages depicting diesel streamliners, name trains, slogans and logos, red/black printing................$8.00
C&O – pad 4 x 7", CHESAPEAKE AND OHIO RAILWAY, slogan – "Ship and Go C and O" and a steam freight train depicted in blue printing, cardboard back has map of System $5.00

C&EI – pad 4¼ x 5", CHICAGO & EASTERN ILLINOIS RAILROAD and logo in black printing $3.00

C&NW – pad 4¼ x 5½", logo, "Ship and Travel" in black on yellow..$4.00

CGW – pad 5 x 7", Chicago GREAT WESTERN Railway in black on orange round logo printed at upper right............$7.50

D&RGW – pad 5¼ x 8", at top is picture of freight train in moutains and slogan "Rio GRANDE the ACTION railroad 100 YEARS of Shipper Service" on yellow/gray stripes, DENVER AND RIO GRANDE WESTERN RAILROAD is on yellow across bottom, pages are lined....................$7.50

EJ&E – pad holder, metal, 5½ x 9", white enamel clip has red/green logo in center, ELGIN, JOLIET & EASTERN RAILWAY and slogan "Where Safety and Service are of the First Importance!" green printing top & bottom $25.00

FRISCO – pad, 5¼ x 7", map of System, diesel freight train and slogan, "SHIP IT on the FRISCO (logo)" in black/red/yellow printing..$4.00

GB&W – pad, 4 x 5", logo and GREEN BAY & WESTERN R.R. in green on yellow $2.50

GN – pad, 4¼ x 7", at top is GREAT NORTHERN RAILWAY goat logo and slogan "Via GLACIER PARK in the MONTANA ROCKIES," at bottom is slogan "Daily BETWEEN CHICAGO and the PACIFIC NORTH-WEST" and name train "The ORIENTAL LIMITED," orange/green printing $8.00

GN – pad, 4¼ x 7", at top is slogan "MEMO Two of America's Finest Transcontinental Streamliners" with orange curved arrow to bottom showing two diesel streamliners, goat logo and name trains EMPIRE BUILDER, WESTERN STAR, orange/green printing, dated 1953 ....$8.00

GN – pad, 5 x 7", cartoon profile of goat and slogan Rocky Says – "GREAT FOR TRAVEL – GREAT FOR FREIGHT" with logo in red/green printing $5.00

GN – pad and holder, green plastic pad, 5¾ x 9" with gold GREAT NORTHERN RAILWAY goat logo imprinted at top, takes 5 x 7" pad..$12.00

GN – pad and holder, white plastic pad, 5¾ x 9", with GREAT NORTHERN and modern version of goat logo in white on sky blue, pad 5 x 7" with GREAT NORTHERN modern goat logo and map of System in white across sky blue top $15.00

IC – pad, 5¼ x 6¼", ILLINOIS CENTRAL RAILROAD logo and slogan "Main Line of Mid-America" in tan/brown printing $3.00

MILWAUKEE ROAD – pad, 4 x 7¼", red box logo and slogan "America's Resourceful Railroad, The Railroad of Creative Crews" in black print across bottom $3.00

MILWAUKEE ROAD – pad, 4¼ x 7¼", at top is red box logo and slogan "IF IT'S FREIGHT IF IT'S TRAVEL we can handle it! We can service you!" red/white on blue; at bottom is The MILWAUKEE ROAD in white print on blue $5.00

MILWAUKEE ROAD – pad holder, 4½ x 9½", black plastic with gold box logo at top..$10.00

M&StL – pad, 4 x 7¼", at top is side view of diesel freight train depicted on red and "The MINNEAPOLIS & ST. LOUIS Railway" in white printing, also "Fast Freight Service" in black on the red field; at bottom left corner is the PEORIA GATEWAY logo printed in red (scarce) $15.00

MP – pad, 4 x 7¼", MISSOURI PACIFIC LINES logo, piggyback freight cars depicted and slogan "Settling the MODERN PACE in transportation," red/black printing....$3.00

NP – pad, 4¾ x 7", map of System, logo and slogan "Ship and Travel NORTHERN PACIFIC" in red/black printing $4.00

NP –pad, 4¾ x 7", NORTHERN PACIFIC RAILWAY in white on black square and yellow/black scene of diesel and caboose passing at night $4.50

NP – memo, 2½ x 5", logo, slogan "Route of the Vista-Dome NORTH COAST LIMITED" and calendar (1969) on cover $5.00

PM – pad, 4 x 6¼", logo and RR agent's name at top left and PERE MARQUETTE RAILWAY in blue across bottom $3.00

READING – pad holder, 5¼ x 8¼", metal, bronze finish, clip with cast metal likeness of READING steam locomotive is bolt-attached at top, READING RAILWAY SYSTEM with two diamond shape logos are raised in front of clip base (scarce) $75.00

SANTA FE – pad, 5 x 7¼", logo with two diesels and slogan "Swift, Sure Freight and Passenger Service is a Santa Fe

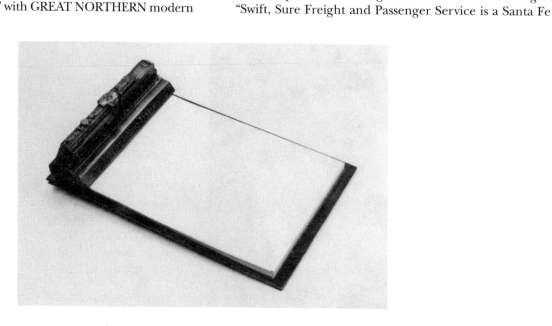

Cast Metal Locomotive Pad Holder

Tradition. The World's Largest Fleet of Diesel-Drawn trains," blue printing $5.00

SANTA FE – memo, 2½ x 4¾", front end of diesel is depicted in center, "Ship ... Travel" above, SANTA FE all the way! below, white/black/blue front cover, back cover has map of System...................................$3.00

SOO LINE – pad, 4¾ x 6", box logo, SOO LINE and names of RR agents across top, bottom edge has "Your Patronage Appreciated" black printing on orange...........$5.00

SOO LINE – pad, 3¾ x 6", two box logos, SOO LINE RAILROAD printed in blue on orange $3.00

SOO LINE – pad, 3¾ x 6", at top is SOO LINE RAILROAD 75 (1883-1958) anniversary round emblem depicted, at bottom are two box logos and slogan "75 years of GOOD SERVICE" blue printing on orange $7.50

SOO LINE – pad holder, 4 x 8¼", red plastic, map of System and logo, SOO LINE Railroad Company in white printing $10.00

SOO LINE – pad holder, metal, gold finish, 4 x 8½", top clip has embossed likeness of diesel pass. train and logo, printed at bottom in red is slogan "Ship –Travel" with logo $15.00

SR – memo, 3¼ x 5¼", SOUTHERN printed diagonally with slogan above, "Gives a green light to innovations that squeeze the waste out of distribution," also SOUTHERN RAILWAY SYSTEM at bottom, black/green printing on cover, inside pages have slogan "Ship via Southern!" in red print at bottom..$4.50

TP&W – pad, 5½ x 5½", dia. shape logo at top left corner, cartoon sketch of Indian smoking pipe at lower left corner and TOLEDO, PEORIA & WESTERN RAILROAD COMPANY in red print across bottom $5.00

UP – pad, 5 x 7¼", FOR DEPENDABLE TRANSPORTATION be SPECIFIC – say "UNION PACIFIC" in red/blue printing, also red/blue shield logo across bottom..........$4.00

UP – pad, 5 x 7¼", GOLDEN SPIKE CENTENNIAL, shield logo and 1869-1969 Golden Spike Centennial emblem printing in red/blue/yellow, pages have blue lines across $5.00

WABASH – pad, 5 x 8", top has 1½" wide cardstock with slogan "THOSE WHO KNOW Ship and Go..." WABASH (logo) in red/blue printing, bottom has Wabash Flag logo, map of System within a heart and slogan "Serving the Heart of America" in red/blue printing, sheets tear along perforations at top, back has map of System.........................$7.50

Stocks, Bonds and Currency

Railroad stock and bond certificates date back to the early days of the railroads, usually having the locomotive in their designs. Some of the engraving companies that did this work went out of business long ago. Many of these certificates feature a magnificent engine vignette and a beautiful ornate engraved border design. There are collectors who specialize only in these. Some railroads issued their own currency, which was also a work of the engraver's art. These interesting paper collectibles of years ago are in demand today with prices steadily on the increase.

Stocks

Note: All stock certificates listed are cancelled unless otherwise noted.

AMERICAN CENTRAL RAILWAY, five shares, Capital, 1869, vignette of early pass. train at top, black border ..$50.00

ATCHISON & NEBRASKA RAILROAD CO., five shares, Capital, 1880, vignette of A&NSRR locomotive at center, black border.............................$30.00

BALTIMORE AND OHIO RAILROAD CO., 100 share, 1903, Common, Tom Thumb train vignette, brown border.........$12.00

BALTIMORE AND OHIO SOUTHWESTERN RAILWAY CO., 10 shares, Preferred Captial, 1894, train and depot in small circle, green border $20.00

BURLINGTON AND NORTHWESTERN RAILWAY CO., three shares, Capital, 1876, illus. of train at depot in center, embossed RR seal, black border $30.00

CHICAGO AND NORTHWESTERN RAILWAY CO., 100 shares, Common, 1958, winged mythological figures each side of Railroad's herald in center, green border....$10.00

CHICAGO BURLINGTON AND QUINCY RAILROAD CO., 100 shares, Capital, 1895, locomotive vignette, brown border $15.00

CHICAGO, BURLINGTON & QUINCY RAILROAD CO., 10 shares, Capital, 1965, illus. of diesel locomotive at top, blue border $7.50

CHICAGO, FORT MADISON & DES MOINES RAILROAD CO., 80 shares, Capital, 1899, pass. train vignette in center, embossed RR seal, black border $30.00

CHICAGO GREAT WESTERN RAILWAY CO., 100 shares, Preferred, 1965, allegorical figures, train in center circle, rust border $15.00

CHICAGO SAINT PAUL MINNEAPOLIS AND OMAHA RAILWAY CO., 20 shares, Common, 1922, illus. of train in center of two scenic ovals, brown border.........$20.00

CHICAGO BURLINGTON AND NORTHERN RAILROAD CO., five shares, Capital, 1885, illus. of U.S. Mail Express train, embossed RR seal, black border $30.00

CINCINNATI, WASHINGTON AND BALTIMORE RAILROAD CO., 10 shares, Common, 1880's, allegorical children, locomotive in center. Not issued $25.00

MK&T 1887 Stock Certificate

COLORADO AND SOUTHERN RAILWAY CO., 100 shares Common, 1971, locomotive vignette at top, green border $18.00

COLORADO AND SOUTHERN RAILWAY CO., 25 shares, Second Preferred Stock, locomotive vignette at top, brown border (not issued or dated) $12.00

GREAT NORTHERN RAILWAY CO., 100 shares, Common, 1969, James J. Hill portrait at bottom, brown border ..$8.50

GULF MOBILE AND NORTHERN RAILROAD CO., 100 shares, Common, 1929, trains in center oval, brown border $15.00

GULF, MOBILE AND OHIO RAILROAD CO., 100 shares, Common, 1941, allegorical figures, train in center frame, blue border $12.00

HARTFORD AND NEW HAVEN RAILROAD COMPANY, five shares, Capital, 1846, illus. of train on dock and ship approaching at top center, black border (rare) $50.00

HOUSATONIC RAILROAD COMPANY, 50 shares, Capital, 1844, small woodcut of early train at top center, red border (rare) $50.00

MINNEAPOLIS & ST. LOUIS RAILROAD CO., 100 shares, Capital, allegorical female and locomotive vignette, olive border, early 1900's. Not issued $15.00

MISSOURI, KANSAS AND TEXAS RAILWAY CO., New York, 10 shares, Capital, 1887, cattle vignette, violet border $22.00

MISSOURI, KANSAS AND TEXAS RAILWAY CO., New York, 100 shares, Common, 1907, locomotive and roundhouse vignette, green border $12.00

NORTHERN PACIFIC RAILWAY CO., five shares, Capital, 1928, logo at top, locomotive at bottom, brown border $12.50

NORTHERN PACIFIC RAILWAY CO., 100 shares, Capital, 1958, vignette of covered wagon at top, purple border $10.00

Bonds

MINNESOTA WESTERN RAILROAD CO. (unissued) Thirty Year Gold Bond, 1924, 30 coupons at both ends, 16½ x 31¼" $60.00

NORTHERN & SOUTHERN WEST VIRGINIA RAILROAD CO. (unissued) State of West Virginia, $1,000 Secured by first mortgage loan $7,000,000 dated 1872, eagle and train vignettes at top, 54 coupons at bottom, 17 x 22¾" ..$80.00

SOUTH MOUNTAIN RAILROAD CO., (unissued) State of Pennsylvania, $500. First Mortgage Gold Bearing Bond, 1873, train on bridge vignette at top, 60 coupons at bottom. 17¾ x 27"...$85.00

TROY & GREENFIELD RAILROAD CO., (unissued) Commonwealth of Massachusetts, $1,000 Dollars, 1854, early train vignette at top, 30 coupons at bottom, 19¾ x 22" $95.00

UTAH AND PLEASANT VALLEY RAILWAY CO. (partially redeemed) Utah Territory, $1,000 First Mortgage Seven Per Cent Gold Loan, 1878, mining scenes and train at top, 45 coupons remain at bottom, 17 x 21½" $75.00

HARTFORD, PROVIDENCE AND FISHKILL RAILROAD CO., State of Connecticut, $1,000 Mortgage and Convertible Bond, 1854, woodcut of primitive train at left side, embossed RR seal below, (not fully redeemed) three coupons remaining at bottom, 11 x 13" (rare) $95.00

Currency

Brunswick & Albany Two Dollar Bill – Obverse

Brunswick & Albany Two Dollar Bill – Reverse

BRUNSWICK & ALBANY RAILROAD CO., Brunswick, Ga., March 4, 1871, Good for TWO DOLLARS for fares, freight and all dues to the Company. Bank bldg. pic. obverse, train at depot reverse $45.00

Central Railroad & Bank'g Co. OF GEORGIA will pay the bearer TWO DOLLARS in Confederate Treasury Notes. Savannah, Dec. 19, 1861. Pic of early train $10.00

ERIE AND KALAMAZOO RAILROAD BANK will pay ONE DOLLAR to bearer on demand, ADRIAN, Aug. 1, 1853, ships vignette in center..$25.00

ERIE AND KALAMAZOO RAILROAD BANK, Five Dollars to the bearer on demand, ADRIAN, Aug. 1, 1853, portrait in center oval, two allegorical females top corners $30.00

ERIE AND KALAMAZOO RAILROAD BANK, will pay TEN DOLLARS to bearer on demand, ADRIAN, Jan. 2, 1854, people waving to train at top, Indian figure – female portrait in corners...$35.00

MISSISSIPPI & ALABAMA RAILROAD CO. Promised to pay TWENTY dollars on demand, Brandon, Oct. 1, 1837, allegorical figures – train at top, male portrait each corner $40.00

MISSISSIPPI AND TENNESSEE RAILROAD CO. will pay FIVE CENTS to bearer, Feb. 20, 1862, American eagle in center circle, Indian figure at left side $8.00

MISSISSIPPI CENTRAL RAILROAD COMP'Y. Will pay TWENTY FIVE CENTS to bearer, Jan. 1, 1862, illus. of early train across center..$6.00

SOUTH CAROLINA RAILROAD, Office of the Receivable as TWO DOLLARS in all payments, vignette of early train in center, portrait of girl in circle at left side, uncirculated, not signed or dated, 1800's......................$8.00

VIRGINIA CENTRAL RAILROAD CO. Promise to pay after date to bearer TEN dollars June 1, 1861, vignette of early pass. train in center......................................$25.00

WESTERN & ATLANTIC R.R. will pay to the bearer FIFTY CENTS, Mar. 15, 1862, early train printed in red across top $6.00

Telephones, Telegraphy, Insulators

The most popular item with the collector of this category appears to be the telegraph key and sounder. The telephone was also a part of the Station Agent's equipment, which included the scissors phone, candlestick desk phone, box-type wall phone, bell boxes and miscellaneous-related accessories. A lineman's portable phone with its box-like leather case and shoulder strap is also included. All of this fast disappearing old depot telegraph and telephone equipment of years past is collectible today. Seldom railroad marked, prices vary depending on their physical condition.

Telephones & Misc. Related

Depot Phones – Candlestick and Scissors Types

DESK PHONE – brass candlestick type, 12" tall, with headset earpiece and special RR design hook for headset, WESTERN ELECTRIC COMPANY, Pat. dates to Jan. 26, '15 on base...$150.00

DESK PHONE – candlestick type, black finish, 11¾" tall, with hand-held earpiece receiver and standard hook, AMERICAN TEL. & TEL. CO., Pat. Jan. 14, 1913 on mouthpiece $125.00

DESK PHONE – brass candlestick type, 11½" tall, with hand-held earpiece and standard hook, dial in base, WESTERN ELECTRIC, Pat. dates to Sept. 21, 1920 on base ..$100.00

DESK PHONE – oval base type with dial, black finish, 5½" high, hand-held ear/mouthpiece unit, center post hook, BELL SYSTEM, ca. 1930-1940 ....$75.00

SCISSORS PHONE – cast iron base for desk mount with brass candlestick phone 10" tall, on extending steel scissors bracket, with headset earpiece and dispatcher's hook, WESTERN ELECTRIC, Pat. dates to Jan. 26, 1915 ....$195.00

LINEMAN'S PORTABLE PHONE – leather case 3½ x 6½ x 9" with shoulder strap, phone unit inside mkd GREAT NORTHERN RY. Signal Dept. Lines East, hand-held 9"L

nickel-plated ear mouthpiece, WESTERN ELECTRIC CO. Pat. Aug. 18, 1909 ....$150.00

WALL PHONE – long box style, 9 x 20" back panel, headset earpiece and dispatcher's RR type hook, "Push to talk – Release to listen" button above mouthpiece, WESTERN ELECTRIC, ca. 1915 ....$245.00

WALL PHONE – short box style, 6½ x 9" back panel, headset earpiece and dispatcher's RR type hook, "Push to talk – Release to listen" button next to mouthpiece, WESTERN ELECTRIC, ca. 1915 ....$145.00

BELL RINGER BOX – wall mount, oak, 6 x 7" back panel, two bells on front of box, mkd CGW RY on inside, NORTHERN ELECTRIC, bells are black enameled $85.00

BELL RINGER BOX – wall mount, oak, 4¾ x 5¾", two bells on front, mkd CM&StPRY, no maker's ID, Type 43 A Special $85.00

BELL RINGER BOX – wall mount, oak, 6½ x 9" back panel, two bells on top, WESTERN ELECTRIC, Type 295A, Pats. to Apr. 30, 1907 ....$65.00

JACK HOLE BOX – oak, 3 x 6½ x 7", with four holes front end to insert brass Jack plugs, No ID, stamped SFB on back $30.00

JACK HOLE BOX – oak, 2¾ x 4½ x 6", with three holes on top for brass Jack plugs, WESTERN ELECTRIC, Pat. May 20, '13, model 385B $35.00

CONDENSER BOX – oak, wall mount, 5½ x 6½" back panel, complete with inside wiring, WESTERN ELECTRIC, model 501-B $20.00

PEG SWITCHBOARD – hardwood slatted panel 10 x 12" with four separate vertical brass strips each with rows of holes to insert metal pegs, marked C.M.& ST.P.RY., J.H. BUNNELL & CO., complete with terminal posts and pegs $150.00

Bell Ringer Boxes

Telegraphy

KEY – yellow brass oval base, top mkd-legless key, W.U.TEL.CO, G.N. RY.CO., Chas. Cory & Son, Inc., NY is stamped on sliding circuit bar $75.00

KEY – yellow brass oval base, two threaded legs 1¾"L under base, top mkd B&MR, Bunnell is stamped on key lever bar $85.00

KEY – yellow brass oval base, top mkd – Telegraph Key, AT&TCo., Western Electric is stamped on sliding circuit bar $45.00

RELAY – cast iron rectangular base 3½ x 7½", black finish, G.N.RY. Co., J.H. BUNNELL & Co. NY, 150 OHMS stamped on nickel plated fancy tab......................$75.00

RELAY – wood rectangular base 4¼ x 7½", maple finish, J.H. BUNNELL & Co. NY, 150 OHMS stamped on ½ x 2" brass plate $45.00

RELAY – combination-wood base mt'd on cast iron bottom, 4 x 7¼", black finish, W U T CO 100 OHMS, Pat'd July 21, 1909, Morse Relay 4-C stamped on top of wooden base $55.00

RESONATOR – adjustable type, cast iron base 6"H with two pivoting (7-8") cast iron arms and mounted wooden box (triangular) to house sounder, O.C. WHITE CO., Worcester, Mass. Pat. Aug. 7, 1911 raised on arms $200.00

Telegraph Relay

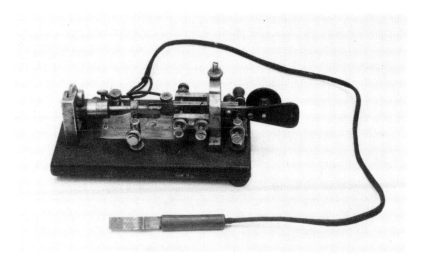

Vibroplex – Telegraph Speed Key

RESONATOR – adjustable type, cast iron base 6"H with three pivoting (6-7-8") cast iron arms and mounted wooden box (triangular) to house sounder, O.C. WHITE CO, Worcester, Mass. Pat. Aug 7, 1911 raised on arms..........$250.00

RESONATOR – stationary type, round iron base with vertical iron pole 9"H and wooden box (curved back) mounted on top without sounder, no maker's name..........$100.00

RESONATOR – stationary type, same model as above, complete with sounder $150.00

SOUNDER – yellow brass unit, J.H. BUNNELL & CO., mtd on varnished wood base 3 x 5½" mk'd on top MAIN LINE SOUNDER 15B, 120 OHMS, stamped on both ends of base – G.N.RY. CO.....................................$80.00

SOUNDER – yellow brass unit, J.H. BUNNELL & Co. Pat. May 7, 1895, mt'd on varnished wood base 3 x 5½" mk'd on top SOUNDER 1-B 400 OHMS, N.P.RY...........$95.00

SOUNDER – yellow brass unit, WESTERN ELECTRIC mt'd on black wood base 3 x 5½", mk'd along edge SOUNDER 3C 140 OHMS $45.00

SOUNDER – yellow brass unit, LIBERTY ELEC. CORP. mt'd on varnished wood base 3 x 5½", mk'd. along edge W U T CO SOUNDER 1-A 50 OHMS $50.00

VIBROPLEX – telegraph vibrating speed key, nickel-plated unit on black crinkle finish cast iron rectangular footed base 3½ x 6½", brass maker's plate depicts "red bug" trademark and Pat. Nos., with brass plug-in cord attached..$75.00

VIBROPLEX – telegraph speed key, yellow brass unit on black enameled cast iron footed base 3 x 6" with gold decor, brass makers plate has "bug" trademark and Pat Nos. early 1900s, complete in black leather case 4 x 4 x 9", ca. 1930's $95.00

VIBROPLEX – Hi-Speed Key, chromium-plated unit on black crinkled finish cast iron 3½ x 6¼" base, "SPEED-X" Standard Model 500 stamped on alum. plate, ca. 1940's..$55.00

Miscellaneous

BOOK – TWENTIETH CENTURY MANUAL OF RAILWAY COMMERCIAL AND WIRELESS TELEGRAPHY, Seventh Edition, 1914, by Fred L. Meyer, h/c, 305pgs..........$35.00

BOOK – TELEGRAPH CODE, MOBILE & OHIO R.R. CO., May 10, 1930, s/c, 94pgs...$25.00

CALL BOX – WESTERN UNION (wall mt'd buzzer) white oval porcelain base, 3½ x 5¾", oval blue steel 1¼"H cover with red turn knob to manually wind spring and activate $50.00

HOLDER – metal, three-tier counter-type for message forms, 6 x 8¾" base, 8½"H, white letters on blue enameled front 5 x 8½" which reads POSTAL TELEGRAPH, Money Telegraphed and Cabled, Messenger Errand Service, etc. (scarce) $265.00

HOLDER – metal, wall-mounted type for single pad of blanks, ½ x 8½ x 6", black finish with enameled yellow front 4 x 8" with words – TELEGRAPH BLANKS, WESTERN UNION, Everywhere (scarce) $175.00

MESSAGE BLANKS – pad WESTERN UNION Telegram blanks, 6 x 8¼", dated 4-54 on back with printed instructions $2.00

MESSAGE BLANKS – pad N.P. blanks 4¾ x 8", has YPL logo upper left corner and TELEGRAM – BE BRIEF printed in large black letters across top, dated 12-24 ....$10.00

MESSAGE BLANKS – stapled soft cover pad of WESTERN UNION blanks arranged for carbon copies, covers show messenger boy holding "Everywhere" blank in his hands, dated 10-42 inside $6.00

SIGN – exterior hanging two-sided porcelainized metal sign, 10 x 17", WESTERN UNION TELEGRAMS white letters on dark blue $125.00

SIGN – depot ticket counter type, 5½ x 9" with easel back, WESTERN UNION TELEGRAMS, white letters on dark blue enameled tin...$55.00

SIGN – exterior hanging two-sided porcelainized metal sign, 12 x 24", WESTERN UNION TELEGRAPH AND CABLE OFFICE, white letters on dark blue.......................$225.00

Telegraph Key, Resonator Box With Sounder

Insulators

Glass insulators used on telegraph poles are also a part of this category, and the collecting of these grew rapidly in the last decade. They were made in clear glass and in various colors, the most common being shades of green and blue. They are generally marked with the manufacturer's name, and many have patent dates. Those that are railroad marked bring good prices; values on others depends on their rarity.

All listed here are glass unless otherwise noted.

AM. TEL. & TEL. CO. – aqua/green, 2½"D, 3¾"H, raised letters around base $6.00

B&O – aqua, 2¾"D, 4"H, B&O and Pat. Jan. 25, 1870 raised on dome top $25.00

CANADIAN PACIFIC RY CO – blue/green, 2¾"D 3¾"H, raised letters around base...$16.00

CANADIAN PACIFIC RY – aqua/green, 2¾"D, 4"H, letters raised around base $15.00

CPR – white porcelain, 2⅞"D, 3¾"H, green initials on dome top $12.00

CPR – white porcelain, 2¾"D, 3¾"H, initials impressed on dome top $12.00

E.R. – (ERIE) aqua/green, 2¾"D, 4"H, raised letters as follows – E.R. and Pat. Nos. around base, CAUVETS PAT July 25, 1865, W. Brookfield, 55 Fulton St. NY around top....$35.00

G.T.P.TEL.CO. – blue/green, 3⅛"D, 4½"H, letters raised around base $20.00

P.R.R. – green, 3¼"D, 4¼"H, initials raised on dome top $10.00

P.R.R. – blue/green, 3¼"D, 4¼"H, initials raised on dome top $12.00

W.U.TEL.CO. – black rubber, 2¼"D, 4", CONTINENTAL RUBBER WORKS USA raised around top $6.00

Tickets and Related Items

A great variety of tickets were issued by the railroads down through the years, such as emigrant passage tickets, various excursion tickets, and small one-thousand mile booklets containing pages of tiny coupons each good for one mile, 50 coupons to a page. When all used up, the empty booklet was surrendered to the conductor, thus making them scarce today. In addition to these, there were daily commutation card tickets to be punched out, half-fare tickets, round-trip tickets which unfolded into a long strip, and an infinite number of small cardboard tickets good for one ride going either First Class or Coach. All these various paper and cardstock tickets put out by the railroads until the end of their passenger business in the 1960s, used or unused, are now in demand and steadily increasing in price.

BOSTON & MAINE R.R. – 1892, Commutation, five rides, Boston and Danvers, cardstock, 2 x 3¼" $12.00

BURLINGTON ROUTE – 1914, Commutation, ten rides, St. Paul – Pullman Ave., cardstock, 1¾ x 3" $10.00

BURLINGTON ROUTE – 1970, Coach, LaCross to Chicago, cardstock, 1¼ x 2¼" $1.50

BURLINGTON ROUTE – (1960's unused) carbonized ticket booklet, blue cover with logo and streamlined Zephyr, 2¾ x 6½" $5.00

CENTRAL VERMONT RAILROAD – 1886, 500 miles ticket, folded cardstock, 3½ x 4¼".......................................$15.00

CENTRAL VERMONT RAILROAD — 1888, First Class, St.

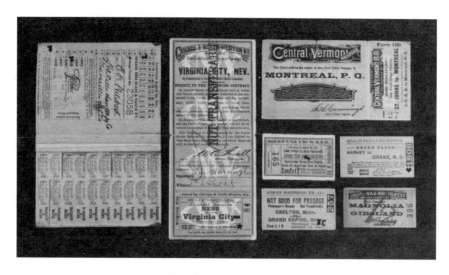

Miscellaneous Tickets

Johns to Montreal, paperstock, 2¼ x 4½".................$9.00

CHICAGO & NORTH-WESTERN RY. – 1877, Emigrant Passage Reno to Virginia City, paperstock ticket with stub, 2¾ x 6" $17.50

CHICAGO & NORTH-WESTERN RY. – 1886, 1,000 mile coupon booklet, partially used, 3½ pages intact, 2½ x 3¾", (scarce) $35.00

CHICAGO & NORTHWESTERN RAILWAY – 1972, One Way Coach, Chicago to Des Plaines, yellow cardstock, 2 x 2½" $1.50

CHICAGO &WESTERN INDIANA R.R. – (1960's unused) ten ride ticket between Dolton and Chicago, cardstock, 2¼ x 4¼" $2.00

CHICAGO GREAT WESTERN RY. – (1903 unused) 1,000 mile ticket booklet, cardstock cover, 3 x 5" (scarce) $35.00

CHICAGO, MILWAUKEE & ST. PAUL RAILWAY – 1917, Coach, Blooming Prairie to Owatonna, Minn., cardstock, 1¼ x 2¼" $7.50

CHICAGO, MILWAUKEE, ST. PAUL AND PACIFICI RAILROAD – 1955, carbonized ticket booklet, cover-pic of Milwaukee Road Super Dome car, 2¾ x 6½" $5.00

CHICAGO NORTH SHORE AND MILWAUKEE RAILWAY (1962-1965 unused) ten ride weekly commutation book between Kenosha and Milwaukee, 2½ x 4½" $5.00

CHICAGO ST. PAUL & KANSAS CITY RY. – 1893, half-fare ticket, Lorimore to Diagonal, Ia. blue paper stock, 2 x 3" $10.00

DULUTH & IRON RANGE R.R. CO. – 1900, Excursion ticket, Lester Park to Eveleth, Minn., brown paper stock, 2¼ x 3¼" $6.00

ERIE RAILROAD COMPANY – 1921, Commutation, 60 rides, Allendale and New York, pink cardstock, 2¼ x 2½" $4.00

FAIRCHILD & NORTH-EASTERN RAILWAY CO. – (unused) First-Class, Foster to Strader, cardstock, 1¼ x 2¼" $4.00

FITCHBURG RAILROAD – 1880, First Class, Troy to Rochester, cardstock, 2¼ x 4½" $10.00

GREAT NORTHERN RAILWAY LINE – 1891, First Class, Minneapolis to St. Paul, cardstock, 1¼ x 2¼" $8.00

GREAT NORTHERN RAILWAY LINE – 1900, Trip Half Fare Permit-First Class, St. Paul to Duluth, violet paper stock with stub, 3 x 6½" $10.00

HUMESTON & SHENANDOAH R.R. – 1893, Half-Fare Ticket, Diagonal to New Market, orange paper stock, 2 x 3" $6.00

LOUISIANA & NORTHWEST RAILROAD – (unused) One Passage Magnolia, Ark. to Homer, La., cardstock, 1¼" x 2¼".................$5.00

MISSOURI PACIFIC R.W. – 1902, Excursion Ticket, Leavenworth (U.D.) Kas. to Kans Cy. and return, violet paper stock with stub, 2¼ x 4¼".................$7.50

MISSOURI PACIFIC LINES – (1960's unused) carbonized ticket booklet, cover – pic of "Eagles" streamliner, 3 x 6½" $8.00

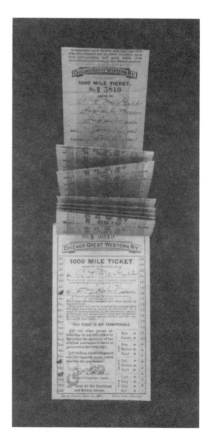

1,000 Mile Ticket Booklet

MINNEAPOLIS & ST. LOUIS RY. CO. – (unused) Round Trip Coach Ticket, lt. green, with stubs attached, paper stock, 2½ x 8"..$10.00

MINNEAPOLIS, ST. PAUL & SAULT STE MARIE RY. – 1936, Banana Messenger's Ticket Book, coupons for ten trips, partially used, cardstock cover with description of messenger, 3¼ x 5¼" (scarce)............................$40.00

MONON – (1960's unused) carbonized ticket booklet, red/grey cover with pic of streamliner, 2¾ x 6½" ..$8.00

NARRAGANSETT PIER RAILROAD CO. – (unused) good for one continuous passage, Kingston, R.I. to Providence, R.I., pink cardstock with stub, 2½ x 5" $5.00

N.Y.C. & ST. L. RAILWAY – 1886, One Continuous Trip Lorain to Cleveland, cardstock, 1⅛ x 1¼".................$4.50

NEW YORK, NEW HAVEN & HARTFORD RAILROAD CO. – 1890, One passage half-fare, Suffield and New Haven, cardstock, 1¼ x 2¼" $6.50

N.Y.CENT. & HUD. RIV. R.R. CO. – 1876, First Class, Jersey City to Philadelphia, Centennial Excursion Ticket, paper stock, 1⅜" x 2¼" $8.50

NEW YORK, LAKE ERIE & WESTERN R.R.CO. – 1893, First Class Continuous, Cleveland to Pittsburg, Pa. & Return, paper stock with stub, 2½ x 6"....................$10.00

NORTHERN PACIFIC RAILWAY – (1906 unused) 25-Ride Individual Ticket Book, St. Paul, Minneapolis or Stillwater, cardstock cover, 2 x 5" (scarce) $25.00

NORTHERN PACIFIC RAILWAY CO. – (1949 unused) round trip, St. Paul to Portland, Ore., paper stock, unfolds to 2¾ x 17"..$8.00

PENNSYLVANIA RAILROAD CO. – 1926, coach ticket, Philadelphia, Pa. to Bellefonte, Pa., cardstock, 2 x 4"......$4.00

ROCK ISLAND ROUTE – 1885, 1,000 mile coupon booklet, partially used, eight pages intact, red soft cover, 2¾ x 3¾", (scarce) $35.00

ROCK ISLAND – (1950's used) carbonized ticket booklet, cover – pic of Rocket passenger and freight trains, 2¾ x 6½"..$8.00

SIERRA RAILWAY COMPANY OF CALIFORNIA – (unused) First-Class Special Excursion Ticket, Oakdale to, paper stock, unfolds 3¼ x 12"..$7.50

SOO LINE RAILROAD – (1957 unused) Extra Fare Ticket, paper stock, unfolds 2¾ x 11¼"..............................$6.00

SOO LINE RAILROAD – (1957 unused) Special Service Charge Ticket, paper stock, unfolds 2¾ x 13½"......$6.00

ST. PAUL MINNEAPOLIS AND MANITOBA RAILWAY – 1888, Trip Half-Fare Permit, Fargo to St. Paul, violet paper stock with stub, 2½ x 6½" $15.00

ST. PAUL, MINN. & MAN.R'Y – 1888, First Class, St. Paul to Minneapolis, Going Coupon and Returning, cardstock, 1½ x 3½" $12.00

WABASH RAILROAD COMPANY – 1904, (via Canadian Pacific R'y) First Class, Portal to Westminister BC, paper stock, unfolds 3 x 10" $8.00

WINONA & ST. PETER R.R. – 1880, First Class, Tracy to Sleepy Eye Lake, cardstock, 1¼" x 2¼" (scarce) $25.00

Ticket Envelopes and Holders

When purchasing tickets, travelers were ususally handed a small-sized envelope to put them in, or if it was a long paper ticket, a cardstock holder was given to paste the folded ticket inside for safeguarding. Many of the earlier envelopes and holders were ornately done, with picturesque scenes on them. In later years, a regular-size envelope was furnished. Those from the famous name train era with colorful pictures of streamlined trains are especially desirable. The earlier ones, of course, are harder to come by and worth more.

BALTIMORE & OHIO R.R. – 1945, white envelope, front – blue pic of train at depot, map bk., 3½ x 6½" $5.00

BURLINGTON, CEDAR RAPIDS & NORTHERN R'Y. – ca. 1890, white envelope with blue adv. printing, 3¼ x 5½" (scarce) $18.50

BURLINGTON NORTHERN – 1970, green folder with inside pocket, 3¾ x 9"..$2.50

CHESAPEAKE AND OHIO – 1940, white envelope, front – sleeping kitten on green, map back, 3½ x 6¼"........$6.00

CHICAGO GREAT WESTERN RAILWAY – 1883, tan envelope, front – black "Maple Leaf Route" logo, map back, 2½ x 4¼" (scarce) $22.50

CHICAGO MILWAUKEE ST. PAUL AND PACIFIC – 1934, yellow envelope, front – pic of electric pass. train Yellowstone Park scene back, 3½ x 6½" $10.00

CHICAGO MILWAUKEE ST. PAUL AND PACIFIC – 1939, folded cardstock holder to paste ticket inside, yellow, front – pic of electric pass. train, Yellowstone Park scene back, 3" x 6"..$8.00

CHICAGO AND NORTH WESTERN SYSTEM – 1956, white envelope, front – pic of yellow streamliner on Stone Arch bridge, 3¾ x 6½" $6.00

GREAT NORTHERN RAILWAY – 1941, yellow envelope, front – black pic of The Winnipeg Limited steam train, 3½ x 6½"..$10.00

GREAT NORTHERN RAILWAY – 1951, blue envelope with clear plastic window, front – pic of two streamliners, picturesque back, 3½ x 6½" $6.00

GREAT NORTHERN RAILWAY – 1953, front – full-color pic of two streamliners, logo, 3½ x 7" $5.00

GREAT NORTHERN RAILWAY – 1959, front – full color pic of dome car, logo, 3½ x 7" $4.00

ILLINOIS CENTRAL – 1950's, brown envelope, front – pics of five name diesel streamliners, map back, 3½ x 6" $7.00

MILWAUKEE ROAD – 1955, orange envelope, front – full-color pic of Super Dome car, back – pic of Hiawatha streamliners, logos, 3½ x 7" $6.50

MILWAUKEE ROAD – 1963, yellow envelope, front – pic of Super Dome car, back – pic of people in dining car, logos, 3½ x 7" $5.50

MISSOURI PACIFIC LINES – 1950's, grey envelope, front – full-color pic of "Eagles" streamliner, eagle logo back, 3½ x 7" $8.50

NEW YORK CENTRAL SYSTEM – 1951, white envelope, front – green pic Old State House, Boston, logos back, 3½ x 6" $6.00

NORTHERN PACIFIC RAILWAY – 1928, white envelope, front – big red/black logo, passenger ID on back, two logos, 3¼ x 6" $9.50

NORTHERN PACIFIC RAILWAY – 1932, folded cardstock holder to paste ticket inside, front – red with photo Old Faithful Geyser, back – photo of Great Falls, Yellowstone Park, logos, 3¼ x 5¾" (scarce) $12.50

NORTHERN PACIFIC RAILWAY – 1961, red folder with inside pocket, front – photo of Vista Dome cars, logo, logo back, 3¾ x 7½" $5.00

ROCK ISLAND – 1952, red envelope, front – pics of steam and diesel trains, black logo, 3½ x 6½" $6.00

ROCK ISLAND – 1963, red/grey envelope, front – Rocket streamliner going through framed pic, map back, logos, 3½ x 7" $5.00

SOO LINE – 1948, folded cardstock holder to paste ticket inside, front – white with red logo, back – blue dining car illus., 3¼ x 5½" (scarce) $12.00

Cardstock Ticket Holder

SOUTHERN PACIFIC – 1967, white envelope, front – pics of four different diesel trains in green, passenger ID back, 3½ x 7" $4.00

UNION PACIFIC RAILROAD – 1950's, white envelope with clear plastic window with pic of yellow streamliner inside, Hoover Dam pic back, logos, 3½ x 6" $7.50

Seat Checks

These are small cardboard checks, approximately 1 x 3¼", which the conductor gave the traveler when he picked up the ticket. The passenger kept this colored card or check, as it secured the ride on the train. It was good for that trip and train only. These checks had the railroad's and the conductor's name printed on them; some even bore the conductor's signature in ink. They carried such phrases as "Good for this trip and train only," "Please place this in your hat or cap," or "Keep this in plain sight." Some had a cut of an early train, others had a mileage chart on the back. Those with names of early railroads now long gone are the real rarities.

Early Cardstock Seat Checks

ALBANY AND SUSQUEHANNA R.R – 1870's, yellow, "THROUGH CHECK" ink signature $12.00

BUFFALO, NEW YORK & ERIE R.R. – 1880's, yellow, "KEEP THIS IN SIGHT"..$10.00

BURLINGTON, CEDAR RAPIDS & MINNESOTA R'Y – 1870's, blue, "KEEP THIS CHECK IN SIGHT" $15.00

CHICAGO & NORTHWESTERN RAILWAY – 1870's, lavendar, Dakota Division, "Good for this Trip and Train Only"....$12.00

C.W. & E.R.R. – (Catawissa Williamsport & Erie) 1850's, yellow, cut of early train, ink signature $17.50

H. & N.H.R.R. – (HARTFORD & NEW HAVEN) 1860s, purple, cut of early train..$15.00

INDIANAPOLIS, CINCINNATI & LAFAYETTE RAILROAD – 1870's, green, cut of early train, Passenger not allowed TO STOP OVER ON THIS CHECK $13.50

MILWAUKEE & ST. PAUL R'Y. – 1870's, RIVER DIVISION, yellow $12.00

MILWAUKEE & ST. PAUL RAILWAY – I. & M. DIVISION – 1870's, green $12.00

NEW HAVEN & NORTHAMPTON RAILROAD – 1850's, blue, cut of early train $17.50

N.Y. & E.R.R. – (New York & Erie) 1860's, orange, cut of early train $15.00

N.Y. & E.R.R – (New York & Erie) 1870's, yellow, READ! If you wish A Quiet Nap, place this in your hat or cap and always by Day or Night, Please to keep THIS Check in Sight $17.50

N.YORK & N.HAVEN R.R. Check – 1860's, orange, cut of early train...$15.00

N.Y.N.H.&H.R.R – (New York, New Haven & Hartford) 1870's, green, cut of early train, "Please Keep this Check in Sight."...$12.00

WINONA AND ST. PETER RAILROAD – 1870's (unused) green, Stop-Over Check, Good For Ten Days Only....$13.50

Ticket Punches

Each conductor had his own ticket punch with a particular die design for perforating the tickets; it was as good as his signature. Some railroads have used hundreds of different die designs down through the years. These old conductor ticket punches with their various punch marks can make an extremely interesting collection. Those that are railroad marked bring the higher prices.

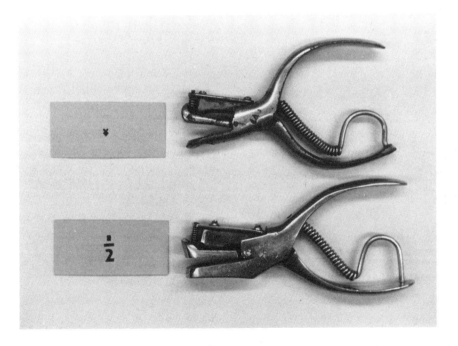

Conductor's Ticket Punches

CGW – punches "L," diagonal spring with finger loop handle, Pat. Apr. 30, '87, L.O. Crocker, E. Braintree, Mass....$50.00

CNW – punches "½", diagonal spring with finger loop handle, Stromberg Allen & Co., Chicago $35.00

GN – punches "2d", diagonal spring with finger loop handle, Poole Bros. Chicago $37.50

PRR – punches cross design, vertical spring in handle, Allen Lanf & Scot, Philadelphia..............................$40.00

Unmarked – punch and stub cutter, top slot punches Satellite design, bottom slot clips off small jagged piece, vertical spring in handle, L.A. Sayre & Son, Newark, N.J., Pat. 4-29-02 ....$15.00

Unmarked – dual design, punches letter "W" and shoe-shape design, vertical spring with finger ring in handle, McGill M.P. Co., Chicago $12.50

Unmarked – punches three-leaf clover, tension-spring handle, L.A. Sayre & Co., Newark, N.J. $10.00

Unmarked – punches "BC," diagonal spring with finger loop handle, Stromberg Allen & Co., Chicago $12.00

Unmarked – punches heart-shape design, vertical spring with finger ring handle, McGill Metal Products Co., Chicago $10.00

Unmarked – punches dagger-shape design, diagonal spring with finger ring handle, Stromberg Allen & Co., Chicago $8.00

Unmarked – punches "B," vertical spring only in handle, American Rail'y Supply Co., N.Y. $15.00

Unmarked – punches "L," diagonal spring with finger loop in handle, Poole Bros., Chicago........................$12.00

Unmarked – punches crescent design, diagonal spring with finger loop in handle, Stromberg Allen & Co., Chicago $10.00

Unmarked – punches arrowhead design, diagonal spring with finger loop in handle, L.O. Crocker, E. Braintree, Mass., Pat Apr 30, 1867...$15.00

Ticket Dater Validating Machines

These were used in the railroad's ticket offices and depots to stamp the railroad's name, location and date on the traveler's ticket, validating it. Those from the last century, in fine condition, complete with ink ribbon and die, have the greater value. Spare dies for these machines can also be found, and they are priced according to the rarity of the railroad's name on them.

Ticket Dater Validating Machine

CENTENNIAL DATER, Made By Independent Mfg. Co., Brass Die Imprints – C.G.W.RY. GRAF, IA., date wheels 1958 to 1969 ....$175.00

COSMOS MODEL No. 2, Dater & Die Set, Imprints – C.R.I. & P.RY. LEWIS, IA., dates 1910 to 1959, black enamel finish, floral decor, A.D. Joslin Mfg. Co., Manistee, Mich $135.00

COSMOS MODEL NO. 3, Dater & Die Set, Imprints – ERIE R.R. CO. DECATUR, IND., dates 1910 to 1969, black enamel finish, floral decor, A.D. Joslin Mfg. Co., Manistee, Mich $130.00

COSMOS MODEL NO. 4, Dater & Die Set, Imprints three railroads – C.M.ST.P.&P.R.R., SOO LINE, C.R.I.&P.RY., MINNEAPOLIS DEPOT, perpetual dating wheels, adjusts any year, black enamel finish, floral decor, A.D. Joslin Mfg. Co., Manistee, Mich $200.00

HILL'S MODEL A CENTENNIAL DATER & Die Set, imprints GREAT NORTHERN RAILWAY, PEKIN, N.D., dates 1946 to 1957 ....$150.00

MODEL AD CENTENNIAL DATER & Die Set, Pat. Oct. 18, '09, Mar 24 '14, Imprints – NOR.PAC.RY. RITZVILLE, WASH., dates 1952-1963, has black rubber cushion cap mkd. with NORTHERN PACIFIC logo, fits over metal striking head $185.00

Spare Ticket Dater Dies

C.R.I. & P.RY., NORTHFIELD, MINN $65.00

D.S.S. & A.R.R., TROUT CREEK MICH $125.00

MAINE CENTRAL R.R., BRUNSWICK, MAINE $55.00

M.ST.P.& S.S.M.R.R., THERESA, WIS $85.00

"SOO LINE" M.ST.P.& S.S.M.RY., LAKE CITY, S.D. $75.00

Ticket Cabinets

Oak, slant roll front, 23 x 35½", 14" deep bottom, 7½" at top,
    Poole Bros. Mfrs., Chicago $375.00
Oak, vertical roll front, 8 x 15 x 28", National Ticket Case Co.,
    Chicago $275.00

Rubber Hand Stamps

Hand stamps with rubber dies were often used to imprint additional words in ink on tickets, such as First Class,
Coach, Ticket Office, Clergy, name of town, etc. Those bearing a railroad ID are worth much more.

Note: All stamps listed are one-piece narrow finger-
molded grip type unless otherwise noted.

Rack of Rubber Hand Stamps

CLERGY $2.50
EMPIRE BUILDER (name train – GN RY) $4.00
FIRST CLASS BETWEEN ST. PAUL & OMAHA COACH
    BEYOND OMAHA $4.50
HALF FARE $2.00
HOT SPRINGS, ARK (town name) $1.75
INTERMEDIATE GOOD ONLY IN TOURIST SLEEPING
    CARS OR COACHES $3.50
LIMIT-THIRTY (30) DAYS – upright handle atop rubber die
    base..$4.00
ONE WAY COACH – upright handle atop rubber die
    base..$5.00

ONE WAY FIRST CLASS – upright handle atop rubber die
    base $5.00
ROOMETTE $1.75
SPECIAL COACH 15-DAY LIMIT – upright handle atop rub-
    ber die base...$6.50
¼ EXTRA FARE ACCOUNT OCCUPANCY DRAWING
    ROOM..$5.00

Railroad Marked

CHICAGO, BURLINGTON & QUINCY RAILROAD COM-
    PANY – upright handle atop rubber die base, 3¾"
    length $15.00
C.M.ST.P. & P. – upright handle atop rubber die
    base..$12.00

D.& R.G.W.RY $6.00
R.I. TO S.ROSA SOU.PAC $10.00
R.I. TO BURL C.B. & Q $8.00
S.P. & S...$5.00

Time Tables

The colorful time tables previous to the 1940's picturing trains, legendary figures, ornate logos and interesting slogans
on their covers generally bring the higher prices, as do those from short lines, narrow gauge and defunct roads. The early
fold-out pictorial time tables from the last half of the nineteenth century are highly prized and continue to increase substan-
tially in price. Many of these were a large single sheet with a colored map on one side with illustrations, advertising and train
schedules on the other side, folding into a pamphlet. The earliest time tables, such as the small card or single sheet of paper
listing train schedules, are the rarities.

Public

Note: Most of the time tables listed here are the standard stapled 8 x 9" booklet type folded in half to make a 4 x 9" pamphlet. The earlier illustrated examples with advertisements, schedules and maps printed on both sides of a single sheet were folded into a TT size; measurements of these are given unfolded.

ALTON RAILROAD COMPANY – TIME TABLES, Effective May 29, 1932, cover – red, pic of engineer/fireman, logo $20.00

ALTON RAILROAD – TIME TABLES, May-June-July-Aug. 1945, cover – red, logo $10.00

AMTRAK – nationwide schedules of intercity passenger service, effective January 16, 1972, cover – white, red/blue wheels motif, logo $4.00

ATCHISON TOPEKA & SANTA FE AND SOUTHERN PACIFIC R.R.'s, 21-Dec.-'82, cover – black/white illustrated train in mountains, unfolds 15 x 28", map back (scarce) $115.00

ATLANTA AND WEST POINT RAILROAD – W. RY. OF ALA., GEORGIA RAILROAD, November 20, 1954, cover – brown/white, The West Point Route logo $8.00

ATLANTIC COAST LINE RAILROAD – Time Tables, Issued September 30, 1951, cover – purple, white logo $6.00

BALTIMORE & OHIO – picturesque B&O WEST AND EAST, June 15, 1884, cover – illustration of frolicking cherubs, unfolds 16 x 32", map back, (rare) $100.00

BALTIMORE & OHIO – B AND O, EAST OR WEST, May, 1886, cover – illustration of conductor holding tickets and passenger with umbrella and grip, unfolds 16 x 32" map back (scarce) $85.00

BALTIMORE & OHIO Railroad System – SCHEDULES OF TRAINS, No. 2, 1912, cover – blue, white Capitol building $15.00

BALTIMORE & OHIO Railroad – System Time Tables, Issued April 26, 1936, cover – blue, white logo $6.00

BALTIMORE & OHIO SOUTH-WESTERN R.R. – TT'S No. 1, 1911, cover – blue, white Capitol building $12.00

BIG FOUR ROUTE – (New York Central System) Effective June 1, 1936, cover – grey pic New Union Terminal at Cincinnati, NYCS logo..$10.00

BOSTON AND ALBANY RAILROAD – (N.Y.C.& H.R.R.CO. LESSEE) LOCAL TIME-TABLE in effect Nov. 23, 1902, Re-issued January 12, 1903, No. 49-c, cover – yellow, pic South Station, Boston $15.00

BOSTON AND MAINE RAILROAD – condensed through TIME TABLES, in effect October 2, 1911, cover – green, white printing $13.00

BOSTON AND MAINE RAILROAD – Portland Division, Local Time Table, in effect June 21, 1915, cover – white, black logo..$10.00

BOSTON AND MAINE RAILROAD – TIME TABLES, Eastern Standard Time, October 29, 1928, cover – green, Minute Man figure $12.00

BURLINGTON, CEDAR RAPIDS & NORTHERN RAILWAY – Official Local Time Tables, April 1900, cover pic – view of Beautiful "Dugway" Drive, Decorah, Iowa (scarce) ..$75.00

BURLINGTON NORTHERN – time table effective October 25, 1970, cover – green, white System map..............$3.00

BURLINGTON ROUTE – TIME TABLES, EVERY WHERE WEST, July-August, 1930, cover – red, black logo..$10.00

BURLINGTON ROUTE – TIME TABLES, Way of the Zephyrs, May-September, 1951, cover – red, black logo, diesel streamliners..$5.00

Four NP Pictorial Folding TT's, pre-1900

NP 1889 Pictorial TT Partially Unfolded

CANADIAN PACIFIC RAILWAY – February 1st, 1913, cover – yellow, red/black beaver atop shield logo $18.00

CENTRAL VERMONT RAILWAY – Green Mountain Route, TIME TABLES, Parlor and Sleeping Car Schedules, July 1, 1913, cover – blue, white printing.....................$15.00

CHESAPEAKE AND OHIO Route – F.F.V. Limited, May 23, 1909, red cover/white printing $20.00

CHESAPEAKE AND OHIO LINES – TIME TABLES, December 10, 1944, cover – red/black kittens, "Sleep like a Kitten" $8.00

CHESAPEAKE AND OHIO RAILWAY – passenger TIME TABLES, May 1, 1951, blue/white cover, pic of sleeping kitten $5.00

CHICAGO AND ALTON R.R. – For Chicago, St. Louis and All Points EAST, NORTH AND SOUTH, February 1882, red cover with depot illustration, unfolds 15½ x 21"....$75.00

CHICAGO AND ALTON Railroad – "THE ONLY WAY" Perfect Passenger Service TIME TABLES, May-June, 1927, maroon cover/pic engineer and fireman $22.00

CHICAGO & EASTERN ILLINOIS RAILWAY – TIME TABLES, corrected to Jan. 1, 1930, yellow cover/red C & E I Ry. engine logo $18.00

CHICAGO & EASTERN ILLINOIS RAILROAD – C & E I, Time Tables, December 12, 1948 orange/blue cov. pic of diesel streamliner $6.00

CHICAGO BURLINGTON AND QUINCY RAILROAD – Feb-June 1878, Now Runs Two Daily Through Trains Between KANSAS CITY AND CHICAGO, white cover with black printing, unfolds 22 x 31", map back (scarce) $95.00

CHICAGO GREAT WESTERN RAILWAY – July 1, 1908, purple cover with white maple leaf map (scarce) $45.00

CHICAGO GREAT WESTERN – March 1, 1912, blue cover with red Corn Belt Route logo................................$25.00

CHICAGO GREAT WESTERN – July 15th, 1923, brown cover with brown Corn Belt Route logo $20.00

CHICAGO GREAT WESTERN – Jan-Feb-Mar, 1929, blue cover with blue Corn Belt Route logo $15.00

CHICAGO GREAT WESTERN RAILROAD – TIME TABLES, June 11, 1933, white cover with black engine logo $10.00

CHICAGO GREAT WESTERN RAILROAD CO. – TIME TABLES, March 1, 1940, white cover with black Corn Belt Route logo $8.00

CHICAGO AND NORTH WESTERN RAILWAY – CHICAGO, ST. PAUL AND MINNEAPOLIS Line, In Effect Aug. 18, 1879, white cover with red/black logos, unfolds 15 x 35½", map back (rare) $135.00

CHICAGO AND NORTHWESTERN Railway – comprising five TRUNK Lines To & From the WEST AND NORTHWEST, 11-12-82, white cover – black/white illustration depot and trainshed, unfolds 16 x 46", map back (rare) $100.00

CHICAGO AND NORTHWESTERN LINE – UNION PACIFIC THE OVERLAND Route shield logo, December 9, 1900, pic of passenger train across entire olive cover, also The NORTH-WESTERN Line logo (scarce) $85.00

CHICAGO AND NORTHWESTERN LINE – UNION PACIFIC THE OVERLAND Route shield logo, Through Train SERVICE, June 11, 1893, black/white illustrations of bridges and rivers on light grey cover, also The NORTHWESTERN Line logo, unfolds 8 x 32" length (scarce)...............$75.00

CHICAGO AND NORTH WESTERN LINE – UNION PACIFIC THE OVERLAND Route shield logo, Complete Passenger Schedules, March 7, 1926, white cover – black/white pic Chicago Passenger Terminal, also C&NW logo........$20.00

CHICAGO AND NORTH WESTERN LINE – Serves The WEST NORTHWEST PACIFIC COAST, June 21, 1936, white cover – black/white logo and train $15.00

CHICAGO AND NORTH WESTERN LINE – September 15, 1942, white cover with three black/white streamliners abreast $10.00

CHICAGO MILWAUKEE & ST. PAUL RY. – LOCAL TIME TABLES, June 1, 1888, white cover – red logo above black/white train (rare) $110.00

CHICAGO MILWAUKEE AND ST. PAUL RAILWAY – 1-1-91, white cover, red logo, black/white pic of train, girl waving hanky, unfolds 22½ x 37½", map back (rare) $95.00

CHICAGO MILWAUKEE AND ST. PAUL RAILWAY – THE FAST MAIL LINE, SOLID VESTIBULED TRAINS, 8-1-97, white cover, red logo, black/white pic of dining car interior, unfolds 8 x 22½", map back (scarce) $75.00

CHICAGO MILWAUKEE & ST. PAUL RAILWAY – passenger train schedules, May, 1906, yellow cover, red logo $15.00

CHICAGO MILWAUKEE & ST. PAUL RAILWAY – passenger train schedules, April, 1915, yellow cover, red logo $12.00

Public Time Tables — Steam and Diesel Era

CHICAGO MILWAUKEE ST. PAUL AND PACIFIC – The Milwaukee Road, June-July 1937, yellow cover, red logo $10.00

CHICAGO MILWAUKEE ST. PAUL AND PACIFIC – The Milwaukee Road, May-June 1939, yellow cover, four black/white loco pics, Hiawathas, Olympian ..$8.00

CHICAGO ROCK ISLAND AND PACIFIC RY. – May, 1883, white cover, grey horseshoe logo, black printing, unfolds 20 x 41", map back (rare) $125.00

CHICAGO, ST. PAUL AND KANSAS CITY – July 28, 1889, cover – black with light green Maple Leaf map, unfolds 16 x 31½", map back (scarce) $85.00

COLORADO MIDLAND RAILWAY – Midland Route, TIME TABLES, July, 1909, cover – black with red-white logo (scarce) $75.00

DELAWARE & HUDSON – "The D&H" Leading Tourists' Line of America, Summer Time Table, 1907, cover – grey with night train $18.00

DENVER AND RIO GRANDE Railroad – scenic line of the world, September, 1893, cover – white, black/white pic trains in moutains, unfolds 8 x 31½", map back (scarce) $65.00

DENVER AND RIO GRANDE WESTERN – descriptive time tables, summer and fall, 1925, cover – black with red printing, unfolds 10½ x 34" (scarce) $30.00

DULUTH MISSABE & NORTHERN – THE "MISSABE" ROAD, Time Table No. 39, July 1912, cover – white with red logo $22.00

DULUTH MISSABE AND IRON RANGE – THE MISSABE ROAD Time Tables, November 30, 1947, cover – white with red-green logo...$15.00

DULTUH, SOUTH SHORE & ATLANTIC RAILWAY – time tables, corrected to December 15, 1940, cover – white with black The SOUTH SHORE logo $18.00

EASTERN RAILROAD – ESSEX RAILROAD, SOUTH READING BRANCH, Summer Arrangement, June 10, 1861, single sheet TT, 18¾ x 23½", black/white pic of early train, black printing on white paper (rare) $110.00

ERIE – TIME TABLES, June 24, 1906, cover – grey, black/white diamond logo.....................................$15.00

FITCHBURG RAILROAD – Hoosac Tunnel Route, Dec. 1884, cover – white with illustration of trains near the Hoosac Tunnel, unfolds 15 x 22", map back (rare)...........$120.00

FLORIDA EAST COAST Railway – TIME TABLES, Issued September 30, 1951, cover – red/yellow with diesel streamliner..$6.00

FRISCO SYSTEM – through the SOUTHWEST and the SOUTHEAST, February, 1903, cover – black with red logo $12.00

FRISCO LINES – (St. Louis-San Francisco Ry.) Great Railroad 5,000 miles, JUNE 1946, cover – red with black logo $8.00

GRAND TRUNK PACIFIC – time tables, June 6, 1915, orange cover with black logo $10.00

GREAT NORTHERN RAILWAY – corrected to November 1898, brown cover with white letters (scarce) $50.00

GREAT NORTHERN RAILWAY – July 15, 1901, green cover with black pic train leaving Cascade Tunnel (scarce) $45.00

GREAT NORTHERN RAILWAY – LOCAL TIME TABLES, Revised to May 1916, pink cover with black logo and printing (scarce) $35.00

GREAT NORTHERN RAILWAY – Nov. 18, 1917, green cover with black logo, red chk. oriental motif border design $20.00

GREAT NORTHERN – TIME TABLES, March, 1924, grey pinstripe cover with white goat logo $15.00

GREAT NORTHERN – TIME TABLES, August, 1926, red cover with red squares in white border design, mountain goat logo $12.00

GREAT NORTHERN RAILWAY – passenger train schedules, April-May-June 1948, orange cover with map and diesel line-up, goat logo $8.00

GREAT NORTHERN RAILWAY – passenger train schedules between Chicago and The Pacific Northwest, October 28, 1962, blue cover with logo and diesel streamliners......$6.00

GULF MOBILE AND OHIO RAILROAD – April 15, 1947, red cover with white map and streamliners $6.00

HARLEM EXTENSION R.R. – TIME TABLE Commencing May 29, 1871, single sheet 8½ x 15" yellow with illustration of primitive train, black printing (rare) $95.00

ILLINOIS CENTRAL RAILROAD – route of the southern fast mail, effective April 20, 1899, white cover, red/black circle/diamond logo..$25.00

ILLINOIS CENTRAL – TIME TABLES, issued June 19, 1931, green cover, white/black circle diamond logo $12.00

INDIANA RAILROAD SYSTEM – effective September 6, 1938, grey/orange cover with pic of electric train..............$6.00

IOWA CENTRAL ROUTE – Short Line Between St. Paul, Minneapolis, St. Louis, 4-20-90, white cover, black logo, unfolds 14¾ x 16¼" (scarce) $45.00

IRON MOUNTAIN ROUTE – 10-20-85, white cover with black illustration front and side view of Buffet Sleeping Car interior, unfolds 16 x 29", map back (rare) $120.00

JERSEY CENTRAL RAILROAD – time tables, effective March 12, 1944, white cover with blue train and map $5.00

KANSAS CITY SOUTHERN Lines – Route of the Southern Belle, June 22, 1947, blue cover with red logo, diesel streamliner $5.00

LACKAWANNA RAILROAD – corrected to September 1, 1901, white cover, blue logo $12.00

LACKAWANNA RAILROAD – time tables, September 28, 1952, cover – full pic of the Phoebe Snow streamliner $6.00

LAKE SHORE and Michigan Southern RAILROAD LINE – 1857, Condensed Time Table, taking effect March 31, card type, 3 x 5" (rare) $50.00

LAKE SHORE & MICHIGAN SOUTHERN RY – spring time tables, May 12, 1878, white cover with illustration of Fast Mail train, unfolds 14 x 21½", map back (rare) $150.00

LAKE SHORE AND MICHIGAN SOUTHERN RAILWAY – December 1, 1882, white cover with illustration Niagara Falls and double track trains, unfolds 15 x 32", map back (rare)..$80.00

LAKE SHORE AND MICHIGAN SOUTHERN RAILWAY – corrected March 9, 1890, yellow cover with illustration trains and depot, unfolds 17 x 39½", map back......$70.00

LAKE SHORE AND MICHIGAN SOUTHERN RAILWAY– May, 1897, tan cover with logo and five mail sacks.............$50.00

LAKE SHORE AND MICHIGAN SOUTHERN RAILWAY – April 1901, brown cover with pic of mail sack between two classical figures $30.00

LEHIGH VALLEY RAILROAD – corrected to August 18, 1901, green cover Pan-Am Expo. 1901 round emblem, Flag logo $20.00

LEHIGH VALLEY RAILROAD – complete time tables, May 14, 1905, green cover with white printing and logo $15.00

LEHIGH VALLEY RAILROAD – The Route of The Black Diamond, January 14, 1945, green cover with white printing and logo $5.00

LOUISVILLE AND NASHVILLE RAILROAD – TIME TABLES, December 17, 1944, green cover with red L&N logo $8.00

LOUISVILLE AND NASHVILLE RAILROAD – passenger train time tables, winter – 1956-57, blue cover with red L&N logo $6.00

MAINE CENTRAL RAILROAD – in effect May 1, 1899, full cover illustration of sailboats and mountains........$45.00

MEXICAN NATIONAL R.R. – MEXICO, 9-9-97, light grey cover with Loredo Route crossed flag emblem, unfolds 23½ x 24", map back $25.00

MICHIGAN CENTRAL AND GREAT WESTERN AND DETROIT AND MILWAUKEE RAILWAY LINES – winter time table, Dec. 1 of 1871-1872, white cover with blue printing, unolds 11 x 20½", map reverse side (rare)............$130.00

MICHIGAN CENTRAL – "The Niagara Falls Route," summer folder, season of 1885, full cover pic of train at Niagara Falls, unfolds 16 x 31", map reverse side (rare) $120.00

MICHIGAN CENTRAL – The Niagara Falls Route, revised to October 21, 1896, maroon cover with pic of train at Falls (scarce) $75.00

MINNEAPOLIS & ST. LOUIS RAILROAD CO. – summer edition, 1907, red cover with Albert Lea Route logo......$35.00

Rare Time Table, Postcard Size

MINNEAPOLIS & ST.LOUIS RAILROAD CO. – time tables, summer edition, 1916, light green cover with black Albert Lea Route logo $20.00

MINNEAPOLIS & ST. LOUIS RAILROAD – passenger train TIME TABLES, issued 1932, blue cover with The Peoria Gateway Line logo..$15.00

MISSOURI KANSAS & TEXAS RAILWAY – The "KATY FLY-ER," MISSOURI, KANSAS, INDIAN TERRITORY, TEXAS, January 1901, blue cover with red logo and figure of lady KATY (scarce) $50.00

MISSOURI KANSAS & TEXAS RAILWAY – time tables, effective March 1, 1948, blue cover with red M-K-T Katy Lines logo $12.00

MISSOURI PACIFIC LINES – issued January 15, 1939, black cover with red logo, black/white trains illustrated $15.00

MISSOURI PACIFIC LINES – issued February 2, 1941, white cover with red logo and blue steam/diesel trains $12.00

MISSOURI PACIFIC LINES – Route of the Eagles, issued November 24, 1946, full cover illustration of diesel streamliner $8.00

MOBILE AND OHIO R.R. – between the NORTH and the SOUTH, 11-22-14, blue cover with red logo..........$15.00

MONON ROUTE – (Chicago, Indianpolis & Louisville Ry) corrected to November 17, 1946, yellow cover with black logo on red $8.00

NASHVILLE CHATTANOOGA AND ST. LOUIS RAILWAY – time tables, spring 1957, dark green cover with red NC&StL logo $6.00

NATIONAL RAILWAYS OF MEXICO – time tables and general information, October-November, 1929, blue cover with white letters on red squares $12.00

NEW HAVEN RAILROAD – time table, effective April 30, 1967 – daylight time, white cover with pic of NH 2001 diesel $5.00

NEW YORK AND NEW HAVEN RAILROAD – time table 1855, card type, 3 x 5" (rare) $50.00

NEW YORK NEW HAVEN AND HARTFORD RAILROAD – local time table, revised to March 17, 1913, white cover with black printing, unfolds 8 x 27½" $15.00

NEW YORK NEW HAVEN AND HARTFORD RAILROAD CO. – summer schedule, June 17, 1945, white cover with black train illustrated $6.00

NEW YORK CENTRAL – time tables, effective September 27, 1931, grey cover with pic of train, logo $15.00

NEW YORK CENTRAL SYSTEM – time tables, effective July 15, 1936, grey cover with pic of Grand Central Terminal and Niagara Falls..$12.00

NEW YORK CENTRAL – system time tables, effective August 13, 1944, white cover with green pic of streamline steam train $10.00

NEW YORK CENTRAL – The Scenic Water Level Route, effective April 25, 1948, blue cover wih pic of passing trains, black logo..$8.00

NEW YORK CENTRAL AND HUDSON RIVER RAILROAD – November 11, 1884, tan cover with two pics, Grand Central Depot, trains on Four Track Route, unfolds 15½ x 31¾", map back (rare)..$95.00

NICKEL PLATE – (New York, Chicago & St. Louis R.R.) TIME TABLE, in effect May 28, 1893, white cover with blue scene within diamond, unfolds 16 x 31½" map back..........$45.00

NICKEL PLATE ROAD – time tables, August 13, 1936, light grey cover with black logo and train illustration ..$10.00

NORFOLK SOUTHERN RAILROAD – time table, steam division, corrected to July 5, 1929, white cover with black printing $8.00

NORFOLK AND WESTERN RAILWAY – time table, June 7, 1953 – No. 3, maroon cover with black pics two Indians and loco front $6.00

NORFOLK AND WESTERN RAILWAY – time table, April 30, 1961 – No. 1, maroon cover with black pics of two Indians $5.00

NORTHERN PACIFIC RAILROAD – September 1880, and its connections – FORT KEOGH & MILES CITY Mail and Stage Lines, or Missouri and Yellowstone River Steamers for DAKOTA & MONTANA, white cover with blue/black printing, unfolds 8½ x 29½", map back (rare) $185.00

NORTHERN PACIFIC R.R. – fall, 1883, September, white cover with black illustration of Falls and Geyser, unfolds 16 x 43½", map back (rare) $175.00

NORTHERN PACIFIC RR – The Dining Car Route between the EAST and PACIFIC COAST, July, 1887, white cover with sketchs of dining car chef, rifle/fish scene, unfolds 16 x 31½", map back (rare) $145.00

NORTHERN PACIFIC R.R. – The DINING CAR LINE To Montana and the PACIFIC COAST, August, 1889, green cover with black illustration of dining car waiter, Yellowstone Park Falls scene, unolds 24 x 34½", map back (rare) $125.00

NORTHERN PACIFIC – revised to June 9, 1897, white cover with red/black logo, unfolds 24 x 34½", map back (scarce) $75.00

NORTHERN PACIFIC – revised to May 5, 1901, white cover with sketch of strong man holding logo with train between feet (scarce) $45.00

NORTHERN PACIFIC – local time tables, issued August 25, 1909, light green cover with black logo and illustration $35.00

NORTHERN PACIFIC – TIME TABLES, effective September, 1912, red cover with black logo and pic of Mount Raineer-Tacoma $25.00

NORTHERN PACIFIC – time tables, April-May 1925, white cover, red/black logo $18.00

NORTHERN PACIFIC – North Coast Limited, summer, 1937, white cover red/black logo $15.00

PENN CENTRAL – EAST/WEST TIME TABLE, effective March 3, 1971, white cover with blue map $3.00

PENNYSLVANIA RAILROAD – GREAT TRUNK LINE and U.S. MAIL ROUTE, January, 1877, white cover with red/black printing, unfolds 14 x 27½", map back....$75.00

PENNSYLVANIA RAILROAD – GREAT TRUNK LINE of the UNITED STATES, May 23, 1887, orange cover with black illustration of eagle, trains on Horse Shoe Curve, unfolds 17 x 35½", map back (rare) $100.00

PENNSYLVANIA RAILROAD – issued September 30, 1945, full cover pic of locomotive on turntable $12.00

PENNSYLVANIA RAILROAD – issued April 27, 1952, full cover pic of trains on Horseshoe Curve $8.00

PENNSYLVANIA RAILROAD – issued February 10, 1963, maroon cover with white line drawing of trains......$6.00

PERE MARQUETTE RAILWAY – passenger time table, corrected to August 10, 1946, blue cover with pic of diesel streamliner $6.00

PHILADELPHIA & READING RAILWAY – in effect Nov. 29, 1903, grey cover with black P&R The Royal Route emblem, unfolds 16½ x 33", map back..................$35.00

PITTSBURGH AND LAKE ERIE – TIME TABLES, corrected to April 30, 1933, grey cover with pic of LaSalle Street Terminal, New York Central Lines logo $15.00

READING RAILWAY SYSTEM – effective September 28, 1947, light blue cover with dark blue Crusader streamliner emblem $6.00

RICHMOND, FREDERICKSBURG AND POTOMAC Railroad – time tables, December 16, 1954, blue/grey cover with white printing and logo $4.00

RUTLAND RAILROAD – schedule of June 22, 1913, white cover, black logo and printing $20.00

ROCK ISLAND – time tables, corrected to June 22, 1924, orange cover with black logo, world globe $18.00

ROCK ISLAND – time tables, January 1941, red cover, black logo, steam and diesel locos.....................................$12.00

ROCK ISLAND – time tables, May 1954, red cover, black logo, pics of Rocket freight and passenger trains at depots ..$8.00

ROCK ISLAND – passenger time tables, spring-summer 1966, pink cover with red logo and diesel train $4.00

ROME WATERTOWN AND OGDENSBURG RAILROAD – TIME TABLE, in effect Monday, July 6, 1885, pink cover, black printing, unfolds 14 x 21", map reverse side $65.00

SEABOARD RAILWAY – TRAIN SCHEDULES, effective January 15, 1945, white cover with red/black heart logo $6.00

SEABOARD RAILROAD – condensed time tables, effective December 14, 1956, red cover with pic of two streamliners and logos $4.00

ST. LOUIS SOUTHWESTERN RAILWAY LINES – SCHEDULES to and from the great SOUTHWEST, effective December 21, 1947, red cover with blue Cotton Belt Route logo...$5.00

SAINT PAUL & DULUTH RAILROAD – July 1896, white cover with black DULUTH SHORT LINE triangle logo, unfolds 8¾ x 19¾", map back (rare) $95.00

ST. PAUL MINNEAPOLIS & MANITOBA R'Y – July 18, 1886, RED RIVER Valley Line, white cover with black illustration St.PM&MRy Double Track Stone Arch Bridge, Minneapolis, Minn., unfolds 24¾ x 30½", map back (rare) $135.00

SOO – SOUTH SHORE LINES – (Minneapolis, St. Paul & Sault Ste Marie and Duluth, South Shore & Atlantic Rys.) January, 1892, blue cover with red banner logo, unfolds 8 x 34¾", map back (rare) $85.00

SOO LINE – LOCAL TIME TABLES, August 1, 1905, white cover with red Banner logos..................................$35.00

SOO LINE – LOCAL TIME TABLES, August 21, 1910, white cover with green Banner logos..................................$30.00

SOO LINE – primer 3, 3-17-15, orange cover with red Box logos...$25.00

SOO LINE – folder A, May 12, 1929, green cover with red Box logos $20.00

SOO LINE – local time tables, October 2, 1933, white cover with blue logo, train $15.00

SOO LINE TIME TABLES, May 15, 1945, blue cover with red logo...$10.00

SOO LINE – TIME TABLES, January 30, 1955, blue cover with red logo, diesel train.....................................$5.00

SOUTHERN PACIFIC – December 1912, red cover with Sunset Ogden and Shasta Routes logo in white on blue..$15.00

SOUTHERN PACIFIC – TIME TABLES, June-July, 1935, blue cover with white Southern Pacific Lines logo $10.00

SOUTHERN PACIFIC – S.P. time tables, May 16, 1948, blue cover with pic of orange steam streamliner, two logos $8.00

SOUTHERN RAILWAY SYSTEM – time tables of passenger trains, August 5, 1951, yellow/black cover with pics of The Southerner, The Crescent streamliners...........$8.00

SOUTHERN RAILWAY SYSTEM – passenger train schedules, January 10, 1960, green cover with pic streamliner crossing river bridge, logo $5.00

STONINGTON LINE AND RAIL – (Boston and Providence R.R. New York Providence and Boston RR, Providence and Stonington S.S.Co.) ca. early 1800's, yellow cover with black illustration of boat and train, unfolds 7½ x 14", map back (rare) $115.00

SPOKANE PORTLAND AND SEATTLE RY. – TIME TABLES, January 1, 1957, green cover with three logos – SP&S RY, NP RY and GN RY.....................................$10.00

TEXAS AND PACIFIC RAILWAY CO. – time table no. 6, April 15, 1926, yellow stripe cover with T and P diamond logo $12.00

TEXAS AND PACIFIC – time table November, 1948, full cover pic of streamliner at depot..............................$6.00

THE NORTH-WESTERN LINE – (F.F.&M.V. and S.C.&P.R.Rds.) logo, February 1, 1893, grey cover with elk's head, unfolds 18 x 39½", map back (rare) $95.00

THE NORTH WESTERN LINE – condensed schedules, August 22, 1909, orange cover with black pic of passenger train, logo, unfolds 18 x 28", map back (scarce) $50.00

THE NORTH WESTERN LINE – (Chicago, St. Paul, Minneapolis & Omaha, Chicago and North Western Railways) corrected to May, 1917, yellow cover with red-gold logo $25.00

TROY & BOSTON & FITCHBURG R.R.ds – HOOSAC TUNNEL ROUTE, 13-Mar-'83, blue cover, illustration of trains at Hoosac Tunnel, unfolds 15 x 21½", map back (rare) $100.00

UNION PACIFIC – local and through time tables, summer edition, June, 1895, cover – red/white, World's Pictorial Line logo, unfolds 18 x 44½", map back (scarce) $40.00

UNION PACIFIC – (Union Pacific R.R. Co., Oregon Short Line R.R. Co., Oregon R.R. & Navigation Co.) corrected to October 1, 1901, blue cover with World's Pictorial Line logo $35.00

UNION PACIFIC – PATHFINDER, local and through TIME TABLES, January, 1901, blue pinstripe cover, World's Pictorial Line logo $25.00

UNION PACIFIC – (Oregon Short Line, Oregon R.R. & Navigation Co., Southern Pacific) revised to March 1, 1908, red cover, The Overland Route logo $22.00

UNION PACIFIC SYSTEM – time tables, corrected to November 15, 1922, white cover with black shield logo $16.00

UNION PACIFIC SYSTEM – time tables, revised to April 2, 1935, white cover with black shield logo, pic of steam and diesel trains $14.00

UNION PACIFIC RAILROAD – time tables, March 1, 1963, grey/yellow cover, shield logo, pic of steam-diesel trains $8.00

WABASH SYSTEM – February 1906, cover – red/white, pic of Niagara Falls...$25.00

WABASH – time tables, January-February, 1926, blue cover, red Flag logo, train..$18.00

WABASH – time tables, August-September, 1935, blue cover, Red Flag logo, train $15.00

WABASH – November 18, 1945, Those Who Know SHIP and GO WABASH, white cover, red Flag logo and heart map $10.00

WABASH – April 26, 1953, MODERN SERVICE In the Heart of America, blue cover, red Flag logo with two diesel trains, red heart map $8.00

WESTERN PACIFIC – time tables, April 28, 1957, white cover with red feather, black logo.....................................$6.00

WHEELING & LAKE ERIE RAILWAY – time tables, February 15, 1894, cover – red/black, with pics of train on bridge, depot, unfolds 8 x 28" $55.00

WISCONSIN CENTRAL LINES – (Northern Pacific Railroad Co. Lessee) issue of April 15, 1891, cover – black with map of route, red logo, unfolds 16 x 23½", map back (rare)..$85.00

WISCONSIN CENTRAL RY. CO. – February, 1900, cover – red/black, logo & map (scarce) $55.00

WISCONSIN CENTRAL RAILWAY – December, 1901, cover – white with black map (scarce) $45.00

Employee Time Tables

Employee time tables also evolved from a single sheet to booklet and folder types. They were plain and unattractive, and were issued for the government and information of employees only in their daily operation of the trains, and were not for distribution to the general public, as they contained restricted information. Employees were instructed to destroy them as soon as an updated issue was received. Many collectors make a specialty of these and pay good money for those from early now defunct roads.

Employee Timetables

BURLINGTON NORTHERN – twin cities region, TT 27, Oct. 1, 1979...$5.00

C&NW – Wisconsin Division, TT no. 441, April 30, 1950....$8.00

CGW – Western Division, TT 39-A, Jan. 26, 1930, 11¼ x 16", seven pages $15.00

CGW – Minnesota Division, TT no. 43, Nov. 23, 1930 ..$12.00

CGW and CRI&P – joint TT no. 20, Between Manley, Iowa and Clear Lake Junction, Iowa, Oct. 30, 1966 .....$10.00

CSTPM&O – Western Division, TT no. 133, Dec. 5, 1915, 10¾ x 15", seven pages, map back page $20.00

CSTPM&O – Western Division, Supplement "A" TT no. 2, Oct. 30, 1955..$8.00

CMSTP&P – LaCrosse and River Division, Second District, TT no. 67, Sept. 8, 1957.....................$6.00
CRI&P – Des Moines Division, no. 4, Oct. 31, 1965 ......$5.00
GN – Willmar Division, TT no. 99, Oct. 11, 1908, 11¼ x 16¾", ten pages, map back page $18.00
GN – United States Railroad Administration, W.D. Hines, Director General of Railroads, Willmar Division, TT no. 2, Feb. 23, 1919, GNR logos on cover, 11¼ x 16¾", 15 pages, map back page (scarce) $45.00
GN – Twin City Terminals, Willmar Division, TT no. 138, Nov. 1, 1931, 11¼ x 16¾", three pages, GREAT NORTHERN goat logo on cover $15.00
GN – Willmar Division, TT 124, Oct. 30, 1966 ....$5.00
IC – Iowa Division, TT no. 26, April 26, 1959 ....$5.00
M&StL – Central Division, no. 10, June 24, 1917 ....$15.00
MStP&SSM – Twin City Terminal Division, TT no. 9, July 12, 1931 ....$12.00

MStP&SSM – Minnesota Division, TT no. 183, Sept. 3, 1950 ....$8.00
MKT – North Texas Division, TT no. 28, Jan. 8, 1956 ..$8.00
MP – Omaha and Northern Kansas Divisions, TT no. 35, Mar. 2, 1958 ....$6.00
NP – Idaho Division, TT 36, Jan. 1, 1912, 12 x 16¼", ten pages, map bavk $15.00
NP – St. Paul Division, Special Instructions no. 9, Jan. 1, 1950 ....$4.00
SOO LINE – Central Division, TT no. 3, Feb. 16, 1964 ..$6.00
SP – Oregon Division, TT no. 8, May 16, 1971 ....$4.00
WILLIAMSPORT & ELMIRA RR – TRAINS MOVING North and South, TT no. 4, Takes Effect Monday May 25, 1857, single sheet 8½ x 12" (rare) $50.00
WINONA & ST. PETER RR – TT no. 113, For the GOVERNMENT and INFORMATION of Employees Only, Takes effect at 3:00 o'clock p.m. on Sunday, Nov. 25, 1883, 11 pages, 9¼ x 12½" (rare) $75.00

Tools, Steam Era Vintage

Collecting old railroad marked tools from the steam era used by workers in the roundhouses, shops, depots and for track maintenance, has become a hobby for many. Some specialize in the small hand-tools only, while others collect all types, both large and small. The railroad marking is found somewhere on the metal or on the wood handle.

Adz

GNRY – track work, flat head with curved blad 5" wide by 6" long, original handle, mfr. HACK-DEVIL $15.00

Axes (with original wood handles)

CMSTP&PRR – flat head, 4¾" wide cutting blade, no mfr. ID $25.00
CMSTP&PRR – double-faced, 4¾" wide blades, no mfr. ID $35.00
G.N.RY. – flat head, 4½" wide cutting blade, TRUE TEMPER FLINT EDGE $30.00

Box Car Mover

NPR – cast iron mechanical acting jack 3 x 19", that abuts car wheel and is attached to wooden leverage pole 58" long, mfr'd by ADVANCE CAR MOVER CO., Appleton, Wis...$45.00

Brakeman's Clubs – used to wind down box car brakewheel spoke handle

BN INC – oval stick 1¼ x 1¾", length 28", indented gold initials..$10.00
GN RY – oval stick, 1¼ x 1¾", length 28", indented black initials..$16.00
M & ST L RY Co – oval stick, 1⅜ x 1⅞", length 28", HARTWELL HICKORY trademark, indented silver letters $25.00
NPR – oval stick 1¼ x 1¾", length 30", AM.HDWE CO., indented gold letters................................$20.00

SOO LINE – oval stick with squared end 1⅛ x 1⅜", length 26", indented gold letters $22.00

Brakemen's Clubs

Chisels

CB&NRR – track chisel, length 8", mt'd on wood handle, square striking head one end, sharp cutting edge on other, VERONA..$15.00

CRI&P – cold steel, octagon, 7¾" long with sharp cutting edge $8.00

CSTPM&ORY – cold steel, octagon, 13½" long with sharp cutting edge $10.00

M&STLRY – cold steel, octagon, 8½" long with sharp cutting edge $12.00

NPR – cold steel, octagon, 12" long with beveled gouger end $10.00

SOO LINE – cold steel, octagon, 8" long with sharp pointed end $8.00

Hack Saw

CM&STPRY – rigid cast iron frame with wood handle, wing nut at end to tighten blade, STAR..........................$20.00

Hammers (with original wood handles)

CMSTP&PRR – claw top for nail pulling, TRUE TEMPER FALLS CITY No. 120..$15.00

CMSTP&PRR – ball pein, knob top, TRUE TEMPER ..$12.00

G.N.RY. – ball pein, knob top, FAIRMOUNT $10.00

N.P.R.R. – ball pein, knob top, TRUE TEMPER FLINT EDGE No. 1224...$12.00

N.P.R.R. – double faced, octagon, 4½"L, TRUE TEMPER $15.00

ROCK ISLAND LINES – ball pein, knob top, CHAMPION DE-ARMENT..$12.00

SOO LINE – claw top for nail pulling, TRUE TEMPER No. 216 ....$15.00

Hand Saw

N.P.R.R. – metal saw, 21" blade, 2-5" wide, carved wooden handle with three screws, C.T. ATKINS & CO $25.00

Hatchets (with original wood handles)

CMSTP&PRR – claw head with 4" wide cutting blade, TRUE TEMPER FLINT EDGE No. TC....................$25.00

G.N.RY. – claw head with 3¾" wide cutting blade, TRUE TEMPER, No. TC $35.00

RY.EX.AGY. – flat head with 3½" wide cutting blade, all metal with wood grips on handle, no mfr. ID $45.00

SOO LINE – flat head with 4" wide cutting blade, AMERICA-NAX, Classport, Pa $30.00

Lining Bar

ST.P.CY.RY. – botton end has 1½ x 14" pinch bar, the middle portion is octagonal and the opposite end has a round section, overall length 58½" $20.00

Mattock

C&O – steel head 15½" long with cutting blade one end, grub hoe other, 35" handle, no mfr. ID $15.00

Monkey Wrenches

BR – smooth jaws, hexagon tightening nut, all steel, length 12", BILLINGS $12.00

C.&N.W.RY.Co. – smooth jaws, round tightening nut, all steel, length 12", J.H. WILLIAMS & CO. $18.00

C.M.&ST.P.RY. – smooth jaws, round tightening nut, all steel, length 18" INTERMEDIATE $20.00

Monkey Wrenches

C ST P M & O RY – smooth jaws, hexagon tightening nut, wood handle, length 12½", B&C Trademark $22.00

G.N.RY. – jaws with teeth round tightening nut at angle, all steel, length 10", LAWSON....................................$15.00

I.C.R.R. – smooth jaws, hexagon tightening nut, all steel, length 15", BEMIS & CALL $12.00

M & ST L – smooth jaws, round tightening nut, wood handle, length 12", THE H.D. SMITH & CO. Pat. Feb. 26, 1901 ....$25.00

M.T.RY. – smooth jaws, hexagon tightening nut, all steel, length 16", BEMIS & CALL $20.00

N.P.R. – open jaws with set of bottom teeth, tubular tightening nut, wood handle, length 16", BEMIS & CALL $25.00

OMAHA RY – smooth jaws, round tightening nut, wood handle, length 8½", THE H.D. SMITH & Co. Pat Feb. 26, 1901 ....$22.00

W.U.TEL.CO. – smooth jaws, round tightening nut, wood handle, length 12", no mfr. ID.............................$16.00

Picks (with original wood handles)

CMSTP&PRR – double end points designed for surface work, curved length 27", no mfr. ID $12.00

G.N.RY. – double end points for surface work, length 20", no mfr. ID $15.00

M&STLRR – point one end, 1¼" wide tamping blade other, length 21", BEALL BROS., Alton, Ill.....................$30.00

SOO LINE – point one end, 1¼" wide tamping blade other, length 21", no mfr. ID...$20.00

Shovels (with original standard RR wood handles)

CMSTP&PRY – track shovel, blade 8½ x 11½", no mfr. ID $15.00

GNRY – track shovel, blade 9 x 11", mfr. HUSKEY on shank $18.00

G.N.RY.CO. – track shovel, blade 9½ x 11½", mfr. AMES HUSKEY on shank $20.00

G.N.RY.CO. – snow shovel, blade 13¼ x 15¼", mfr. AMES 4 on shank, long 36" handle $25.00

GN – coal scuttle shovel, cast iron, scoop end 5 x 8" with 13" long handle, mkd. GN P1760 (scarce) $50.00

NPRR – coal yard shovel, scoop blade 12½ x 17", mfr. AMES RED EDGE No.8 on shank.......................................$22.00

NPR – locomotive fireman's coal shovel, scoop blade 11 x 16", mfr. ZENITH 4U, Featherweight $25.00

R-I-LINES – coal scuttle shovel, cast iron, scoop end 4½ x 7" with 9" long handle, no mfr. ID (scarce) $65.00

SOO LINE – track shovel, blade 8¾ x 10", mfr. TRUE TEMPER 2, Heat Treated Railroad Weight on shank $22.00

Sledge (with original wood handle)

SOO LINE – octagon striking face one end, rounded pointed top other, length 8¼" no mfr. ID $18.00

Soldering Iron

CM&STPRY – hexagon pointed copper tip, iron rod to wood handle, overall length 16", no mfr. ID....................$12.00

Spike Mauls

CMSTP&P – double end round striking faces, 1¼"D and 1¾"D, length 15", no mfr. ID $20.00

NP RY – double end round striking faces each 1⅝"D, length 14", no mfr ID $18.00

NOR PAC RY – double end octagonal striking faces, ⅞" and 1½", length 12", VERONA $22.00

Tie Tongs

R.I. LINES – flat steel ⁵⁄₁₆" x 1¼" with loop handles at top, two sharp points lower end, painted red, 29" long, ALDUSHT CO., CHGO $30.00

Welding Torch

NPR – oxygen-acetylene, yellow brass handle with turn knobs and press lever, two nickel-plated tubes to nose tip, length 20", AIRCO $35.00

Wrenches – Double-End with Jaws, "S" shape

C & N W RY CO – 12" long, J.H. WILLIAMS & CO., Brooklyn, NY $15.00

C.M.& ST.P. – 9½" long $10.00

C.ST.P.M.&O.RY. – 11" long $12.00

D.M. & N.RY. – 17¼" long..............................$20.00

L S & M S – (raised letters) 12" long $25.00

M. C. R.R. – 13½" long $12.00

ROCK ISLAND – (big letters) 11½" long $15.00

SOO LINE – 12½" long...................................$12.00

UNION PACIFIC – 24¼" long (track wrench) J.H. WILLIAMS & CO., Brooklyn, NY...............................$20.00

N.Y.C. & H.R. – 19" long, 1⅛" and 1¼" jaws $25.00

Double-End Wrenches

Tourist Guides and Brochures

Eastern Railroad Guides were published as early as the 1850's. Transcontinental travel by train became a reality in America on May 10, 1869, and before long, hard cover guide books were being published and sold to railroad travelers. These contained illustrations, maps, train schedules, mileage charts and general information about the scenes along the way. Those published in the 1870's and 1880's are very much sought after as they are of special interest to the historian as well as the railroadiana collector, and rarities go on the auction block. Some railroads put out their own souvenir picture albums which were smaller in size than the regular guide books to show views along their routes. These had hard covers too, with the name of the railroad embossed on them, containing pages of sepia tone pictures with descriptive captions. Several examples are listed here.

Guide Books

Two Official RR Hard-Cover Guide Books

APPLETON'S NORTHERN and EASTERN TRAVELER'S GUIDE, 1853, illustrated with numerous railroad maps and plans of cities, 303 pages, red h/c, 4¼ x 6½", rare $85.00

CROFUTT'S Trans-Continental TOURISTS' GUIDE, 1871, Union and Central Pacific RR, Their Branches and Connections by Stage and Water, Atlantic to Pacific Ocean, illustrated, 215 pages, green h/c, 5 x 6¾"..............$65.00

CROFUTT'S NEW OVERLAND TOURIST and PACIFIC COAST GUIDE, 1883, Railway Edition, Around the Circle, description over the lines of UNION, KANSAS, CENTRAL AND SOUTHERN PACIFIC RAILROADS, 275 pages, illustrated, blue s/c, 5¼ x 7¾".......................$50.00

BALTIMORE & OHIO R.R. ALBUM OF SCENERY, 1881, Wittemann Bros. 45 Murray St. N.Y., contains 12 pages sepia engraved views on the railroad's line, green h/c, 3½ x 5" $25.00

HARPER'S NEW YORK AND ERIE RAILROAD GUIDE, 1852, description of scenery, rivers, towns, villages and most important works on the RR's road, illustrated, 176 pages, brown h/c, 4½ x 7½", rare $95.00

HITTELL'S HAND BOOK of PACIFIC COAST TRAVEL, 1885, notable views along the line of the Union and Central Pacific RR's visiting the Pacific Slope of No. America, illustrated, 263 pages, green h/c, 4¾ x 6¾" $45.00

NELSONS' PICTORIAL GUIDE BOOKS 1871, THE CENTRAL PACIFIC RAILROAD, A trip across the North American Continent from Ogden to San Francisco, 32 pages, with 12 color illustrations, green h/c, 4 x 6½" $60.00

NELSONS' PICTORIAL GUIDE BOOKS, 1871, THE UNION PACIFIC RAILROAD, A trip across the North American Continent from Omaha to Ogden, 46 pages with 12 color illustrations, brown h/c, 4 x 6½" $60.00

OVER THE RANGE TO THE GOLDEN GATE, 1891, A complete tourist's guide to Colorado, New Mexico, Utah, Nevada, California, Oregon, Puget Sound and the Great NorthWest, 351 pages, illustrated, reddish tan h/c, 5¾ x9".........$35.00

PENNSYLVANIA R.R. ALBUM OF SCENERY, 1888, Ward Bros., Columbus, O., contains ten pages of sepia-tone engraved views on line of RR., includes map in back, brown h/c, 5 x 6" $30.00

RAILROAD AND TOURIST GUIDE by A. T. Sears and Effie Webster, 1879, Popular Routes for Summer and Winter Tourists, Colorado, East & South, N. West, 188 pages, illustrated, grey h/c, 7¾ x 11¾" $45.00

THE NORTHERN PACIFIC TOUR, From the Lakes and Mississippi River to the Pacific including Puget Sound and Alaska, 1888, W.C. Riley Publisher, St. Paul, Minn., contains 29 pages of sepia-tone engraved views from Minnesota to the Pacific Coast, purple with gold design hard cover, 5¾ x 7½" $85.00

THE NORTHERN PACIFIC, 1884, photographed and published by F. Jay Haynes, Fargo, Dakota, contains 18 sepia views from Duluth Harbor to Portland, Oregon, red h/c, 3½ x 5", rare $50.00

THE OFFICIAL NORTHERN PACIFIC R.R. GUIDE, 1893, for use of tourists and travelers over the lines of the railroad, its branches and allied lines, illustrated, 439 pages, red h/c, 5 x 6¾" $100.00

WILLIAMS PACIFIC TOURIST AND GUIDE across the continent, 1880, a complete traveler's guide of the Union and Central Pacific RR's to the scenery, resorts and attractions of the Pacific Coast, 355 pages, illustrated, maroon h/c, 7 x 9¼".................................$50.00

Three Early Soft-Cover Tourist Guides

Travel Brochures

Thousands of travel brochures were distributed by the railroads down through the years. They came in various types of publications, such as booklets, folders, pamphlets and descriptive timetables. Many were discarded by travelers or vacation tourists after the trip ended, making them scarce today. Those from around the turn of the century are much in demand, copies in fine condition bringing good prices.

B&O – "Reasons Why," booklet, 3¾ x 8", cover – blue, printing and logo, June, 1901, 33+ pages $10.00

B&O – "EASTERN Summer Trips via Baltimore & Ohio RAILROAD," folder, 4 x 9", cover – green, black/white photos, summer 1931, unfolds 18 x 32" sheet, map opposite side.................................$7.50

B&M – "Boston and Maine RAILROAD, Among the Mountains," booklet, 4 x 8", cover – grey with pic stagecoach and mountains, 1905, 66 pages with fold-out map.........$15.00

BCR&N – "A MID-SUMMER PARADISE, SPIRIT LAKE" Reached by the Burlington, Cedar Rapids and Northern Railway, booklet, 5½ x 7½", cover – tan with boating illustration, 1890, 30 pages (rare) $75.00

BURLINGTON ROUTE – "MISSISSIPPI RIVER Scenic Line," folder, 4 x 9", cover – yellow with pic of two streamliners, logo, 6-15-54, 15 pages.................$7.50

CENTRAL IOWA RY – "The Great NORTHWEST," Compliments of the Passenger Department, booklet, 5½ x 8", cover – multi-color with flowers, back cover – logo, 1887, 30 pages (rare) $75.00

C&NW – "HUNTING AND FISHING along the NORTHWESTERN LINE," booklet, 5¾ x 8", cover – light grey with pic of two men hunting and fishing, 1895, 96 pages with fold-out map (rare).................$65.00

C&NW – "The Only Double Track Railway between CHICAGO and the MISSOURI RIVER," Chicago & North-Western Railway, booklet, 5¼ x 7½", cover – red/black printing, logo on yellow, 1902, 28 pages with fold-out map (scarce) $35.00

CM – "Early Days," NOTED OCCURRENCES on the line of the COLORADO MIDLAND RAILWAY, hard-cover book, 9 x 11", cover – gold with litho of standing Indian holding shield with RR's logo, contains 12 litho scenes along the route traversed by the C M Ry., 1902 (very rare)....$175.00

CM – "THRU THE ROCKIES OF COLORADO" pamphlet, 7¾ x 10", cover – two circled pics and Colorado Midland logo, back cover – mountain lion, ca. 1915, 8 pages (scarce) $50.00

CM&STP – "Kilbourn and the Dells of the Wisconsin" with Views En Route Chicago to St. Paul and Minneapolis, booklet, 6¼ x 8¼", cover – grey with white mythological figures on black, red logo on back cover, 1901, 25 pages of black/white titled photos $22.50

CM&STP – "Kilbourn and the Dells of the Wisconsin" Chicago, Milwaukee & St. Paul Railway, booklet, 6 x 8", cover – dark green with oval photo, red logo on back cover, 20 pages of colored titled photos, 1907.....................$17.50

CM&STP – "KILBOURN AND THE DELLS OF THE WISCONSIN" Chicago, Milwaukee & St. Paul Railway, booklet, 6¼ x 8¼", cover – light green with rectangular photo, red logo on back cover, 1912, 20 pages of colored titled photos $15.00

CM&STP – "THE TRAIL OF THE OLYMPIAN" 2000 Miles of Scenic Splendor – Chicago to Puget Sound, CHICAGO, MILWAUKEE & ST. PAUL RAILWAY, booklet, 6¼ x 8½" cover – yellow with rectangular color mounted pic., 1917, 20 pages, titled sepia photos $12.00

CMSTP&P – "THE TRAIL OF THE OLYMPIAN" booklet, 6¼ x 8½", cover – tan with color pic of train in mountains, logo, ca. 1930, 20 pages, titled sepia photos.........$12.00

CRI&P – "THE SUMMER RESORTS OF IOWA AND MINNESOTA Reached by the ALBERT LEA ROUTE," booklet, 5¼ x 7¾", cover – tan with two black pics, CRI&P monogram on back cover, 1884, 61+ pages with fold-out map (rare)................$55.00

D&H – "The ADIRONDACKS Our Great National Playground" hotels, resorts, "The D&H," camps, lakes, folder 4 x 9", cover – color pic – boat/trains/mountains, 1920's, unfolds to 24 x 27" sheet.........$12.00

D&RG – "Panoramic Views Along the Line of the DENVER & RIO GRANDE Railroad," The Scenic Line of the World, folder, 4 x 8", cover – white, black/white illustration of train in mountains, map opposite side, 1893, unfolds 51" length $22.50

FEC – "EAST COAST OF FLORIDA" hotel list and information folder, published by Florida East Coast Railway, 4 x 8¾", cover – grey with pic of Ponce de Leon Hotel, season of 1900-1901, 32 pages, with fold-out map $17.50

GN – "HOTELS & TOURS GLACIER NATIONAL PARK" folder, 4 x 9", cover – multi-colored, tourist hotel in mountains, black/white box logo, 1915, 25 pages $15.00

GN – "To the Scenic Northwest" GREAT NORTHERN RAILWAY (box logo) "See America First," folder, 4 x 9½", cover –orange with mountains, sunset on lake, St. Mary – Glacier National Park, 1910, 23 pages $22.00

GN – "The Oriental Limited The Perfect Train," booklet, 4½ x 8½", cover – green with pic of observation car, box logo, 1914, eight pages with fold-out schedule in back $25.00

GN – "The SCENIC NORTHWEST" GREAT NORTHERN A Dependable Railway, folder, 4 x 9", cover – multi-colored two trains, passing, two goat logos, ca. 1930's, 24 pages $20.00

LV – "IN THREE STATES" LEHIGH VALLEY RAILROAD, booklet, 6 x 8½", cover – tan, with litho scenes, back cover – little girl holding hour glass "The LEHIGH runs on TIME" ca. 1880's, 14 pages (rare) $75.00

NYC – "AMERICAN TOURISTS HAND BOOK UNITED STATES and CANADA," Travel via NEW YORK CENTRAL LINES stop over at NIAGARA FALLS, booklet, 4 x 8", cover – pic of train, ship, Falls and logo, ca. 1920's, 31 pages, with fold-out map $15.00

NYC – "HUDSON RIVER" New York Central, folder 4 x 9", cover – colored pic of trains and river scene, 1934, 46 pages $12.00

NP – "A ROMANCE OF WONDERLAND" NORTHERN PACIFIC R.R., The WONDERLAND ROUTE to the PACIFIC COAST, folder, 3¾ x 8¼", cover – litho of girl seated at desk with Boston Globe paper, 1890, unfolds to 18½ x 24½" sheet, map opposite side, (rare) $125.00

NP – "THE YELLOWSTONE NATIONAL PARK" Via the Northern Pacific Railroad, folder, 3¾ x 8", cover – white, American flag motif, pine trees, 1895, unfolds to 18½ x 24½" sheet, map opposite side (rare) $65.00

NP – "ALONG THE SCENIC HIGHWAY" Through the Land of Fortune, booklet, 5¾ x 8½", cover – train, mountain, logo, Indian seated by fire looking on back cover, 1914, 84 pages.........$25.00

Tourist Travel Brochures

NP – "2000 MILES of Scenic Beauty," booklet, 4½ x 8", cover – red with logo and black engine, 1933, 63 pages......$15.00

PRR – "Eastern Tours," SUMMER – 1929, Low Fares to ATLANTIC CITY NEW YORK BOSTON and Other Eastern Resorts, Pennsylvania Railroad, folder, 4 x 9", cover – white with photo of Atlantic City Beach and Boardwalk, 16 pages $18.00

ROCK ISLAND SYSTEM – "Across the Continent in a Tourist Sleeping Car," folder, 4 x 9", cover – red with black logo, girl and lady boarding car, February 1903, 20 pages $20.00

ROCK ISLAND LINES – "CALIFORNIA" booklet, 6 x 8½", cover – beige with oranges and colored rectangular pic., 1912, 46 pages.........$15.00

SANTA FE – "The California Limited," booklet, 4 x 9", cover – cl'd. pic of Indians and train, back cover – Indians on canyon cliff – Santa Fe All the Way, 1914-1915, 22 pages $12.00

SANTA FE – "GRAND CANYON OUTINGS," folder, 4 x 9", cover – white with pic of canyon, Santa Fe logo, March 1927, 62 pages.........$8.00

SANTA FE – "ALONG YOUR WAY," facts about stations and scenes on the Santa Fe, booklet, 8 x 9", cover – cl'd. pic. of streamliner at station, 1949, 44 pages.........$7.50

SP&S – "The Scenic COLUMBIA River through the CASCADE Mountains to the PACIFIC," folder, 4 x 9", cover – blue with illustration of train in mountains, and SPOKANE PORTLAND & SEATTLE logo, ca. 1920's, unfolds to 32" length $15.00

SOO LINE – "BY WAY OF THE CANYONS," booklet, 5 x 9¼", cover – pic of river in canyon and footbridge, logo, June 17, 1907, 36 pages with fold-out map in back $22.50

SOO LINE – "SOO PACIFIC LINE" True Scenic Transcontinental Route, Scenic Short Line to Spokane, descriptive time table, 4½ x 9", cover – blue with red/black logo and printing, July 1, 1907, 94 pages $20.00

SOO LINE – "SEE EUROPE IF YOU WILL BUT SEE AMERICA FIRST," folder, 4½ x 9¾", cover – blue with tan mountain peaks, June 17, 1907, unfolds to 36"L.........$15.00

SOO LINE – "HOTELS & HYDROS EAST AND WEST," pamphlet, 6½ x 8¾", cover – pic of hotel at Winnipeg within oval, 1906, 27 pages.....................................$12.50

UP – "A Glimpse of the GREAT SALT LAKE ON THE (logo) UNION PACIFIC," booklet, 7 x 9", cover – white, illustration of lady tourist and beach scene, 1894, 36 pages, and fold-out map, logo on back cover (rare) $65.00

UP – "CALIFORNIA CALLS YOU" UNION PACIFIC, booklet, 6 x 9", cover – colored pic of girl sitting on grassy knoll with umbrella, pic of mother and children on back cover, logos, 1922, 38 pages $18.50

UP – "Along the Union Pacific System," folder, 4 x 9", cover – pic of 1861 The Overland Stage, back cover – mother and children, logos, 1922, 38 pages $15.00

UP – "ZION, BRYCE CANYON, GRAND CANYON, THREE NATIONAL PARKS," booklet, 7 x 10", cover – with two embossed scenes, gold letters, logo, 1929, 56 pages $10.00

String-Tied Scenic Guide Books

These soft-cover albums from the early 1900's, approximately 9 x 12", have a scenic color photo glued in the center of the cover with the railroad's name surrounding the picture. They contain around 15-22 string-tied pages, each with a single mounted picturesque view of a scene along the route. The date of the publication usually appears on the title page or is found on the map on the back page.

String-Tied Scenic Guide Book

CM&STP – "LAKE MICHIGAN TO PUGET SOUND," cover photo – Mount Rainer and Reflection Lake, Ranier National Park, Washington, title page dated 1914......$35.00

CM&STP – "LAKE MICHIGAN TO PUGET SOUND," cover photo same as above, dated 2-12-24 on front page map $20.00

CP – "CANADIAN ROCKIES – CANADIAN PACIFIC RAILWAY," cover has colorful artistic mountains and pines design, contains 24 pages of sepia views, ca. 1930's $15.00

D&RGRR – "HEART OF THE ROCKIES IN COLORADO," cover photo – Observation Car In Royal Gorge, Colorado, dated 1913 on back page map $27.50

D&RGW – "ROCKY MOUNTAIN VIEWS On the RIO GRANDE – The Scenic Line of the World," cover photo – train with smoke in Royal Gorge, dated 1917 on title page $25.00

D&RGW – "ROCKY MOUNTAIN VIEWS On the RIO GRANDE – The Scenic Line of the World," cover photo – train without smoke in Royal Gorge, dated 1910 on back page map $30.00

SANTA FE – "THE GREAT SOUTHWEST" cover photo – "The First Santa Fe Train" title page – THE GREAT SOUTHWEST ALONG THE SANTA FE, Published by Fred Harvey Kansas City Mo. 1914 (scarce) $65.00

SP – "THE OVERLAND TRAIL," cover photo – "Crossing Great Salt Lake At Sunset" dated 1913 on back page Explanation of Views.......................................$25.00

SP – THE SHASTA ROUTE," cover photo – "Mount Shasta From Reservoir Lake," dated 1923 on second photo $17.50

WP – "FROM SALT LAKE CITY TO SAN FRANCISCO BAY," cover photo – "Golden Gate at Sunset, California," dated 1915 back of title page $25.00

Settler's Advertising Brochures

B.& MR.R. – "B & M LANDS IN NEBRASKA," folder 3¾ x 8¾", opens to 18 x 25½" sheet, maps one side, 1883 (rare) $50.00

BURLINGTON ROUTE – "FREE GOVERNMENT LANDS WYOMING," folder 4 x 9", opens to 27 x 27" sheet, map one side, 1916 ....$15.00

BURLINGTON ROUTE – "FREE GOVERNMENT LANDS" in Nebraska, Colorado, Wyoming, Montana, and South Dakota, folder 4 x 9", opens to 17½ x 32", map one side, 1908 ....$20.00

BURLINGTON ROUTE – "HOME-SEEKERS EXCURSIONS"
To the …West, Northwest and Southwest, folder 4 x 9",
opens to 15¾ x 18½" sheet, map one side, 1908 ....$15.00

C&NW – "CHEAP FARMS AND GROWING TOWNS, MIN-
NESOTA AND DAKOTA," folder, 4 x 8½" opens to 18 x
24½" sheet, maps one side, 1884 (scarce) $40.00

CM&STP – "MONTANA," THE TREASURE STATE, folder, 4
x 9", 60 pages with fold-out map in back, 1915 ....$20.00

CM&STP – "THREE FORKS COUNTRY MONTANA," folder,
4 x 9", 23 pages, 1913 ....$15.00

CM&STP – "The GRANARY of the NORTHWEST," booklet,
6¼ x 8½", 48 pages, 1916 ....$12.00

GN – "ZONE OF PLENTY," Minnesota, North Dakota, Montana, Washington, Oregon, Idaho, booklet, 8½ x 11", 37
pages, 1929 ....$10.00

GN – "NORTH DAKOTA," booklet, 8½ x 11¼", 36 pages,
1915 ....$12.00

M&O – "LANDS IN ALABAMA AND MISSISSIPPI," booklet,
4 x 8¼", 35 pages, 1901..$22.00

NP – "New Homes in the PRODUCTIVE NORTHWEST RE-
GIONS," folder, 4 x 9", opens to 35" x 38" sheet, map one
side, 1891 ....$20.00

Settler's Brochures

SP – "CALIFORNIA for the SETTLER," booklet, 6½ x 9½", 63
pages, 1922 ....$10.00

Toy Trains

Collecting toy trains is one of today's most popular hobbies. In the early years, these toy trains were made out of wood, tin, or cast iron, to be pushed or pulled along the floor. As time went on, a friction model engine was made containing a fly-wheel, which when pushed, would run a short distance under its own power. It did not take long before steam power, wind-up (clockwork spring driven) and electric trains came on the scene, with flanged wheels to run on tracks. Some collectors are interested only in the early pre-1900 toy trains, while others specialize in the various wind-ups and electrics. Names most sought after are Ives, American Flyer and Lionel. Condition plays an important role in determining value. An early set complete in the original box brings a very high price. Reproductions are being made.

PULL TYPE – wood, three-piece set (locomotive, two passenger cars) black litho details on yellow paper glued to
sides and roof, legend reads "Grand Excursion Train to
Rocky Mountains and California. This is the car in which

good little boys and girls may ride." 2½H, 31½"L, ca.
1870 ....$300.00

PULL TYPE – wood, three-piece set (loco, baggage and passenger car) color litho details on yellow paper glued to

Early Wooden Coaches With Glued-On Paper Details

sides, entitled ADIRONDACK RAIL ROAD #61, lift-off roofs, 4½"H, 27"L, ca. 1880 ....$250.00

PULL TYPE – tin, four-piece set (loco, three passenger cars) 2½"H, 21"L, original paint colors – yellow, red, blue cars, black/red/green loco, ca. 1860's $250.00

PULL TYPE – cast iron, freight train, four pieces (loco, tender, two open cars) 21"L, original black/red paint, loco has PAT'D JUNE 8 '80, bottom of cars has PAT. MAY 26, 1880, REISS'D MARCH 14, 82 ....$375.00

PULL TYPE – cast iron, passenger train, five-pieces (loco, tender, three cars) 3"H, 31"L, original paint – black loco, red/white/blue cars, PAT. JUNE 19, '88 on loco $325.00

PULL TYPE – cast iron, passenger train, four pieces (loco, tender, two cars) 3½"H, 41"L, bright metal finish, #1101 on tender, CHICAGO ROCK ISLAND & PACIFIC RR on cars, ca. 1890's $425.00

PULL TYPE – cast iron, freight train, five pieces (loco, tender, two cattle cars, caboose) 3½"H, 43"L, original paint, yellow/orange cars, black loco trimmed with colors, M.C.R.R. on caboose, 999 on loco, sliding doors on cars, ca. 1890 ....$475.00

PULL TYPE – cast iron, passenger train, three pieces (loco, tender, car) loco 3½"H, 14"L, #19, black with red/gold trim, car 3½"H, 14½"L, yellow with CHICAGO LIMITED in red, ca. 1890's...$250.00

PULL TYPE – cast iron, passenger train, six pieces (loco, tender, four cars) 3¾"H, 57"L, original paint, black loco with red wheels and gold trim, #857, black tender with PENNSYLVANIA raised, three red cars with PENNSYL-VANIA RR CO., #44 WASHINGTON in gold, observation car named NARCISSUS, ca. 1927 ....$450.00

PULL TYPE – cast iron, two pieces, locomotive and tender, 4½"H, 12"L, BIG 6 under loco cab window, original metal patina, ca. 1890 ....$200.00

PULL TYPE – tin/iron, freight train, five-piece set (loco, tender, gondola car, box car, caboose) BIG FOUR on tender, S.T.& N.CO. 1911 SPECIAL on caboose, 7"H, 61"L, black loco with gold trim, yellow cars, red caboose, ca. 1911 ....$250.00

PUSH TYPE – wood/metal, friction locomotive, "Hill Climber," 7"H, 13"L, original red paint with gold trim, ca. 1890 ....$300.00

PUSH TYPE – tin/wood, two pieces, loco and tender, 7"H, 25"L, lithographed details, loco has #1900 and likeness of Engineer/Fireman in cab window, RECORD BREAK-ER plus 1900 on tender, ca. 1900 ....$225.00

PUSH TYPE – tin, friction, two pieces, loco and tender, 6½"H, 25"L, cut-out face of engineer in cab window, orig-inal red paint with gold trim, ca. 1925 ....$100.00

LIVE STEAMER – passenger train (loco, tender, baggage, two passenger cars) 35" long, VULCAN made in Ger-many, loco is brass and tin, cars are tin, original paint decor, tops of cars lift open to show seated figures inside, ca. 1890 - 1900...$1,500.00

WIND-UP – tin plate, "American Flyer" passenger train, four-piece set (loco, tender, two cars) 3½"H, 27"L, black cast iron loco, tin cars enameled in blue, orange and gold, original box with circle of tracks, ca. 1920's $200.00

WIND-UP – MARKLIN, passenger train, five-piece set (loco, tender, three cars) 3½"H, 29"L, tin/metal loco. No. R 890, tin cars, enameled in black, red and green with orange trim, original box with tracks, ca. 1920's $175.00

WIND-UP – tin plate, Hafner's "Overland Flyer" passenger train, five-piece set (loco, tender, baggage, two cars) 3"H, 33"L, enameled in red and yellow, red letters on cars, bat-tery powered headlight in loco and tail-end car, ca. 1930's $150.00

ELECTRIC – IVES, O gauge, three pieces, electric-type loco-motive, motor 3200, "THE IVES RAILWAY LINES," (black cast iron loco is 3"H, 6¾"L) two tin passenger cars with lithographed details, ca. early 1900's............$300.00

ELECTRIC – IVES, O gauge, 5 pieces, coal burning type (loco No. 1117, tender, 3 pass. cars) 3½"H, 43"L, black cast iron loco, tin tender and cars, LIMITED VESTIBULE EX-PRESS, lithographed details, ca. 1920-1930's........$400.00

ELECTRIC – LIONEL, O gauge, five-piece set (loco #258, tender, three passenger cars – two Pullman, one Obser-vation) 3½"H, 43"L, metal loco, tin cars, enameled col-ors, original box with transformer and circle of tracks, ca. 1930's $450.00

ELECTRIC – LIONEL, 027 gauge, six-piece set (No. 1666 loco, tender, gondola car, box car, milk car, caboose) 3"H, 52"L, diecast metal loco, Bakelite cars with printed details, original box complete with accessories, ca. 1950's $185.00

ELECTRIC – MARX, diesel-type electric train, UNION PA-CIFIC streamliner, five-piece set, tin, 3"H, 34"L, loco and cars in silver and red colors with blue letters, loco M-10005, original box, complete, ca. 1940's $85.00

ELECTRIC – MARX, "Commodore Vanderbilt" streamline electric train, six-piece set, all tin (loco, tender, three freight cars, caboose) 3"H, 41"L, enameled colors with printed details, original box complete, ca. 1950's $75.00

Tin "Hill Climber" Friction Locomotive

ⵈⵈⵈ Watches, Watch Fobs and Emblem Charms ⵈⵈⵈ

American watchmakers were required to meet certain rigid standards established by the railroads, including inspection and servicing routinely performed by qualified jewelers. It would be wise for the collector not knowledgeable of authentic railroad pocket watches to make a thorough study in this field before investing in them. The fact that a watch may have a train engraving on the case or movement, for instance, does not necessarily mean that the watch is an approved railroad grade. Watches not in running order, or having dial cracks, or cases badly worn or dented, must be discounted. All railroad pocket watches listed here are in perfect running condition and have the regular standard Arabic digits dial.

Key to Abbreviations

ADJ – movement has been adjusted to railroad specifications.
17J – number of jewels in the movement, 21J, 23J, etc.
5P – adjusted position of movement, as five positions, six positions, etc.
992 – numbers denote model of movement and railroad grade.
16S – size of watch movement and case, 18 size large, 16 size smaller.

MONT – Montgomery minute marginal numeral dial.
RGP – rolled gold plate case.
YGF – yellow gold filled case.
WGF – white gold filled case.

BALL – (Elgin) 333, 17J, ADJ, 18S, silverode case $285.00
BALL – (Hamilton) 17J, ADJ, 18S, Keystone Ball model silveroid case $250.00
BALL – (Hamilton) 999, 17J, 5P, 18S, Keystone Ball model silveroid case $300.00
BALL – (Waltham) 17J, 5P, 16S, YGF case $225.00
BALL – (Illinois) 19J, 5P, 16S, Keystone Ball model YGF case $275.00
BALL – (Hamilton) 999, 21J, ADJ, 18S, sterling case, gold inlaid locomotive...$450.00
BALL – (Hamilton) 999B, 21J, 6P, 16S, MONT, Ball 10K YGF case $350.00
BALL – (Hamilton) 21J, 5P, 16S, Ball Model 14K WGF case $245.00
BALL – (Hamilton) 23J, 5P, 16S, Keystone 10K YGF case $600.00
BALL – (Swiss) 21J, 6P, 16S, 10K RGP case $275.00
ELGIN – B.W. RAYMOND, 19J, 5P, 18S, Up & Down indicator dial, YGF case...$750.00
ELGIN – B.W. RAYMOND, 21J, 5P, 16S, YGF case $185.00
ELGIN – Father Time, 21J, 5P, 16S, MONT, Elgin 10K RGP case $180.00
ELGIN – 349, 21J, 5P, 18S, YGF case $185.00
ELGIN – Veritas, 21J, 5P, 16S, YGF case $195.00
ELGIN – Veritas, 23J, ADJ, 18S, YGF case, fancy design engraved on back $300.00
ELGIN – Veritas, 23J, 5P, 18S, YGF case $325.00
ELGIN – Father Time, 21J, 5P, 16S, 12K YGF case $180.00
ELGIN – 571, B.W. RAYMOND, 21J, 9P, 16S, Elgin 10K YGF case $195.00
HAMILTON – 996, 19J, 5 P, 16S, YGF case $275.00
HAMILTON – 940, 21J, 5P, 18S, MONT, YGF case $185.00
HAMILTON – 992, 21J, 5P, 16S, MONT, YGF case $175.00
HAMILTON – 992B, 21J, 6P, 16S, Hamilton 10K YGF case $300.00
HAMILTON – 950, 23J, 5P, 16S, Wadsworth 10K YGF case $425.00
HAMILTON – 950B, 23J, 6P, 16S, dial marked "23 Jewels-Railway Special," Hamilton 10K YGF case $485.00

HAMILTON – 992B, 21J, 6P, 16S, dial marked "Railway Special," Hamilton stainless steel case........................$175.00
HAMILTON – 992, 21J, 5P, 18S, MONT YGF case, fancy engraved design on back $185.00
HAMPDEN – New Railway, 21J, 5P, 16S, Dueber 14K WGF case $195.00
HAMPDEN – John Hancock, 21J, ADJ, 18S, silveroid case $175.00

Uncommon Up-Down Winding Indicator Dial

HAMPDEN – Railway Special, 21J, ADJ, 18S, sterling case, gold inlay locomotive $300.00
HAMPDEN – Special Railway, 21J, 5P, 18S, Dueber YGF case $250.00
HAMPDEN – New Railway, 17J, ADJ, 18S, Keystone 14K YGF case $225.00

18 Size and 16 Size Watches

HAMPDEN – Special Railway, 23J, 5P, 18S, Keystone 14K YGF case $350.00

HAMPDEN – railway, 19J, ADJ, 16S, Challenge nickel case $175.00

HOWARD – railroad chronometer series 10, 21J, 5P 16S, YGF case $300.00

HOWARD – railroad chronometer Series 11, 21J, 5P, 16S MONT, Keystone 10K YGF case $325.00

ILLINOIS – A. Lincoln, 21J, 5P, 18S, MONT, YGF case $185.00

ILLINOIS – Abe Lincoln, 21J, 5P, 16S, Ferguson dial, YGF case (scarce) $425.00

ILLINOIS – Bunn Special, 21J, 6P, 16S, YGF case, locomotive engraving $225.00

ILLINOIS – Bunn Special, 21J, 6P, 18S, Canadian dial (inner red digits) silveroid case $235.00

ILLINOIS – Bunn Special, 60 Hour, 21J, 6P, 16S, Wadsworth 10K YGF case $325.00

ILLINOIS – Burlington Special, 21J, ADJ, 16S, MONT, YGF case $195.00

ILLINOIS – Sangamo Special, 21J, 6P, 16S, YGF case, fancy engraved design $265.00

ILLINOIS – Sangamo Special, 23J, 6P, 16S, MONT, Panama YGF case...$450.00

ILLINOIS – Santa Fe Special, 21J, ADJ, 16S, MONT, Illinois 10K YGP case $275.00

ROCKFORD – 545, 21J, 5P, 16S, YGF case $185.00

ROCKFORD – 505, 21J, 5P, 16S, YGF case $210.00

ROCKFORD – 918, 21J, 5P, 18S, MONT, sterling case, locomotive engraving $325.00

SOUTH BEND – 227, 21J, 5P, 16S, MONT, YGF case....$180.00

SOUTH BEND – Studebaker, 21J, 8P, 16S, star nickel case $190.00

SOUTH BEND – 295, 21J, 5P, 16S, MONT, YGF case, fancy engraved design on back $195.00

WALTHAM – Riverside, 19J, 5P, 16S, MONT, Keystone YGF case $195.00

WALTHAM – Vanguard, 21J, 5P, 18S, Canadian dial, YGF case $215.00

WALTHAM – Crescent Street, 21J, 5P, 16S, MONT, WGF case $195.00

WALTHAM – 645, 21J, 5P, 16S, Keystone YGF case ..$275.00

WALTHAM – 845, 21J, 5P, 18S, YGF case $165.00

WALTHAM – Vanguard, 23J, 6P, 16S, Canadian dial, Keystone base metal case, train engraving on back $245.00

WALTHAM – Maximum, 23J, ADJ, 16S, 18K gold case $985.00

WALTHAM – Vanguard, 23J, ADJ, 18S, Monitor YGF case, fancy engraved design on back $325.00

WALTHAM – Vanguard, 23J, 6P, 16S, Up & Down indicator dial, Star 10K YRGP case $850.00

WALTHAM – Crescent Street, 21J, 5P, 18S, Up &Down indicator dial, Keystone 10K YGF case $800.00

Non-Approved Railroad Watches

Back in the days, cheap watches were made to sell as bonafide railroad watches at a lower price to the unsuspecting buyer. A locomotive would sometimes be depicted on the porcelain dial or be shown on the movement, also on the back of the case, with such names as "Trainmen's Special," "Engineer's Special," and "R.R. Special." Some collectors make a specialty of these old bogus RR watches, paying good money for them. Some examples are listed here.

MARIAN WATCH CO. – "R.R. SPECIAL," locomotive on dial and movement, 17J, ADJ, 18S, regular digits, silveroid

case $145.00

NEW ERA – 7J, Roman numeral digits, 18S, silveroid case,

locomotive engraved on back $45.00
SWISS MADE – "ENGINEER'S SPECIAL" on dial and movement, 21J, Specially Adjusted, 18S, brass hunting case,
   embossed design $100.00
No Mfr's Name – blue locomotive and regular digits on dial,
   NEW ERA USA on movement, nickel silver case with
   train engraved on back $55.00
No Mfr's Name – "ENGINE SPECIAL," locomotive on dial
   and movement, 23J, ADJ, regular digits, 18S, Fahys ore
   silver case $165.00
No Mfr's Name – "TRAINMEN'S SPECIAL," locomotive on
   dial and movement, Chicago USA, 23J, ADJ, Roman
   numerals, 18S, big Alaska silver case $175.00
No Mfr's Name – "GRAND TRUNK PACIFIC SPECIAL" on
   dial and movement, 21J, 5P, 18S, Roman numerals, silveroid case, copper inlay locomotive on back $145.00
No Mfr's Name – "A.T.& S. Fe TRAIN DISPATCHER" on dial
   and movement, 21J, 3 ADUTS. Montgomery dial, brass
   case, locomotive engraved on back $150.00

Non-Approved RR Watch With Locomotive Engraving

Watch Fobs and Emblem Charms

      Thousands of Railroad and Brotherhood emblem charms were made to be worn on a gold watch chain across the vest. They were also made to be hung from a woven wire mesh or black satin ribbon fob. Various other metal emblems or fobs were made to be hung on a leather strap from the pants watch pocket. These authentic old Brotherhood and Railroad emblem charms and fobs are now much in demand and bring very good prices. There are current reproduction railroad logo watch fobs, leather strap type, on the market, and these should not be confused with the old.

Watch Fobs, Leather Strap Type

BROTHERHOOD RAILWAY CARMEN OF AMERICA – ornate V shape, BRCA blue enamel symbol in center, silver
   on copper, Bastian Bros., Rochester, NY...............$45.00
DAVENPORT LOCOMOTIVE WORKS, DAVENPORT,
   IOWA – oval, silver-plated copper, embossed locomotive
   in center, hmkd. Greenduck Co. Chicago $125.00
INT'L. ASSN. OF RWY. SPECIAL AGENTS AND POLICE –
   round, bronze, train encircled by SAFETY FIRST on blue
   enamel, hmkd. Gustave Fox Co. Cin. O $85.00
KANSAS CITY SOUTHERN – bronze disc 1" diameter, Gold-
   en Spike Anniversary, 1897-1947, vest chain fob ..$25.00
NORTHERN PACIFIC – monad logo, enamel on bronze,
   black satin ribbon type, B&B, St. Paul Minn.........$85.00
O.R.C. LADIES AUXILARY, Chickasaw Div. 195, Memphis
   Div. 175, May 1907 – ornate bronze, Whitehead & Hoag
   Co. $65.00
PRR – VETERANS' ASS'N PHILA. DIV. around keystone
   logo center, Harrisburg, Pa. on back, silver on copper,
   ornate, Whitehead & Hoag Co. $75.00

RAILWAY SIGNAL ASSOCIATION – round, brass, train and
   semaphores in center, F.H. Noble & Co. Chi-
   cago $55.00
STANLEY MERRILL & PHILLIPS RY. CO., STANLEY, WISC.
   – oval, bronze, locomotive center, "1909" above, "Spur 5"
   below $125.00

Emblem Charms for Watch Chains, Wire Mesh
and Black Silk Ribbon Fobs

ASSOCIATED SOCIETY OF LOCOMOTIVE ENGINEERS &
   FIREMEN, ESTAB'D 1880 – white/blue enamel on
   brass, ornate emblem charm for vest chain $95.00
BROTHERHOOD OF RR BRAKEMEN – gold shield shape,
   enameled BRRB insignia center, engraved locomotive
   on back, for woven wire mesh fob $75.00
BROTHERHOOD OF LOCOMOTIVE FIREMEN AND EN-
   GINEERS – ornate gold/enamel emblem charm for vest
   chain $75.00
BROTHERHOOD OF RAILWAY TRAINMEN – ornate
   gold/enamel BRT emblem charm for woven wire mesh
   type fob $65.00

Watch Chain and Emblem Charms

BROTHERHOOD OF RAILWAY TRAINMEN – maltese cross type, gold/black enamel, BRT insignia at center, emblem charm for vest chain $60.00

NORTHERN PACIFIC – inlay enamel Monad logo on gold-filled disc, 1⅛" diameter, logo emblem charm for vest chain...$80.00

Wax Sealers and Accessories

These are small hand tools approximately 2½"-4" tall used by Railroad Station Agents to safeguard envelopes and packages containing currency or valuable items with wax seals. They were made with either a fancy or plain wood handle attached to a bronze or brass matrix – or "head" as referred to by collectors. They also came in a one-piece unit, brass or bronze. The head had indented letters and digits stamped in reverse, producing a legible impression in the wax seal. Wax sealers were discontinued shortly after World War II. Those from early now defunct roads have the higher value. Those with the head badly scratched, nicked or defaced, or with cracked, chipped or replaced handles must be discounted in price.

Note: All wax sealers listed here have attached handles unless noted a one-piece unit.

AT&SF – THE A.T.& S.F.RY.CO. AGENT, GAGE, OKLA. on round head, iron handle $175.00

B&M – AGENT, B. & Me. R.R. CHARLESTOWN, N.H. on round head, maple wood handle $195.00

B&MR – B.& M.R.R.R.CO. NO. 59 on oval head, two-tone fancy wood handle $235.00

B&MR – B.& M.R.R.R., NELSON, IN NEB. on round head, brass toadstool handle $395.00

B&NW – B.& N.W.R.R. BELLS, TENN. on round head, black wood handle $185.00

C&EI – C.& E.I.R.R. FOUNTAIN CREEK, ILL. on oval head, black wood handle $165.00

C&G – C.& G.RY.CO. AGENT, ELIZABETH, MISS. on round head, black wood handle.....................................$175.00

CB&Q – C.B.& Q.R.R. BUSSEY, IOWA on oval head, two-tone fancy wood handle $225.00

CB&Q – C.B.& Q.R.R.CO. AGENT, FREMONT, NEB. on round head, maple finish wood handle $200.00

CB&Q – C.B.& Q.R.R.CO. RANDOLPH, IA. on oval head, one-piece brass hollow bulb handle $250.00

CGW – C.G.W.R.R. 142 NEW HAMPTON, IA., on round head, one-piece brass hollow bulb handle $275.00

CGW – C.G.W.R.R. FORREST PARK, ILLINOIS on round head, black wood handle $225.00

CI&S – C.I.& S.R.R.CO. CONDUCTOR 7, DANVILLE DIV. on round head, pine wood handle, hmkd. J.H. Fleharty, Engraver, Cleveland, O...$250.00

CM&STP – C.M.& ST.P.RY., C. & C. B. DIV., PERRY, IA. on round head, brass toadstool handle $200.00

CM&STP – C.M.& ST. P.RY., W.V.DIV., PORT EDWARDS on round head, brass toadstool handle $225.00

CM&STP – C.M.& ST.P.RY., MITCHELL STATION on oval head, maple wood handle $200.00

CM&STP – C.M.& ST.P.RY.CO., S.M.DIV., FEDORA, on round head, black wood handle $195.00

CM&STP – C.M.& ST.P.RY.CO. FRT. OFFICE, MINNEAPOLIS, MINN., on oval head, fancy walnut wood handle $225.00

CMSTP&P – C.M.ST.P.& P.R.R.CO., MADISON, S.D., S.M.DIV. on oval head, black wood handle $195.00

CRI&P – AGENT, C.R.I.& P.RY., BANKS, ARKS., on oval head, one-piece brass hollow bulb handle $295.00

CRI&P – AGENT, C.R.I.& P.RY. EAGLE LAKE JCT. IOWA, on oval head, one-piece brass hollow bulb handle ..$250.00

CRI&P – AGENT, C.R.I.& P.RY., HAVELOCK, NEB. on oval head, black wood handle......................................$175.00

CRI&P – AGENT, C.R.I.& P.RY., HOPE, MINN. on oval head, black wood handle $185.00

C&NW – C.& N.W.RY., STATION, FAULKTON on oval head, brass toadstool handle $325.00

C&NW – C.& N.W.RY.CO., THREE LAKES WIS. STATION on oval head, brass toadstool handle $350.00

C&NW – C.& N.W.RY., AGENT, GENEVA, NEB. on oval head, one-piece brass hollow bulb handle $250.00

CSTPM&O – C.ST.P.M.& O.RY.CO., HERMAN, NEB. on round head, nickle-plated toadstool handle, hmkd. Northwestern Stamp Works, St. Paul, Minn........$275.00

GC&SF – G.C.& S.F.RY., BALLINGER, TEX. on oval head, brass toadstool handle $245.00

GF&A – G.F.& A.RY., AGENT, LOCAL, ALA. on round head, one-piece brass toadstool handle $235.00

Railroad Wax Sealers

GN – G.N.RY.CO., A-13, DINING CAR DEPT., on round head, black wood handle $350.00

GN – GREAT NORTHERN RY., TREASURER, on round head, brass toadstool handle $325.00

GN – GREAT NORTHERN RY. CO., ANOKA, MINN. on round head, brass toadstool handle....................$230.00

GT – G.T.R., GROVETON, on round head, one-piece brass toadstool handle $245.00

IC – I.C.R.R.CO., LE ROY, ILL. on oval head, brass toadstool handle $225.00

IC – I.C.R.R., TICKET OFFICE, HILLS, MINN., on oval head, one-piece brass hollow bulb handle $325.00

IC – AGENT, BARNES, I.C.R.R., on oval head, fancy two-toned wood handle $200.00

IC – FREIGHT AGENT, BLOOMINGTON, ILL., I.C.R.R., on oval head, tall two-toned wood handle $225.00

ILL SO – THE ILLINOIS SOUTHERN RAILWAY CO., FLAT

RIVER, MO., on oval head, brass toadstool handle $300.00

IND SO – IND. SO. RY., AGENT, BLOOMINGTON, IND., on oval head, brass toadstool handle $375.00

KCM&B – K.C.M.& B.R.R, SULLICENT, ALABAMA, on round head, iron bulb handle $200.00

KCSTJ&CB – K.C.ST.J.& C.B.R.R., AMAZONIA, MO., on oval head, one-piece brass hollow bulb handle $250.00

KCS – KANSAS CITY SOUTHERN RY. JOPLIN FREIGHT STATION, on round head, black wood handle $200.00

LS&MS – L.S.& M.S.RY.CO., CONDUCTOR 52, WESTERN DIV. on round head, pine finish wood handle, hmkd. J.H. Fleharty, Engraver, Cleveland, O $300.00

MKT – M-K-T R.R.CO., AGENT, DEERFIELD, MO. on round head, one-piece brass toadstool handle $175.00

MKT – M.K.& T.RY.CO. AGENT, BARTLESVILLE, OKLA. on round head, one-piece brass toadstool handle ..$300.00

M&NW – M.& N.W.R.R.CO. NEW HAMPTON, IA. on round head, nickle-plated toadstool handle $375.00

M&STP – M.& ST.P.RY., MCGREGOR, CONDUCTORS on oval head, large maple wood bulb handle $300.00

M&STP – M.& ST.P.RY., ALGONA on oval head, large maple wood toadstool handle................................$275.00

MO PAC – THE MO.PAC.RY.CO. 168 on oval head, iron bulb handle $195.00

MO PAC – THE MO.PAC.RY.CO. LOCAL FRT. OFFICE on round head, one-piece brass toadstool handle ..$225.00

MO PAC – MO.PAC.R.R.CO. AGENT, CHATFIELD, ARK. on round head, one-piece nickel-plated toadstool handle $235.00

NYC – THE NEW YORK CENTRAL RAILROAD CO. 181 on oval head, black wood handle $175.00

NYC – NEW YORK CENTRAL R.R. B 134, ALBANY, N.Y. on round head, two-tone brown wood handle $185.00

NYC&STL – N.Y.C.& ST.L.RY.CO., 403 on round head, two-tone wood bulb handle $200.00

NP – NOR.PAC.RY.CO. MADDOCK, N.D. on round head, brass toadstool handle $275.00

NP – NOR.PAC.R.R. ANOKA, on round head, brass toadstool handle, hmkd. Northwestern Stamp Works, St. Paul, Minn $300.00

NWP – N.W.P.R.R., WILLITS, on round head, black wood handle $200.00

PW&B – P.W.& B.R.R.CO., 212 on round head, pewter toadstool handle $225.00

RRI&STL – R.R.I.& ST.L.R.R., BUSHNELL on oval head, fancy two-tone wood handle $300.00

STLSF – ST.L.S.F.R.R., AGENT, CLARKDALE, ARK. on round head, one-piece brass toadstool handle................$200.00

SCR – S.C.R.R.CO., 29, AGENCY on round head, two-tone wood bulb handle..$195.00

STP&SC – ST.P.& S.C.R.R., KASOTA on small oval head, fancy two-tone wood handle $325.00

SP – SOU.PAC.CO., MARSHFIELD, ORE. on round head, black wood bulb handle....................................$185.00

SR – SOUTHERN RY. CO., BRANCHVILLE, S.C. on round head, black wood bulb handle $195.00

TSTL&KC – T.ST.L.& K.C.R.R., 144 on oval head, fancy dark wood handle $295.00

UP – UNION PACIFIC 548 on oval head, black wood handle $195.00

WAB – THE WABASH R.R.CO. 37 on round head, one-piece nickel-plated toadstool handle $225.00

WAB – DINING CAR DEPARTMENT, WABASH R.R. on round head, black wood bulb handle.................$325.00

W&STP – W.& ST.P.R.R., REDWOOD FALLS STATION on oval head, one-piece brass hollow bulb handle ..$300.00

WSTL&P – W.ST.L.& P.RY. DINING CAR NO. 197 on round head, one-piece brass toadstool handle $325.00

Y&MV – Y.& M.V.R.R.CO., ISOLA, MISS. on oval head, brass toadstool handle...$295.00

Express Company Wax Sealers

These parallel those of the railroads. The most commonly found are the ones from the now defunct Railway Express Agency, which had widespread use throughout the country and can still be realized at minimal prices. Those that are dual marked, with both railroad and express company names on them, and those with territorial markings, are the rarities and bring big money.

Express Company Wax Sealers

ADAMS EXPRESS COMPANY 5186 BURLINGTON, IOWA on round head, one-piece brass toadstool handle $135.00

AM.EX.CO. No. 2 ATALISSA, IOWA on oval head, iron bulb handle, hmkd. Meyer & Wenthe, Chicago...........$100.00

AMERICAN EXPRESS CO. MILROY, MINN. on oval head, nickel-plated bulb handle $95.00

AMERICAN RAILWAY EXPRESS CO. FINGAL, N.D. on round head, one-piece brass hollow bulb handle ..$75.00

AMERICAN RAILWAY EXPRESS CO. 2154 Messenger on round head, black wood handle..............................$55.00

AMERICAN RAILWAY EXPRESS BEAVER CITY, NEBR. on round head, black wood handle..............................$65.00

AMERICAN RAILWAY EXPRESS CO. PUBLIC WABASH, IND. on oval head, black wood handle $90.00

CANADIAN PACIFIC EXPRESS 653 on round head, one-piece brass toadstool handle.................................$200.00

NATIONAL EXP. CO. WILLSHIRE, OHIO on oval head, two-tone wood bulb handle....................................$125.00

NATIONAL EXPRESS CO. WASHBURN, ILL. on oval head, nickel-plated bulb handle $135.00

NOR.PAC.EX.CO. 746 GOVAN, WASH. on round head, brass toadstool handle, hmkd. Northwestern Stamp Works, St. Paul, Minn $225.00

RY.EX.AGY.INC. PUBLIC HASTINGS, MINN. on oval head, black wood handle $55.00

RY.EX.AGY.INC. 6775 MESSENGER on oval head, black wood handle $45.00

RY.EX.AGY.INC. DUMONT, MINN. on round head, one-piece brass hollow bulb handle $50.00

SOUTHERN EX. CO. 6261 CONWAY, N.C. on round head, tall iron handle, hmkd. E.J. Brooks & Co. New York $165.00

SOUTHERN EX. CO. 4797 WHITAKERS, N.C. on round head, one-piece brass toadstool handle $175.00

WELLS FARGO & CO.'S EXPRESS HAMPTON, MINN. on round head, maple wood bulb handle $185.00

WELLS FARGO & CO. EXPRESS 442 on round head, nickel-plated bulb handle..$150.00

WELLS FARGO & CO. EXPRESS SOUTHARD, OKLA on round head, one-piece brass hollow bulb handle...........$175.00

WELLS FARGO & CO. EXPRESS 1758 Messenger on round head, one-piece brass hollow bulb handle $150.00

Railroad and Express Dual Marked

AM.RY.EX.CO. C. & N.W. MERRILL IOWA on round head, black wood handle $235.00
NAT'L.EX.CO. NO.7 C&A RR on oval head, black wood handle...$225.00
NOR.PAC.EXP. N.P.R.R.CO. CLEAR LAKE MINN on oval

head, one-piece brass hollow bulb handle $350.00
RY.EX.AGY.INC. CGW CLARKSVILLE, IOWA on round head, black wood handle $210.00
RY.EX.AGY.INC. G.N. CARLISLE, MINN. on round head, black wood handle $195.00

Territorial

THE A.T.& S.F.RY. AGENT BARTLESVILLE, I.T. on oval head, fancy wood handle $350.00

S.C.& D.R.R. SIOUX FALLS D.T. on round head, fancy wood handle $350.00

Wax Sealing Accessories

The various torches, lamps and other implements used in melting the sealing wax, the sticks of sealing wax, and the early money package envelopes forwarded by railroads and express companies are also being collected and bring good prices too.

Sealing Wax – sticks measure ⅝ x 10½" unless otherwise noted.

Single stick, mkd. M.K.&T., brown partially used $4.00
Box of four sticks, mkd. WABASH R.R., brown, unused, Princeton Sealing Wax Co. $20.00
Box of four sticks, mkd. NORTHERN PACIFIC, green, unused, Princeton Sealing Wax Co.......................$20.00

Box of two sticks, mkd. RAILWAY EXPRESS AGENCY, brown, unused, Dennison Mfg. Co. $10.00
Box of 20 sticks, mkd. AMERICAN EX. No. 2 red, ⅜ x 7½", unused, Dennison Mfg. Co....................................$20.00

Utensils For Melting Wax Stick

Utensils For Melting Sealing Wax Stick

Round, squatty type, brass, 2¼"D, 2½"H, red enameled, finger ring grip cap for wick on screw top, Bradley & Hubbard Mfg. Co. #728...$75.00
Mini-coffeepot type, tin 1¾" bottom diameter, 2¼"H with 3" long spout with wick, hook handle, hinged lid, C.L. Anton, Mfgr $50.00

Tray type, brass, 3½ x 5½", complete with alcohol burner, ladle, trough for wax and holder for sealer, no mfgr's. name $85.00

Money Package Envelopes – used, with original wax seal impressions on backside.

AMERICAN EXPRESS COMPANY – brown 4 x 9" envelope, five seals with American Express Co. Burliington, Iowa, ca. 1850's $35.00

CHICAGO AND NORTH WESTERN SYSTEM – brown 4¼ x 9¼" envelope, three seals – C.& N.W.RY.CO. Freight Agent,, Council Bluffs, Iowa, ca. 1900's................$20.00

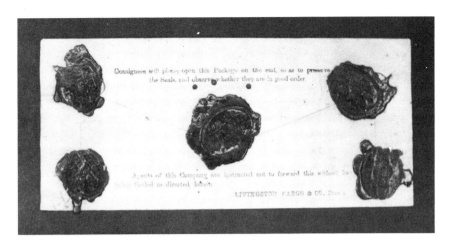

Early Express Cover With Wax Seals Intact

TERRE HAUTE, ALTON & ST. LOUIS R.R. – orange 3¼ x 5½" envelope, ca. 1856-1861, five partially legible seals (rare) $75.00

UNITED STATES EXPRESS COMPANY – brown 4 x 8½" envelope, dated 1865, five illegible seals $30.00

UNITED STATES & CANADA EXPRESS – brown 4 x 8½" envelope, dated 1888, two seals – American Express Company, Treasurer's Office, New York........................$25.00

Money Package Envelopes – unused.

All listed are standard 4¼ x 9½" manila envelopes Agents used these in remitting money to home office or bank. Reverse side has printed circles over flap where wax seals should be applied. 1900's.

A.T.& S.F.RY. CO. – two printed circles on flap for seals $5.00

CHICAGO & EASTERN ILLINOIS RAILROAD – three printed circles on flap for seals $6.00

CHICAGO GREAT WESTERN RAILWAY COMPANY – three printed circles on flap for seals.............................$10.00

NORTHERN PACIFIC RY. CO. – three circles, one for cross stitch $8.00

REA EXPRESS – three printed circles on flap for wax seals $5.00

Wood Tokens

Wood tokens were made of brass or copper, varying in size from a nickel to a half-dollar. They had the denominations of ¼ to one cord wood stamped on them, along with the engine number. Some also had the railroad's ID included on them. In the early days of wood-burning locomotives, these were used by the railroads as payment for cord wood supplied by farmers and others at fueling stops along the railroad's right-of-way. The railroads had money in the home office or on deposit in various banks where they could be redeemed. These tokens are very rare and carry a premium price.

"M.C.R.R..112" – stamped on obverse, ½ CORD on reverse, milled border, brass, 1"D $125.00

"M.C.R.R." – stamped on obverse across center, ½ CORD, 13 (engine No.) on reverse, brass, 1¼"D $110.00

"M.S. & N.I.R.R." – E&N DIV – raised on obverse, ¼ CORD, 48 (engine No.) on reverse, star border, copper, 1"D $135.00

"WOOD" – Eng No. 136, ½ Cord – stamped on obverse, reverse is blank, brass, 1¼"D $100.00

Brass Token Good for ½ Cord Wood

Miscellaneous Things

There will always be miscellaneous things and odds and ends turning up. The question is "What price will they bring?" Here are a number of them not included in the foregoing categories.

BELL – horse, early street railway, cast brass, raised letters LOUISVILLE CITY RAILWAY around bottom skirt, 3"H, 3"D, original iron clapper......................................$125.00

BELL – horse, early street railway, cast brass, raised letters ST. P. CITY RY. CO. around bottom skirt, 3"H, 3"D, original iron clapper $150.00

BOTTLE – clear glass, 1½ x 1⅞ x 4½", embossed SOUTHERN PACIFIC CO. HOSPITAL DEPARTMENT, cork stopper $25.00

BROOM – depot, handle length 38" with 16" yellow straws, marked C&NW, Made by O.K. Broom Co., Chicago......................................$30.00

BROOM – track, handle length 34" with 6" metal tip, 14" heavy duty brown straws, marked CRI&P, O.K. Broom Co., Chicago $35.00

BRUSH – coach seats, wood, rounded top handle, bristles below, mk'd. N.Y.C.&H.R.R.R, early 1900's.............$25.00

BRUSH – clothes, flat oval top, wood, with bristles below, mk'd. GREAT NORTHERN RY. on extended handle $35.00

BULLETIN BOARD – depot, train arrival and departures, wood, black finish, 30 x 36", mk'd. UNION PACIFIC with two UP shield logos and BULLETIN BOARD across top $235.00

Railroad Police Whistles

CLOCK – depot, wall hanging, eight day, octagon oak case, pendulum case below, height 24", SETH THOMAS on dial, mk'd SOO LINE on back..............................$500.00

CLOCK – depot, wall mounted, square oak case 6 x 21 x 21", battery power mechanism (two dry cells) inside, brass plate on front inscribed STANDARD TIME, A.L. Haman Co., Chief Watch Inspectors, mk'd SOO LINE on dial $400.00

CLOCK – alarm, BIG BEN, nickel-plated, 5"D, made by Westclox, LaSalle, Ill., Pats. 1902-1914, J.J. Allin, SOO LINE and NP Watch Inspector, Mpls. on dial................$100.00

DOOR HOOK – wrought iron, for roundhouse door, 6½" long, with 3 x 3" eye plate, mk'd NPR FM 930 ......$25.00

DOOR PLATE – depot, cast iron, 3 x 10", beveled sides, two round holes, one for door knob other for key lock, NORTHERN PACIFIC logo at top, mfr. SARGENT $250.00

DOOR PLATE – depot, cast iron, 3 x 10", beveled sides, two round holes, one for door knob other for key lock, GREAT NORTHERN RAILWAY box logo at top, mfr. SARGENT 250.00

DOOR PLATE – depot, cast brass, 3½ x 16½", beveled sides, one round hole for key lock, SOO LINE banner logo at top, hm'kd. Yale & Towne on back $300.00

DRINKING CUP – aluminum, collapsible, round, 2½"D, 3"H, GREAT NORTHERN RY.CO. NEWS SERVICE, 15 cents embossed on removable cover $35.00

DRINKING CUP – aluminum, collapsible, round, 2½"D, 2½"H, SAFETY FIRST Duluth Missabe & Northern printed in black on removable cover....................$40.00

DRINKING CUP – aluminum, collapsible, round, 2½"D, 2¼"H, black lithographed pic of G.N.RY. "Oriental Limited" train on Stone Arch Bridge, Mpls. on removable cover $45.00

FEATHER DUSTER – coach, wood handle with turkey feathers, 24" long, mkd. NYC $25.00

FIRE EXTINGUISHER – glass tube, chemical type, 2½"D, 18"L, sealed top, embossed C&NW Ry. on length of tube, two cast iron wall brackets $85.00

FLASHLIGHT – Bakelite, black, 7¾" long, printed in white PROPERTY OF RAILWAY EXPRESS AGENCY, made by Bright Star $25.00

FLASHLIGHT – Bakelite, black, two cells, 7" long, incised AT&SF RY CO $30.00

HARD HAT – yellow plastic shell, adjustable size, mk'd. with white/black G.N.RY. goat logo at front, Wilson Product, style No. 9 STC $15.00

HARD HAT – yellow plastic shell, adjustable size, mk'd. with green BN BURLINGTON NORTHERN logo at front, Bullard, Model 5100 ....$8.00

HARD HAT – white plastic shell, adjustable size, mk'd. with red SOO logo at front, AO, Model BX21 ....$12.00

HOLSTER – leather, mk'd. RY.EX.AGY., for .38 Colt revolver, 12" long, Jos. Kantor, maker, CHGO $50.00

LAMP – depot platform, bracket or pole mounted, kerosene, burns 24 hours, adjustable self-extinguishing device, Dietz "PIONEER" height 24", early 1900's $300.00

LAMP SHADE – ceiling, depot, metal, green enameled outside, white inside, 14" diameter $12.50

LEAD SEAL PRESS – nickel-plated cast iron, shaped like pliers with side lever, 3 x 8", imprints W.F. & CO. and location on lead slug, used for sealing cloth money sacks, PORTER SAFETY SEAL CO. CHGO. Pat. June 10, 1902........$75.00

LEAD SEAL PRESS – cast iron, black enamel, shaped like pliers 9½" long, imprints AM.EX.CO. and location on lead disc, used for sealing cloth money sacks, J. BROOKS & CO. NY., Pat. Dec. 7, '97 ....$55.00

LITHOGRAPH PLATE – copper, rectangle, ⅛ x 5 x 7½" with etched N.P. diesel locomotive $25.00

MAIL BAG – canvas, 15 x 21", leather bottom and top with handle, hinged hasp for padlock, mk'd. G.N.RY., CAR A-6......................$35.00

Ry. Ex. Agy. Bakelite Flashlight

PAINT BRUSH – cml. type, bristles vulcanized in rubber, 3" wide, 11" long, mk'd. G.N.RY. on wood handle, MAENDLER $10.00

PAINT BRUSH – com. type, pure bristles, 2" wide, 8½" long, mk'd. PRR logo on wood handle, RUBICO $8.00

POKER CHIPS – set of 100 in box, blue, red, white plastic, both sides mkd. with gold G.N.RY. goat logo, (100 @ $2.00 ea.) $200.00

POCKET SAVER – for shirt pocket to clip pens and pencils, red plastic with NP logo imprinted on overhang tab........$5.00

POLICE WHISTLE – brass, B&ORR incised on top....$25.00

POLICE WHISTLE – black plastic, PRR monogram inlaid at side $20.00

PRINTER'S TYPESETTING BLOCK – metal die on wood, 1 x 2½ x 2½", Great Northern Railway goat logo $10.00

PROPERTY PLATE – brass, oval, 1½ x 3", CB&Q (raised) stamped letters and digits, two mt. holes..............$12.00

PROPERTY PLATE – brass, 1½ x 3½" with rounded ends, N.P.RY. (raised) stamped letters and digits, two mt. holes $12.00

RAILROAD SPIKE – narrow gauge road, Colorado, 4½" long $5.00

RAILROAD SPIKE – standard gauge, 6" long, gold-plated, souvenir of steam excursion trip, BURLINGTON ROUTE $8.00

SCALE – counter type, two-sided dial, weighs up to 60 lbs., pan-marked RY. EX.AGY., cast iron base, 6" wide, 17" long $145.00

SEMAPHORE SIGNAL ARM – metal, original paint, three colored glass lenses, red, yellow, green, 72" long $175.00

STEEL RAIL – narrow gauge road, from Colorado, cut and polished desk piece 3"H, 3"L, dated 1882 ....$22.00

STONEWARE JUG – 11¼"H, 7"D, brown top and finger hold handle, Property of CHICAGO & NORTHWESTERN RY. CO. in blue letters on light grey $225.00

STONEWARE JUG – 11¼"H, 7"D, brown top and finger hold handle, Property of GREAT NORTHERN RAILWAY CO. in blue letters on light grey $235.00

STOVE – cast iron, approx. 28" tall, has stove pipe collar, square base, pot bellied with lids on top, weight approximately 250 lbs., old style, mk'd. PRR....................$500.00

SURVEYOR'S INSTRUMENT – brass unit complete with compass, levels, telescope, wooden carrying case, and tripod, mk'd G.N.RY., Pat. Nov. 13, 1900, BUFF MFG. CO. Boston $350.00

TETHER WEIGHT – cast iron, 8"D, 2½"H, 20 lbs., raised letters around top NOR.EX.CO., 6' long leather hitching strap $175.00

TETHER WEIGHT – cast iron, 8"D, 2½"H, 30 lbs., raised letters around top AM.RY.EX.CO., with serial number $150.00

TIME TABLE HOLDER – wall type, metal, 8¾ x 12", for depot use, mk'd. C&NW front................................$65.00

THERMOMETER – wall, metal, 2½ x 10", G.N.RY. with indented black numerals on brass background. Taylor $50.00

TOILET PAPER HOLDER – cast iron, two pieces, nickel-plated, wall mt'd., 6 x 6", UNION PACIFIC SYSTEM raised across top plate $85.00

Collapsible Aluminum Drinking Cups

Hard Hats

TOILET PAPER HOLDER – wire frame with wood roll holder, wall mount plate embossed CMSTP&P RR $75.00

TRAIN ORDER DELIVERY HOOP – bentwood style, oval 13 x 18" with 30" long straight handle, metal clip at oval joint to hold paper train orders..............................$45.00

TRAIN ORDER DELIVERY HOOP – "Y" shape, wood pole 4 ft. long with metal top piece to hold two sticks apart with string-tied train orders, HI-SPEED DELIVERY FORK, SHELBYVILLE, IND $35.00

WALLET – leather, black, railroad name and/or logo with slogan imprinted in silver on frontside. Example – "B&O, Linking 13 States with the Nation." $20.00

WASTE BASKET – wire grill type, tin pie-plate bottom, 14" tall...$18.00

WHISTLE POST SIGN – cast iron, shield shape, with big "W" raised inside rolled rim, 16 x 18", original black/yellow paint $85.00

WOOD HANDLE – spiking maul, 36" long, BN INC indented gold letters, unused $6.00

WOOD HANDLE – axe, 36" long, CGW indented red letters, unused $8.00

WOOD HANDLE – hammer, 16" long, CB&QRR indented blue letters, mfr.'s paper label reads O.P. LINK HANDLE CO. Salem, Ind., unused $12.00

WOOD HANDLE – hatchet, 15" long, GNRY, indented in brown, DUNLAP, unused $7.00

RAILROAD DATE NAIL – C&NW, STEEL, SQUARE HEAD, 7 indented, stubby shank $2.00

RAILROAD DATE NAIL – MILW. ROAD, copper, round head, 36 raised, short shank....................................$4.00

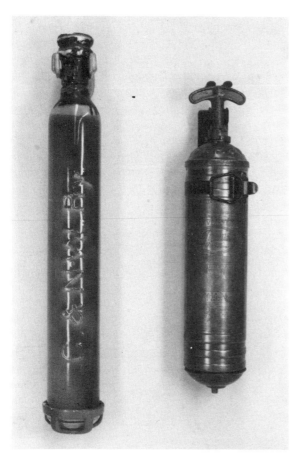

Fire Extinguishers – wall mounted

Toilet Paper Holder

Railroad-Related Collectibles

There are a number of objects in the form of the locomotive and many different things pertaining to the railroads that were made. While these are not authentic railroadiana items, those who generalize will usually include some of them in their collections. Here is a representative listing with their tentative values.

BANK – locomotive, 3½"H, 7"L, pot metal, bronze finish, RAILROADMEN'S FEDERAL, ca. 1950's, Banthrico, Chicago $35.00

BANK – locomotive, two pieces, 11"L, pot metal, copper finish, GENERAL, W&ARR, Banthrico, Chicago, 1974 ....$20.00

BANK – locomotive, 5"L, pot metal, copper finish, CASEY JONES $15.00

BIRTHDAY CANDLE HOLDER TRAIN – six pieces, ceramic, locomotive, circus cars and caboose, Japan $15.00

BOTTLE – Maccoboy Snuff, RAILROAD MILLS, dark amber, 4½"H, train on label $30.00

BREAD PLATTER – clear glass, 9 x 12", leaf border design, 350 Fast Mail Train impressed in center, ca. 1880's $75.00

CALENDAR – cardstock 11 x 14", black/white engraved, 12 mos., 1885, locomotive scene at top, TRAVELERS LIFE & ACCIDENT INS. CO., Hartford, Conn $75.00

CANDY BOX – cardboard, 2½ x 7½ x 9½", Pearson's CHOO CHOO 5 cents Salted Nut Roll Bars, pic of speeding passenger train on cover, ca. 1930's $8.00

CANDY CONTAINER – locomotive, 4"L, glass with lithographed tin closure depicting cab interior $35.00

CANDY CONTAINER – locomotive, 4½"L, glass, "999" tin screw cap closure rear $45.00

CANDY CONTAINER – railroad lantern, red glass, tin flared base and screw-on top, wire handle, 3¾"H, mk'd V.G. Co $15.00

CANDY CONTAINER – signal lantern, green glass, tin screw top closure, wire handle, 3½"H, mk'd AVOR 1 oz. USA $15.00

Glass Locomotive Candy Container

CHOCOLATE MOLD – early six-wheel locomotive, hinged, 4½ x 6", bright tin $65.00

CIGAR BOX – wood, 2 x 6 x 9¼", HORSE SHOE CURVE, CROOKS, Wine & Rum Treated, two for five cents, pic of streamliner rounding curve of tracks, 1930's ..$25.00

CIGAR BOX – wood, 2¼ x 4¾ x 7½", SOO LINE, mfr'd by S.A. Cutter, pic of old-time train inside cover, ca. 1880's..$30.00

Tin RR Heralds – Cereal Premiums, 1950's

Desk Ornament – Pot Metal RR Cars

CIGAR BOX – wood, 2½ x 5½ x 9¼", NORTH WESTERN, look-a-like C&NW logo inside cover which reads "The North Western Leader," ca. 1930's $30.00

COLLAPSIBLE DRINKING CUP – aluminum, round, 2½" tall, GREATER GALVESTON CAUSEWAY, Galveston, Tex., black pic of trains on bridge $35.00

COVER – U.S. 1895, "Largest Single Shipment Oil Stoves Ever Made," has freight train across full length with ad copy, used $25.00

COVER – U.S. 1900, "RAILWAY EQUIPMENT" has pic of locomotive at left side, M. Mitshkun Co., Detroit, Mich., used $10.00

CRACKER JACK PRIZE – tin locomotive, 2" long, No. 512, ca. 1920's $50.00

CRAYONS – DIXON Railroad, 888 White Chalk Crayons, box of one gross 4" long sticks for marking freight cars......$15.00

CUP & SAUCER – pottery, old time locomotive and coaches, Portland Pottery Ltd., England, ca. 1930's $35.00

DESK ORNAMENT – match holder (stick matches) porcelain base 3½ x 4½" with holder and tray, adv. LOCOMO-TIVES, CARS & RAILS, James T. Gardner, Chicago, made by Union Porcelain Works, NY., early 1900's $65.00

DESK ORNAMENT – pot metal, tank and refrigerator car coupled on felt padded base, 1¾"W x 7"L, NORTH AMERI-CAN CAR COMPANY, CHICAGO, ca. 1925 ....$145.00

DESK ORNAMENT – cast aluminum railroad track joint, 1¼ x 1½ x 6¼", The American Rail Joint Co., Niagara Falls, NY $55.00

DESK ORNAMENT – nickel-plated tie plate, 3 x 4½", THO-MAS RAIL ANCHOR TIE PLATE, Chicago Mall Casting Co., West Pullman, Ill $45.00

DESK ORNAMENT – coal hopper car, pot metal on felt padded base 2 x 6", with embossed words FRAME FRIEND & STINEMAN INC., Miners and Shippers.................$145.00

DESK ORNAMENT – hopper car, pot metal on felt padded base 2 x 6", embossed The Pittsburg & Midway Coal Mining Co., Kansas City, Mo $145.00

DOMINOES – box, 1¼ x 3½ x 10¼", DOUBLE TWELVE EXPRESS DOMINOES, litho. of full length passenger train on cover, locomotive embossed on dominoes, The Embossing Company, N.Y., early 1900's................$45.00

DOMINOES – box, 1½ x 2 x 12", DOUBLE NINE EXPRESS DOMINOES, litho. of full length passenger train on cover, engine embossed on dominoes, The Embossing Company, N.Y., ca. 1910 ....$35.00

FLASK – LOWELL RAILROAD, horse-drawn cart, eagle and stars on reverse, amber, ½ pint, early 19th century $200.00

FLASK – SUCCESS TO THE RAILROAD, horse-drawn cart on both sides, olive green, pint, early 19th century $180.00

GAME – "Across the Continent," map of U.S. on which Tootsie Toy zephyr cars are moved along routes, played with dice, original box, Parker Brothers, 1952 ....$18.00

GLASS SLIDE – for magic lantern, 3¼ x 9½", colorful scene of train at depot, Germany, early 1900's $10.00

GLASS SLIDE – for magic lantern, 1¾ x 6½", colorful railway scene, Germany, early 1900's................................$5.00

JIGSAW PUZZLE – C&I litho., AN AMERICAN RAILWAY SCENE AT HORNELLSVILLE, ERIE RAILWAY, puzzle size 17 x 25", original box, PAGER INDUSTRIES, N.J. 1974................................$10.00

MATCH SAFE – pewter, ½ x 1 x 2½" long, early locomotive, ornate designs embossed both sides....................$50.00

MEDALLION – THE LOCOMOTIVE FINISHED MATERIAL COMPANY, bronze, 3½"D, 75th Anniv. 1872-1947, diesel and steam locos. depicted, factory buildings on reverse $55.00

MIRROR – pocket, oval, advertising, THE TRAVELER'S IN-SURANCE COMPANY, HARTORD, CONN., picture of passenger train at night................................$37.50

MOVIE PLACARD – 11 x 14", "Rails Into Laramie," 1954, color shot of old-time steam engine.....................$25.00

MUG – pottery, 4" tall, 4"D, litho. illustration of old-time locomotive and coaches, B&T hm'k., England, ca. 1890's $65.00

PAPERWEIGHT – steel, locomotive wheel, 4"D, red/black finish, LOCOMOTIVE AND CAR WHEEL TIRES, The Standard Steel Works, Phila. Pa $27.50

PAPERWEIGHT – bronze, 3"D, HIPOWER NUT LOCKS, train speeding through lock washer raised in center, The National Lock Washer Co., Newark, N.J. $37.50

PAPERWEIGHT – bronze, 3"D, AMERICAN RAILWAY EN-GINEERING ASSOCIATION, 50TH Anniv. 1899-1949, rail end depicted $30.00

PAPERWEIGHT – thick glass, octagonal shape, 4"L, illustration of ditching machine on white, Mahoney R.R. Ditching Machine Co., Vincennes, Ind........................$20.00

PAPERWEIGHT – thick glass, rectangular, 4¼"L, pic. of steam and electric train on bridge, The Galveston Causeway, Galveston, Texas, mirror back.............$37.50

PLATE – pottery, 10¼"D, CHICAGO RAILROAD FAIR, depicting early locomotives, Vernon Kilns, USA, 1949......$50.00

PLATE – pottery, 10¼"D, litho of Currier & Ives American Express Train, ADAMS hm'k. England, ca. 1930's ..$75.00

POCKET KNIFE – two blades, 4¼"L, photo of mallet locomotive, Aerial Cut Mfg. Co. Marinette, Wis., ca. 1910 ....$50.00

POCKET KNIFE – The Traveler's Ins. Co., Hartford, Conn. Ticket Dept., full-length embossed steam train, 3¼"L, ca. 1910 ....$45.00

PLAYING CARDS – UNION TANK CAR CO., standard cards complete in original case, backs depict blueprint specs of tank car.................$5.00

PLAYING CARDS – game of CUPPLEUP, 56 cards of various cars and eight engines to be coupled up into GNRY trains, original case, Pub. by Railway Education Co., St. Paul, 1925 ....$45.00

PLAYING CARDS – double deck standard cards, complete in original box, backs depict depot scene – freight train and baggage cart, ca. 1950's $20.00

POSTER – motion picture, 14 x 36", ROCK ISLAND TRAIL, early locomotive in format, ca. 1950's $35.00

POSTER – circus, 26 x 39", Ringling Bros., Barnum & Bailey, railroad scene unloading circus cars.................$150.00

RAILROAD HERALDS – tin, complete set of 28, cereal premiums, 1950's.................$155.00

RAILROAD HERALDS – tin, set of 25 only, re-run late 1970's.................$110.00

RAILROAD HERALDS – tin, cereal premium, single from original set $8.00

SHAVING MUG – occupational, locomotive engineer, name in gold and pic of old-time steam engine, ca. 1875 ....$275.00

SHAVING MUG – occupational, baggage handler, name in gold and pic of old-time baggage car, ca. 1875 ....$275.00

SHAVING MUG – occupational, telegrapher, name in gold and illustration of telegraph key, ca. 1890 ....$175.00

SIGN – tin, 13¾ x 17¾", advertising, Chew PAYCAR SCRAP The Best Flavor, Chewing Tobacco, litho of railroad pay car $65.00

SIGN – tin, 9¼ x 11" advertising, ALTOONA BEERS, 36 Pilsener, 36 Lager, litho of Horseshoe Curve and trains, 1930's.................$85.00

SOUVENIR TIN ART PLATE – 10"D, litho of train crossing Great Salt Lake in oval scene at top, Souvenir Novelty Co. Salt Lake City, 1911 ....$60.00

SOUVENIR CHINA ART PLATE – 8"D, hand-painted pic of UNION STATION, St. Louis, Mo. The Jonroth Studios, Germany, early 1900's $30.00

SOUVENIR CHINA NAPPY DISH – 6 x 7", painted scene of Old Union Station, White River Jct., Vt. Germany, early 1900's $250.00

SOUVENIR CHINA MINI MUG – 2¾"H, painted scene of G.N. Depot, St. Cloud, Minn. Germany, early 1900's $15.00

SOUVENIR CHINA TRAY – 3 x 4", painted scene N.P.R.R. Bridge near Lindstrom, Minn. Germany, dated 1907...........$10.00

SOUVENIR SPOON – sterling, Louisiana Purchase Exposition, St. Louis, 1904, front end of steam loco. on handle $35.00

SOUVENIR SPOON – sterling, ALTOONA, embossed loco and car on handle, Horse Shoe Bend tracks raised in bowl, dated 1906 ....$45.00

STEVENSGRAPH – original mat and frame, "The Present Time" 60 Miles an Hour, old time train woven in silk, England.................$150.00

STEIN – porcelain, 10" tall, lithopane base, "Corps. of Ry. Const. Engineers," steam locomotive on pewter lid, Germany, 1882-1884.................$185.00

STICKPIN – 2½"L, The Traveler's Ins. Co., Hartford, Conn. Ticket Dept., raised locomotive on small gold plated oval, early 1900's $25.00

THE IRON FIREMAN – ashtray, white pot metal, oval felt padded base, 4 x 6½", standing mechanical man 4"H with coal shovel, ca. 1930's $65.00

TOBACCO TIN – FAST MAIL Chewing Tobacco, 2¼ x 3½", litho. of mail train on cover, J.J. BAGLEY & CO., dated Sept. 24, 1878 (rare) $250.00

TOBACCO TIN – cut plug, 1 x 2 x 3½", loook-a-like NP logo on cover reads PLAYERS CUT PLUG, The Surbrug Co. Richmond & NY, early 1900's $12.00

TOOTHPICKS – cardboard box, 1¼ x 2½ x 3", look-a-like C&NW logo on cover and sides reads THE NORTH-WESTERN BRAND, Warfield, Pratt, Howell Co., Des Moines, Ia., early 1900's.................$10.00

WATCH FOB – The Travelers Ins. Co., Hartford, Conn. Ticket Dept., ornate metal fob with raised likeness of speeding passenger train, leather strap type $85.00

WATCH FOB – C.T. Ham Mfr.Co. Rochester, NY, cut-out metal lantern fob with HAMLIGHT raised across globe, leather strap type $75.00

TRINKET BOX – locomotive, 2½"L, white porcelain with gold trim, Staffordshire, ca. 1890's.................$55.00

If you'd like to keep yourself up to date on railroad collectible finds, you should join the Railroadiana Collectors Association Incorporated. Contact Joe Mazanek, 795 Aspen Drive, Buffalo Grove, Illinois 60089 – 1359.

Schroeder's
ANTIQUES
Price Guide

. . . is the #1 best-selling antiques & collectibles value guide on the market today, and here's why . . .

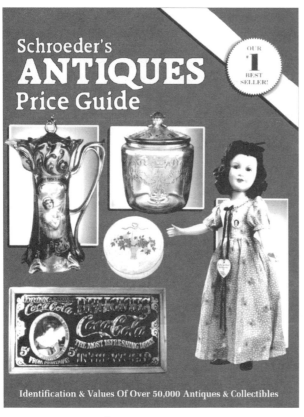

Identification & Values Of Over 50,000 Antiques & Collectibles

8½ x 11, 608 Pages, $14.95

• More than 300 advisors, well-known dealers, and top-notch collectors work together with our editors to bring you accurate information regarding pricing and identification.

• More than 45,000 items in almost 500 categories are listed along with hundreds of sharp original photos that illustrate not only the rare and unusual, but the common, popular collectibles as well.

• Each large close-up shot shows important details clearly. Every subject is represented with histories and background information, a feature not found in any of our competitors' publications.

• Our editors keep abreast of newly developing trends, often adding several new categories a year as the need arises.

If it merits the interest of today's collector, you'll find it in *Schroeder's*. And you can feel confident that the information we publish is up to date and accurate. Our advisors thoroughly check each category to spot inconsistencies, listings that may not be entirely reflective of market dealings, and lines too vague to be of merit. Only the best of the lot remains for publication.

Without doubt, you'll find
SCHROEDER'S ANTIQUES PRICE GUIDE
the only one to buy for
reliable information and values.

COLLECTOR BOOKS
A Division of Schroeder Publishing Co., Inc.